SHOOTING TO KILL

The present book brings together perspectives from different disciplinary fields to examine the significant legal, moral and political issues which arise in relation to the use of lethal force in both domestic and international law. These issues have particular salience in the counter terrorism context following 9/11 (which brought with it the spectre of shooting down hijacked airplanes) and the use of force in Operation Kratos that led to the tragic shooting of Jean Charles de Menezes. Concerns about the use of excessive force, however, are not confined to the terrorist situation. The essays in this collection examine how the state sanctions the use of lethal force in varied ways: through the doctrines of public and private self-defence and the development of legislation and case law that excuses or justifies the use of lethal force in the course of executing an arrest, preventing crime or disorder or protecting private property. An important theme is how the domestic and international legal orders intersect and continually influence one another. While legal approaches to the use of lethal force share common features, the context within which force is deployed varies greatly. Key issues explored in this volume are the extent to which domestic and international law authorise pre-emptive use of force, and how necessity and reasonableness are legally constructed in this context.

Oñati International Series in Law and Society

A SERIES PUBLISHED FOR THE OÑATI INSTITUTE
FOR THE SOCIOLOGY OF LAW

General Editors
Rosemary Hunter   David Nelken

Founding Editors
William L F Felstiner   Eve Darian-Smith

Board of General Editors
Carlos Lugo, Hostos Law School, Puerto Rico
Jacek Kurczewski, Warsaw University, Poland
Marie-Claire Foblets, Leuven University, Belgium
Roderick Macdonald, McGill University, Canada

Recent titles in this series

Feminist Perspectives on Contemporary International Law:
Between Resistance and Compliance?
edited by Sari Kouvo and Zoe Pearson

Challenging Gender Inequality in Tax Policy Making: Comparative Perspectives
edited by Kim Brooks, Åsa Gunnarson, Lisa Philipps and Maria Wersig

Emotions, Crime and Justice
edited by Susanne Karstedt, Ian Loader and Heather Strang

Mediation in Political Conflicts
Soft Power or Counter Culture?
edited by Jacques Faget

Criminological and Legal Consequences of Climate Change
edited by Stephen Farrall, Tawhida Ahmed and Duncan French

Challenging the Legal Boundaries of Work Regulation
Edited by Judy Fudge, Shae McCrystal and Kamala Sankaran

For the complete list of titles in this series, see
'Oñati International Series in Law and Society' link at
www.hartpub.co.uk/books/series.asp

Shooting to Kill

Socio-Legal Perspectives on the Use of Lethal Force

Edited by

Simon Bronitt
Miriam Gani
and
Saskia Hufnagel

Oñati International Series in Law and Society

A SERIES PUBLISHED FOR THE OÑATI INSTITUTE
FOR THE SOCIOLOGY OF LAW

·HART·
PUBLISHING

OXFORD AND PORTLAND, OREGON
2012

Published in the United Kingdom by Hart Publishing Ltd
16C Worcester Place, Oxford, OX1 2JW
Telephone: +44 (0)1865 517530
Fax: +44 (0)1865 510710
E-mail: mail@hartpub.co.uk
Website: http://www.hartpub.co.uk

Published in North America (US and Canada) by
Hart Publishing
c/o International Specialized Book Services
920 NE 58th Avenue, Suite 300
Portland, OR 97213-3786
USA
Tel: +1 503 287 3093 or toll-free: (1) 800 944 6190
Fax: +1 503 280 8832
E-mail: orders@isbs.com
Website: http://www.isbs.com

© Oñati IISL 2012

British Library Cataloguing in Publication Data
Data Available

ISBN: 978-1-84946-292-1

Typeset by Compuscript Ltd, Shannon
Printed and bound in Great Britain by
TJ International Ltd, Padstow, Cornwall

Acknowledgements

The editors would like to acknowledge the support of the sponsors and various institutions involved in the creation of this volume of essays: first and foremost, the International Institute for the Sociology of Law (IISL) in Oñati, Spain, (and especially the then Director Carlos Lista and the administrator Malen Gordoa) for generously hosting the workshop at which the papers presented formed the foundation for this publication; secondly, the Australian Research Council Centre of Excellence in Policing and Security (hosted by Griffith University) which generously made available the research assistance needed to complete the book through its Legal Frameworks programme (Use of Force); and finally, the ANU Centre for European Studies and the ANU College of Law at the Australian National University, which provided an institutional home for the editors in which the project was conceived and much of this work was done.

The editors thank all the authors for their high quality contributions, inordinate patience and cheerful cooperation throughout the process of turning the presentations into an edited collection. The editors and authors acknowledge the contributions of the workshop participants whose presentations did not end up being published here, who nevertheless made a significant contribution to the workshop discussions—Johannes Krebs, Schlomit Wallerstein, Tim Bakken, Aniceto Masferrer and Prita Jobling.

Two of the editors, Simon and Miriam, would like to acknowledge the extraordinary efforts of their co-editor, 'Dr Hugnagel (sic)' who bore the bulk of editorial coordination with good humour (mostly) and with only an occasional air of scholastic resignation. Danke schön!

The editors would also like to thank Hart Publishing and in particular Rachel Turner (Assistant to Richard Hart, Managing Director) for their commitment to the project, wonderful support and infinite patience during the process.

In particular, we would like to thank Thea Coventry for her meticulous work on this volume as a research assistant and for very generously sacrificing a large part of her honeymoon in New Zealand to finish the project.

Contents

List of Contributors

Simon Bronitt is Director of the ARC Centre of Excellence in Policing and Security and Professor at Griffith University in Brisbane. His research interests include criminal justice issues, including counter terrorism law and human rights, covert policing, telecommunications interception and international criminal law.

Tom Campbell is Professor of Philosophy in the Centre for Applied Philosophy and Public Ethics, an ARC funded Special Research Centre at Charles Sturt University, Canberra. He specialises in legal philosophy and business ethics and writes on justice, legal positivism, democracy and rights.

Miriam Gani is an Associate Professor at the ANU College of Law at the Australian National University in Canberra. Her teaching and research interests are in criminal law, especially Australian federal criminal law.

Ian Gordon OBE QPM is a former Chief Police Officer, with experience of police investigation and professional standards. He is Convener of the Standards Commission for Scotland and an Associate Professor in Policing at Charles Sturt University, Canberra working on ethical standards, leadership and work related stress in police forces.

Douglas Guilfoyle is a Senior Lecturer at the Faculty of Laws, University College London. His research interests include international criminal law and the law of the sea, with a particular interest in piracy.

Russell Hogg is an Associate Professor in the School of Law, University of New England, Armidale. His research interests include criminological theory, collective violence, punishment and law and order politics.

Saskia Hufnagel is a Research Fellow at the ARC Centre of Excellence in Policing and Security at Griffith University in Brisbane. Her research focuses on comparative criminal and human rights law, EU and Australian police cooperation, emergency law and art crime.

Tziporah Kasachkoff is Professor Emerita in the Department of Philosophy at the Graduate School and University Center, City University of New York. Her research interests are in political and social philosophy, theoretical and applied ethics, and the teaching of philosophy.

David Kinley holds the Chair in Human Rights Law at Sydney University and is an Academic Panel Member of Doughty Street Chambers in London.

His research and publications focus on the intersections between human rights and the global economy.

John Kleinig is Professor of Philosophy in the Department of Criminal Justice, John Jay College of Criminal Justice, City University of New York, and Professorial Fellow in Criminal Justice Ethics, at the Centre for Applied Philosophy and Public Ethics, Charles Sturt University. His research interests are broadly in moral, social and political philosophy, most recently on the topics of loyalty and means and ends.

Ian Leader-Elliott is an Adjunct Professor at the University of South Australia School of Law and Emeritus Fellow at the University of Adelaide School of Law. His current research interest is codification of the criminal law with particular reference to Macaulay's Indian Penal Code.

Seumas Miller is a Professorial Research Fellow at the Centre for Applied Philosophy and Public Ethics (an Australian Research Council Special Research Centre) at Charles Sturt University (Canberra) and the 3TU Centre for Ethics and Technology at Delft University of Technology (The Hague). His recent books include *The Moral Foundations of Social Institutions: A Philosophical Study* (Cambridge, Cambridge University Press, 2011) and *Terrorism and Counter-terrorism: Ethics and Liberal Democracy* (Oxford, Blackwell, 2009).

Kai Möller is a Lecturer in Law at the London School of Economics and Political Science. His research interests include constitutional rights theory, comparative constitutional law, and legal, moral and political theory.

Andrew Murdoch was, at the time of writing, a legal adviser in the UK's Royal Navy. He is now a legal adviser in the Foreign and Commonwealth Office. His research interests include maritime security, law of the sea and international humanitarian law.

Odette Murray is a Senior Legal Officer with the Office of International Law in the Australian Attorney-General's Department, Canberra. She previously practised in plaintiff class action litigation. She holds a BA (Hons) and LLB from Sydney University and an LLM from Cambridge University, specialising in public international law.

Mary Ellen O'Connell is the Robert and Marion Short Chair in Law and Research Professor of International Dispute Resolution—Kroc Institute, University of Notre Dame in Indiana, US. She teaches and writes in the areas of international legal theory, international law on the use of force, and peaceful dispute resolution.

Andrew Vincent is Emeritus Professor (Sheffield University); Honorary Professor Cardiff University and Professorial Fellow of Collingwood and

British Idealism Centre, Cardiff University. His research interests include contemporary political, moral and legal philosophy; modern political ideologies; nationalism; state theory; and philosophical idealism.

Kylie Weston-Scheuber is a supervising lawyer with the Office of the DPP (ACT). She has recently been awarded her PhD from the Australian National University, Canberra. Her research interests include criminal law, sexual assault law reform, terrorism, domestic violence and international humanitarian law.

Introduction

There was only one catch and that was Catch-22, which specified that a concern for one's own safety in the face of dangers that were real and immediate was the process of a rational mind. Orr was crazy and could be grounded. All he had to do was ask; and as soon as he did, he would no longer be crazy and would have to fly more missions. Orr would be crazy to fly more missions and sane if he didn't, but if he was sane, he had to fly them. If he flew them, he was crazy and didn't have to; but if he didn't want to, he was sane and had to. Yossarian was moved very deeply by the absolute simplicity of this clause of Catch-22 and let out a respectful whistle.

Joseph Heller, *Catch-22* (1961)

Joseph Heller's famous satirical war novel *Catch-22* captures some of the absurdities of war, the soldiers' dilemma and specifically the pervasive fears of those flying B-25 bombers. Yossarian, a member of one such squadron, experiences the constant fear of being a target of lethal force—in effect, the 'killer' fears being killed—but fears even more the bureaucracy steering him. His fears underscore legitimate justifications of acting in self-defence and necessity, but also reveal the psychological coercion arising through the system of military chain of command and superior orders. Musing about the insanity arising from that constant fear of being killed, which he regarded as a form of sanity, in turn justifies further killing, as legally cemented in the 'Catch-22'. Yossarian's dilemma illustrates the instability of the legal categories of justification or excuse, as well as the malleability of the distinct legal subjects of 'culpable offender' and 'innocent victim'. This conceptual instability is one that recurs throughout this edited collection.

The 'Catch-22' has acquired new significance in the debates in the decade post-9/11. The 'War on Terror' provides a new context in which legal systems have struggled to determine the legitimate boundaries on the use of force to prevent acts of terrorism, including the deployment of lethal force. Much of the academic debate has focussed on the legal questions of necessity, reasonableness and proportionality including inter alia the extent to which the law authorises the pre-emptive uses of lethal force in both policing and military operations. Legal concerns about unjustified or illegitimate uses of force are not limited to terrorist situations. The authors of this collection examine the myriad of ways in which the state and the law (both domestic and international) sanction the use of lethal force across a wide spectrum of contexts. Authors in this edited collection traverse a wide terrain—from violence perpetrated in the name of the state by military or police, to private forms of self-defence in the 'domestic' context. The law across all these domains seeks to regulate—to define, limit and legitimate (or not)—these acts of violence.

Failures to take action against unjustified violence perpetrated by military or police personnel undermines the rule of law, as well as the legitimacy of the state in whose name the violence is perpetrated. The recent shooting of Osama bin Laden by US Special Forces in Pakistan on 2 May 2011 raised questions of necessity, reasonableness and proportionality of the force used by the US Special Forces. The focus on the legality of that action has centred around the language of self-defence, respect for the rule of law and compliance with the military's rules of engagement.[1] The operation was described by US Attorney General Eric Holder as a 'kill or capture mission', so that 'if there was the possibility of a feasible surrender, that would have occurred'.[2] Despite revised official descriptions of the event indicating that bin Laden was in fact unarmed,[3] in the absence of a clear indication of surrender from him, it has been concluded that the Special Forces acted 'in an appropriate way'. As one senior military officer involved in the operation noted, 'the protection of the force that went into that compound, was I think uppermost in our minds'.[4] How legal systems, both national and international, respond to such security threats is crucially important. Getting it 'wrong' can have serious and devastating consequences, as illustrated in the Jean Charles de Menezes shooting by counter terrorism police and more recently, the UK riots in August 2011 that followed in the week after the police shooting of Mark Duggan. The authors of this collection are under no illusion that the difference between on the one hand, the use of force being a justified act of heroism, or on the other hand, an abuse of power or serious criminal offence, is highly contingent on context.

New and nuanced insights into use of force require legal rules to be examined in a variety of contexts. Legal doctrine and theory must be interrogated through a range of critical and applied perspectives (which include military and policing practitioners). While some chapters approach the topic using a theoretical or ethical perspective, others have a predominantly doctrinal and sociological perspective on the law. The use of the case study method in some of these chapters enables a highly contextual picture of the law relationship with state-authorised or state-sanctioned violence to emerge.

---

[1] See R Khatchadourian, 'Bin Laden: The Rules of Engagement', *New Yorker*, 4 May 2011, www.newyorker.com/online/blogs/newsdesk/2011/05/bin-laden-the-rules-of-engagement.html.
[2] See BBC report, 'Bin Laden death "not an assassination"—Eric Holder', *BBC*, 2 May 2011, www.bbc.co.uk/news/world-us-canada-13370919.
[3] Khatchadourian, above n 1.
[4] BBC report, above n 2.

For thematic coherence and convenience, the book adopts a tri-partite structure (although we recognise that many of the themes and perspectives are overlapping and interrelated). Part I deals with Theoretical and Ethical Perspectives; Part II examines Legal Frameworks for Shooting to Kill; and Part III looks at Shooting to Kill in Context: Case Studies.

Part I examines the core concepts surrounding the use of lethal force such as state of emergency (Campbell), the limits of necessity claims (Kleinig and Kasachkoff), the core principles of proportionality and the right to life (Möller). It also examines the broader philosophical question of whether the state can be held responsible for criminal uses of force by its agents (Vincent), and how political and juridical discourses use language to legitimate lethal force in the war on terror (Hogg). Campbell's chapter on 'The Rule of Law, Legal Positivism and States of Emergency' focuses on the question of how domestic states of emergency could be hedged in by utilising the traditional patterns of checks and balances within a constitutional state. Using the example of police use of lethal force, he examines whether expanded police powers and competences in the field of terrorism response are held at bay by the rule of law or whether they are, in fact, consolidated by it. Kleinig and Kasachkoff, in their chapter on 'Civil Emergencies and the Claims of Innocence' also focus on powers and competences attributed to state officials in the fight against terrorism, in the particular context of the use of lethal force against hijacked aircraft. The validity of legislation (moral, legal and ethical) enacted in many countries after the 9/11 attacks authorising the use of pre-emptive lethal force in a 9/11 World Trade Centre (WTC) scenario is examined in several of the contributions to this book. Kleinig and Kasachkoff approach this problem from the perspective of the moral dilemmas of key decision-makers. Other authors adopt a different approach to the scenario, focussing on the constitutional, legal and practical issues. Möller, in chapter three, for example, reviews the legality of shooting down hijacked aircraft from a distinctly legal constitutional perspective, drawing on hypotheticals from the field of applied ethics. Using this extreme example, Möller investigates the constitutional principle of proportionality in relation to the use of lethal force and offers some fresh insights into whether certain 'absolute' constitutional rights—such as the right to human dignity—do, in fact, exist.

Drawing on his field of political philosophy, Vincent approaches the topic by asking the deceptively simple (but ultimately complex) question, reflected in the chapter title, 'Can States Commit Crimes?'. While the legal answer to the question might appear relatively straightforward, the disciplinary lens of political philosophy reveals multiple facets of the issue of how far the state can legitimately go in its efforts to protect its citizens. Part I concludes with a chapter on 'Death and Denial in the "Global War on Terror"' by Hogg. Referring to the specific issue of terrorism, but this time from a distinctly socio-legal and criminological perspective, Hogg focuses on the international rather than domestic aspect of the 'global war on terror' and compares the strategies used to deny the 'resemblances between similar sets of facts' in contemporary violent conflicts, in particular those connected with global terrorism.

Part II delves into further detailed analysis of the 'common' legal concepts that serve to legitimise the use of lethal force, such as necessity, reasonableness, proportionality, as well as exploring how these concepts are given effect in substantive legal defences and how these are operationalised in police administrative guidelines. Leader-Elliot provides a structured analysis of Australian model criminal law defences and how these affect the criminal liability of individuals who use lethal force. This involves a detailed analysis of all existing defences under Australian criminal law. He stresses, however, that what all defences have in common is the requirement of a 'reasonable response', which serves as a limit to state abuse of power. This however hands the assessment to the judges rather than the legislature. The next chapter (Bronitt and Gani) moves to the frontline decision-making of those who use force, exposing the fact that decisions to use force are highly contextual, shaped by legal norms as well as administrative practices and guidelines. A gender perspective is offered in a comparison of the law's treatment of police who use lethal force to combat violent crime and terrorism, and of women who kill to escape from violent partners (Weston-Scheuber). The contours of law's doctrines are undeniably shaped by gender, but also by legal culture—this is apparent in relation to the paramount status of human dignity in German law that has severely limited the scope for using lethal force pre-emptively in counter terrorism operations (Hufnagel). Adopting a comparative legal methodology, this chapter returns again to the 9/11 WTC scenario, but the approach adopted is an applied legal focus (rather than legal theoretical) on the operation of available criminal law defences in German and Australian law.

Part III concludes with a series of case studies, providing the opportunity for further contextualisation of both domestic and international law governing the use of lethal force. While the governing legal doctrines share 'common features' (legal rules authorising the use of necessary, reasonable and proportionate force in self-defence and defence of others, or to prevent crime and disorder, or to protect property, etc), the *contexts* within which lethal force is deployed vary greatly. The first chapter by Gordon and Miller asks the question 'The Fatal Police Shooting Of Jean Charles de Menezes: Is Anyone Responsible?'. The authors employ an innovative methodological approach to analyse the shooting of de Menezes (and the use of force protocols applied in Operation Kratos) that melds philosophical and ethical insights (Miller) with practical perspectives of a former operational senior police officer (Gordon). The chapter also provides an in-depth assessment of the criminal law, human rights, ethical and moral arguments raised by this tragic case. The next chapter by Guilfoyle and Murdoch is a case study addressing the use of lethal force in counter-piracy operations off Somalia that similarly combines applied practitioner and academic perspectives on law enforcement operations by the military. It assesses international law and domestic criminal law approaches to the use of lethal force against pirates and concludes that the interaction between these different types of laws still poses considerable problems in the field. The penultimate chapter by O'Connell examines the legality of combat drones deployed in Pakistan (2004–09) by the US military from an international law perspective. The final chapter by Kinley and Murray, titled 'Corporations that Kill: Prosecuting Blackwater', raises the question whether outsourcing of military and policing services to the corporate sector permits states to evade or escape liability for the harms and crimes caused by private military contractors corporations. The transnational and global dimension of private security offers another perspective on the topic, providing an epilogue on future trends of global corporate misuse of power.

Part I

Theoretical and Ethical Perspectives

1

The Rule of Law, Legal Positivism and States of Emergency

TOM CAMPBELL

POLICIES RELATING TO the use of lethal force by the state cover a wide range of circumstances, ranging from routine police procedures for dealing with physically dangerous and perhaps deranged individuals to sophisticated actions by trained specialists to prevent major terrorist activities. The former may be considered routine while the latter may be viewed as exceptional. If, indeed, shoot to kill policies in the context of anti-terrorist procedures are not, any longer, to be considered 'exceptional', in the sense of unusual, then there are important points to be raised about how legitimising these measures can be handled in a way that conforms to, rather than opts out of, the rule of law.

This is currently a very difficult question to approach within the ambit of contemporary legal and political philosophy, for there are few concepts within this field that are as contested as that of 'the rule of law'. The relatively simple formalist model of the rule of law as a doctrine requiring that the acts of executive government must be in accordance with valid legal rules, is being displaced by a more substantive concept according to which legitimate government actions must not violate certain fundamental moral standards. In this chapter I do not enter into this wider constitutional debate, but explore, instead, how far 'exceptional' anti-terrorism measures could be subsumed under a formal model of the rule of law. This exercise is undertaken on the assumption that this might be a significant legal, and ultimately also political check, on the unwarranted use of lethal force in allegedly exceptional circumstances. The thought is that having emergency laws which require courts to determine whether or not there is an emergency as defined in formally good laws, may be a more effective and more democratic way of curbing abuses of such anti-terrorist powers, rather than requiring courts to make a moral assessment of the merits of the policies in question.

I. THE RULE OF LAW

This section indicates how the 'rule of law' should be defined and institutionalised. We proceed to examine how far my preferred model can be usefully deployed to provide controls on the use of lethal force in the context of policing with respect to counter terrorism. My line is that a legal positivist construction of the rule of law can be used to generate a strategy that affords relatively effective and democratically legitimate modes of protecting and promoting defensible conceptions of rights to life in the context of counter terrorism. The model commended is that of a separation of powers that approximates to a system in which executives are held to account in terms of democratically enacted laws by courts whose duties are confined to applying specific laws to concrete situations defined in terms amenable to objective assessment by courts through evidence-based decision-making. In other words, I endorse normative legal positivism and exclude human rights constitutionalism.

In the case of defensible uses of lethal force for counter terrorism purposes that depart from those applicable to other spheres of policing, I explore how far this could be accommodated by limiting their applicability to periods of terrorism-defined states of emergency whose authorisation requires court approval based on positivist rule of law standards. In brief, the morally legitimate authorisation of counter terrorism lethal force can and therefore should be accommodated within a constitution of democratic rule-governance.

While my concerns are ultimately moral ones as to the proper uses of political power my involvement in these debates arose from participation in a symposium designed to explore what might be called the legal theory of emergencies, in which we were asked to reflect on the contrasting approaches of Oren Gross and David Dyzenhaus to counter terrorism law, the former taking the view that the de facto emergencies involve permitting governments to act beyond the limits of legality, the latter holding to the view that 'emergency action' can and should be accommodated within the limits of law or legality. On that occasion I sided with Dyzenhaus while demurring from his conception of legality, which incorporates substantive as well as formal values in the manner characteristic of contemporary post-democratic legal constitutionalism.[1]

Despite taking place within the rarefied strata of legal theory, questioning the legality of counter terrorism involves us in an emotive debate that takes us back to the Nazi philosopher, Carl Schmitt, who argued that the true character of the liberal state is revealed in 'emergencies' in which its

---

[1] See P Craig, 'Formal and Substantive Conceptions of the Rule of Law: An Analytic Framework' (1997) *Public Law* 467.

governments depart from law and govern by decrees backed by force.[2] The philosophy of liberal democracy was undermined, for Schmitt, by the fact that there remains the power within the liberal democratic state to suspend the constitution and rule by dint of emergency powers. Highly discretionary shoot to kill policies that involve powers not normally exercised in the course of standard police practice, could be regarded as an example of such lawlessness. On the other side of the debate, it is insisted that emergencies, however grave, do not warrant the exercise of effectively unlimited and legally unsupervised discretionary coercive power, which would be to negate all that has been achieved in the field of civil liberties. On this account, anti-terrorism 'shoot to kill', like any official policy, must be subjected to a regime of legitimate law.

This blossoming debate is riddled with confusions that need to be transcended before theory impacts on practice. For instance, there are a number of blind alleys that are to be avoided. One such is the confusion of the legality debate with the issue of whether the same rules apply to all situations at all times, including emergencies. Thus, it may be argued, for instance, that if habeas corpus is the law, then it is the law within that jurisdiction at all times. That is, however, with apologies to Dicey, neither a requirement of rule governance nor accurate with respect to the historical application of habeas corpus.[3] Arguably, rule governance is indeed incompatible with constant frequent changes of the rules for this negates their regulatory function, but there is nothing extra-legal in rule-change as such. More generally, there is clearly no formal problem with rules defining the temporal or other limits of their applicability. That is commonplace. Positivist rule governance does not require universality of application and changing rules is not equivalent to abandoning rule-governance. Changing rules can be rule-governed and formally good rules can be temporally restricted.

Similar dead-end diversions apply to the debate as to whether the same rules apply to everyone in a polity, be they police, military, government ministers or Joe Soap. Some rules obviously should be universal in this sense, but equally obviously many should not, which has considerable relevance to our topic since police and the military have some legal power relating to use of lethal force not available to the ordinary citizen. The question as to which should apply to all, and which should not, is to be distinguished from the question as to whether or not there should be rules at all.

So what is at stake in the Gross–Dyzenhaus debate? The theoretical issue seems to be a particular constitutional problem that arises in the North American context, and no doubt in other jurisdictions with barely

---

[2] C Schmitt, *Legality and Legitimacy* (Durham, Duke University Press, 2003); see also G Agamben, *State of Exception* (Chicago, University of Chicago Press, 2005).

[3] AM Gregg, 'Shoot to Kill—How Far is Too Far in Protecting Citizens?' (2006) 25 *Pennsylvania State International Law Review* 295.

amendable constitutions and involving areas of judicial supremacy. Gross, an American resident, is exercised by the fact that the measures he deems necessary to deal with terrorist activities are or may be in conflict with the constitution, which does not have any provision for formal states of emergency and does provide for judicial invalidation of counter terrorism and other laws that are deemed to violate its Bill of Rights. Gross holds that in such circumstances presidents can and should depart from the constitution and act outside the law, and do what is necessary to 'save the nation'. In his words 'Public officials, like everybody else, ought to obey the law, even when they disagree with specific legal commands. However, there may be extreme exigencies when officials may regard strict obedience to legal authority as irrational or immoral. Public officials who believe that the law is so fundamentally unjust as to be devoid of both legitimacy and legality, may exercise their discretion and refuse to apply, or seek actively to undermine, such law'.[4]

After the event, it is then for the people to decide whether to respond by punishing the president and his staff or by approving of their actions, with the uncertainty involved acting as a deterrent for officials contemplating the use of their 'extra legal' powers,[5] an optimistic scenario that awaits instantiation.

Dyzenhaus has an alternative theoretical framework which involves ascribing to law a moral content that can be drawn upon to cope with extreme circumstances by rendering the apparently illegal legal through constitutional interpretation. This requires a substantive conception of legality that is not tied to prevailing legal institutions but can readily be found within contemporary constitutional law which regards constitutional rights as providing a moral input into the validation of positive law and is not fazed by departures from the traditional separation of powers between executives, legislatures and courts that are involved in this process. This enables Dyzenhaus to come up with a model whereby there is never a need for executives to resort to illegalities.

In this chapter I bypass the apparent reductio ad absurdum of US constitutionalism set out by Gross, in which it appears that, at the very time judicial constraint on executive action is most important, it can be set aside by extra-legal executive decision-making.[6] I do take up the debate

---

[4] O Gross, 'Extra-legality and the ethic of political responsibility' in VV Ramraj, *Emergencies and the Limits of Legality* (Cambridge, Cambridge University Press, 2008) 60–93.

[5] O Gross, 'Chaos and Rules: Should Responses to Violent Crises Always be Constitutional?' (2003) 112 *Yale Law Journal* 1011; O Gross, 'Stability and Flexibility: a Dicey Business' in VV Ramraj, M Hor and K Roach (eds), *Global Anti-Terrorism Law and Policy* (Cambridge, Cambridge University Press, 2003) 90–106; also O Gross and F Ni Aolain, *Law in Times of Crisis: Emergency Powers in Theory and Practice* (Cambridge, Cambridge University Press, 2006).

[6] Thereby, perhaps, endorsing the analysis in G Agamben, *State of Exception* (Chicago, University of Chicago Press, 2005).

with Dyzenhaus in regard to the nature of the relative inputs of courts, legislatures and executives to the determination of the laws that apply in emergency situations, formal or de facto. This requires a brief outline of the philosophical basis of my rejection of the 'constrained democratic constitutionalism' to which Dyzenhaus adheres.[7]

The theory of law I adopt but do not have space here to defend is called 'prescriptive legal positivism' (or, sometimes, 'ethical positivism') to distinguish it from theories which reduce positivism either to a descriptive theory or to an analytical or conceptual thesis about the necessary separations between law and morality.[8] The prescriptive version of legal positivism does presuppose a lot of empirical theory and utilises rigorous analytical tools but also incorporates a significant measure of normative theory. The normative thrust of prescriptive legal positivism is that there are major social and individual benefits to be derived from adopting an aspirational model of law in terms of an integrated system of action guiding and coordinating rules that are clear, empirical in content, specific and practicable, and yet deal with generalities not particulars. The benefits include harm control, collective achievement, social justice, transparency and democratic control. The key institutions are independent courts for the fair and accurate application of the rules, professional bureaucracies and enforcement agencies for their effective and incorrupt implementation, and legislatures accountable to citizens under conditions of free speech, adequate information, education and association.

This thin conception of the rule of law focuses on formally good rules rather than on good substance and involves a separation of powers rather than a division of powers.[9] The functions and conditions of legislation, adjudication and administration are distinct but not distributed (although they may be devolved). It does not, however, allocate all political power to elected governments. The substance of the law is a matter for legislatures, but the form is not. Citizens or their representatives, after open debate, may make law, but they cannot apply it. Executives administer the laws but cannot change them and must act within them. Courts have a monopoly on settling disputes as to what the law is and using authorising coercive implementation, but are excluded as far as possible from law-making.

---

[7] D Dyzenhaus, *The Constitution of Law: Legality in a Time of Emergency* (Cambridge, Cambridge University Press, 2006) 11–12.

[8] T Campbell, *The Legal Theory of Ethical Positivism* (Brookfield, Dartmouth, 1996); T Campbell, *Prescriptive Legal Positivism* (Portland, Cavendish, 2004).

[9] If it seems rather too thin, it may be worth noting that this is the sort of rule of law that EP Thompson, in *Writing by Candlelight* (London, Merlin Press, 1980) 230, held to be an 'unconditional good: It concerns the conduct of social life, the regulation of conflicts, according to rules of law which are exactly defined and have palpable and material evidences.'

This crude statement of a somewhat utopian model of law and government cannot be adequately expounded or defended here.[10] However, it is important for this discussion to make the point that prescriptive legal positivism does not assume that whatever is democratically decided is thereby morally right. Democratic decision-making does generate prima facie political obligation independently of the content of the decisions in question. In fact the full benefits of institutionalised prescriptive legal positivism in its democratic form depend on more than law-abidingness, requiring a certain threshold quantum of ethical attitudes, such as that voters vote and legislators legislate in accordance with their conceptions of the right and the good, while executives govern and courts adjudicate in the spirit of commitment to the letter of the law and citizens commit to following in good faith the enacted rules as adjudicated by the courts.[11]

The moral rationale for adopting this conception of law is a mixture of the fairness and efficiency which follows from the public capacity to know in advance what a person's legal obligations and permissions amount to, and the instrumental significance of such a legal system to empower governments to govern effectively, but to do so in a way that is not arbitrary in the sense that it involves case by case and therefore inconsistent decision-making at the point of enforcement. These valued outcomes have particular moral force when the government in question is democratic in the sense that it seeks to maximise the equal power of all individuals within the decision-making processes of the state.

One other point to make is that the position is firmly positivist in relation to the exclusion of moral norms from the content of the rules that are created to achieve moral and other purposes. Morality relates to the choice of rules and to their proper application but ought not to be directly involved in the process of officials and courts deciding what the law is. That is a fundamental part of the separation of legislative and adjudicative powers. It therefore excludes natural law intrusions into the concept of legality according to which a law is not a law unless it meets certain substantive criteria, a position that would condone the creation of constitutions that give courts the power not to implement duly enacted statutes that they deem to be morally defective on specified grounds.

We have a major terminological gulf here in that legal theory is populated by persons who make such substantive moral requirements an essential feature of the rule of law or 'legality' while others regard this as undermining the fundamental moral rationale of the rule of law ideal. Undoubtedly, as emerges below, this gulf affects the approaches taken by different theorists

---

[10] For more see T Campbell, 'The Point of Legal Positivism' (1998) 7 *King's College Law Journal* 63.

[11] T Campbell, *The Legal Theory of Ethical Positivism* (Brookfield, Dartmouth, 1996) ch 5.

to the debate as to how to facilitate and yet limit and control the exercise of governmental powers of exception.

II. PREVENTING TERRORIST CARNAGE

What guidance flows from the prescriptive legal positivist to the policy-maker designing a system of enabling and yet controlling anti-terrorist measures? If the rule of law is a formal matter, then in itself legality has nothing to exclude practices that involve the abrogation of normal legal protections of suspected persons, provided the emergency policies are articulated in the form of good positivist rules. However, this immediately confronts the problem that, perhaps, in such extreme times with significant terrorist threats, such rules would inhibit the discretionary conduct of police protection and apprehension of terrorists in violation of their duties with respect to the protection of life. In which case, should ethical positivism bow to the higher moral demands of saving lives and endorse extra-legal discretion? On the other hand is the situation one in which the emphasis on publicly known and enforced rules can play a vital part in both controlling and facilitating official action in situations where moral rights-based judicial review has been traditionally an ineffective protection against abusive police conduct?

The first major question in this regard is whether or not the rules of engagement or police guidelines for the use of firearms relating to 'shoot to kill' are capable of being expressed in terms that can be clear guides which can be useful in the moment of action and objectively adjudicated after the event. The broad principles may be clear enough: lethal force is justified if it is necessary in the self-defence of the user of lethal force or if it is necessary to protect third parties from death or serious injury, and perhaps also, if it is necessary to secure the apprehension of a dangerous person or known perpetrator of serious crime.[12] Specific triggers of the reasonable assumption of such circumstances can include the possession of lethal weapons on the part of the target and the extent and nature of the evidence as to the dangerousness and identity of the targeted persons.[13]

Clearly there are particular needs for clarity and specificity in rules that are to be applied in the heat of dramatic events. If we rely on concepts such as 'reasonableness' and 'proportionality' to set the standards then this must be seen as a drafting failure on the part of the enactors of the legislation or directives. On the other hand it is necessary that the directives are such that

---

[12] 'Shoot to kill' may be taken to mean only a licence to kill persons without due process of law and without the need to provide any justification, such as self-defence. This may apply in military combat in times of war. I am assuming that 'shoot to kill' also covers killing for some further purpose, such as self-defence or prevention of harm.

[13] For a lucid summary of these points see S Miller and J Blackler, *Ethical Issues in Policing* (Burlington, Ashgate, 2005) ch 3.

can be followed in dramatic and fast-moving circumstances. Nevertheless, in this context we are talking about personnel who have been, or should have been, thoroughly trained in the use of lethal force, its controlling norms and the handling of stressful and dynamic scenarios.[14]

A second major question is whether the rules of engagement with respect to counter terrorism are likely to require significantly different conduct on the part of those involved in other types of prevention and containment. I suggest that they are, for a number of reasons, including: (1) the potential extent of the harm to third parties both in numbers and degree; (2) the fear and alarm caused by terrorism to entire populations; (3) the suffering caused by the economic damage resulting from acts of terror; (4) the extended undiscriminating aggressive motivation of terrorism in contrast to ordinary criminality; (5) the complexity of the calculations of risk involved in taking perhaps necessary pre-emptive action against suspected terrorists, and (6) the evident nature and extent of the potential limitations to civil liberties involved in counter terrorist tactics, such as preventive detention and, of course, shoot to kill policies.

While these circumstances are clearly overlapping with those which arise in the prevention of spousal violence,[15] violence in the context of theft and the potential harm done by psychologically disturbed persons, the scale of the danger in individual cases, and the public harms that result from terrorist activities and threats, make it at the very least plausible to argue that, outside war and the threat of war, the prevention of imminent terrorist attacks is different in several morally relevant aspects.[16]

This conclusion is likely to be supported by those who argue that post 9/11 there is a different style of policing emerging, at least in the security branches, which is more proactive, militaristic, covert, operational and top down, rather than locally negotiated, in its command structure, as was exhibited in the killing of the suicide bomber suspect Jean Charles de Menezes in a London underground train in July 2005. This is an event which has been traced back to the shoot to kill security policies adopted as part of Operation Kratos which developed guidelines for the British security police to follow in the pursuit of suicide bombers.[17] At the same time military personnel are now seen as appropriately involved in security policing activities to combat terrorism.[18]

---

[14] See this volume, ch 10.

[15] See this volume, ch 8.

[16] Z Baumann, *Liquid Fear* (Cambridge, Polity Press, 2006).

[17] P Kennison and A Loumansky, 'Shoot to kill—understanding the police use of force in combating suicide terrorism' (2007) 47 *Crime Law and Social Change* 151, drawing on GT Marx, *Under Cover: Police Surveillance in America* (Berkeley, University of California Press, 1988).

[18] See S Bronitt and D Stephens, 'Flying Under the Radar—The Use of Lethal Force against Hijacked Aircraft: Recent Australian Developments' (2007) 7 *Oxford University Commonwealth Law Journal* 265, which deals with the use of the military in aid of civil power, now extended in Australia to the authorisation of the Defence Force to shoot down civilian aircraft.

This takes us to possible positivist responses to these differences. The most obvious is that there should be careful articulation of a distinct set of rules to deal with suspected terrorist activities. These include making allowance for the greater risks involved to police and the public and the difficulty of knowing whether or not the target persons are in fact a major danger. I suggest, for instance, that there may be less reason to give as much priority to the safety of the police, who might be expected to take greater risks with their own lives in terrorism situations than in normal criminal work.

There may also be more reason to take suspects alive in the cause of identifying dangerous terrorist groups. On the other hand the degree of likelihood of horrendous outcomes required to justify killing a suspect who might be about to perpetrate a serious act of terrorism must be less than in situations that have less significant outcomes in quantitative terms.

In this case we might reasonably expect to see more tolerance of false positives, such as the de Menezes case, and more acceptance of superior orders and a looser definition of 'necessity' in the legal defence to charges of unlawful killing, and less reliance on absolute rights in the framing of policy directives.[19]

Something here will depend on a relevant definition as to what constitutes 'terrorism', however in this context what matters is mainly the nature and extent of the potential damage that might be perpetrated by the target persons rather than their motivations. In this context, I note, in support of the positivist thesis, the significance of the critiques of anti-terror laws which utilise unnecessarily vague and open-ended definitions of terrorism.[20]

It follows from all this that the content of the rules which, I have suggested, might flow from the distinctive features of counter terrorism are likely to generate anxiety on the part of civil libertarians, of whom I am one, since the suggestion is that such rules would anticipate less protection for suspects and increased likelihood of abuse of counter terror powers by their application to other police activities. This is exacerbated by the evident pressure on police to be seen to be acting decisively in suspected terrorism scenarios.

On the basis of the democratic credentials of prescriptive legal positivism, it is of course open to the legislatures to put aside these considerations on such grounds as that the preservation of life and control of state power outweigh the alleged and perhaps exaggerated danger of terrorism. It may be

---

[19] See this volume, ch 6. As an exception see the discussion of the German Federal Constitutional Court relating to Luftsicherheitsgesetz (Aviation Security Act) of 2005 discussed in J Kleinig, 'Civil Emergencies and Claims of Innocence', this volume, and in Bronitt and Stephens, 'Flying Under the Radar, The Use of Lethal Force against High Jacked Aircraft: Recent Australian Developments'.

[20] Consider, for instance the detailed definition provided in the Australian Criminal Code 1995 (Cth) s 100(1); See also JL Hiebert, 'Parliamentary Review of Terrorist Measures' (2005) 68 *MLR* 676.

that the benefits of a sense of security are over-valued and the possibilities of learning to live with terrorism are underestimated.[21] Further, it may well be that citizens in general and their representatives are given to panic and alarm, and are insufficiently concerned as to the plight of erroneously killed suspects. What, in such circumstances, does the prescriptive legal positivist have to offer?

III. STATES OF EMERGENCY

If circumstances appear to justify a different set of rules and procedures for the use of lethal weapons in relation to the prevention of terrorism, one obvious path for the democratic legal positivist is to work at getting the special rules required into as good formal shape as possible, particularly with respect to the nature of the risk, the system of command and the evidence that is legally required to justify lethal intervention on the part of trained and authorised personnel. However, it would appear that there are some grounds for acknowledging that, in some respect at least, operational directives are likely to be too loosely worded and discretionary to meet positivist standards of clarity and decisiveness.

In these circumstances one further move is to make the application of these formally unsatisfactory rules conditional on the prior existence of an officially declared state of emergency. The suggestion is that a precondition of such civil liberty threatening rules should require the declaration of a state of emergency or danger on terrorism grounds. This would enable us to draw on the pacifying effect which is occasioned by taking some of the vital decisions out of the heat of the moment so that, while the occasions for the use of lethal force are likely to be in the cauldron, the assessment of the possible outcomes of terrorism can be subject to more measured consideration.

Uninformed comment on this device is likely to fasten on the alleged fact that instantiating states of emergency is inevitably within the discretionary power of the executive and therefore provides no controlling dynamic against the mistaken and abusive use of enhanced shoot to kill powers.[22] There are plenty of historical examples of governments declaring states of emergency as a self-protecting anti-democratic device. However, there are

---

[21] L Zedner, 'The Pursuit of Security' in T Hope and R Sparks (eds), *Crime, Risk and Insecurity* (London, Routledge, 2000) 200.

[22] G Agamben, *States of Exception* (Chicago, University of Chicago Press, 2005) demonstrates the vulnerability of all states to arbitrary takeovers in times of crisis, a fact that is overlooked by those who put their trust in human rights guarantees, but this does not exclude the possibility of the declaration of states of emergency being formally subject to judicial oversight on the basis of specific emergency laws.

plenty of counter-examples of various emergency provisions that are precise in their requirements and subject to judicial oversight.[23]

I take the potential benefits of formal states of emergency to be: (1) avowal that the measures involved are exceptional and are likely to be temporary or, if extended, subject to periodic review; (2) the requirement that objective evidence be presented that there is a de facto emergency of the sort envisaged in the statute, and (3) the fact that it can operate in tandem with the requirement that the relevant parliament make a similar judgment after having had the opportunity to challenge such information and evidence as the government lays before it.

The state of emergency mechanism will seem unattractive to those who know of the history of courts in many jurisdictions in deferring to the judgment of the executive in the determination as to whether or not there is a state of emergency. This follows the Schmitt model where it is assumed that it is the de facto executive government that has the power to initiate the imposition of a state of emergency that suspends some or all existing laws and enables legislation by degree. However, there is nothing in the concept of a state of emergency that rules out the clear identification of what is to count as an emergency within the legislation in question. While emergencies themselves might require decisive flexible action, this does not mean that what constitutes an emergency cannot be articulated with precision and applied to particular situations with some precision. This can be readily illustrated in relation to the declaration for formal emergencies in response to natural disasters.

In the case of counter terrorism there could be a requirement that a state of emergency requires either actual instances of lethal terrorist activities or hard evidence of serious potential terrorist attacks on the scale, for instance of 9/11. Given the criteria set out for good positivist law there is a need to be much more specific than the indeterminate category of an 'emergency'. However, there are plenty of exemplary instances of suitably specific criteria for the existence of an emergency of one sort or another. The generic term may not suffice but the nature of an emergency is susceptible to linguistic capture as well as most conceptions. The objection that part of the nature of an emergency is that it is unpredictable and therefore undefinable is belied by the existence of precise criteria for natural emergencies and the contingencies of war.

Very similar factors are evident in analyses of the mechanism of derogation. Thus, the European Convention on Human Rights (ECHR), article 15(1) allows derogation from particular specified rights 'in times of war or public emergency threatening the life of the nation'. Both arms of the requirement,

---

[23] See T Campbell, 'Emergency Strategies for prescriptive legal positivists: anti-terrorist law and legal theory' in VV Ramraj (ed), *Emergencies and the Limits of Legality* (Cambridge, Cambridge University Press, 2008) 201.

particularly the second, are capable of more precise formulation, and herein lies one of main challenges to the prescriptive legal positivist who wishes to suggest that formal states of emergency can enable courts to judge objectively whether the necessary conditions exist, as defined in the statute, without having recourse to speculative or moral considerations. This may result in a multiplicity of stand-by emergency legislation for different types of crisis, but that may be an acceptable price to pay for democratic control of liberty threatening police powers.

All this must be put into the context of the wider debate concerning courts versus legislatures as the better path for the effective protection of human rights in the context of terrorism. We are dealing here with perhaps the most fundamental human right, the right to life, with respect both to suspected terrorists and the victims of actual terrorist activity, as well as, of course, the lives of those involved in counter terrorist organisations. It therefore seems appropriate to consider whether this is not a paradigmatic example of the sort of practice that ought to be subject to the strongest form of whatever sort of judicial review is available within a jurisdiction together with whatever oversight can be obtained through the operations of international human rights law. Further, police powers are in that realm of state activity with which courts have a working familiarity.

On the other hand, the scope and limitations of the right to life are amongst the more controversial aspects of human rights jurisprudence. Even if we put to one side the issue of capital punishment, there are conflicting authorities as to whether the saving of life is a negative or a positive duty. The decisive life or death questions are even more contested in the context of moral debate about the proper content of such law. Moreover, when it comes to security measures designed to protect lives of innocent persons against terrorist attack, this is not a field of judicial expertise. There are considerable problems about judicial access to security information that cannot be divulged in open court without endangering lives. Additionally, there is an extensive literature on the historical inadequacies of courts in the exercise of such powers as they have in the face of illiberal legislation in times of emergency.

I touch briefly on this rapidly spawning debate through the work of Mark Tushnet on emergency powers. Tushnet, uncharacteristically for someone from the home of strong judicial review, comments on the superior efficacy of political process on such matters.[24]

Tushnet's thesis is that political controls on emergency powers in democracies can in certain conditions be more effective than legal controls in real time. He defines an emergency as occurring 'when there is general agreement

---

[24] M Tushnet, 'The political constitution of emergency powers: parliamentary and separation-of- powers regulation' (2007) 3 *International Journal of Law in Context* 275.

that a nation or some part of it faces a sudden and unexpected rise in social costs, accompanied by a great deal of uncertainty about the length of time the high level cost will persist'. This enables him to rule out 'manufactured emergencies' when governments invent emergencies for self-serving reasons. By 'emergency powers' he means 'the expansion of governmental authority generally and the concomitant alteration in the scope of individual liberty, and the transference of important "first instance" law-making authority from legislatures to executive officials' so they can act quickly, coordinated and on adequate information, while 'control' means 'measures taken to ensure that whatever alternations in government power and individual liberty that occur, do not produce a higher rate of violations of fundamental human rights than happens under non-emergency conditions'.[25]

The control question, Tushnet argues, requires knowledge as to whether or not the new practices violate fundamental rights, while acknowledging that it cannot simply be assumed that *any* diminution of rights is a violation of such rights. He then sets out the evidence that courts are normally slow and weak at the time of apparently unwarranted restrictions on liberty in national emergencies. Politics, he thinks, can work better than courts in the US unless the same party holds the Presidency and controls Congress. Courts lack the necessary speed and information to intervene effectively, while 'executive governments have an array of lawful techniques they can use to retard the pace of judicial proceedings, including withholding of information until ordered to do so by the highest court'.[26] He then draws on evidence that the US style separation of powers impedes the initiatives of executive power in this sphere.[27] He goes on further to extend his claims to what he calls 'constrained parliamentary systems' where some sort of rights-based judicial review is available, such as the UK, pointing to instances of effective parliamentary impact on the terms of the Prevention of Violence Act 1939 and the lifting of the suppression of the *Daily Worker* newspaper during the Second World War in 1942 and, more recently to the activities of the parliamentary Joint Committee on Human Rights. He then passes to his main example of political effectiveness, the Arar Commission in Canada relating to the Canadian citizen of Syrian origin who was intercepted by the US security services and deported to Syria for questioning as an al-Qaeda suspect who was released and compensated as the result of press and political activities.

---

[25] Ibid 276–77.

[26] Ibid 277.

[27] M Tushnet, 'The Political Constitution of Emergency Powers: Some Lessons from Hamdan' (2007) 91 *Minnesota Law Review* 1451; see also M Tushnet, 'The political constitution of emergency powers: some conceptual questions' in VV Ramraj (ed), *Emergencies and the Limits of Legality* (Cambridge, Cambridge University Press, 2008).

Evaluating such historical material is beyond my competence, but what I can do is identify some of the options in this tangled empirical debate as to institutional competence. The comments follow Tushnet's paper in the same volume of the journal in which his article appears. Colm O'Cinneide of University College London responds that effective political action on these matters depends on the existence of 'a vibrant constitutional culture where the potential abuse of emergency powers is recognised', where 'legal and supranational controls plays an important role', which he exemplifies in the impact of the ECHR through the implementation of the UK Human Rights Act 1998.

Similarly Andrew Lynch, Director of the Terrorism and Law Project at the University of New South Wales claims that the absence of a Human Rights Act in the Australian federation demonstrates that the sort of political controls identified by Tushnet do not operate in the absence of legal controls. His evidence is the way in which the Howard Government was able to enact its counter terror legislation almost without modification. Finally Phillipe Sands, of University College London, identifies the case of *Abbassi v Secretary of State for Foreign and Commonwealth Affairs* as an example of the way in which a relatively ineffective legal decision can, by its use of human rights analysis, have a political impact of considerable significance.[28]

The consensus of Tushnet's critics is that political and legal controls in times of emergency should not be seen as alternatives but as supplementations of each other. What seems to be missing, however, is precisely what the contributing role of the courts should be. Tushnet's critics, by assuming that human rights-based judicial review is what courts can offer, assume that what we are dealing with here is some sort of moral safety-net based on moral judgements as to the proportionality between desirable objectives and undesirable means, such as civil rights restrictions. However, the sort of impact they are looking for might be derived from a more traditional administrative form of judicial review which turns on the black letter legality of the official action in question.

Thus, in the *Abbassi* case the legal decision or opinion was founded on the clear law of habeas corpus that prevents imprisonment without legal justification deriving from black letter law. This has none of the controversiality of the sort of 'legal controls' that Lynch has in mind when he declares Australia to be without 'any formal instrument of rights protection', or those features of the *Belmarsh* decision that have been hailed as the high point of judicial activism under the UK Human Rights Act when the

---

[28] Mr Abbassi, a British national, was released from Guantanamo after the Court of Appeal's finding that he was being detained arbitrarily in a 'legal black hole'.

Law Lords found that certain detention and deportation powers under UK immigration law were incompatible with the ECHR.[29]

Given the ultimate ineffectiveness of the *Belmarsh* decision which merely landed the detained persons under rather less attractive home detention under hastily enacted 'control orders', we might instead take a lead from the minority view of Lord Hoffman in the same case, who found that the government had not made their case that there existed a state of emergency which would then justify their derogation from the European Convention. If we follow this lead, and if we obtain emergency legislation in which there are more precise criteria for what constitutes a relevant state of emergency than is the case with the derogation clause in the ECHR, then we would have a more legitimate form of courts' oversight of emergency practices which could play a more effective because less controversial part in focusing political attention on rights-threatening legislation and administrative practice. I suggest that this is an appropriate rule of law mechanism for steering elected governments towards acceptable shoot to kill policies with respect to counter terrorism.

---

[29] *A v Secretary of State for the Home Department* [2004] UKHL 56.

2

Civil Emergencies and the Claims of Innocence

JOHN KLEINIG AND TZIPORAH KASACHKOFF

I. INTRODUCTION

O N SEPTEMBER 11, 2001, while the four terrorist attacks were still taking place, US Vice-President Dick Cheney is reported to have authorised the 'taking out' of any further hijacked aircraft.[1] Had that order been acted upon, passengers travelling in those planes would have almost certainly been killed. In 2005, after a person, later discovered to be mentally disturbed, threatened to crash a plane into a high-rise building, the German parliament passed a law to permit the Federal Minister for Defence to authorise the shooting down of an aircraft were there ample reason to believe that it was being used as a weapon.[2] A year later, however, the German Federal Constitutional Court declared the law unconstitutional in response to an appeal by a German citizen who argued that, as a potential passenger on a civilian plane, the shooting down of a suspicious plane on which he was travelling would treat him—an innocent person—as a means to the saving of others which, he claimed, would violate both his right to life and his right to be treated with dignity. The Constitutional Court agreed that, inter alia, the ruling authorising the shooting down of civilian but suspicious planes would violate Articles 2.2 and 1.1 of the Basic

---

[1] D Milbank, 'Cheney Authorized Shooting Down Airplanes', *Washington Post*, 18 June 2004, A01, www.washingtonpost.com/wp-dyn/articles/A50745-2004Jun17.html; *cf* also, www.mediamatters.org/research/200409240007. Much of the discussion of V-P Cheney's action focused on whether he really had the authority to do what he did or instead usurped a role reserved for the President.

[2] The relevant clause was included as §14(3) of the Luftsicherheitsgesetz (Aviation Security Act) of 2005: 'the direct use of armed force [against an aircraft] is permissible only where it must be assumed under the circumstances that the aircraft is intended to be used against human lives, and where this is the only means to avert the imminent danger'. The translation used is that found in the Federal Constitutional Court's ruling.

Law, which recognise the right to life and the inviolability (*Unantastbarkeit*) of human dignity.[3]

The German law and its subsequent overturning have generated a great deal of legal and constitutional discussion.[4] We have no desire or competence to add to that debate. However, the moral questions raised by the possibilities just referred to are of great interest and here we propose to focus on several of them.

We will consider (in section III) the 9/11-type scenario described above, in which an appropriately authorised government official is faced with giving an order for a hijacked passenger plane to be shot down. The aircraft is believed to be heading towards a major metropolis where it will be deliberately crashed into a symbolically important building, and, if it makes its destination, will almost certainly cause considerable loss of life there in addition to that of the aircraft's passengers. Then (in section IV) we want to consider some variants on that case—one in which the pilot of the hijacked plane decides to defy the hijackers by crashing it before it reaches their intended destination, even though the lives of those on board will be

---

[3] Germany's Basic Law of 1949 includes as part of its opening article: 'Human dignity shall be inviolable.' Deutsches Grundgesetz (hereafter GG), official translation available at www. btg-bestellservice.de/pdf/80201000.pdf. The Federal Constitutional Court's judgment also draws significantly upon Article 2.2, sentence 1, which states that 'Every person shall have the right to life and physical integrity.' However, because there are provisions for overriding the latter ('These rights may be interfered with only pursuant to a law.' sentence 3), the decisive work is done by Article 1.1. The judgment can be found in BVerfG, 1 BvR 357/05 of 15 February 2006, paras 1–154, available at www.bundesverfassungsgericht.de/entscheidungen/ rs20060215_1bvr035705en.html.

[4] For some articles in English, see R Geiss, 'Civil Aircraft as Weapons of Large-Scale Destruction: Countermeasures, Article 3bis of the Chicago Convention, and the Newly Adopted German "Luftsicherheitsgesetz"' (2005) 27 *Michigan Journal of International Law* 227; M Bohlander, '*In Extremis*—Hijacked Airplanes, "Collateral Damage" and the Limits of Criminal Law' (2006) *Criminal Law Review* 579; O Lepsius, 'Human Dignity and the Downing of an Aircraft: The German Federal Constitutional Court Strikes Down a Prominent Anti-terrorism Provision in the New Air-transport Security Act' (2006) 7 *German Law Journal* 761; M Bohlander, 'Of Shipwrecked Sailors, Unborn Children, Conjoined Twins and Hijacked Airplanes—Taking Human Life and the Defence of Necessity' (2006) 70 *Journal of Criminal Law* 147; K Möller, 'On Treating Persons as Ends: The German Aviation Security Act, Human Dignity, and the German Federal Constitutional Court' (2006) 51 *Public Law* 457; M Ladiges, 'Comment—Oliver Lepsius's Human Dignity and the Downing of Aircraft: The German Federal Constitutional Court Strikes Down a Prominent Anti-terrorism Provision in the New Air-transport Security Act' (2007) 8 *German Law Journal* 307; T Hörnle, 'Hijacked Airplanes: May They Be Shot Down?' (2007) 10 *New Criminal Law Review* 582; S Bronitt and D Stephens, '"Flying Under the Radar"—The Use of Lethal Force Against Hijacked Aircraft: Recent Australian Developments' (2007) 7 *Oxford University Commonwealth Law Journal* 265; A Walen, 'Striking Down the German Air-transport Security Act; Pragmatics over Philosophical Coherence', unpublished paper available at www.publicpolicy.umd. edu/faculty/Walen/Works%20in%20Progress/Striking%20Down%20the%20German%20 Airtransport%20Security%20Act, %20clean.doc; R Youngs, 'Germany: Shooting Down Aircraft and Analyzing Computer Data' (2008) 6 *International Journal of Constitutional Law* 331; S Hufnagel, 'German Perspectives on the Right to Life and Human Dignity in the "War on Terror"' (2008) 32 *Criminal Law Journal* 100.

sacrificed (section IV A); another in which several of the passengers decide to try to overpower the hijackers to prevent them from reaching their target (section IV B); and a third in which a private citizen, hearing of the hijacking over the radio, has an opportunity and the means to shoot the plane down before it reaches the hijackers' target (section IV C).

Before we consider those cases, however, we want to spend some time discussing three issues that are common to each account. Arguably, these factors give the cases much—even if not all—of their moral potency. First, the deliberate downing of the aircraft will almost certainly result in the loss of what are called, in a sense to be explained, 'innocent' lives (section II A). Second, whether or not the aircraft is shot down, the passengers will shortly be killed (section II B). And third, if the aircraft reaches its intended target, more lives will be lost than if it is brought down beforehand (section II C).[5]

II. THREE MORAL CHALLENGES

A. The Claims of Innocent Human Life

Deliberately downing the aircraft will result in the loss of innocent lives.[6] What is meant by 'innocence' in this context is that (apart from the hijackers themselves) the passengers on the plane bear no responsibility—either causal or moral—for initiating or perpetuating the threat posed by the hijacking. They are akin to trapped bystanders.[7]

These innocents have certain important moral claims by virtue of, first, their being *human*, second, their being human *lives*, and third, their being *innocent* human lives.

(1) *Human Standing.* Because of their standing as moral agents,[8] humans are owed special regard. As moral agents, they have important rights to self-determination. They are thus owed (and owe to others) some degree of non-interference. Moreover, they (especially the passengers in the cases at hand) have a significant claim to be involved in decisions that will affect their interests.[9]

---

[5] At this point we leave open the question whether that will be morally worse.

[6] We are not concerned with a case in which hijackers evict both the crew and passengers and are now flying towards their target. In these circumstances, few would question the permissibility of shooting it down, though questions would obviously need to be raised about where this should take place.

[7] Here we leave the aircraft's (official) pilot out of the equation.

[8] We leave aside the complications that may be introduced by marginal cases in which humans are not (yet) moral agents. That discussion belongs elsewhere.

[9] The actual scope of a right to be involved in decisions affecting one is subject to some dispute. For a provocative discussion, see C Cohen, 'Have I a Right to a Voice in Decisions that Affect My Life?' (1971) 5 *Nous* 53.

Admittedly, rights to self-determination are not absolute and some instantiations of those rights are more demanding than others.[10] Nevertheless, it is ordinarily expected that in cases in which liberty or liberties are to be constrained, people who are subject to constraint should have an opportunity to review and challenge the grounds on which such constraints are to be based.

(2) *Claims of Life.* The most foundational claim that people have is to life itself. Although life is likely to be valued for itself, it also undergirds everything else and thus, when what is at stake is human life, a most demanding right comes into play. Violating the right to life permanently disables or extinguishes one's other rights.[11]

Even if we allow that some rights of agency (such as the right not to be tortured) are more stringent than the right to life, reasons for overriding a person's right to life will generally need to be much stronger than those required to limit liberty and liberties.

The strongest case that can be made for taking human life is that such a killing is necessary for self-defence or, in certain circumstances, for the defence of the lives of others.[12] In these cases, there is sufficient reason for terminating the life of those who threaten one's own or others' lives—assuming, of course, that there exists no less drastic means for the saving of one's own life or others' lives. But though there is widespread agreement on this general position, there is also considerable disagreement over its details, for example:

— the conditions under which such self-defensive behaviour may take place (whether the perception of threat must be reasonable; whether the threat in question must be to life or may extend to serious injury; whether the threat must be 'imminent'; etc);
— the rationale for such defensive behaviour (and whether the aggressor forfeits his right to life, has it suspended, or only has it overridden);

---

[10] Our desires to travel on the road at whatever speed we wish and to construct on our property whatever kind of house we want are socially constrained and morally more easily constrained than our right to marry whomever we wish, or our rights to free speech and religious freedom. In US constitutional law, this is reflected in the differing degrees of scrutiny to which constraints on self-determination are subjected.

[11] The point is put a little too starkly: (1) it operates with a narrow understanding of the right to life—others may wish to argue for a more expansive understanding; (2) one's right to have one's will honoured is not extinguished or disabled upon death—at most what is disabled is the waivability that is normally associated with rights; (3) the claim is not intended to imply that the right to life is stronger than all other rights (eg, the right not to be tortured); and (4) we leave to one side other ways in which the right to life and right to self-determination may be connected (whether, eg, should the capacity for self-determination be destroyed, the right to life would be diminished).

[12] Though often run together as 'defence of life', killing in self-defence and killing in defence of others may not be morally equivalent. For an exploration, see this volume, ch 6.

— whether the rationale justifies, warrants, permits, or excuses the taking of life; and

— whether the aggressor is active or passive, and deliberately or only negligently threatening.

We shall not rehearse these and other controversies,[13] though some of the arguments that appear in these debates will also reappear in the present case.

As we have already hinted in adverting to the controversy over the scope and conditions for the defensive taking of life, speaking generally of aggressors is apt to conceal the different ways in which others' lives may be placed at risk. The standard case of self-defence is one in which A wilfully and deliberately attacks B, and B, to defend himself, must seriously injure or kill A. But not all aggressors, even when causally threatening, are morally responsible for the threat they pose, and in such cases there is considerable controversy, not only about whether one would be morally justified in taking the life of the person who poses the threat, but also about the rationale for such justification if there is one.

In this type of situation, what can be and often is argued is that though the lives of the morally non-culpable aggressor and person threatened cannot be differentiated in terms of their *intrinsic* worth, the fact that one party is causally responsible for the threat posed to the other gives the threatened party a moral edge or standing that can be used, if not to justify, then either to permit or excuse shifting the cost of death onto the aggressor.[14]

(3) *Claims of Innocence.* In the hijacked aircraft case, however, the passengers are not aggressors at all, but hostages to others' aggression. Their inherent claim to self-determination and life is as strong as any can be. It is mere happenstance that they are on a plane that hijackers have

---

[13] For an overview of many of these issues, see S Uniacke, *Permissible Killing: The Self-Defence Justification of Homicide* (Cambridge, Cambridge University Press, 1994).

[14] We can imagine a case in which A is falling from a building towards B, who is standing on the pavement. B will be killed if and when A hits him. Should that occur, however, A will survive the impact though, without B as a cushion, A will be killed. In the envisaged case there is no suggestion that one life is more valuable than the other; nevertheless, B may step aside, for A has no rightful claim on B's remaining where he is. (Were B's life not at stake, B might have a moral ('Good Samaritan') obligation to do something to assist A.) A more problematic case is one in which B, seeing A falling towards him, decides to shift A's trajectory by shooting him with a weapon that will throw him off course. Opting for that solution rather than stepping aside might be viewed as opting for a causally (and morally?) more potent alternative (given the equal probabilities of death in each case), but it raises a question about B's own agency in bringing about A's death. Further, we might want to distinguish (a) the case in which shooting A (with a foam dart) does not injure A but simply moves him away from B where he will die on impact with the ground from (b) a case in which shooting A injures B but it is the impact with the ground that causes death and (c) a case in which shooting A is the cause of his death—he is dead by the time he hits the ground. Would it make a difference were C, who sees what is taking place, to become the agent who changes A's trajectory?

commandeered and are now using as a *weapon* against others.[15] The latter fact has considerable weight. Were we to know that the hijackers intended only to leave the country, the question of preventing them by shooting down the plane would hardly arise as a moral option. But the hijackers are targeting a site that they view as strategic to their cause, and we are to presume (with some discussion of this to come) that 'significantly greater devastation' will be caused if they are not stopped than if they are stopped by being shot down.

We now indicate a number of considerations that might be thought relevant to the morality of a decision to shoot down the aircraft.

(a) *The Appeal to Dignity.* One consideration—one that was advanced by the German Federal Constitutional Court—might be to argue that the dignity of the passengers would be violated were the plane to be shot down. In that case, because their situation is deemed to come within the provisions of Article 1 of the Basic Law, the issue is effectively settled, since the Basic Law affirms the inviolability of human dignity. As the Court puts it:

> Such a treatment [shooting down the plane] ignores the status of the persons affected as subjects endowed with dignity and inalienable rights. By their killing being used as a means to save others they are treated as objects and at the same time are deprived; with their lives being disposed of unilaterally by the state, the persons on board the aircraft, who, as victims, are themselves in need of protection, are denied the value which is due to a human being for his or her own sake.[16]

But although the Constitutional Court believes that in such cases the state would treat the passengers' lives 'as mere objects of its rescue operation for the protection of others', this seems mistaken. The passengers' lives are not being targeted *as a means* of thwarting the hijackers. Rather, the hijackers are being targeted, and it is tragic that they cannot be effectively targeted

---

[15] Of course, it is possible that the hijackers chose their aircraft because it had innocent passengers on board and they wished to deter the authorities from shooting it down. But, as likely as not, a regular commercial flight was a convenience to them rather than a morally strategic choice. We do not explore the possibility that the manipulative use of innocents might alter the moral equation, though the strategic consequences and moral implications of refusing to shoot down an aircraft carrying innocent passengers should not be ignored. See CAJ Coady, *Morality and Political Violence* (Cambridge, Cambridge University Press, 2008) 149.

[16] German Constitutional Court, BVerfG, 1 BvR 357/05, para 122. That would not necessarily be the case were human dignity seen instead as an important, but not necessarily overriding consideration (such as the right to life), as it is in the constitutional documents of some other countries (Israel, eg). See Israeli Basic Law: Human Dignity and Liberty (1992, as amended 1994) Article 1A: 'The purpose of this Basic Law is to protect human dignity and liberty,' available at www.knesset.gov.il/laws/special/eng/basic3_eng.htm. What is more critical in the present context, however, is the moral status that human dignity should be accorded. The absolute rejection of torture is often yoked to the way in which it violates human dignity.

without the passengers also losing their lives.[17] It is the fact that they will be killed that makes it tragic. Describing it as 'tragic' would be less apt were their lives thought to be of no or reduced value. If the plane is shot down, it is not the passengers' dignity that is unrecognised but their right to life that is invaded and the critical question is whether their weighty right to life is infringed in a defensible or excusable way.[18]

(b) *Intended v Foreseen Harm*. The foregoing suggests a further consideration that is sometimes advanced, namely, that the deaths of the innocent passengers should be seen as 'collateral damage'—the foreseen but unintended (and indeed unavoidable) side effect of shooting down the plane.[19] This way of construing the matter reflects a long tradition of debate, going back at least to Thomas Aquinas and usually conducted under the rubric of 'the doctrine of double effect' (DDE).

We have no wish to add to the huge literature on double effect.[20] However, we note the following:

— The distinction between that which is intended and that which is merely foreseen does not seem to possess uniform moral significance, and it may be necessary to consider whether this is one of those cases in which what is foreseen and what is intended are all but morally indistinguishable.[21]

— Even when the intended/foreseen distinction appears to play an active moral role it does not do so on its own but only in conjunction with certain other considerations. In Joseph Mangan's widely cited formulation of DDE:

---

[17] Some might be unwilling to accept this assumption. The German legislation and some other commentators countenance the possibility of intermediate measures, eg, damaging the aircraft or otherwise forcing it to land so that it cannot endanger others, but without killing the passengers. We are assuming that this is like expecting police to shoot the gun out of a criminal's hand rather than shooting the criminal—morally relevant only when we have the technology or capacity to do it. To the extent that it becomes technically feasible, then the principle of the least restrictive alternative would come into play.

[18] To appreciate the contingent relation between the shooting down of the aircraft and the deaths of the passengers, consider the following possibility: the missile used to shoot down the plane destroys one of the engines. The hijackers, seeing that they will not reach their target, determine that there will be no survivors and so, as the stricken plane heads for a crash landing, they detonate bombs that blow up the plane and kill all aboard.

[19] We shall later say more about the unfortunate euphemism of 'collateral damage'.

[20] For a valuable, brief overview of that literature, see A McIntyre, 'Doctrine of Double Effect' in EN Zalta (ed), *The Stanford Encyclopedia of Philosophy* (Spring 2009 edn) www.plato.stanford.edu/archives/spr2009 /entries/double-effect.

[21] Glanville Williams famously uses the example of a person who blows up a passenger plane in order to collect the insurance. We are unlikely to say that, because the deaths were only foreseen and not intended, they should count differently in our decision about what charges to lay. Williams, however, was excessively sceptical about the distinction's moral significance. See G Williams, *Criminal Law: The General Part* (London, Stevens and Sons, 1961); see also G Williams, 'The *Mens Rea* for Murder: Leave it Alone' (1989) 105 *Law Quarterly Review* 387.

A person may licitly perform an action that he sees will produce a good effect and a bad effect provided that four conditions are verified at one and the same time:

(i)   that the action in itself from its very object be good or at least indifferent;
(ii) that the good effect and not the evil effect be intended;
(iii) that the good effect not be produced by means of the evil effect; and
(iv) that there be a proportionately grave reason for permitting the evil effect.[22]

Does shooting down the aircraft satisfy these conditions? It probably does, though that leaves us with the complex issue of the doctrine's acceptability—including whether the DDE renders an otherwise evil action 'licit' or at best diminishes the wrong done.[23]

(c) *Doing v Allowing Harm*. Those who are unpersuaded by what are asserted to be the moral implications of the intended/foreseen distinction may be moved by another distinction that is intuitively appealing—one between *doing harm* (to the passengers, should the aircraft be shot down) and *allowing harm to eventuate* (both to the passengers on the aircraft that is crashed into the target site as well as to those at the target site). For they may consider that it is morally worse for someone to harm another than to allow another (or perhaps different others) to suffer harm.[24]

The doing/allowing harm distinction has an intuitive appeal. But it is not altogether clear whether the distinction is generally sustainable, and in the particular cases in which it is sustainable whether it has moral significance, and when it does have moral significance, what that significance is.[25]

(i) Consider the distinction's intuitive appeal. Suppose A pushes B off a jetty to drown him. C happens to pass by, observes B flailing in the water, but, though capable of rescuing him, does not do so and allows B to drown. Though we would most likely consider both A and C responsible in B's death, it is only A whom we would consider a murderer. Our differential

---

[22] J Mangan, 'An Historical Analysis of the Principle of Double Effect' (1949) 10 *Theological Studies* 41, 43.

[23] For a recent critique, see A McIntyre, 'Doing Away with Double Effect' (2001) 111 *Ethics* 219.

[24] For the time being we are bracketing the potential relevance of our previously canvassed distinction between intending the harm that one causes and merely foreseeing the harm that one causes. We also bracket the fact that, from the perspective of someone who can order the plane to be brought down, two different harms must be taken into consideration: if the aircraft is brought down, only the innocent passengers will be harmed; but if the aircraft is not brought down, harm will be allowed to befall not only the innocent passengers, but also those who are located at the hijackers' target site. We will address the issue of numbers later (section I C).

[25] For a brief overview, see F Howard-Snyder, 'Doing vs. Allowing Harm', *Stanford Encyclopedia of Philosophy* (Fall 2008 edn) www.plato.stanford.edu/entries/doing-allowing.

judgement of A and C might be taken to support the view that there *is* a moral difference between doing harm and allowing it to occur.

But it is at least arguable that in an example such as this, it is not the distinction between doing/allowing that makes for our tendency to judge A and C differently, but reasonable presumptions concerning the intentions/ motivations of those involved. Such differences in presumptions concerning intentions or motivations might be thought generally to distinguish the 'doer' and the 'allower'.[26]

But even if the intentions and motivations typical of the doer of harm versus those typical of the allower of harm play a powerful role in our differential judgements concerning the morality of their respective acts, they do not seem to tell the full moral story. To see this, consider the following case: A and C are equally desirous of B's death and both would readily bring about B's death if given the opportunity. However, A is the first to get the opportunity, and when he does he pushes B off the jetty. The trumped C watches from the shore as B drowns. Perhaps we would view both A and C as equally *despicable*, but only A, as the agent of B's death, should be held to have murdered him. So agency must also be factored into moral assessment.[27]

---

[26] If A pushes B off the jetty to drown him, A can be presumed to intend B's death (for foul motives), whereas C is not likely to intend B's death or have a particularly foul motive for allowing him to die (perhaps he is in a hurry, or does not want to wet his new clothes or, more excusably, fears that he may himself drown). We can see the powerful role played by intention and motivation should the case be one in which A pushes B off the jetty only accidentally or carelessly, but in which C secretly rejoices when he sees B flailing in the water. In such circumstances we might judge A no more harshly than C, even though A does the harm and C only allows it to occur. This would comport well with a pair of hypotheticals made famous by James Rachels. Adapting Rachels' example to the present case, A, wanting B dead, pushes B off the jetty to drown him, and C, also wanting B dead and on his way to push him off the jetty, arrives to find B already in the water, and lets him flail and sink (all the while being prepared to push B back under if he looks as though he might survive). See J Rachels, 'Active and Passive Euthanasia' (1975) 292 *New England Journal of Medicine* 278. Should we judge A more severely than C? We need not accept either Rachels' conclusion that doing and allowing are thereby to be seen as morally equivalent or the more general view that no moral work is done by the doing/allowing distinction.

[27] But what is involved in being the agent of another's death, and is agency what makes a moral difference between doing and allowing harm? Answering this question in any depth is likely to take us too far afield. Nevertheless, we should at least make some gestures toward its importance and complexity. For example, is A the agent of B's death because A is causally responsible for the harm that is visited upon B, whereas C is not the agent of B's death because C is causally unconnected with the harm that B suffers? We might think that C was causally unconnected to B's death because, had C not been in the vicinity, B would still have died. But is that enough to show C's lack of causal connection? Might it be the case that, when discussing agency, determinations of causal connectedness incorporate considerations of moral responsibility, thus begging the question whether A's causing harm provides an independent basis for judging agency? Might we want to argue that, had C not failed to do what he could and should have done, B would not have drowned and therefore that he had some causal role in B's death? However, a moralised account of causal connectedness cannot be the whole story. Consider our response should A accidentally push B off the jetty. In such circumstances, A would harm B no less than had he intentionally pushed him: the causal link is as strong in one case as in

It might be tempting to conclude from this that the notion of agency resurrects something of the doing/allowing distinction, attracting assignment of greater responsibility to the agent of harm—that is, the doer of harm—than to the allower of harm. But this is a temptation that we should resist because the notion of agency does not always track commissions of acts as opposed to failures to act. A mother who neglects to feed her child such that the child dies of starvation is someone who has failed to act. But by virtue of her special responsibility to her child (along with the presumption that she is able to meet that responsibility) this failure attracts the judgement that she is the agent of the child's death. In this situation, doing and allowing may be thought to converge, or even disappear. All that is likely to remain in the doing/allowing distinction may have to do with differences in motivation that usually, though not invariably, accompany what takes place. That is, a mother who deliberately starves her child will more likely be judged to have been the agent of that child's death than if she fails to feed it because of some other reason.[28]

(ii) Let us now return to the aircraft case and see whether it is reasonable to employ the doing/allowing distinction in deciding whether or not the hijacked aircraft should be shot down.[29] Does the fact that in one case the decision-maker would bring about the deaths of some and in the other case would simply allow those deaths to occur have any moral relevance?[30]

Because the decision-maker in this case is an official who bears a public responsibility for the protection of citizens, then what he allows if he decides not to order the shooting down of the aircraft is for a course of

---

the other. And A may be less culpable than C should C fail to perform the rescue of which he is capable (assuming A is not). Nevertheless, agency clearly plays *some* significant role in these cases, however we try to characterise it. We may not hold A morally responsible for B's drowning if the push is accidental. However, if A is no less able than C to save B, but fails to do so for similar reasons, we will regard A more culpable than C for B's death.

[28] Special responsibility may not always lead to a convergence between actively subverting a duty and negligently failing to fulfil it. It will depend on the kind of responsibility that the agent has. If A accidentally pushes B off the jetty and C is a lifeguard who observes what happens, but neglects to rescue B, we will not be tempted to say that A caused B to drown. However, we might consider C also to have been an agent in what occurred by virtue of the responsibility that he had. Agency is here distributed, though moral responsibility may still need to be determined. Agency may not itself be sufficient to settle that question.

[29] We are, remember, leaving out of account the possible relevance of the intention/foresight distinction and the possibly different magnitudes of harm involved.

[30] Obviously there is the contingent relevance of intention/motivation, though in this case their relevance would not be typical. We might imagine that the person who orders the plane to be shot down does not do so out of any malice toward the aircraft's passengers, but out of a concern to ensure that those at the hijackers' target site are protected. Likewise, we might imagine that the person who refrains from shooting down the aircraft (or ordering it to be shot down) does so out of a concern not to be the agent of the passengers' death. Each motive has a good deal to be said for it, even though we might wonder whether the concern for moral purity—a concern, that is, not to be an agent of evil—might (in the circumstances) be thought a bit self-indulgent.

events to unfold that goes contrary to the terms of his public office—namely, protecting citizens against the predations of others. He *can* protect those at the hijackers' target site. There is *nothing* he can do to protect those who are on the hijacked aircraft. He cannot protect them by allowing the hijackers to continue or (obviously) by ordering the plane to be shot down. At best he can ensure that they have an extra 30 minutes of life.

(d) *Killing v Letting Die v Allowing To Be Killed.* It might be argued that what we have in the above case is not a choice between killing and letting (or allowing to) die but rather a choice between killing and allowing to be killed. The distinction between 'doing harm and allowing harm to eventuate' covers two sets of differences: on the one hand, the difference between A killing B and A allowing B to die; and, on the other, the difference between A killing B and A allowing B to be killed by someone else. Whether or not it matters morally that in the example we are discussing the official's choice is best described as one between killing (by shooting the plane down) and letting (those at the target site) *be killed*, rather than a choice between killing and letting those at the target site die, will depend on the moral difference between the two.

We suggest that the difference lies in this: in the case in which one allows another to be killed, as opposed to the case in which one allows another to die, what one allows is not only the death of another human being but that their death be brought about through the evil intentions and actions of another. What one allows, therefore, is not only the undeserved death of an innocent but the additional evil of someone unjustifiably bringing about that death. Consider the possibility that a (non-hijacked) aircraft with an identical number of passengers to the one we have been considering develops an irreparable mechanical problem, or gets caught up in a tornado, such that the plane is now heading uncontrollably, but inexorably, towards the same site as the one targeted by the hijackers. In such a case an official who orders the aircraft to be shot down to prevent it from crashing into the site in question would be killing the passengers, rather than allowing those at the target site to die, whereas an official who orders the hijacked plane shot down would be killing the passengers, rather than allowing those at the target site to become the victims of the killers on board.

This difference between allowing to die and allowing to be killed and our sense that the latter is morally worse than the former is reflected in our belief that our duty to defend (to the extent that we are able to do so) those who are lethally attacked by others is more stringent and pressing than our duty to help those who will die absent our intervention. (This latter obligation is sometimes referred to as a 'Good Samaritan' duty.) For this reason, though it is morally incumbent upon us to save lives wherever and whenever we are able, we are under a stronger moral obligation not to let someone be killed than not to allow someone to die and so there are stronger reasons for intervening in the former than in the latter.[31]

B. The Imminence of Death

A second controversial consideration that obtains in the aircraft case is the relevance of the inevitability and imminence of the passengers' deaths. Because the plane's crashing into its intended target or its being brought down beforehand exhausts the possible alternatives in the case that we are considering, the passengers will soon perish. For convenience, let us suppose that we are talking about half an hour—leaving it open that, were the period shorter or longer, we might wish to return to the question of the moral significance of the time left for the passengers. What moral relevance might an imminent death have?

(1) *The Relevance of 'Contingencies'*. The German Federal Constitutional Court refused to give *any* moral significance to the imminence of the passengers' deaths.[32] It took the view that each human life should be accorded equal value and, therefore, that appeals to factors such as 'has only half an hour to live' as a basis for making decisions as to which human beings should live and which not would open the door to a way of thinking about what constitutes worthwhile human life that—one suspects—the Court wished to put behind it.[33]

A critic of the Court's reasoning might argue that, given their circumstances, the passengers are unlikely to have more fulfilled lives as a result of the extra half hour. Whether they are shot down or killed 30 minutes later, the quality of their lives is likely to be the same. Moreover, a small increment in quantity without added quality does not amount to anything

---

[31] We leave open the question of whether *for the official who is professionally charged with protecting citizens from harm*, there are stronger reasons for one intervention than there are for the other.

[32] Referring to Article 2.2, which 'guarantees the right to life as a liberty right,' it asserted:

> With this right, the biological and physical existence of every human being is protected against encroachment by the state from the point of time of its coming into being until the human being's death, independently of the individual's circumstances of life and of his or her physical state and state of mind. Every human life as such has the same value.

German Constitutional Court, BVerfG, 1 BvR 357/05, para 83.

[33] During the reign of National Socialism, the idea of lebensunwertes Leben was used to discount the value of lives on the basis of contingencies such as disability, race, political opinions and sexual preference. The Court appears to have thought that once we begin to make normative distinctions among lives based on 'contingencies' we will find ourselves on a slippery slope on which it may be difficult to stop. Therefore, the Court decided that the contingency that the aircraft passengers would have only a short period of life remaining to them should not be permitted to enter the equation.

of moral significance when it is set against the substantial number of lives that will be saved if the plane is shot down.

A likely reply to this line of argument is that it is not for others to determine what, to the passengers, would be the value of their having only an extra 30 minutes to live. The value of a life to a person is for *that* person to determine, and some of the extra 30 minutes might be taken up with matters of great significance to the passengers—such as phone calls to loved ones, prayer, or even meditation. Of course, for some of the passengers, the extra period might only prolong their terror, and for them the sooner the ordeal is over the better. But in each case we recognise the appropriateness of the passenger as a decision-maker and determiner of the value that the extra 30 minutes have.

The idea of consulting the passengers is not entirely fanciful. On United Airlines Flight 93 (9/11/2001), at least some of the passengers knew how dire their situation was.[34] We can speculate on the passengers being asked to vote on whether an official attempt to bring the plane down is one they could endorse. Some might decide that, in the absence of viable alternatives, this would be an honourable thing to do, though we should not underestimate the psychological challenge involved in agreeing to be sacrificed so that others might live. Of course, one might wonder whether such issues as these should be decided by vote at all.[35] But should it be thought appropriate to vote on the matter, one might also wonder whether participation should be limited to the passengers on the aircraft given that those at the target site would be vitally affected should a passenger vote go against government intervention.[36]

(2) *A Rawlsian Strategy.* Might we instead approach the issue via a Rawlsian hypothetical? Suppose we put to a group of people who are charged with drawing up social rules—and who are ignorant of whether they might be passengers or located at the target site—whether there should be a rule permitting a duly authorised official to order an aircraft to be shot down in circumstances such as those envisaged. It is certainly arguable that such people might reasonably determine that, given what was left for them as passengers on a hijacked aircraft and what would be left for them were they in the target group, they should permit—even require—a responsible official to order their plane to be shot down. Although those who found themselves passengers would be denied the opportunity to decide whether to extend their lives for 30 minutes, they

---

[34] There was mobile phone contact between some passengers and their families, contact that enabled the former to learn about the assault on the Twin Towers of the World Trade Center.

[35] Even though in liberal democratic societies voting is a strategy for determining social action in circumstances in which unanimity is unlikely to be achievable.

[36] In addition, we should not overlook the ethical implications of the fact that a vote would leave no space for conscientious objection or other forms of radical dissent.

could accept the reasonableness of having a social rule that would permit an official to make such a determination. Nevertheless, the 'arguability' of this position should not blind us to the fact that one of the challengers to the German legislation was a citizen who objected to the idea that such a decision should be permitted—presumably on the grounds that the government had no business making such determinations concerning the lives of its citizens.[37]

(3) *Triage Situations.* The question of whether or not to shoot down the aircraft need not be viewed as one that involves the question of whether the lives of passengers are to be valued less because they have only 30 minutes to live. For in cases such as this we are not concerned with judging the *relative worth of lives* but with the *relative worth of saving lives.* Although the lives of all may have equal worth, when we have to choose whether or not to save some at the cost of shortening the lives of others who, in the circumstances, will not in any case be able to live out their lives, the question is no longer one of the relative *worth of the various lives involved* but of the worthwhileness of saving those who *can* be saved against the worthwhileness of desisting from shortening lives that in any case *will* shortly be extinguished.

In some respects, the decision to be made here is akin to decisions made in medical triage situations. We do not condemn physicians who pass over patients who cannot be saved to attend to patients who have a chance for survival. Nevertheless, there are important differences between medical triage cases and the situation we are here considering: the physician does not

---

[37] Obviously, were a rule of this kind to be adopted behind a Rawlsian veil of ignorance, it would have to come with significant safeguards. Any official charged with making such a decision would need to have a rank/role commensurate with its social gravity. Not only that, there would need to be ways of ensuring that the aircraft in question was indeed a hijacked one and heading towards a strategic target of enough importance to 'warrant' such a decision. This is not a situation that could easily brook mistakes. And mistakes there have been. Among them have been the shooting down of El Al Flight 402 by Bulgarian MIG fighters (27 July 1955), killing all 58 passengers and crew; Libyan Arab Airlines Flight 114 by Israeli F-4 Phantom fighters (21 February 1973), killing 108 of the 113 on board; Korean Airlines Flight 007 by Soviet jets (1 September 1983), killing all 269 passengers and crew; and Iran Air Flight 655 by the USS *Vincennes* toward the end of the Iran-Iraq war (3 July 1988), killing all 290 passengers and crew. The original German legislation included a number of safeguards, though the Constitutional Court did not find them persuasive. See German Constitutional Court, BVerfG, 1 BvR 357/05, paras 121 et seq. Nevertheless, one cringes at the thought of someone like Dick Cheney making such decisions, especially in the light of events after 9/11. It might be argued that it would be better were there no policy or rule governing such situations. A public rule of permission might be an invitation or temptation to reliance on it, and a Rawlsian strategy might function better as a way of thinking about the reasonableness of a decision already taken then as an ex ante policy. There are some parallels here in debates about torture and ticking bombs, especially in the aftermath of the 1999 decision by Israel's High Court to outlaw torture, but to leave a ticking bomb provision. See especially the post-1999 report by the Public Committee Against Torture in Israel, '1999 to the Present', available at www.stoptorture.org.il/en/skira1999-present.

kill some patients in order to assist other patients to survive.[38] And both the decision to pass over some to attend to others and the criterion used in making those decisions—who have the better chance of survival?—are communally acknowledged as both right and rightly grounded. Matters are not so clear outside the medical context, however: we have no developed conventions concerning the proper prerogatives of government authorities regarding decisions about the worthwhileness of saving lives when not all can be saved; nor have we developed traditions concerning the appropriate criteria for making those decisions. This is why, although the triage physician makes a medical decision that has community endorsement, we are less certain that government officials who are faced with the circumstances under consideration should have our support should they decide to shoot down the aircraft.

The responsibilities of a public official include community protection, and the decision may be viewed as one of minimising the devastation caused by a terrorist attack. However, not only must such an official consider the number of lives to be saved from destruction (at the target site) against the number of lives extended (unfortunately, only by minutes on the doomed aircraft), he must also consider the moral cost of bringing about the death of his own innocent citizens. This may be thought by some—and perhaps inevitably so by those who realise that their deaths will be brought about by their own government—as a profound betrayal of trust. That the very officials who act on behalf of one's government and who are charged with the protection of citizens will be the ones who order their deaths may be hard to accept, if not intellectually, then psychologically.[39]

C. Comparing Devastation

A third factor that applies to each case is the 'greater devastation' that will be caused if the plane is not shot down than if it is shot down. This might initially appear to be a simple matter of numbers. Suppose there are 50 passengers in the aircraft and that 150 people will remain in the building that has been targeted. In that case 200 people will be killed, whereas the deaths will be limited to 50 if the plane is shot down.[40]

But the comparison is not as simple as a tally of numbers might incline us to think. For one thing—though this is the lesser consideration—there is

---

[38] The effect of shooting down the aircraft will be the certain deaths of the passengers, but it need not be seen as directly killing them. Within a double effect framework this constitutes a morally significant distinction.

[39] We return to this point below. There is, however, an argument for trying to avoid paralysis or foolish decision-making by initiating public officials into their roles via simulated role plays. Thanks to Brandon del Pozo for this suggestion.

[40] For simplicity of reference, we are leaving out of account the crew and hijackers.

the strategic significance of the target for the hijackers. Suppose the hijackers were headed for the Washington Capitol building. Not only might those killed there include many with important roles in the national administrative framework, but the infrastructure that will be destroyed could create administrative chaos for an extended period of time. No doubt, this would add weight to the case for shooting the aircraft down. But in addition—and much more critically—if the aircraft is shot down, the government will be responsible for—the agent—bringing about the deaths of a significant number of its own citizens: it will have knowingly sacrificed—and not merely risked the lives of[41]—a number of its people in prosecuting a 'war on terror'. These are important moral costs that add significantly to the weight of the case for not shooting down the plane. What emerges here is that we do not have simple consequentialist costs in which the two sides of the equation can be added up and compared (as might be the case were we able to translate everything into units of Benthamite utility).[42]

III. THE BASE CASE

Let us turn to the case as we originally described it. The hijacked aircraft carries 50 innocent passengers, leaving out of account pilots and other crew members.[43] We have excellent reason to believe that the hijackers' target is a building with substantial symbolic significance. Apart from its symbolic significance the building is currently occupied by a reasonably large number of people (say, 200), and it will be impossible to evacuate most of them before the plane hits. If it hits, 150 of its occupants will be killed.[44]

We are, finally, to assume that the authorities have very good (even if not incontrovertible) reason to believe that the plane in question has been hijacked

---

[41] As we noted earlier, we do not think that at present we can realistically differentiate disabling the plane from bringing about the deaths of the passengers.

[42] Consider the possibility that the plane is headed towards the Capitol building at night with only a single security guard on duty. Now only 51 people will die instead of 50, but the government would have taken a decision to shoot down the aircraft to ensure that the Capitol would not be hit. Even though the passengers would have shortly died, authorising the aircraft's shooting down for this reason might have seemed morally disproportionate, both because the building was given undue importance, and because of what it showed the state would be prepared to do to its citizens to secure what it took to be its national interest. We leave to one side the problematic nature of references to 'national interest'. J Kleinig has said more about them in 'Liberty and Security in an Age of Terrorism' in B Forst, J Green and J Lynch (eds), *Criminologists on Terrorism and Homeland Security* (New York, Cambridge University Press, 2011) ch 15.

[43] The actual 9/11 passenger numbers were as follows: AA Flight 11, 81 (including five hijackers); UA Flight 175, 56 (including five hijackers); AA Flight 77, 58 (including five hijackers); and UA Flight 93, 37 (including four hijackers).

[44] In the case of AA Flight 77, which was directed at the Pentagon, 125 of those killed were inside the Pentagon.

and is heading for a strategic target.[45] We do not want to underestimate the challenges involved in making such an assumption. Although there are cases in which we could clearly say that a particular aircraft has been hijacked and is heading towards a strategic target, once one embeds this in policy, officials will be strongly tempted both to overestimate what they know and also to overstate those estimates.[46]

Nevertheless, the assumptions are defensible. Let us imagine—given the events of 9/11—that this is the fourth hijacked aircraft. Three other planes have already hit their targets with devastating consequences, and mobile phone calls made by passengers have indicated that this particular aircraft has also been hijacked. Might an appropriately authorised government agent give orders to have the plane shot down?

Our response is to argue that this is a fairly standard 'dirty hands' case.[47] That is, it is a case in which whatever the official decides to do, the decision will result in his doing something that will involve him in the violation of an important moral principle.[48] If the official decides that, as awful as the decision will be, his public responsibility obligates him to authorise the shooting down of the plane, he will have to carry the burden of authorising an action that will result in the deaths of 50 innocents. On the other hand, if he believes that he cannot order the shooting down of a plane carrying 50 innocent passengers (citizens, moreover), he will have to bear the burden of permitting, on his watch, the killing of an additional 150 innocent citizens. Because, by virtue of his role, the official has a positive protective obligation both to those who occupy the target building and to those on the plane, no matter what he does or decides not to do, he will not be able to avoid being complicit in the terrible events that will follow.

---

[45] As noted earlier, in the German Aviation Security Act, a continuum of efforts to verify and deflect was required before shooting the plane down—not foolproof but fittingly demanding.

[46] If the past nine years have taught us anything, it is the fallibility of supposedly informed officials and the ease with which ideological and other factors have been able to skew their judgement. Think, eg, of what turned out to be false or exaggerated assessments of ticking bombs, the benefits of torture, weapons of mass destruction, and Iraq/al-Qaeda links.

[47] We do not dispute that 'dirty hands' cases differ from one another. See KI Winston, 'Necessity and Choice in Political Ethics: Varieties of Dirty Hands' in DE Wueste (ed), *Professional Ethics and Social Responsibility* (Lanham, Rowman and Littlefield, 1994) 37.

[48] This is, of course, a somewhat pared down account of dirty hands. The critical point is that the hijackers have constructed a morally impossible situation for the official, so that even if he does 'what the situation calls for,' he will have brought about the deaths of 50 passengers who neither deserve to be killed nor constitute innocent threats. For additional literature on the complexities surrounding the dirty hands issue, see P Rynard and DP Shugarman (eds), *Cruelty and Deception: The Controversy over Dirty Hands in Politics* (Ontario, Broadview Press, 2000); S Wijze, 'Dirty Hands: Doing Wrong to do Right' in I Primoratz (ed), *Politics and Morality* (Basingstoke, Palgrave Macmillan, 2007) 3; CAJ Coady, 'The Problem of Dirty Hands', *Stanford Encyclopedia of Philosophy* (Spring 2009 edn) www.plato.stanford.edu/entries/dirty-hands.

Of course, one might argue that if a person is not willing to make hard decisions as a public official, he should not accept such a role.[49] This seems to have been the position taken by Max Weber in his classic essay, 'Politics as a Vocation'.[50] Someone who 'is to be allowed to put his hand on the wheel of history must have passion, a feeling of responsibility, and a sense of proportion'.[51] The ethics of politics, Weber claims, needs to take into account the fact that it 'operates with very special means, namely power backed up by *violence*.' This gives political ethics its distinctive character.

Weber outlines what he takes to be two competing but irreconcilable approaches to political ethics—an ethic of ultimate ends (or, better, conviction—*Gesinnungsethik*) and an ethic of responsibility (*Verantwortungsethik*).[52] The first he associates with Christian belief, specifically the Sermon of the Mount—with its putatively unconditional requirements.[53] This ethic is concerned with purity of heart, with doing right whatever the consequences. As Weber expresses it: 'The Christian does rightly and leaves the results with the Lord.'[54] He considers such an ethic to be disastrous, likely to subvert the very ends that it is intended to serve. However, this is unlikely to faze the proponent of such an ethic: 'If an action of good intent leads to bad results, then, in the actors' eyes, not he but the world, or the stupidity of other men, or God's will who made them thus, is responsible for the evil.'[55] 'The believer in an ethic of ultimate ends

---

[49] Some further expansion is required here. One of the things with which even a public official concerned with the issue of his agency must come to terms is the way in which an opponent might continue to 'up the ante' should the official not be willing to make hard decisions. A desire for moral purity may transmogrify into perverse moral self-indulgence. See B Williams, 'Utilitarianism and Moral Self-Indulgence' reprinted in *Moral Luck: Collected Papers 1973–1980* (Cambridge, Cambridge University Press, 1981) ch 3; see also discussion within n 15 above.

[50] M Weber, 'Politics as a Vocation' in HH Gert and CW Mills (eds), *From Max Weber: Essays in Sociology* (New York, Oxford University Press, 1973) 77. For an alternative translation, see D Owen and TB Strong (eds), R Livingstone (trans), *The Vocation Lectures* (Indianapolis, Hackett, 2004) 32. Weber's predecessor, Niccolò Machiavelli, observes that a successful (he does not say morally praiseworthy) prince must learn moral compromise: 'Because a man who might want to make a show of goodness in all things necessarily comes to ruin among so many who are not good ... it is necessary to a prince, wanting to maintain himself, to learn how to be able to be not good and to use this and not use it according to necessity', N Machiavelli, A Codevilla (trans), *The Prince* (New Haven, Yale University Press, 1996) ch 15. Machiavelli does not say that the prince has to be a bad person, but that he has to *learn* to be able to act badly. *cf*: 'it is necessary that [a prince, especially a new prince] have a spirit disposed to turn as the winds and the variations of fortune command him, and ... not to depart from good when he can, but to know how to enter into evil when he needs to' (ch 18); 'a prince who wants to keep the state is often forced to be not good' (ch 19). However, unlike Weber's politician, Machiavelli's prince does not show evidence of the moral struggle appropriately involved in such decisions.

[51] Weber, above n 50, 115.
[52] Ibid 120.
[53] Ibid 119–20.
[54] Ibid 120.
[55] Ibid 121.

feels "responsible" only for seeing to it that the flame of pure intentions is not quelched.'[56] 'If ... one chases after the ultimate good in a war of beliefs, following a pure ethic of absolute ends, then the goals may be damaged and discredited for generations, because responsibility for consequences is lacking'.[57]

In an ethic of responsibility, however, 'one has to give an account of the foreseeable results of one's action.'[58] Unlike the advocate of an ethic of ultimate ends, the proponent of an ethic of responsibility 'takes account of ... the average deficiencies of people ... He does not feel in a position to burden others with the results of his own actions so far as he was able to foresee them; he will say: these results are ascribed to my action.'[59]

It is Weber's belief that, *to some degree at least,* a politician must observe an ethic of responsibility. Nevertheless, he recognises that this has ethical costs: 'No ethics in the world can dodge the fact that in numerous instances the attainment of "good" ends is bound to the fact that one must be willing to pay the price of using morally dubious means or at least dangerous ones—and facing the possibility or even probability of evil ramifications. From no ethics in the world can it be concluded when and to what extent the ethically good purpose "justifies" the ethically dangerous means and ramifications.'[60]

And yet, when all is said and done, Weber draws back from exclusive advocacy of an ethic of responsibility. 'One cannot prescribe to anyone whether he should follow an ethic of absolute ends or an ethic of responsibility, or when the one and when the other.'[61] It is, he says

> immensely moving when a *mature* man—no matter whether he is old or young in years—is aware of a responsibility for the consequences of his conduct and really feels such responsibility with heart and soul. He then acts by following

---

[56] Ibid.

[57] The sentence continues: 'and two diabolic forces which enter the play remain unknown to the actor.' These are 'the trained relentlessness in viewing the realities of life, and the ability to face such realities and the measure up to them inwardly', ibid 126–27. However, we think Weber's differentiation of the two ethics is somewhat schematic, and, as we observe below, a public official is likely to have a share of each.

[58] Ibid 120.

[59] Ibid 121.

[60] Ibid. Weber thinks that even the proponent of an ethic of ultimate ends does not eschew all violence. He notes that the tension between means and ends is particularly acute in politics, because 'the decisive means for politics is violence', ibid 121. What tends to happen politically, is that the defender of an ethic of ultimate ends turns into a 'chiliastic prophet', ibid 122. He calls for one great act of violence in order to get rid of violence: 'If one makes any concessions at all to the principle that the end justifies the means, it is not possible to bring an ethic of ultimate ends and an ethic of responsibility under one roof or to decree which end should justify which means', ibid. 'The genius or demon of politics lives in an inner tension with the God of love, as well as with the Christian God as expressed by the church', ibid 126. 'Everything that is striven for through political action operating with violent means and following an ethic of responsibility endangers the "salvation of the soul"', ibid.

[61] Ibid 127.

an ethic of responsibility and somewhere he reaches the point where he says: "Here I stand; I can do no other." That is something genuinely human and moving. And every one of us who is not spiritually dead must realise the possibility of finding himself at some time in that position. In so far as this is true, an ethic of ultimate ends and an ethic of responsibility are not absolute contrasts but rather supplements, which only in unison constitute a genuine man—a man who can have the "calling for politics".[62]

The base case, then, is not one in which a person who acts in an official capacity can argue that he was justified in authorising the shooting down of the plane simply as the lesser of two evils. Rather, the responsibilities of his office made it morally obligatory that he view his actions, at least to a large extent, through the lens of his role. And this perspective, he may argue, required of him that he order the shooting down of the plane and, in consequence, his bringing about the deaths of innocent passengers—citizens, no less, for whom he was responsible. He may believe, and we may agree, that this means that, as consequence of his decision to accept the responsibilities of his office he incurred the risk of tarnishing his soul.[63]

Contrary to the view of many who discuss the issue, characterising the case as a 'dirty hands' one does not resolve the moral issue.[64] For it is not at all clear what we should say about dirty hands—whether, for example, we should say that doing right sometimes requires doing wrong,[65] or that

---

[62] Ibid.

[63] Here we may also recall Bernard Williams's challenging story of Jim and the Indians in which, if Jim is to save 19 of the 20 Indians about to be shot, he must shoot one of them himself. Jim's moral integrity is at stake. See B Williams, 'A Critique of Utilitarianism' in JJC Smart and B Williams, *Utilitarianism: For and Against* (Cambridge, Cambridge University Press, 1973) 97. If Jim shoots one to save the 19, he will violate a deeply held commitment against the killing of innocents. On the other hand, if he refuses, all 20 will be killed, albeit not by him. The point of Williams's example is to make us aware that whatever option is chosen it will have moral costs. He does not say whether Jim should accept the moral cost of refusal and its known consequences. But Williams's Jim is not an official, and in the hijack narrative the official has additional moral responsibilities that stem from his role—responsibilities that may affect the responsibility that each of us has not to be an agent of killing. The official has a strong role obligation to those at the target site. For some of the extensive literature that discusses Williams's story, see M Hollis, 'Jim and the Indians' (1983) 43 *Analysis* 36; P Railton, 'Alienation, Consequentialism, and the Demands of Morality' (1984) 13 *Philosophy and Public Affairs* 134; HA Bedau, 'Jim and the Indians in the Jungle Clearing' in *Making Mortal Choices: Three Exercises in Moral Casuistry* (New York, Oxford University Press, 1997); A Miller, 'Lenin's Anticipation of Bernard Williams's Integrity Objection to Utilitarianism' (1997) 31 *Journal of Value Inquiry* 503; J Lenman, 'Utilitarianism and Obviousness' (2004) 16 *Utilitas* 322; and T Chappell, 'Bernard Williams', *Stanford Encyclopedia of Philosophy* (2006) plato.stanford.edu/entries/williams-bernard/.

[64] For a development of the topic of dirty hands and related distinctions, see J Kleinig, *The Ethics of Policing* (Cambridge, Cambridge University Press, 1996) 52–64.

[65] As M Walzer suggests; see M Walzer, 'Political Action: The Problem of Dirty Hands' (1973) 2 *Philosophy and Public Affairs* 160. Walzer uses a variety of locutions, suggesting that he is not quite sure how to make his point (my italics): 'I *don't think I could govern innocently*; nor do most of us believe that those who govern us are innocent— ... even the best of them. But this doesn't mean that it isn't possible to do the *right thing* while governing' (161); 'a particular

sometimes the circumstances 'call for' us to do what is wrong, leaving aside the question whether what we did was also 'right' or 'permissible', 'excusable', or simply 'understandable'.[66]

We are inclined to favour the latter approach and view the case we are considering as one in which the official is called upon by his office to make a decision that carries a terrible moral cost, but with the strong proviso that an official who makes such a decision should then be held to account for his decision.[67] Holding the official to account is not to (implicitly) impugn his decision or his motives, but to determine whether, when he acted, he acted with due diligence and due regard—whether he did as much as his office required of him and with appropriate regard to the moral dimensions of what confronted him. In the case at hand, we may choose not only to refrain from taking action against the official, but also to acknowledge that he bore a heavy moral penalty *on our behalf*—namely, of authorising a course of action that would lead to the deaths of 50 innocent persons. The latter point is important, because, in a liberal democratic community, those who occupy positions of power are ordinarily chosen by us to act *for us*. They take upon themselves burdens that *we* choose not to bear and perhaps could not stomach.[68]

Here we want to make use of an argumentative strategy that seems peculiarly appropriate to moral relations, one in which decision-makers and those affected by their decisions are seen as answerable to each other. So we hypothesise the possibility of an alternative after-life in which the official, having decided not to shoot down the aircraft, is then confronted by the 150 people killed in the targeted building. What might he say to them? Would it be enough for him to say that because the passengers on the aircraft were citizens (for whom he had a *direct* responsibility) he did not think it right that *he* be the agent of their deaths? Is it enough for him to say that the distinction between, on the one hand, *his* acting to bring about the deaths of those on the aircraft and, on the other hand, allowing those

act of government ... may be exactly the *right thing to do in utilitarian terms* and yet leave the man who does it *guilty of a moral wrong*' (ibid); the person who 'remains innocent ... not only fails to do the right thing (in utilitarian terms), he may also fail to measure up to the duties of his office' (ibid); 'the defenses we offer are not simply justifications; they are also excuses ... an excuse is typically an admission of fault; a justification is typically a denial of fault and an assertion of innocence' (170); 'we know that we have *done something wrong* even if what we have done was also *the best thing to do on the whole in the circumstances*' (171).

[66] See, eg, CAJ Coady, 'Messy Morality and the Art of the Possible' (1990) 64 *Proceedings of the Aristotelian Society* 259 and Coady, above n 48.

[67] Although we are not always sympathetic to Walzer's characterisation of dirty hands decision-making, it has the considerable merit of addressing the question of how we should respond to an official who dirties his hands. See also, N Levy, 'Punishing the Dirty' in I Primoratz (ed), above n 48, 38.

[68] D Thompson, 'Democratic Dirty Hands' in *Political Ethics and Public Office* (Cambridge, Harvard University Press, 1987) 11.

at the target site be killed *by others* was of such moral importance that it was better that the plane (with its doomed occupants) be crashed by those others into their intended target rather than that he, the official, order the plane to be shot down? [69]

The official certainly would not be justified in arguing that he had responsibility only for his commissions and not for his omissions; nor would he be justified in arguing that he had responsibility only for what he himself did and not for what he allowed others to do. Clearly, there is more than one question whose answers are germane to determining the contours of the official's moral responsibilities: (1) Is there, in *this* particular case, sufficiently greater weight to be given to what the official *does* as opposed to what *he allows to be done* to make those at the target site capable of appreciating his decision not to shoot down the plane as a morally conscionable decision? And (2) Is it morally understandable—and perhaps even morally called for in *this* particular case—that the official refuse to be the *agent* of grievous harm albeit knowing that his refusal will allow an even greater harm to be brought about through the *agency of others*?

The distinctions on which these questions focus, namely, between doing harm and allowing harm to be done, and between being the agent of harm and refusing that agency at the cost of enabling greater harm to be perpetrated through the agency of others, must be distinctions that not only have moral validity, but are of sufficient moral importance that they can bear the enormous moral weight of the decision not to shoot down the plane that will, if not shot down, be used as the weapon that kills many more others at the target site. Whatever the validity and weight of these distinctions, it is not clear that those at the target site can be expected to appreciate them as morally determinative.

Now consider the further possibility of an after-life in which those at the target site confront the innocent passengers in the plane who argue against being shot down (as did the complainant in the German Constitutional Court case who hypothesised that he could have been one of the doomed passengers). Might they accuse the passengers of extreme selfishness in insisting on an extra 30 minutes of life at the cost of the lives of 150 of their fellow citizens? And might the passengers who so insisted, agree to this characterisation while at the same time claiming that being selfish about one's final moments is not altogether condemnable by others not so situated?[70]

---

[69] There is, however, the interesting possibility in which the target site is in a different jurisdiction. Does the official have responsibility for people there? In such a case we might want to draw upon the distinction between formal and moral responsibility.

[70] Here we encounter, but duck, the large literature that addresses 'a right to do wrong'. See, eg, J Waldron, 'A Right to Do Wrong' (1981) 92 *Ethics* 21; W Galston, 'On the Alleged Right to Do Wrong: A Reply to Waldron' (1983) 93 *Ethics* 320; J Waldron, 'Galston on Rights' (1983) 93 *Ethics* 325; M Strasser, 'Conscience and the Right to do Wrong' (1987) 17

IV. VARIANTS

Up until now, the account we have provided trades—to a significant extent—on the ethical obligations of a government official.[71] Do we reach similar results if the decision to bring the plane down comes from some other source? We consider three variants.

A. The Defiant Pilot

On one variant, the pilot of the hijacked plane decides to *thwart* the hijackers by prematurely crashing it, albeit at the cost of the lives of those on board.[72] We can suppose a situation in which the hijackers put a gun to the head of the pilot and tell him to change course. Might the pilot thwart the hijackers by crashing the plane?

Schematically, we are considering a situation in which A threatens B with death unless B kills innocent C. May B kill C? We would ordinarily say no: strong though the claims of self-preservation may be, they do not justify the deliberate killing of non-threatening innocent others. Not even duress will ordinarily excuse the killing of innocent others.[73] What our judgement in this case reflects is acknowledgement of the strong moral claims to life of non-threatening innocent persons.

In the present case, however, the hijacker threatens to kill the pilot if he does not kill innocent others (those at the target site), and the pilot, to avoid killing those innocent others, *though not to save his own life*, acts to save them, but at the cost of doing what will kill his innocent passengers.[74] In this case, the pilot takes defensive measures to preserve the lives of some

---

Philosophia 411; D Enoch, 'A Right to Violate One's Duty' (2002) 21 *Law and Philosophy* 355; G Øverland, 'The Right to Do Wrong' (2007) 26 *Law and Philosophy* 377.

[71] We have resisted a consideration of the moral situation of the person who would be expected to carry out the will of the government official. See, in general, Y Dinstein, *The Defence of 'Obedience to Superior Orders' in International Law* (Leyden, AW Sijthoff, 1965).

[72] The accounts we have suggest that the 9/11 hijackers took over the flying themselves, eliminating the pilots from such decisions.

[73] This scenario may recall the situation famously exemplified in *R v Dudley and Stephens*: there—to simplify—two people, facing death by starvation, kill (and eat) another in order to survive. Though they acted under extreme duress, we would likely be unsympathetic to what the killers did (though there could be circumstances, such as the victim's already being close to death, that might ameliorate our judgement). See *R v Dudley and Stephens* (1884) 14 QBD 273; *cf* the discussion in AWB Simpson, *Cannibalism and the Common Law* (Chicago, University of Chicago Press, 1984).

[74] Though of course the pilot will also be killed.

innocents at the cost of the lives of others, a measure that will also cost him his own life.[75]

We might consider whether the pilot, by virtue of his professional role and the obligations that are implicit in it, has a special moral responsibility *for his passengers*. Just as we might want to argue that a governmental official, by virtue of his public role, must think in broad terms about others in his constituency, it might be that the pilot has the passengers as *his* moral constituency. This is not an unreasonable position, but it probably does not go far enough. The pilot could also reason as follows: Although I have a special responsibility for my passengers, there is nothing I can do in the circumstances that will relieve their situation to any significant degree. Moreover, by virtue of my professional licensing, I also have a wider responsibility to fly my aircraft with as little risk as possible to the public; I should therefore act in a way that minimises that risk.[76] We might ask of course whether the pilot's responsibility to his passengers is significantly greater than to those on the ground, and whether this greater responsibility gives him a strong enough reason to favour their lives over the lives of those at the target site (even though the passengers' lives will soon be lost in any case).[77]

Might it be better for the pilot to crash the aircraft deliberately (and thus to thwart the hijackers) rather than seek to *defy* them—leading, presumably, to their shooting him for his defiance, even though that would also be likely to lead to the aircraft crashing prematurely? One might argue for the preferability of *his* crashing the aircraft. Although it is reasonable to assume that if the pilot defies the hijackers they will shoot him and the plane will crash, we do not know that this will be the outcome, and so his deliberate crashing of the aircraft might be seen as the preferable option. So long as he retains control of the aircraft he can determine that the crash will minimise ground casualties—thus better fulfilling his larger responsibilities.

---

[75] This is perhaps reminiscent of, though different from, the classic trolley case, in which a person, seeing a runaway trolley heading toward five innocent people, pulls a lever to divert it to another line on which other but fewer innocent people are sitting. Though both cases are similar in that the innocent deaths that are caused in each are not intended, but only the foreseen outcome of the diversionary action, in the hijacking case, but not in the trolley case, the diversionary measure is undertaken in the context of coercion. Moreover, although the five innocent people will not be killed if diversionary measures are not taken in the trolley case, in the hijacking case the innocent passengers will not survive despite the brief respite they will have.

[76] Consider the dual concern of Chesley B Sullenberger III, the US Airways pilot who recently downed his disabled plane into the Hudson River, NY. See Wikipedia, 'Chesley Sullenberger', www.en.wikipedia.org/wiki/Chesley_Sullenberger. Although Sullenberger felt a primary responsibility for his passengers, he was also concerned about the danger he posed to those on the ground.

[77] Even were this granted, the numbers at risk could be so different that a less demanding responsibility would override a more stringent one—not to forget that the passengers will in any case shortly die.

Imagine that, miraculously, the pilot is the only person to survive the impact of the crash that he himself has caused. What might we say to him? No doubt, we will share his regret—or more—that the passengers were sacrificed, but because they would have been sacrificed anyway, believe he acted as well as we might have expected of someone in his circumstances. We could hardly accuse him of selfishness or of lack of regard for the passengers. Had he continued to pilot the plane, albeit under coercion, he would have been causally responsible for the deaths both of his passengers and those at the target site. At some level, his decision to crash the plane reflects a heroic, if tragic, moral choice.

B. Heroic Passengers

On another variant, several of the passengers decide to overpower the hijackers and prevent them from reaching their target by bringing the plane down.[78]

What exactly happened on the fourth plane that was hijacked on 9/11 remains unclear. However, we know that several of the passengers became aware that the plane was one of a number that had been hijacked, that they too were destined to be used as a weapon against a significant target, and so they banded together and sought to thwart the hijackers. It is not clear whether they were trying to regain control of the plane—for the pilot appears to have been killed and the plane was being piloted by one of the hijackers—or whether, by prematurely bringing the plane down, they were seeking only to avert the outcome that the hijackers had planned (which, one presumes, was the crashing of the plane into the Washington Capitol, White House, or some other symbolically significant target). In any case, from what we know there appears to have been some form of agreement on the part of at least some of the passengers to derail the hijackers from using the plane as a weapon of destruction.

What would be the morality of these passengers choosing to do this? In the case as described, we might argue that the passengers had consented to place themselves at risk of dying sooner rather than later, or even that they consented to die sooner rather than later. They were, therefore, justified in doing what they did. It was a heroic decision on their part and any moral

---

[78] We have attempted to keep in mind the events of United Airlines Flight 93 as recorded in the 9/11 Commission Report, which, though not perfect, is a reasonable attempt to reflect on the events of that day. It appears that the passengers 'voted' to try to thwart the attackers. Some effort is made to reconstruct the events in National Commission on Terrorist Attacks Upon the United States, *The 9/11 Commission Report*, available at www.gpoaccess.gov/911/pdf/fullreport.pdf, 13.

blame for the death of innocents fell squarely on the hijackers.[79] But there are (at least) two further variants on these sub-variants:

(a) *Voting Majority.* According to one, a vote is taken on whether or not to attack the hijackers, but only a majority of voters is found to be in favour of the attack, an outcome that seems reasonable enough given that (as we noted earlier) voting is a legitimating decision-making strategy we employ in situations that would not be likely to yield unanimity. The hijacked plane situation might well be one such situation (though complicated by the fact it may be difficult to imagine what passengers who vote against the proposed attack of the hijackers might hope to gain, given the options that are known to be available to them). On one account, once a positive vote is obtained, a group will attack the hijackers in an attempt to regain control of the aircraft so that it can be diverted—admittedly at great risk—from its intended target and with some prospect of saving the passengers. On the other account, the group tries to crash the plane so that it cannot be used as the hijackers intend.

(b) *Assertion of Dignity.* According to the other variant, there is no vote of the passengers. Rather, several of the passengers take it into their own hands to thwart the hijackers and crash the plane themselves so that it cannot be used as the hijackers intend. The group does not consult with others but, recognising what is happening, decide to ensure that they will not passively allow themselves—or the other passengers—to be used by the terrorists to further their terrorist aims. The group plans to 'go down fighting', their resistance constituting an assertion of their dignity as agents who, to the greatest extent possible in the circumstances, direct their own fate.

With respect to this last scenario, we might want to consider whether the loss of the lives of all of the other passengers, as a result of bringing down the plane, might appropriately be viewed as damage that is 'collateral' to the bringing down of the plane. The description of the damage as 'collateral' is in no way meant to suggest any attenuation of the tragedy involved in the loss of innocent lives. It is meant rather to emphasise that these deaths of (say) 40 innocent people are, though foreseen, not the intended outcome. The intention in crashing the plane is to resist its use as a diabolical means for terrible ends, ends that include the killing of innocent others (though the group would not have been in a position to know how many at the target site would thereby be spared). But though not intended, the deaths of the passengers on the plane are, of course, foreseen. Indeed, it is the fact that they are foreseen, and foreseen with trepidation, that makes the decision

---

[79] We leave out of account (here) any moral blame that might have accrued to others for allowing the hijacking to have occurred in the first place—misuse of intelligence, poor screening, and so forth. As *The 9/11 Commission Report* indicates, there was plenty of blame to go around for the events of 9/11. Blame is not a fixed moral quantity, like the liquid in a hydraulic pump.

to bring down the plane so fraught with moral poignancy. Bringing down the plane under these circumstances thus appears to be an act that is public spirited, self-sacrificial, and done with what must surely be heavy hearts.

C. A Public-Spirited Citizen

On the third variant, a private citizen, learning of the hijackings over the radio or TV, has an opportunity and the means to shoot down a commandeered aircraft before it reaches its target.

Although private citizens may well have 'Good Samaritan' moral obligations to assist others—and, in certain jurisdictions, even have a legal obligation to render assistance, where it would be easy to do so, to those in dire straits—a case of this kind would clearly fall well outside what could be reasonably expected. However, suppose, for the sake of continuing our analysis, that the citizen hears over the radio that a fourth hijacked aircraft is heading towards Washington to cause additional damage to that which has already been reported concerning the three other planes. The citizen sees an aircraft—presumably *the* aircraft—heading over his property in the direction of Washington. He uses his private rocket launcher to bring it down. If he is successful, and it is indeed the aircraft about which he has heard, we might well be grateful for what he managed to do. At the same time, however, we ought to express considerable concern about a private citizen pursuing this kind of task on his own. For the epistemic challenges in such a case are considerable. Even though the citizen may correctly judge that this is the aircraft commandeered by terrorists, it may still be fortuitous that he is correct about this. Such a major act of intervention should have much better epistemic grounds than the citizen has or is likely to have. This is why we generally argue that, for interventions of this kind, there needs to be someone in *authority*—that is, someone who could be presumed to *know* that this would be an appropriate intervention.[80,81]

---

[80] Social authority is closely tied to the idea of a 'presumption to know'. See J Kleinig, above n 64, ch 1, where an account of authority is developed in the following terms: *Authority* is not a property that people possess, such as body weight or skin colour, but a *social relation*, an accorded status. Someone who is in authority, or is an authority, or who has authority, is acknowledged by others as being in a position to do or require or know whatever happens to be the object of that authority. Yet authority is not simply a socially sustained relation that links positional, actual, and expert authority (ie, being *in* authority, *having* authority, and being *an* authority). Underlying every recognition of authority is a presumption that the person (or officeholder, or group member) is 'in the know'. The bearer of authority is presumed to be informationally equipped to engage in or require certain conduct, or to pronounce on particular matters. It is only a *presumption* of knowledge that sustains authority, not the *possession* of knowledge that would justify it.

[81] There are some parallels here with discussions about the right of citizens to bear arms. Leaving aside the tangled US debate on that issue, freighted as it is with ideology, it is normally considered good social policy to restrict the public bearing of firearms to a limited group

In the case we are now looking at, when we focus—as we must—on the fact that the hijacked aircraft has 50 innocent passengers on board, the prospect of a private citizen choosing to act in a manner that could foreseeably result in their deaths should give us great pause. Even if, in the particular case, we might want to relieve the citizen of some penalty for his act, we would have strong social reasons for deterring such behaviour. A private citizen who wrongly judged a matter of this kind could not expect to go free on the basis of 'public spiritedness'.[82]

V. CONCLUSION

The innocent passengers on a hijacked aircraft need to be accorded their full rights as human beings—including rights to self-determination and life, even though their lives will soon be terminated. This is what makes the decisions of those who are in a position to make decisions—governmental officials, the pilot, some or all of the passengers, and even civilian outsiders—so problematic, indeed, compromising. Any action to save those targeted by the hijackers will violate the rights of the hijacked passengers. That said, no less than the innocent passengers on the aircraft, those at the target site also have full rights to life and self-determination and, although a decision not to shoot down the aircraft will effectively be a decision to allow them to be killed, we wonder whether the doing/allowing distinction can bear so much moral weight that it would rule out completely the moral 'legitimacy' of someone with appropriate role authority giving overriding weight to the claims of those on the ground. If the role obligations of decision-makers give added and even determinative weight to the claims of those on the ground, it will not be because those who were (foreseeably, but not intentionally) killed in the effort to protect them have counted for naught.[83]

of trained personnel because the tasks of law enforcement or military intervention will be effected more efficiently and fairly if such weaponry is confined to those with the skills, training, and—we trust—the judgement to use it. If adult citizens in general are permitted to make their own determinations about the bearing and use of weapons, they are as likely as not to use them inappropriately. That is not to say that, if weapons are permitted, they would never be used appropriately, but that we do better, *as a matter of social policy*, to restrict their use to those with appropriate authority.

[82] In addition, one might argue that unlike those with some formal responsibility for passengers and potential victims at the target site, the public-spirited citizen had a lesser obligation to secure the well-being of the latter.

[83] Among others, we are particularly grateful to Christian Barry, Brandon del Pozo, Miriam Gur-Arye, Igor Primoratz, and participants at the Oñati workshop for perceptive and clarifying comments on earlier drafts.

3

The Right to Life Between Absolute and Proportional Protection

KAI MÖLLER

O NE OF THE puzzles of human rights and constitutional law is
whether there are any rights which are absolute, that is, rights
which must never be interfered with. Some of the candidates which
come to mind are the right not to be tortured[1] and the right to life. The
question of absolute rights touches upon issues which have become highly
relevant in practice especially since the terrorist attacks of 11 September
2001 and the subsequent changes in the attitudes of some states towards
torture and killings, and this alone would merit a close analysis. However,
the issue is also important with regards to the theory of human and constitutional rights. Few ideas have spread as quickly and pervaded an entire
area of law as thoroughly as the proportionality approach in constitutional
rights law around the world. Robert Alexy's model of rights as principles
which have to be balanced against conflicting principles is one of the most
influential theoretical accounts of this development.[2] While I am critical of
some aspects of Alexy's model,[3] I do accept and subscribe to the desirability
of balancing in constitutional rights law.[4] This does of course not imply
that *all* constitutional rights are open to balancing in *all* situations; rather,
it may turn out that some are and some are not, or some are in most but
not all situations. We therefore need a theory which distinguishes absolute
from non-absolute rights.

This chapter will try to shed some light on this question by focussing
on the right to life. It will proceed by first presenting an account of the
leading case in this area, namely the judgment of the German Federal
Constitutional Court (FCC) in the Aviation Security Act case, where the

---

[1] *Cf* Article 3 of the European Convention on Human Rights.

[2] R Alexy, *A Theory of Constitutional Rights*, Julian Rivers (trans) (Oxford, Oxford
University Press, 2002).

[3] See K Möller, 'Balancing and the Structure of Constitutional Rights' (2007) 5 *International
Journal of Constitutional Law* 453.

[4] By which I mean balancing as involving trade-offs between a right and a competing value.

Court held that shooting down an aeroplane which was likely to be used as a terrorist weapon was a violation of the right to life in conjunction with the human dignity of the innocent passengers aboard. I will then offer a few thoughts on the Court's reasoning, specifically with regard to what it has to say about the idea of absolute rights. Having concluded that the judgment offers little help in illuminating this problem, I will present some approaches to absolute rights from moral philosophy and apply them to human and constitutional rights law. My conclusion will be that the right to life will under certain circumstances be absolute or near-absolute, but that these circumstances will be rarer than sometimes thought.

I

One of the German laws passed as a response to the attacks of 11 September 2001 is the Aviation Security Act (Luftsicherheitsgesetz). Its most controversial part was §14(3) which gave the minister of defence permission to order the shooting down of passenger planes if, according to the circumstances, it had to be assumed that the aircraft was to be used against the lives of people and if the shooting down was the only effective defence against the threat. This part of the statute was declared void by the FCC in 2005.[5] To understand the decision, some doctrinal background regarding German constitutional jurisprudence is helpful. First, according to the wording of the Basic Law (BL), the right to life is not an absolute guarantee, but can be interfered with pursuant to law.[6] Taken literally, this would mean that as long as there is an authorising law, the state could kill unrestrictedly. This is where the doctrine of proportionality comes in. It means that each interference with constitutional rights must not only be prescribed by law, but must also be proportional, that is, it must serve a legitimate goal; it must be suitable to further this goal; it must be necessary in that there is no other, less restrictive but equally effective means to reach the goal; and it must be proportionate stricto sensu in that it must not impose a disproportionate burden on the right-holder. Applying the proportionality test to the case of a hijacked airplane seems to indicate that the shooting down could easily be justified at least in those cases where the number of people likely to die in the terrorist attack for which the plane is being used exceeds the number

---

[5] For an analysis of the case, *cf* K Möller, 'On Treating Persons as Ends: The German Aviation Security Act, Human Dignity, and the Federal Constitutional Court' (2006) 51 *Public Law* 457.

[6] Basic Law for the Federal Republic of Germany or Deutsches Grundgesetz Basic Law, Article 2(2):'Every person shall have the right to life and physical integrity ... These rights may be interfered with only pursuant to a law.'

of passengers on board.[7] But it is exactly this conclusion that the petitioners opposed. Relying on a well-established principle of German criminal law according to which lives must never be balanced, they argued that the proportionality principle has no application in the case of the intentional killing of innocents.

Article 1(1) of the Basic Law accords a special place to human dignity.[8] The official English translation[9] does not quite capture a subtle difference of language made in the original text. In German legal terminology, there is a distinction between 'inviolable' (*unverletzlich*) and 'untouchable' (*unantastbar*), the former meaning that the state may sometimes interfere with the object of the right, provided that it comes up with a legitimate justification, and the latter meaning that any interference will automatically amount to a violation of the right. Human dignity, as the 'superior value' of the Basic Law, is 'untouchable', and an interference can therefore never be justified. Note the radical consequences of this approach: in principle, even when one could save the lives of thousands by one violation of human dignity, it must not be carried out. Furthermore, even when one could prevent the violation of the *dignity* of thousands by violating one person's dignity, this would not be permissible.[10] Therefore, it does not come as a surprise that in light of this doctrinal approach to human dignity it seems necessary to interpret dignity quite narrowly. No general theory of what is and is not part of human dignity has yet been successfully put forward. The most widespread definition, employed by the FCC in many decisions, is the one first proposed by Günter Dürig in the 1950s who, employing the Kantian distinction between treating persons as ends and as means to an end, argued that dignity required treating persons as subjects rather than objects.[11] The notorious difficulty in defining human dignity has not, however, prevented the concept from becoming both one of the cornerstones of German constitutional jurisprudence and a major export, in particular to the new South

---

[7] There is an additional problem, namely whether those aboard the plane should count, which may be disputed in light of the fact that they are going to die in the attack anyway.

[8] There is an ongoing discussion in German academia as to whether Article 1(1) stipulates a right to human dignity or merely dignity as a (nevertheless binding and justiciable) constitutional value. The debate is of no practical relevance, however, as there is a consensus to the effect that wherever human dignity is violated, there will necessarily also be a violation of one of the explicit rights in the subsequent articles of the Basic Law.

[9] Basic Law, above n 6, Article 1(1): 'Human dignity shall be inviolable. To respect and protect it shall be the duty of all state authority.'

[10] This is the traditional doctrine which is still endorsed by the majority of commentators but has been challenged in the *Jakob von Metzler* case and the ticking bomb case to which I will briefly refer below; cf W Brugger, 'May Government Ever Use Torture? Two Responses from German Law' (2000) 48 *American Journal of Comparative Law* 661.

[11] G Dürig, 'Der Grundrechtssatz von der Menschenwürde' (1956) 81 *Archiv des Öffentlichen Rechts* 117, 127.

African[12] and Eastern European[13] constitutions. The German FCC regards human dignity as the basis of all constitutional rights and the central value of the Basic Law, and has referred to dignity as a principle guiding the interpretation of other provisions of the Basic Law in many contexts, for example in its abortion decisions[14] and its privacy jurisprudence.[15]

The Court based its decision in the *Aviation Security Act* case on two grounds. First, it argued that the law was unconstitutional because the Federation lacked the legislative competence for it.[16] The second and more spectacular ground concerns the violation of constitutional rights. The Court held that §14(3) of the Aviation Security Act violated both human dignity and the right to life insofar as it permitted the shooting down of aircrafts in situations where there were innocent persons on board.

The Court begins its assessment with some general remarks on the right to life and human dignity. It stresses that the right to life is guaranteed only pursuant to law, but moves on immediately to argue that any law which interferes with it must be interpreted in light of both the right to life and human dignity: 'Human life is the vital basis of human dignity as the primary structural principle and superior constitutional value.'[17] This assumed close connection between the right to life and the right to human dignity is the bridge which enables the Court to leave the right to life behind and concentrate, in what follows, on dignity. It does not give a general definition of human dignity but stresses the necessity to decide on a case-by-case basis. However, it then relies on the old doctrine of treating persons as subjects rather than objects. Citing its own jurisprudence, the Court declares:

> Starting from the ideas of the founders of the Basic Law that it is a part of human nature to determine oneself in freedom and to freely develop oneself, and that the individual can demand as a matter of principle to be recognised in the community as an equal member with his own value, the duty to respect and protect human dignity generally excludes the possibility of making human beings the mere object of the state. Thus, any treatment of persons by public authorities which categorically questions their quality as subjects, their status as subjects of the law ... is plainly prohibited.[18]

---

[12]   Constitution of the Republic of South Africa 1996 (South Africa), s 10.
[13]   *Cf* C Dupré, *Importing the Law in Post-Communist Transitions: The Hungarian Constitutional Court and the Right to Human Dignity* (Oxford, Hart Publishing, 2003) ch 3.
[14]   BVerfGE 39, 1, 88, 203.
[15]   *Cf* W Schmitt Glaeser, 'Schutz der Privatsphäre' in J Isensee and P Kirchhof (eds), *Handbuch des Staatsrechts,* vol 6 (Heidelberg, CF Müller, 1989) 41, 46–47.
[16]   BVerfG, 1 BvR 357/05 of 15/02/2006, [89]–[117].
[17]   Ibid [119].
[18]   Ibid [121].

Having set out the doctrine in general, it now takes the Court a mere two paragraphs to apply the formula to the facts of the case:

> The passengers and crew members who are exposed to such a mission are in a desperate situation. They can no longer influence the circumstances of their lives independently from others in a self-determined manner. This makes them objects not only of the perpetrators of the crime. Also the state which in such a situation resorts to the measure provided by §14(3) of the Aviation Security Act treats them as mere objects of its rescue operation for the protection of others ... Crew and passengers cannot sidestep these actions of the state ... but are defencelessly and helplessly at the mercy of the state with the consequence that they will be shot down together with the aircraft and therefore be killed with near certainty. Such a treatment ignores the status of the persons affected as subjects endowed with dignity and inalienable rights. By their killing being used as a means to save others, they are treated as objects and at the same time deprived of their rights; with their lives being disposed of unilaterally by the state, the persons on board the aircraft, who, as victims, are themselves in need of protection, are denied the value which is due to a human being for his or her own sake.[19]

In the following section, the Court relies on an additional reason. It argues that it will be practically impossible to judge whether the statutory conditions for the shooting down have been met. The Court considered that in light of the fact that Germany is a relatively small country and that accordingly the time window in which to make the decision will be very small, there was an immense pressure to decide quickly and therefore a very real danger of rash decisions.[20]

The Court then sets out to consider and refute some objections to its conclusion. It rejects as unrealistic the proposition that passengers who enter an aircraft knowing that they will be shot down should it be hijacked thereby implicitly consent to being shot down.[21] The argument that those who are on board an aircraft are going to die anyway if the aircraft is used as a terrorist weapon is dismissed on the ground that human life and dignity must enjoy the same degree of protection with no regard of the probable remaining lifespan.[22] The assumption that someone who is in an aircraft which is used as a weapon is himself part of that weapon and has to accept being treated accordingly 'shows blatantly that the victims of such an incident are no longer regarded as humans, but as a part of a thing, and are therefore made objects'.[23] The idea that an individual is under a duty to sacrifice himself where this is the only option to prevent attacks on the community which aim at its destruction is regarded by the Court as being

---

[19] Ibid [123]–[124].
[20] Ibid [125]–[129].
[21] Ibid [131].
[22] Ibid [132].
[23] Ibid [134].

too far removed from the point of the Aviation Security Act which was not concerned with attacks on the state as such.[24] Finally, the argument that there is a positive duty towards those who would be the victims should the terrorist attack be carried out is refuted with the counterargument that although such a duty exists, the means used to comply with the duty must be constitutional and not violate human dignity.[25] Each of these objections raises serious issues and could have been the basis of long discussions; however, the Court does not engage with them any more than absolutely necessary and in most cases restricts itself to one counterargument.

In the final section of the judgment, the Court sets out why in cases where only the hijackers are on board the aircraft, the shooting down would in fact be justified. In such cases, the Court does not regard the shooting down as a violation of dignity because the criminals are not being treated as objects: 'On the contrary, it corresponds to the position of the aggressor as a subject to make him accountable for the consequences of his autonomous actions.'[26] Therefore, as dignity is not involved, proportionality analysis becomes applicable. In a lengthy analysis, the Court concludes that in those cases where there is reason to assume that the aircraft will be used to kill people, the shooting down would be proportionate. For the Court, this follows from the fact that, although the shooting down would be a 'serious' interference with the basic rights of the hijackers (because it would almost certainly lead to their deaths), the interference would be justified given that the hijackers themselves caused the necessity of the state interference and that it would lie in their hands to give up their criminal plan and thus prevent being shot down.[27]

II

Courts often find themselves in a difficult position when dealing with national security issues: if they make a mistake and overprotect human rights at the cost of national security, the price in terms of human lives to pay for this mistake might be very high. Their composition as bodies of unelected judges as well as the fact that they are not experts on issues of national security, explains their tendency to be very careful in these matters. But this is only one side of the story: in a constitutional democracy, it is the proper role of the courts to enforce constitutional rights, and they cannot simply abdicate that responsibility on the ground that they feel incompetent to do so, that they are not elected, or that the majority might disagree

---

[24] Ibid [135]–[136].
[25] Ibid [137]–[139].
[26] Ibid [141].
[27] Ibid [144]–[153].

with their conclusions. This is particularly true when an important right, such as the right to life, is at stake. For reasons whose analysis and defence is beyond this chapter, the German FCC does not normally hold institutional deference in high regard, nor does it normally regard the fact that it is made up of unelected judges as a problem. Broadly speaking, it sees its role as enforcing the basic rights of the Basic Law, interpreted in a way which focuses on the *substance* of these rights, as opposed to considerations of institutional competence or democratic accountability. This explains, negatively, why the Court will not shy away from interfering with the will and expertise of the elected branches. But positively, it does not yet answer the question of what, if anything, justifies determining the right to life of the innocent passengers aboard the plane to be absolute, as a matter of the substance of human rights.

Nothing in the wording of Article 2(2) BL indicates that the right to life could be absolute. The constitutional 'default' in this case is therefore the proportionality doctrine. In order to avoid the proportionality principle and come to the conclusion of an absolute right, the Court needs a special doctrinal tool, and it finds this tool in the principle of human dignity: since human dignity is absolutely protected, whenever a killing amounts to a violation of human dignity, it must be constitutionally illegitimate. The problem here is that the content of the dignity clause is notoriously unclear. The Court itself relies on the old Kantian formula of treating people not as means but as ends to justify its conclusion that human dignity is violated. This formula is not only the most common approach to human dignity, but it has also been criticised for its lack of substance and guidance and the corresponding danger of delivering exactly the answer that happens to suit the interpreter's personal moral or political views best.[28] The Court itself had noticed its vagueness and declared in an earlier judgment that 'it is not rare for persons to be mere objects not only of the circumstances and social developments but also of the law in that they must comply without regard to their interests'.[29] From a doctrinal perspective, it is disappointing that the Court did not even attempt to provide some clarity in this area.

III

I will come back to what I regard as the main mistake in the judgment further below. In this and the following sections, I will take a step back from the *Aviation Security Act* case and address the more general question of whether there is sometimes an absolute right not to be killed. The

[28] *Cf* N Hoerster, 'Zur Bedeutung des Prinzips der Menschenwürde' (1983) *Juristische Schulung* 93, 95.
[29] BVerfGE 30, 1, 25–26.

respective philosophical debates take place in the context of discussions about consequentialism (according to which the moral rightness or wrongness of an action depends exclusively on its consequences) versus deontology (according to which consequences are at least not the only thing that counts).[30] Take the example of whether it is permissible to kill one innocent person to prevent five innocent persons from being killed. Under a straightforwardly consequentialist approach, what counts are outcomes, and it seems that we should prefer the outcome of one dead person over the outcome of five dead. Therefore, killing the one would be permissible.

This conclusion seems to be problematic. The point is not so much that it would necessarily be wrong to kill the one person; rather it seems that coming to this result simply by comparing numbers ('five dead is worse than one dead') misses some important moral considerations. Intuitively, it seems that killing an innocent person is morally wrong, even if this killing leads to an outcome that is overall preferable. Killing innocent persons may be morally impermissible as an *action* independently of the *outcomes* produced. Robert Nozick's theory of rights illustrates such a deontological approach. He provides the following example:

> A mob rampaging through a part of town killing and burning will violate the rights of those living there. Therefore, someone might try to justify his punishing another he knows to be innocent of a crime that enraged a mob, on the grounds that punishing this innocent person would help to avoid even greater violations of rights by others, and so would lead to a minimum weighted score for rights violations in the society.[31]

Nozick presents two possible routes to the solution of this problem. The first he calls 'utilitarianism of rights'. While classical utilitarianism is interested in maximising happiness, this new version would have the goal of maximising rights protection: the non-violation of rights is simply built into the desirable end state to be achieved. Under this version punishing the innocent man would be justified because, although punishing him violates his rights, the number and weight of rights that would otherwise be violated by the mob is even greater.

Nozick prefers the second view according to which rights function as 'side constraints upon action'. Under this view, rights determine which actions are permissible independently of the outcomes produced. So, according to this approach, violating the right of one person is impermissible even if this

---

[30] I do not wish to imply—indeed I think it would be simplistic to assume—that proportionality analysis is linked to consequentialism and absolute rights are linked to deontology. The reason why the philosophical debates take place in the context of those two moral theories is that deontological theories have often been developed in response to certain perceived deficits in the dominant strands of Anglo-American moral theory, namely utilitarianism and consequentialism.

[31] R Nozick, *Anarchy, State, and Utopia* (Oxford, Blackwell, 1974) 28–29.

would prevent a larger number of rights being violated. Thus, punishing the one innocent person would be impermissible. How does Nozick justify his view?

> Side constraints upon action reflect the underlying Kantian principle that individuals are ends and not merely means; they may not be sacrificed or used for the achieving of other ends without their consent. Individuals are inviolable.[32]

> But why may not one person violate persons for the greater social good? Individually, we each sometimes choose to undergo some pain or sacrifice for a greater benefit or to avoid a greater harm: we go to the dentist to avoid worse suffering later; we do some unpleasant work for its results; some persons diet to improve their health or looks; some save money to support themselves when they are older. In each case, some cost is borne for the sake of the greater overall good. Why not, similarly, hold that some persons have to bear some costs that benefit other persons more, for the sake of the overall social good? But there is no social entity with a good that undergoes some sacrifice for its own good. There are only individual people, different individual people, with their own individual lives. Using one of these people for the benefit of others, uses him and benefits the others. Nothing more. What happens is that something is done to him for the sake of others. Talk of an overall social good covers this up. (Intentionally?) To use a person in this way does not sufficiently respect and take account of the fact that he is a separate person, that this is the only life he has. He does not get some overbalancing good from his sacrifice, and no one is entitled to force this upon him—least of all a state or government that claims his allegiance (as other individuals do not) and that therefore scrupulously must be neutral between its citizens.[33]

This understanding of rights as side constraints may have intuitive appeal; however, the reason Nozick gives is deficient.[34] Assume that his argument (violating a constraint treats a person as a means and not as an end) was correct and treating people in a certain way disrespects them. But then, one could similarly conclude that we should minimise instances of disrespect. By disrespecting the one innocent person in Nozick's example, we can prevent many instances of disrespect to the people whose rights would otherwise be violated by the mob. Similarly, in the example of whether it is permissible to kill one to prevent five from being killed, we can prevent five instances of disrespect by committing one such instance. Nozick may be right in everything he says about the need to treat people as ends, but he does not show a link between this and his claim that treating people as means is always morally wrong independently of the consequences.

---

[32] Ibid 30–31.
[33] Ibid 32–33.
[34] *Cf* A Walen, 'Doing, Allowing, and Disabling: Some Principles Governing Deontological Restrictions' (1995) 80 *Philosophical Studies* 183, 185–86.

Nozick's failure is instructive about the traps on the way to a coherent justification of an absolute right not to be killed. The problem is that if one focuses on the interests of the potential victims, one can set their interests against the interests of those who would be saved. Focussing on the prevention of suffering and pain, the respect owed to them as human beings, their chances to live their life, and so on, does not help because the same points can be used on the other side of the equation. If there is a sound way to defend an absolute right not to be killed, it must avoid this fallacy.

IV

It may be helpful to separate the arguments justifying an absolute prohibition to kill into two categories. First, the justification may lie in something relating to the person who commits the killing, for example her integrity, responsibility, or intention (let me call these *agent-focussed approaches*). Second, one can turn to the victim and ask whether there is something pertaining to the victim which gives the victim the right not to be killed even if by killing him one could save more from being killed (I shall refer to these as *victim-focussed approaches*). In this section, I will examine two agent-focussed approaches.

One possible agent-focussed consideration relies on the distinction between actions and omissions: arguably, it is impermissible to actively kill one person, but it is permissible to let five die. While this argument may have some intuitive plausibility, it is however partly question-begging. If I come to a lake and see my son who has just fallen into the water, I am morally obligated to pull him out of the water, just as I am morally obligated not to push him into the water in the first place. The real issue is one of responsibility. Often, we are responsible for what we do and not for what we let happen; but as the example shows, this is not always so. Therefore we need a theory which explains under which conditions we are responsible for preventing a particular outcome. While the distinction between actions and omissions might be relevant within that theory, it cannot in itself do all the moral work.

Another approach is to draw a distinction between two points of view: an objective and a subjective one. In his book *The Rejection of Consequentialism*, Samuel Scheffler defends an agent-centred prerogative:

> It might be suggested that ... consequentialism ignores the independence of the personal point of view. This suggestion might be developed in the following way. Each person has a point of view, a perspective from which projects are undertaken, plans are developed, events are observed, and life is lived. Each point of view constitutes, among other things, a locus relative to which harms and benefits can be assessed, and are typically assessed by the person who has the point of

view. This assessment is both different from and compatible with the assessment of overall states of affairs from an impersonal standpoint.[35]

Scheffler's idea has some plausibility in the world of personal ethics because it limits the seemingly endless demands that consequentialism imposes upon every person. But his approach cannot be applied to the state. The state, as an abstraction, does not have a personal point of view. The people acting in the name of the state (for example the minister of defence who wonders whether he ought to order the shooting down of a plane) do of course have such a personal point of view, but when acting in their capacities as representatives of the state we demand of them to take an objective as opposed to personal perspective. We think that if it were objectively the right thing to shoot down the plane or to kill one innocent person to prevent five from being killed, then the government official in charge must leave worries about his personal viewpoint aside and do what is objectively right. If he is not prepared to do this, then he is the wrong person for the job. A further reason why the idea of an agent-centred prerogative is unhelpful is that it does not capture the real concern of those opposed to state-conducted killings, who want to argue that such killings are impermissible, whereas Scheffler's argument just defends a prerogative not to kill.

V

With regard to victim-focussed approaches, could it plausibly be argued that there is something about the victim which makes it impermissible to kill him, even if by doing so one could prevent five other killings? Frances Kamm has made an important contribution to this debate. For her, one must distinguish between the persons actually being killed on the one hand, and the person's *status as inviolable* on the other hand. She admits that when it is permissible to kill one person to prevent five killings, one might save lives. However, even if lives are saved, something else suffers: the general status of persons as inviolable.

> The realm of status is *not* what happens to people. If many are killed in violation of their rights because we may not kill one to save them, their status as individuals who should not be killed does not change. If it were permitted to kill the one to save them, their status would change. We may be concerned about what happens, but be unwilling to prevent it in a way that is only consistent with a change in status. It is a mistake to see an opposition between the rights of the one person and the rights of all others, since the status of everyone is affected by the way it is permissible to treat one person. [Emphasis in the original.][36]

---

[35] S Scheffler, *The Rejection of Consequentialism* (Oxford, Oxford University Press, 1982) 20.
[36] FM Kamm, *Morality, Mortality*, vol 2 (Oxford, Oxford University Press, 1996) 272.

Kamm is interested not in what is done (one killing rather than five), but what is allowed to be done. For her, if it were *permissible* to kill one to prevent five killings, this would imply that persons are violable. This would mean that they had a lower status compared to a situation where it was not permissible to kill one to prevent five killings. Therefore, she concludes, if we want to protect people's status as inviolable, we must accept that we must not kill one to prevent five killings. This obviously involves a sacrifice: sometimes we must let people die where we could save a greater number of lives. What is it about the status that justifies this sacrifice?

> If we are inviolable in this way, we are more important creatures than more violable ones; this higher status is in itself a benefit *to us* ... It is having the status itself which is a benefit, not just its being respected ... Having the status is a benefit, in part, because it makes one worthy of respect, owed respect ... Furthermore, the world is, in a sense, a better place for having more important creatures in it. Our having higher status is a benefit to *the world*. [Emphasis in the original.][37]

Two points have to be noted to clarify the theory and avoid misunderstandings. First, inviolability is not an all-or-nothing concept: one can be more or less inviolable. Kamm discusses the example that it is permissible to kill one to prevent 10 killings.[38] Compared to a case where it is only permissible to kill one to prevent one million killings, the inviolability of the person is low in this case. However, compared to a situation where it is permissible to kill one to prevent two killings, it is high. Second, it is important to see that Kamm's point is not that her status argument applies to all instances of killings. For example, it surely does not apply to a killing carried out in self-defence: nobody would claim that in order to preserve the status of humans as inviolable, one must tolerate being killed by an aggressor rather than kill the aggressor in self-defence. Similarly, it is not obvious whether Kamm's argument applies to the *Aviation Security Act* case (more on this below). So her argument is not that the permissibility of each and every killing affects the status of humans as violable; rather it is an argument justifying the general, deontological claim that *sometimes* an action *may* be impermissible even though it would lead to better outcomes. But the argument as to when this is the case still needs to be made independently: 'Simple talk about inviolability is not enough. Restrictions and constraints are better explained by inviolability against impositions that create inappropriate relations between victim and beneficiaries.'[39]

So the question is under what circumstances would the killing of one to prevent five from being killed lead to an inappropriate relationship between persons? There exists a vivid, controversial, and ongoing debate about these

---

[37] Ibid 272.
[38] Ibid 275.
[39] Ibid 274.

questions in moral theory, which is too vast and complex to be dealt with in its entirety within the limits of this chapter. Much of this debate focuses on some of the countless variations of the so-called 'Trolley Problem':[40] suppose a trolley is heading towards a group of five people. It is going to kill them unless it is redirected to a second track where it will kill one person instead. Is it morally permissible or required to redirect the trolley? Compare this case to the Fat Man Case: again, a trolley is heading towards the five, but this time the only way to stop it is to take a fat man and throw him onto the tracks. The trolley will crash into the man and come to a halt; the fat man will die, but the five will remain uninjured. In both cases one has the possibility of killing one in order to prevent five from being killed; yet most people agree that it would be permissible to redirect the trolley in the first scenario but not to throw the fat man onto the tracks in the second. The trolley cases come in countless modifications whose purpose is to show the appeal or rejection of the various principles which have been suggested to find satisfactory solutions to the question of when it is permissible to kill some in order to save many from being killed.

Mattias Kumm has recently subscribed to one of these approaches as particularly helpful for the discussion of whether there are absolute rights in human rights law.[41] He refers to an idea first presented by Alec Walen, who draws a distinction between enablers and disablers.[42] This distinction can be explained with regard to the two trolley cases introduced above. In the first scenario, it would doubtless be permissible (or required) to redirect the trolley if there was no person on the other track. The claim of the one person on that track is therefore that his being on the track should *disable* the otherwise permissible rescue action. Compare this to the Fat Man Case: here the fat man is instrumental to the success of the rescue action. He is being *used as a means* to stop the trolley and thus *enable* the rescue action. Kumm argues that as a matter of human rights law, proportionality analysis applies to the case of disablers being killed, but that there is a deontological constraint against killing an enabler.[43] Applying this logic to the case of the Aviation Security Act he concludes that the German FCC got it wrong: the Court argued that the innocent people aboard the plane are being used as a means. However, in reality their claims are only those of disablers: there is no doubt, indeed the FCC itself expressly states, that the shooting down would be justified if there were no innocent passengers on board. Therefore the claim of the passengers is that their presence on the

---

[40] Ibid ch 6; J Thomson, 'The Trolley Problem' (1985) 94 *Yale Law Journal* 1395; Walen, above n 34.

[41] M Kumm, 'Political Liberalism and the Structure of Rights: On the Place and Limits of the Proportionality Requirement' in G Pavlakos (ed), *Law, Rights, and Discourse: The Legal Philosophy of Robert Alexy* (Oxford, Hart Publishing, 2007) 131, 153–64.

[42] Walen, above n 34.

[43] Kumm, above n 41, 154.

plane should make the otherwise permissible shooting down impermissible. The passengers are, contrary to the argument of the German FCC, not being used as objects or means. They are not being used at all because their presence makes no difference to the rescue action, and their death is only a regrettable side effect.[44]

On this point, the *Aviation Security Act* case is quite a spectacular failure. Note that this failure does not affect the outcome of the case because, as explained above, the relevant part of the Aviation Security Act was also declared unconstitutional for other reasons. However, imagine a scenario in which a misguided interpretation of the Kantian formula controls the outcome: not only would the Court protect a right which does not exist, but it would also put national security at risk. This outcome could not be fixed by the legislature amending the statute, and worse, it could not even be fixed by amending the constitution: under German constitutional law, the guarantee of human dignity in Article 1(1) BL is irreversible according to the so-called 'eternity clause' of Article 79(3), which states that '[a]mendments to this Basic Law affecting ... the principles laid down in Articles 1 and 20 shall be inadmissible'.

I agree with much of Kumm's methodology; in particular he deserves credit for taking the discussion about absolute rights in human rights law in a very promising direction by linking it to current debates in moral theory. However, I also think that the matter, especially with regard to the *Aviation Security Act* case, might be even more complex. While it seems to be uncontroversial that it is indeed impermissible to kill enablers, it is not clear that it is always permissible to resort to balancing in the case of disablers. In the Car Case, a person is rushing to the hospital to save five, foreseeing that he will run over and kill one person on the road.[45] The one person on the road is a disabler: his claim would have to be that his presence on the street makes the otherwise permissible rescue action impermissible. Yet it seems impermissible to kill him.[46] Another case introduced by Kamm is the Grenade Case: a runaway trolley will kill five people unless we explode a

---

[44] Ibid 155–56.

[45] The example was first used by Philippa Foot; see P Foot, *Moral Dilemmas* (Oxford, Oxford University Press, 2002) 81. The formulation used here derives from FM Kamm, *Intricate Ethics: rights, responsibilities, and permissible harm* (Oxford, Oxford University Press, 2007) 22.

[46] Walen, above n 34, 203, discusses this case and modifies his understanding of disablers to the effect that while the one 'seems to be a disabler since you could save the five perfectly well if he were not in your way' at 204, 'you are only free to respond to the needs of some if you have a right to use the necessary means' at 205, and 'the means of saving the five includes getting to them, and that aspect of the means is what would kill the one' at 207. While this reasoning may explain the correct outcome of the case, I wonder if, in substance, it abolishes the distinction between enablers and disablers and introduces a new, more complex principle, evaluating which is beyond the scope of this chapter.

grenade that will kill an innocent bystander as a side effect.[47] Again, the bystander would be a disabler; yet Kamm argues it would be impermissible to explode the grenade.

There is a remarkable parallel between the Grenade Case and the *Aviation Security Act* case. One difference between them is that in the *Aviation Security Act* case, the passengers are part of the weapon. I wonder whether the real reason for the permissibility of balancing in the *Aviation Security Act* case is not that the innocent passengers are disablers, but rather that they are part of the weapon. Kamm stresses that for the doctrine of double effect, which is closely related to the distinction between enablers and disablers, to have any plausibility, one must allow 'for the permissibility of intending harm to the guilty and in self- or other-defense against even moral innocents who are threats'.[48] I cannot resolve the issue here; nor am I sure that the debates in moral theory would provide us with a resolution to this moral puzzle (mainly because real life scenarios as the one envisaged by the Aviation Security Act tend to be more complex than those discussed in moral philosophy); rather, I would like to point out the complexity of the issue. Intuitively, I agree with Kumm's conclusion that there is no deontological constraint against shooting down the plane; but I think that the reason for this lies not in the role of the passengers as disablers but rather in the fact that the passengers are part of the weapon.

Here is a further puzzle. Kumm applies his approach to torture cases.[49] The most widely discussed case in this context is the imaginary 'Ticking Bomb Case': the police have caught a terrorist who has hidden a bomb in the centre of a city, and the only way to prevent the bomb from going off and killing many people is to torture the terrorist in order to make him reveal the whereabouts of the bomb. Kumm explains, to my mind convincingly, that our focus, at least initially, should not be on the number of people we could save by torturing the terrorist.[50] Rather, it should be on the special relationship between the terrorist and the victims, and this relationship is independent of whether there are one or one million victims. So it might be helpful to focus on a case with only one victim, and as it happens, there is a real and, again, German case at hand. In the notorious *Jakob von Metzler* case, the police had threatened a suspect accused of kidnapping a young boy with torture (and were prepared to carry out that threat) should he not reveal the whereabouts of his victim who was erroneously believed to be still alive. Under the threat, the suspect confessed.

As a preliminary point, Kumm is aware of the fact that there might be good policy reasons for prohibiting torture in all cases, such as reasons

---

[47] Kamm, above n 36, 151.
[48] Ibid 150.
[49] Kumm, above n 41, 158–64.
[50] Ibid 160.

relating to the extreme suffering of the victim, slippery slope arguments, and practical or symbolic concerns.[51] His question is therefore whether there is a deontological constraint against torture in this case, and this he denies: while it is true that the kidnapper is used as a means—one of the terrible things that torture does is to coerce people to commit self-betrayal in order to serve the purposes of the torturer—the deontological constraint is, according to Kumm, neutralised because of the personal responsibility of the kidnapper for the threat.[52]

I believe that this is partly but maybe not entirely correct. Let us modify the example. Suppose that the kidnapper is not captured by the police but by the father of the boy. There is no time left to call the police, and the only way for the father to save his son is to torture the kidnapper in order to make him reveal the whereabouts of his son. I think that most would agree (although I acknowledge this would require further argument) that it is permissible for the father to torture the kidnapper. So for this scenario I believe that Kumm is correct to say that because of the personal responsibility of the kidnapper for the boy there is no deontological constraint against torturing the kidnapper. But I am not sure about what is right when the kidnapper is in the custody of the police. There may be a difference between what is permissible to do in the name of the state, and what is permissible for a private person, and I do not think that this difference is explainable only in terms of institutional or policy considerations such as slippery slope arguments. Rather, my intuition is that there is an additional constraint at work here which leads to everyone's, including the kidnapper's, status as inviolable requiring that torture be impermissible if carried out (or authorised) by the state. Put differently: I tend to think that if it were permissible to torture the kidnapper in the name of the state in the *Jakob von Metzler* case, this would affect *everyone's* (and not only kidnappers') inviolability: torture may thereby under certain circumstances become permissible; and my intuition is that this is too high a price to pay for the protection of lives, except maybe in catastrophic scenarios (eg a nuclear bomb in London). Again, this does not even come close to a watertight argument because one could reply that the permissibility to torture the kidnapper concerns only kidnappers and comparable aggressors, and does not affect everyone's status. I repeat that I do not claim to resolve the issue here, but only point out some of the puzzles in the area of deontological constraints. It appears to be a possibility that deontological constraints apply in different ways to private persons and the state.

[51] Ibid 159.
[52] Ibid 161.

VI

In spite of the many open questions, I think that Kumm's and Walen's distinction between enablers and disablers points to one important conclusion: the status of innocent and non-threatening persons as inviolable requires that they not be killed when killing them would involve using them as a means (as enablers). This does not necessarily amount to an absolute right because, as I pointed out above, inviolability is not an all-or-nothing concept; persons can be more or less inviolable. But what can be concluded is that while maybe not absolute, the right to life certainly offers to enablers more than simply proportional protection: enablers cannot justifiably be killed on the ground that this leads to a reduction in the overall number of people killed. It is therefore correct to say that the right to life is sometimes absolute or near-absolute.

For the reasons given above I am not convinced that balancing of rights is always permissible in the case of disablers. I do however think that there are at least some scenarios where it is permissible to kill innocent disablers, such as in the one envisaged by the *Aviation Security Act* case. This conclusion will leave many opponents of state-conducted killings unsatisfied because they want to stop the state from engaging in the business of killing innocent, non-threatening persons altogether. I cannot think at the moment of any realistic case where the state would seriously consider killing enablers (one would have to think of examples such as terrorists threatening to commit a devastating attack unless one innocent person is killed). The fact that such cases are not realistic in the sense that no state would comply with such requests shows that deontological constraints have a firm place in our moral and legal reasoning, including our reasoning about what human rights require. But they cannot be extended to cover all cases of killing innocents.

4

Can States Commit Crimes?

ANDREW VINCENT

A S WILL SOON become clear, this is an unorthodox chapter. My
initial supposition is relatively unproblematic, namely that the use
of lethal force by a state, or state-linked agency, in certain circumstances can be closely connected to the issue of state crime. In this context
the fundamental underlying question arises: can a state commit crime?
The question—can a state commit crime—might appear prima facie to be
a strictly legal question and unquestionably there are quite crucial legal
issues involved, but I approach it as a political philosopher. In this sense
there is a self-consciously experimental and cross-disciplinary dimension to
this chapter; the predominant theme is thus what might be loosely called a
prolegomena to a political philosophy of state crime.

The concept of state crime for a political philosopher is unique and raises,
by default, deep questions about the character of the concepts of responsibility, law, sovereignty, crime and statehood. I will argue that this question
of state crime also relates to another question concerning what it means
to be human. This connection may seem rather obscure at first glance: the
underlying argument is that we become human via politics, politics denoting a mode of association which addresses human plurality in a specific
manner. The 'mode of association' which interests me here is what I call
the civil state, which certainly for the last two centuries at least has increasingly (certainly in the Anglo-European context) been closely identified with
politics. In this sense state crime—by inference—appears to affect the very
character of politics itself and the nature of the civil state and consequently
impinges on an important understanding of our humanity. In a nutshell,
the ground of any limitation on lethal force is linked inferentially to the
question of the character of politics, which is directly linked, in turn, to the
nature of the civil state and ultimately what it is to be human.

I. THE BASIC QUESTION

When we examine the notion of lethal force exercised by a state, or a state-
related agency, we are speaking, on one level, about something self-evident.

The empirical fact that states do exercise lethal force is, in itself, not a crucial issue (unless you are a serious anarchist or state-sceptic), for the simple fact that one crucial reason for the state's existence and raison d'être is to maintain the security of its citizens. The issue of security at times may require the use of lethal force internally or externally; this is a practical detail of the state's function. There are though more interesting questions here: namely, in what context can a state exercise this lethal force and further, are there specific limits to this exercise, and, in addition, how does one ascertain when a state has exceeded these limits? Despite the importance of these questions, they are not my central concern. My discussion rather focuses on another question, that is, when a state does exceed specified limits, can it be said to have committed a crime? This would be the case either, whether one regarded certain individual or group agencies of a state as having acted intentionally, in terms of state policy, or whether one regarded the state as a juristic person, as having committed the act. Thus, it is not lethal force per se which interests me in this chapter, it is rather the fact that if a state has exceeded (what is understood to be) specific limits in the use of lethal force, can be it be said to have committed a crime? In considering lethal force we are thinking (I assume) about the use of *authorised* force, which I presume is distinct from the unregulated use of power and violence.[1] It follows that if these authorised rule-limits are exceeded, then, if the state (a state representative or representative state body) is the agency which has attempted to authorise the action, then it follows that it is the state itself which has committed a crime.[2]

---

[1] I do not think it is fortuitous that we speak of lethal force being exercised by a state, rather than lethal violence. The state does have a monopoly of force, which it is authorised to use. I admit that the empirical description of an act of force (shooting someone) could come under a similar description of an act of violence. However, the intention and constellation of ideas and authorisations surrounding the act of shooting are crucial. Force by a state (or state agency) is authorised, constrained by rules and expectations, and limited to a degree. Force is not a random act reliant upon whims. I admit that this judgement hangs upon an interpretation of the concepts of force and violence, but I see no particular problem here. If violence was the concern we would not be worrying about the 'use of lethal force' as a normative issue. The fact that we are concerned about the limits of lethal force, in itself, distinguishes state action or state agency related action from other types of action denoting violence. Of course one may want to deny this particular distinction and be possibly reconciled to the idea that all force denotes violence, which is another viable interpretation (beloved of anarchists and state-sceptics). However, this presents a different interpretation of political and legal existence which carries its own range of intrinsic problems. Thus, for the sake of the argument, I would at this stage maintain a distinction between violence and force to enable the argument about limits on state action to work. Action by a state agency within regulated limits is denoted as force.

[2] What, in passing, is further implied in this distinction is that the exercise of force is related to the notion of authorisation (as indicated in the previous footnote). In this sense, force is related to authority. This would be distinct from the basic exercise of power—the ability to alter and change actions by threat or coercion. Violence and the threat of violence can coerce human beings and change their activity; in this sense violence or the threat of violence can underpin and maintain power. But this is not necessarily authorised. This means that force

II. GENEALOGY OF STATE CRIME

The issue of state crime has of course a genealogy, with a provenance largely from the mid- to late-twentieth century. The domain in which this debate has mainly taken off is in the sphere of international law. In one sense international law is a prime disciplinary candidate for speaking about the concept of state crime. The very existence of international law is open to a broad ambit of interpretations (some interpretations being much less accommodating to the concept of state crime), but minimally it provides the possibility for the question of state crime to be raised, simply by positing some form of law which exceeds in some manner individual states.

Briefly, 1918, and much more significantly 1945, were crucial moments in thinking about state crime. Attention was focussed largely—at these moments—on the idea of the criminal responsibility of persons or organisations representing the state. In some slightly rarer arguments it was the government or the state itself which was seen to be criminally responsible—or a combination of these. The most decisive moment in this genealogy of state crime was unquestionably the Nuremberg trials. The conclusion of the 1939–45 war saw an Agreement for the Prosecution of the Major War Criminals of the European Axis and a Charter for an International Military Tribunal, indicating three major categories of criminal offence: crimes against peace, war crimes and crimes against humanity (although these were filtered down from earlier lists).[3] The Nuremberg Charter was later used as a working model for attempts at formulating crimes of state, particularly in the Rome Statute (1998). In all such cases, working as a state official or executive, in any capacity, was regarded as providing no exemption from criminal responsibility. It should be noted here that although individual responsibility of state agents figured importantly after the Second World War, nonetheless the extent and range of both organisations, individuals and groups, considered in the post-1945 trials, gave rise to the idea that the state itself was, in large measure, still corporately responsible in some manner, insofar as it encompassed or incorporated these individuals

and authority cannot and do not utilise an aspect of power, but again my argument would be that for the notion of lethal force to be limited or constrained, there must be a minimal acknowledgement that the exercise of power, per se, is not self-sufficient. There must be a recognition that the act is constrained in some manner. In other words, authority supplements and legitimates the exercise of power.

[3] The Charter indicates three categories of offence falling within its jurisdiction: crimes against peace (planning, preparing, initiating or waging a war of aggression or a war in violation of international treaties, agreements or assurances or participating in a conspiracy for the accomplishment of the forgoing); war crimes (violations of laws or customs of war, eg, ill-treatment of prisoners, killing hostages, etc); crimes against humanity (murder, extermination, enslavement, deportation, inhumane acts against civilians on political, racial or religious grounds).

and groups.[4] Post-1945, both individuals and states did become potential subjects for the imputation of responsibility in international law terms, particularly in terms of crimes against humanity or crimes which affected the international community.

III. THE PECULIARITY OF THE CONCEPT OF STATE CRIME

Prior to 1945, as one international law scholar has noted, 'the only active subjects of international law were states'.[5] In this earlier era, the issue of state crime and responsibility were largely nugatory. Although dominating the nineteenth century, this latter understanding was still reflected firmly in the early-twentieth century, for example, as in the main principles of the *Lotus* judgment of the 1920s, where sovereignty figures importantly. In this latter case the Permanent Court of International Justice (*Lotus Case*—7 September 1927) envisaged international law as solely governing the relation between states, with sovereignty taken as the central axiom; further, states were seen in this case to *make* international law.[6] Consequently international law, per se, could not be applied to a state unless it had expressly consented to it. This view underpinned a widely held unease with the concept of state crime, even to the present day. In fact it would still be regarded—I assume—with profound suspicion by many states and indeed certain conceptions of international law.

The reasons for this unease have roots deep in our understanding of the concept and practice of specifically the European state tradition over the last three centuries.[7] One core logically-motivated idea, underpinning this disquiet, is that a state cannot, by definition, commit a crime since the sovereign state is the only valid legal presupposition to the concept of crime. In this sense the concept of crime simply cannot logically transcend or indeed temporally precede the state. Consequently, the idea of state crime is a logical self-contradiction. The temptation is therefore to steer clear of any suppositions of state crime and suggest that it is particular agencies, or individual officials, that have made misjudgements or mistakes, have failed to follow rules, or have just misinterpreted rules. In addition, although

---

[4] 'It seemed more expedient to talk of individual criminal responsibility after the Second World War, although it would seem that, in the case of Germany, given the number of people tried as individual or members of criminal organizations, the entire state apparatus was in effect condemned', NHB Jørgensen, *The Responsibility of States for International Crimes* (Oxford, Oxford University Press, 2000) 25.

[5] Ibid 139.

[6] SS *'Lotus' (France v Turkey) (Judgment)* [1927] PCIJ (ser A) No 9, 18.

[7] It would still be truism to a large degree that 'the idea of states being criminally responsible for acts that violated international law had always been viewed with suspicion', Jørgensen, above n 4, 139.

it is extending this point too far at this stage, there is a strong juridical assumption that effectual law must imply definite legal remedies. Crime by a state, or alternatively human rights violations by a state (to take a cognate example), require remedies. The question is: are there any such remedies when dealing with states? Crimes of state, or violations of human rights by a state, might be regarded therefore as largely unviable propositions, simply because they have no actual consistently enforceable remedies, outside of war, military intervention, economic sanctions, or the direct consent of the state at issue. The latter are obviously feasible, but in all but the most extreme historical scenarios, the international community is usually reluctant to follow these pathways. However, I want to leave this point to one side for the moment.

The above argument does not mean that the concept of state crime is meaningless, far from it. However, when the idea is commonly articulated it relies upon a fairly hard distinction between law and politics—as well as law and morality in a different mode. Thus, one conventional, if quite optimistic, response to the subject of state crime insists that the distinction between politics and law must be maintained, not only on the domestic level, but more acutely on the international level. Thus, the conventional response, in large part, to the idea of state crime is raised within the forum of *international criminal law*. International criminal law, in effect, shows us the limits of lethal action by a state and makes the necessary legal judgments. This might be called the *Rechtsstaat* solution. International criminal law, as presently constituted, is thus the *Rechtsstaat* writ large. This argument presupposes that it is essential to maintain the rule of law at both the domestic and international levels and that this entails keeping politics at arm's length. State crime then becomes a feasible international option under basic rule of law principles.

However, there is a second response which, like the *Rechtsstaat* proposition, also maintains the separation of law and politics. This is though a more sceptical argument. It contends, in effect, that law functions well within a confined territorial frame, where a clear jurisdiction can be identified. Beyond that jurisdiction, that is internationally, there can be no hard law. At most, there is soft law and more pertinently the antagonisms of politics, understood in terms of unregulated power and national self-interest. The more unyielding formulations of this sceptical argument will often go on to deny the very idea of state crime altogether as nonsensical and consequently acclaim the irrelevance of international criminal law (except in the most minimal sense). We might call this the *Realstaat* solution.[8] It follows from this brief overview of arguments that, minimally, an overly rigid distinction between

---

[8] If being a sovereign state means being either able to decide the state of exception or keep law distinct from politics, then there is no legal limitation to lethal force either domestically or internationally; all that might be said to exist is politics.

politics and law is not always helpful in trying to articulate an account of state crime.

One example of the above more sceptical *Realstaat* argument, which relies predictably on the separation of politics and law, identifies law as a self-sufficient rule-governed system within a particular territorial unit. However when, for example, a lethal action is taken by a state which exceeds the rule of law, then sovereignty kicks in, in terms of what Carl Schmitt understood as the 'state of exception'. In this context something, or some entity, 'decides'. This 'state of exception' is largely where 'politics' subsists (decisionism). In this sense, any 'limit' is not a limitation on the state, but is rather a limitation on law—particularly international criminal law—although it also limits domestic law. Sovereignty (as decisionism) decides on the limit of law, and this in turn invokes politics, which decides on the extra-legal questions, such as the use of lethal force. Schmitt's 'state of exception' thus provides no room for legally judging a limit to lethal force, it nonetheless *solves* the problem of lethal force with remarkable ease. Politics, per se, for Schmitt, provides negligible leeway for the concept of state crime to be formulated. It also provides little or no leeway for international law, in toto, except in the more traditional pre-1945 sense of the term that is basically dealing with the customary interrelations between sovereign state entities.[9]

The above argument led Schmitt to a characteristic cynicism with regard to the Nuremberg trials, as a prime decisionist situation, remarking (in somewhat bad taste), for example, that whereas Germany committed crimes against humanity, the allies committed crimes for humanity.[10] The problem here is that Schmitt's view neither takes any full cognisance of the post-1945 world, nor indeed the enormity of the German state's activities prior to 1945. If anything, his argument on politics, sovereignty, and the 'state of exception' harps back to an earlier nineteenth century era of sovereignty and international law, although the core ideas still remain pervasive today.

IV. POLITICS AND LAW IN A DIFFERENT KEY

However, in trying to provide a coherent account of state crime, should politics be separated from law in the international sphere? Another critical, but nuanced and careful response to this question is Martti Koskenniemi's

---

[9] C Schmitt, *The Concept of the Political* (Chicago, University of Chicago Press, 1996) and C Schmitt, *Political Theology; Four Chapters on the Concept of Sovereignty* (Chicago, Chicago University Press, 2005).

[10] See M Salter, 'Neo-Fascist Legal Theory on Trial: An Interpretation of Carl Schmitt's Defence at Nuremberg from the Perspective of Franz Neumann's Critical Theory of Law' (1999) 5 *Res Publica* 161.

work. Bluntly put, international law in general is either considered to be a universal normative order, externally imposed upon the state, or, alternatively, something which has been extrapolated from real state practices. In the former it stands outside state practices and subsists in a utopian world of normative sentiments and propositions; in the latter it is something which simply reiterates existing concrete state practices.[11] From the latter perspective, international law is just stage-managed politics, becoming simply an apology for sovereignty. However, from the former perspective, international law remains utopian, dreaming vaguely of global justice and right. The more the normative autonomy of international law from politics is stressed, the more utopian it becomes.[12] Thus, whereas one perspective concentrates on concreteness and fails to maintain normativity, the other focuses on normativity to the exclusion of concreteness.[13] For Koskenniemi the concreteness argument derives from the earlier nineteenth-century doctrine of sovereignty, entailing the absolute liberty to legislate. Sovereignty is seen as externally imposed upon law. Interestingly he associates this view directly with the 1927 *Lotus* judgment, mentioned earlier.[14] Alternatively, if sovereignty is seen as subject to law—as in the recent 'responsibility to protect' debate—then the utopian normativity vision arises once again.[15]

For Koskenniemi, the bulk of international law over the last two centuries has therefore been a utopian struggle *against* politics.[16] He continues that the rule of law, in international terms particularly, has been continuously pursued to the present day within the basic activities of the United Nations. He describes this pursuit, in toto, as the 'liberal impulse to escape

[11] As he states 'An argument about concreteness is an argument about the closeness of a particular rule, principle or doctrine to state practice. But the closer to state practice an argument is, the less normative and the more political it seems. The more it seems just another apology for existing power. An argument about normativity, on the other hand, is an argument which intends to demonstrate the rule's distance from state will and practice. The more normative a rule, the more political it seems because the less it is possible to argue it by reference to social context. It seems Utopian and—like theories of natural justice—manipulable at will', M Koskenniemi, 'The Politics of International Law' (1990) 1 *European Journal of International Law* 4, 8.

[12] Ibid 9–10.

[13] Koskenniemi also calls these 'the rule and policy approaches to international law'.

[14] Koskenniemi, above n 11, 14.

[15] 'One style consists of preceding the law's substance with an analysis of the character of statehood and that of the international order—the "political foundations". Another starts out by listing the sources of international law and lets the law's substance follow therefrom.' See ibid 14. See also M Koskenniemi, *The Responsibility to Protect: Report on the International Commission on Intervention and State Sovereignty* (Ottawa, International Development Research Centre, December 2001).

[16] 'The diplomatic history of the 19th century is a history of such a fight. Since the Vienna Congress of 1814–15 and the defeat of Napoleon, the relations between European powers were no longer built on one power's search for primacy but on a general pursuit of the maintenance of the balance of power, guaranteed by complicated legal procedures and alliances', Koskenniemi, above n 11, 5.

politics'.[17] He infers that international society will not solve any hard issues by overtly agreed laws. Undoubtedly a common legal rhetoric does exist among international lawyers and philosophers, but, as he comments, 'that rhetoric must, *for reasons internal to the ideal itself,* rely on essentially contested—political—principles to justify outcomes to international disputes'.[18] Consequently, criticising a state (or in my argument indicating that a state has committed a crime) 'is not a matter of applying formally neutral rules'; it rather 'depends on what one regards as politically right'.[19] Abstract agreement on a legal rule can be gained, but when the rule is applied and interpreted it will immediately generate political judgement.

V. A BRIEF ASSESSMENT

My argument follows this usage of the concept of politics in Koskenniemi more systematically and then raises it specifically in the context of state crime. In one sense, I would agree with Schmitt, in small part, and Koskenniemi, in greater part, that international law is concerned with politics. Following the latter argument I would also agree that their separation is way overdone and the stress some lay on the autonomous character of law is a mistake. If international law does act as a limitation on states, it is a political limitation. In Schmitt though the argument is pushed to an extra level—which I regard as suspect. International criminal law is viewed largely as a facade by Schmitt. What does exist is a world of 'states of exception'—that is, multiple sovereignties which minimally shows us the limits of criminal law. In this context, state crime is meaningless. If a state commits a lethal act which exceeds specified limitations, then it is exerting its state of exception.

This latter Schmittian argument takes no cognisance of the political and historical changes of the post-1945 world and cynically avoids the issue of genocide by the German state—which for many was a catalyst of change in the perception of both international law and politics. In my view Koskenniemi makes a more valuable contribution here, particularly by insisting that international law has to be reconceived as a sophisticated form of political judgement, which takes full cognisance of divergence, diversity and social conflict. I would also extend Koskenniemi's argument from international law to domestic state law. His argument, almost by

---

[17] Ibid 6. For Koskenniemi, 'The Rule of Law constitutes an attempt to provide communal life without giving up individual autonomy. Communal life is, of course, needed to check individualism from leading either into anarchy or tyranny. Individualism is needed because otherwise it would remain objectionable for those who feel that the kind of community provided by it does not meet their political criteria' at 28.

[18] Ibid 7.

[19] Ibid 21.

default, moves in this direction, although there are some further qualifications to make.

In summary, I do not accept Schmitt's distinction between 'law' and the politicised 'state of exception'. In post-1945 circumstances, it is historically and politically naive. A much better distinction would be between the ordinary normalities of domestic law and the extra-ordinary aspect of international law. Further, law and politics are blended at both the domestic and international levels. What we think of as law, on the domestic state level, is habituated and institutionalised political judgement. Law is thus formalised and regularised politics. It has been, in this domestic state sense, immensely useful (something that coincides with the development of the 'state form' over the last three centuries and something which accelerated massively in nineteenth-century states) to train a corps of legal practitioners and regularise them into highly formalised political judgement, such that they perceive the world through rules, which can be tested in courts and procedures. However, this should not allow us to philosophically and historically lose sight of the deep political substance of law—a substance which comes to light starkly at certain historical moments, such as immediately post-1945 in the Nuremberg trials. Schmitt's argument thus needs to not only deepen its philosophical and historical understanding of politics, but also take cognisance of the normalisation of politics in domestic law in addition to the political character of the state of exception. Against Schmitt's monotonous notion of politics—as implying automatic antagonism—there is no reason not to see a form of rightness implicit in political judgement, as mooted in aspects of Koskenniemi's work.[20] Politics does not automatically equate with arbitrariness and self-interest, although such ideas are not absent from politics. To equate politics wholly with antagonism, self-interest and arbitrariness is a modernised and somewhat romanticised Augustinianism.[21]

Koskenniemi's argument therefore strikes me as a fruitful contribution to this debate. The concept of politics is, however, the key to its success and to my mind it still remains slightly murky in Koskenniemi's presentation. In one of his uses, politics denotes an arena of conflict where no specific consensual rules exist; a second use describes politics as 'furthering subjective desires'.[22] A third usage, in his work, indicates that in addressing conflict, politics engages with a certain notion of 'rightness' in judgement, as distinct from legal or moral rightness.[23] This latter use is, to my mind, the more productive angle to explore. It entails a form of 'political judgment' which refuses to lay down 'determining rules or ready-made resolutions to future conflict'. It thus accepts that there are 'no determining legal standards'. But

---

[20] This rightness has no foundational aspect.
[21] This is a romanticism of negativity towards politics.
[22] Koskenniemi, above n 11, 5.
[23] Ibid 21.

this is not an argument either for inertia, apology, or simply succumbing to state sovereignty.[24] Koskenniemi interprets politics, in this latter sense, as a move away from the idea of a *Rechtsstaat* towards a more flexible and contextually determinate condition. However, this is not the *Realstaat* solution mentioned earlier in the case of Schmitt. Koskenniemi suggests, in passing, that this whole scenario will also require lawyers—particularly international lawyers—to transform their whole self-image.

One point though, that I would want to argue here—in a Koskenniemian mode—is that the post-1945 change of perception, concerning the nature of state crime, was largely a change in political judgement. In this sense, the Nuremberg trials represented a radical transformation of political judgement, in a more concrete form. The Nuremberg trials, like the Genocide Convention, were a political act and their long term effect was and indeed remains fragile.[25] In saying this I am neither following a standard critique, suggesting that the Nuremberg trials represent a victor's justice, nor the view that there were distinct legal oddities and arbitrary dimensions to the trials.[26] However, I would not want to necessarily deny aspects of these latter critiques. In indicating that these were political trials, I am not therefore suggesting that that it was in any way wrong to consider that the regime in Germany (in 1945) had committed criminal acts.[27] There was, nonetheless, a deeply experimental aspect to the trials, although the chaos of the immediate post-1945 world was a reasonable moment to experiment.[28] In the more tempered reduced environment of the 1990s and 2000s this experimentation has, in smaller part, returned. The International Criminal Court (ICC) of 2002 can thus be viewed as 'a direct descendant of the Nuremberg Military Tribunal, as were the European Convention on Human Rights signed in 1950 and the Genocide Convention'.[29]

VI. POLITICS AND LAW

To return to an earlier critical theme: one immediate objection to the above argument is that it is surely vitally important to keep politics separate

---

[24]   Ibid 28.

[25]   'The trials were without question a political act, agreed at the level of diplomacy, and motivated by political interests ... Yet the final outcome was less prejudiced and more self-evidently just than these objection might imply', see R Overy 'The Nuremberg Trials: International Law in the Making' in P Sands (ed), *From Nuremberg to the Hague: The Future of International Criminal Justice* (Cambridge, Cambridge University Press, 2003) 29.

[26]   Eg, indictable charges only came about after a long period of legal wrangling, many did not even know that they were defendants for many months, see ibid 8.

[27]   Despite the fact that the German government was never branded a criminal organisation, the idea of criminality of the whole 'formed the basis of the trials', see Jørgensen, above n 4, 70.

[28]   Overy, above n 25, 28.

[29]   Ibid 29.

from law. The issue of state crime cannot be political, since it makes the Nuremberg trials (so the argument goes) into a partisan subject, with little or no consistent grounding in rules. This is even more crucial in the international forum where the accusation of political bias in international affairs is an ever present impasse. The recent furore over the ICC indictment of Omar Al-Bashir as a politically motivated act, is yet another in a long litany of such claims. Thus state crime—from an international perspective—needs to be thought of as a strictly legal concern (as clearly distinct from politics) in order to maintain fairness and neutrality.

My argument would be that we need a clearer understanding of politics here. My premise is that politics implies self-interest, plurality, distributive disagreement and uncertainty. This is part of the character of human co-existence. As importantly, though, politics is a way of addressing and mediating this human condition. Politics embodies therefore both plurality and uncertainty and its possible mediation. Politics is not though a means to something else, some higher moral value.[30] Politics can be crude and philosophically defective, amoral, at times frustratingly ineffective, and regularly invokes a range of skills which can, at points, look morally disquieting. As Stuart Hampshire comments, as human beings 'we are not masterpieces in our lives, and the lives of communities are not master classes. We look for some relaxation of tension, but, until death, we do not expect the neat disappearance of conflict and of tension, whether in the soul or in society'.[31] Conflict and uncertainty are not a sign of vice. They are simply a fact of human co-existence. Hampshire refers to this as the Heraclitean view, where 'every soul is always the scene of conflicting tendencies and of divided aims and ambivalence's, and correspondingly, our political enmities in the city or state will never come to an end while we have diverse life stories and diverse imaginations'.[32]

In point, what is distinctive about politics is that it is also the modus operandi through which conflict is taken in hand and mediated. It does not imply total resolution or perfectionism, but rather a process of thoughtful deliberation and engagement. Politics thus constitutes a public setting in which conflicts can be deliberated, often not solved, but certainly addressed. Politics functions in a public setting where differences are mediated, ultimately, if successful, into policy. In both this formal setting, as well as in all processes of adjudication, politics embodies an expectation of what Hampshire called 'hearing the other side' (*audi alteram partem*). This is a dimension of politics as an engagement with difference and pluralism. It implies a habit of both balanced adversarial, as well as dialectical, engagement with difference and

---

[30] Although certain types of institutional arrangement, facilitated by politics in liberal democracies, can and do merge contingently with aspects of such value.

[31] S Hampshire, *Justice as Conflict* (London, Duckworth, 1999) 40.

[32] Ibid 19.

plurality.[33] Politics thus denotes an approach to public affairs concerned with a regularisation of deliberatively 'hearing the other side'. 'Hearing the other side' moves ultimately towards formalising politics in rule-governed procedures (for practicality). Historically, in the Anglo-European setting, a crucial vessel for formalising politics is embedded in the jurisprudence of the civil state tradition.

One further point to add here: politics is a human artifice which has been historically tested and tried, forming the content of a complex body of traditions. However, politics also corresponds with one crucial anthropological factor of being human. It implies, at root, the relatedness of human beings. Humans have and always will exist relationally. At a very basic level one cannot *be* conscious of one's self as a human being, unless one is aware of other human beings, and that one is in turn recognised by them. This awareness enables the individual person to understand what it is to *be* an individual human being. There is no perfect self-realisation here, no perfect notion of a person. There are rather multiple modes of such relatedness and recognition from the family, friendship, neighbourhood and beyond. One crucial mode of relatedness is contained by politics, which in larger social agglomerations embodies the acceptance of humans as relational beings, and yet, at the same time, acknowledges the plurality of memories, interests and differences. The social recognition implicit in politics further implies being mutually acknowledged as independent human agents and not simply as objects. This also entails a sense that large scale relational activity (in states) cannot be moral or intimate. It requires the recognition and acceptance (to different degrees) of distance and formality—what might be called third-party relatedness. This contains an implicit rejection of the idea of any national intimacy. This acknowledgement and recognition in politics embodies a concomitant obligation to 'hearing the other side' in any social conflict.

There is therefore an often understated but nonetheless powerful dialectic at work in politics. Denying recognition is a denial of both our humanity and is consequently a form of oppression. Given that non-recognition implies oppression, it follows that recognition suggests certain type of institutional arrangements, which enable and ensure the conditions for mutual recognition. To be an agent, under these arrangements, is to be granted a specific normative status by others within a political structure. This implies a comprehensive vision of institutional arrangements—which I would associate with the *telos* of the civil state tradition. In this sense politics is essential for achieving our humanity. In this immensely fragile dimension of human co-existence, therefore, the civil state embodies politics in which a prevalent sense of humanity can be made possible.

---

[33] Ibid 21–22.

VII. STATES AND POLITICS

My argument is thus that the most resonant way of institutionalising this mediating aspect of politics is via a conception of civil statehood. Civil statehood embodies politics; it also invokes constitutionality, which is the capacity for constitutional self-limitation implicit in the process of politics itself. That is to say it links with the political virtue of 'hearing the other side'.[34] The self-limitation of the civil state implies that the other side has to be verbalised in a political space. The constitutional facet of politics, within civil statehood, therefore provides the structures and procedures for mediating social conflict, via (always imperfect) formalised procedures. It is thus only *within* civil statehood that the artificial distinction between law and politics is made possible, since it institutionalises and formalises the otherwise implicit fragility of politics (as long as one understands that law is habituated and formalised political judgement). However, in international terms the situation is much more complex and infinitely messier. International law is, at the present moment, an expectation of the habituation and formalisation of politics at the international level.

When we therefore examine the Nuremberg trials, or alternatively if we try to identify what is implicit in the Rome Statute (1998), what we see in fact is extrapolations from the vernaculars of the civil state tradition. Given that the civil state embodies politics, what we therefore see inferentially (at a deeper level) is the political character of state crime.[35] State crime is ultimately a transgression against political existence and our basic understanding of humanity. What state crime embodies therefore is a conscious intentional enterprise to rend the fabric of politics. The full significance of this argument is supplemented by the prior argument, namely that it is in politics that we identify the recognition of a deeply prevalent (but not uncontested) grasp of our very humanity. In this context it would be true to say that international criminal law is parallel to the movement which created human rights post-1945, which I would also see as ultimately political in character.[36]

Still, envisaging state crime as political does sound odd to the juridical ear. However, all crime, in my argument, can potentially be viewed as a falling away from politics, that is, a falling away from conditions of civility in politics. Domestic crime is basically embroiled or immersed in the complexities

[34] This political virtue is implicit, imperfectly, in the practice of all civil states.

[35] Nuremberg was largely 'inspired by treaties, [and] the "customs and practices of states"', A Clapham, 'Issues of Complexity, Complicity and Complementarity From the Nuremberg Trials to the Dawn of the New International Criminal Court' in P Sands (ed), *From Nuremberg to the Hague: The Future of International Criminal Justice* (Cambridge, Cambridge University Press, 2003) 40.

[36] See B Broomhall, *International Justice and the International Criminal Court: Between Sovereignty and the Rule of Law* (Oxford, Oxford University Press, 2004) 42.

and everydayness of habituated politics, which is regularised in legislation, lawyers' talk and the processes of legal judgment and adjudication. The bulk of ordinary domestic crime is not intended to disrupt politics; it derives rather from facets of human fallibility, self-interest, and a complexity of motives. Depending on its intensity, its ultimate effect is not necessarily to wholly disrupt politics, since politics itself is rooted in the acceptance of human fallibility and self-interest (as well as the way to mediate this). Law is therefore regularised politics. Domestic criminal law might in this context be seen as 'shallow crime'. State crime—which I would distinguish from international delicts—is potentially 'deep crime'. Deep crime involves an intended profound destabilisation of politics. Failure in a treaty obligation and genocide are both international wrongs, but they are distinct wrongs.[37] Internationally, state crime has a more confined sphere of operation, but its subject is more fundamental for humanity. It is concerned with issues which rip apart the fabric of politics, in a much deeper and more comprehensive manner.[38] Thus, Article 19 of the 1976 ILC *Draft Article on State Responsibility* argued that 'An international wrongful act ... results from the breach by a State of an obligation so essential for the protection of fundamental interests of the international community that its breach is recognised as a crime by the community as a whole constitutes an international crime'.[39]

VIII. RECONFIGURING *JUS COGENS*

It might be a wholly unorthodox way to formulate this point, but I would argue that this argument underpins the concept of *jus cogens*. *Jus cogens* is a profoundly political concept, which is telling us something fundamental about the character of both the civil state and the nature of humanity.[40] The origin of the term *jus cogens* derives from Article 53 of the 1969 Vienna Convention on the Law of Treaties; although it has been suggested that

---

[37] In 1976 the International Law Commission decided to include in its *Draft Article on State Responsibility* a distinction between normal international wrongful acts (delicts) and exceptionally grave breaches (international crimes). It was still maintained into the 1990s, despite opposition.

[38] These are parallels here with the gist of the famous *Barcelona Traction* case where a distinction is drawn between the obligation of states towards the international community as a whole, and those arising vis-a-vis another state in the field of diplomatic protection.

[39] Quoted in A Pellet, 'Can a State Commit a Crime? Definitely, Yes!' (1999) 10 *European Journal of International Law* 427, Pellet notes 'when a state breaches an international obligation essential for the interests of the international community as a whole, it never acts by chance or unintentionally; therefore, the elements of intent and of fault, which are not necessarily present in other internationally wrongful acts, are part of the crimes, exactly as they are part of penal infractions in domestic law. Moreover, even without a judge, the reactions of the international community to a crime clearly include punitive aspects' at 434.

[40] This would explain the *erga omnes* dimension.

the idea can be found in Hugo Grotius's work.[41] *Jus cogens* conventionally refers to 'a peremptory norm … accepted and recognised by the international community of States as a whole as a norm from which no derogation is permitted and which can be mollified only by a subsequent norm of general law having the same character'.[42] *Jus cogens* thus gives rise to obligations *erga omnes*, that is obligations that appear within all—in my vocabulary—civil states.[43] Despite still being a contested issue (as one would expect given the odd prevalence of sovereignty argument), such norms are often now taken to be binding on and within all states, although in practice the realisation and acceptance of *jus cogens* remains subject to 'uncertainty and resistance'.[44]

Still, for many international lawyers, *jus cogens* norms constitute the clearest basis for the concept of international criminal law. As one scholar remarked, no one now seriously doubts that 'norms of *jus cogens* have a real specificity among international law rules'.[45] However, such norms are still thin and to a degree, rare.[46] There are various ways in which these norms can be conceived: namely as external normative imperatives; associative conditions of membership; or as the customary action of states.[47] My own supposition is that *jus cogens* norms are in essence speaking about the minimal conditions of politics within civil states. These constitute the basic constituent elements of what it is to be human and function politically. An offence against *jus cogens* by a state can thus be conceived as an offence against politics and ultimately therefore an offence against our very

---

[41] International Law Commission, *First Report on State Responsibility,* UN GAOR, 50th sess, UN Doc A/CN.4/490/Add.1 (1 May 1998) para 48.

[42] Pellet, above n 39, 428; see also L May, *Crimes Against Humanity: A Normative Account* (Cambridge, Cambridge University Press, 2005) 25.

[43] All *jus cogens* are *erga omnes*, although certain things are *erga omnes* but not necessarily peremptory norms.

[44] Broomhall, above n 36, 43.

[45] Pellet, above n 39, 428.

[46] For certain scholars there are criteria for identifying such norms. They must be recognised by the international community as a whole; they need to be accepted as serious by all; they need to affect the conscience of humanity; they must be seen to offend against considerations of humanity; they will normally affect international peace and security; they will also entail crimes of individual criminal responsibility under international law, see Jørgensen, above n 4, 161.

[47] Larry May argues that 'there are some principles that transcend national borders and achieve universal binding force', see May, above n 42, 29. May comments that 'all that matters is that there be a philosophical basis for universal or quasi-universal norms grounded in basic human rights, on which the norms of international law might rest. This is the basic insight of moral minimalism as I conceive it' at 34. Thus *jus cogens* norms are seen as 'providing a protection from the treatment by a State that would jeopardize the security of its subjects' at 32. In a different mode, Thomas Franck sees certain deep rules underlying the whole idea of international criminal law; they form associative norms (rather than substantive norms) necessary for membership of the international community. They are not subject to the consent of states and they form part of an 'ultimate canon' of preconditions to the very recognition of sovereignty, see T Franck, *Fairness in the International Legal and Institutional System* (Oxford, Oxford University Press, 1993) 57–61.

humanity. This is what ultimately underpins the understanding of 'crimes against humanity'.

IX. CONCLUSION: STATE CRIME AND POLITICS

What advantage can be gained from seeing state crime in this manner? In my view it begins to tackle a paradox in the legal position on state crime. Law has an ongoing weird and at times inconsistent relation with the concept of sovereignty, both at the domestic and international levels. One can see why many lawyers would like to junk the term; it is in some ways the inconvenient truth about law. Domestically, sovereignty usually implies a supreme competence *within* a state. Thus, internally, sovereignty authorises, recognises and legitimates law. Sovereignty *decides* the limit of law. Externally—in the international realm—sovereignty implies a form of 'plenary competence' and 'the totality of international rights and duties'.[48] In this latter realm, sovereignty exists in a different, but nonetheless still integral relation with international law. International law is either legitimated (externally) by state sovereignty—as in the domestic sphere—or it is soft law, which still requires the decision of sovereignty. Some might wish for hard international law, but again what is the real obstacle here? The answer is straightforward. The reason why there is no hard international law is that there is no international sovereignty. Sovereignty is essentially the problem for law.[49] Even the idea that sovereignty can be contained by making international law internal to sovereignty still implies a decision. Thus, whichever way you configure it, law subsists with sovereignty domestically or internationally. One then asks the question: what is the problem here? The problem in a nutshell is politics. Sovereignty, as decisionism, implies, prima facie, the possibility of arbitrariness, inconsistency, and self-interested exercise of power implicit in a predominant populist understanding of politics. That is to say, sovereignty implies politics as part of the state of exception. One can see, therefore, law as both repelled by and intimately involved with politics, via the unpredictable vessel of sovereignty. Law longs for the *Rechtsstaat* in the midst of the *Realstaat*. In this scenario the concept of state crime remains permanently in a paradoxical limbo.

---

[48] J Crawford, *The Creation of States in International Law*, 2nd edn (Oxford, Oxford University Press, 2006) 32.

[49] Anthony Cassese sensed this conflict profoundly during his time as President of the International Criminal Tribunal for the Former Yugoslavia, arguing in retrospect that international law always remains the austere contrary to the potential irresponsibility of state sovereignty. He complained that even the 1998 Rome Statute has been still far too deferential to state sovereignty, see references in Broomhall, above n 36, 56–57. As HG Niemeyer commented in 1932, international law remains therefore 'an edifice built on a volcano—state sovereignty', quoted in Broomhall, above n 36, 60.

The paradox for law therefore is that it is always subject to sovereignty both internally and externally.[50] In relegating politics to an external dimension it unintentionally links it inextricably to power and sovereignty. In consequence it creates a potential anarchic international realm. Thus, in summary, the refusal of law to accept its inner political substance creates the problem of irresponsible sovereign power, specifically in international terms. In this sense, the demand to focus on law—autonomous from politics—makes law ultimately vanish into decisionism and state sovereignty.

However, if we acknowledge that law is rooted in politics and, further, that politics is being given very short shrift, conceptually, if seen as pure arbitrariness and self-interest, a different scenario is created. Politics, in a richer understanding, *engages* with diverse self-interest and plurality. Further, if we accept the argument that the civil state tradition embodies the *telos* of politics in this richer sense, and this in turn is linked intimately with a prevalent understanding of our sense of humanity, then law can be reconceived as regularised politics, intimately tied to a prevalent sense of our very humanity. State crime—as political—then presupposes the judgement of rightness and civility implicit in politics, thus avoiding the irresponsibility implicit in the penumbra of the legal autonomy perspective. It is via this pathway that the desire for international law might be addressed, namely one which recognises the rightness within politics, that is ultimately the desire to habituate politics on an international level.[51]

---

[50] If we take seriously the argument concerning the separation of law and politics, the problem is that it bypasses the ineffectiveness of international criminal law—even from the *Rechtsstaat* perspective—compared to the effectiveness of sovereignty. It is still the case that much state crime goes unremarked and measures to address it seem remarkably weak. However, more seriously, one key way in which this separation has been articulated—in both the above arguments—is via the use of the concept of sovereignty. Law is viewed as a self-contained system, which functions within a specific boundary; the boundary of law, as well as its core authorisation, is in fact defined by sovereignty. Events beyond the boundary then relate to politics, focussed largely on the externalities of the state. Yet, paradoxically it is the insistence of law on its autonomy from politics which generates the irresponsible and anarchic potential of sovereignty. This is simply because sovereignty defines the limits of law.

[51] The idea is that sovereignty is not constituted in a vacuum but rather by 'recognition of the international community, which makes its recognition conditional on certain standards, has become increasingly accepted in the fields of international law and international relations. ... From this perspective, crimes under international law can be understood as a formal limit to a State's legitimate exercise of its sovereignty', see Broomhall, above n 36, 43.

5

Law, Death and Denial in the 'Global War on Terror'

RUSSELL HOGG

W ITH THE PASSING of the Bush administration in the US (and the Howard government in Australia) the rhetoric of the Global War on Terror (GWOT) subsided, although the first of the two major armed conflicts to which it gave birth, in Afghanistan, continues and Iraq remains riven by sectarian violence. When, in the aftermath of the September 11 attacks, George Bush declared war on terrorists and their supporters throughout the world[1] this was an accurate and literal statement of US intent. No mere metaphor in the tradition of some past US wars (on poverty, crime, drugs and so on), the term 'war' was used on this occasion as a precise legal category, as soon became clear with the military invasions of Afghanistan in October 2001 and Iraq some 18 months later.

At the same time, a new paradigm for the conduct of international armed conflict was asserted by the US, centred on two core notions: first, a doctrine of preventive war that enlarged the (*jus ad bellum*) grounds for resorting to armed force in self-defence; and secondly, the need to curtail the (*jus in bello*) restrictions on the manner in which war was to be conducted, in particular in relation to the treatment of enemy combatants apprehended and detained in the course of the conflict. These changes were justified to meet the altered conditions of armed conflict in the twenty-first century, in particular the advent of unconventional threats from non-state actors and rogue regimes. Bush administration lawyers were put to work on refining the legal arguments and doctrinal adjustments needed to support the paradigm shift. The GWOT became very much a lawyers' war, a series of struggles over both the status and requirements of existing international

---

[1] National Commission on Terrorist Attacks upon the United States, *The 9/11 Commission Report—Final Report of the National Commission on Terrorist Attacks Upon the United States* (New York, WW Norton and Company, 2004) ch 10.

law and the need (or otherwise) to radically reform both international law and domestic criminal and security laws.[2]

This chapter for the most part steers away from these debates over the legal rules. Although they are important, so too is the recognition that rules never operate in a political and cultural vacuum. Law has a 'cultural life', as Ian Loader has put it,[3] and it is heavily and unavoidably conditioned by power and politics. This is true of the domestic law setting. It could hardly be less so in the fraught world of international security. For much of the twentieth century states claimed fidelity to international laws (including the laws of war) although frequently, and systematically, flouting them in practice. Atrocities proliferated along with the laws designed to stop them. It is true that without the legal efforts things might have been even worse. But the paradox does underline the need to consider the 'meanings-in-use' of rights and rules,[4] the inevitable ambiguity and contestability of law in context. It is therefore necessary to also inquire into the mechanisms by which in everyday life worlds, states and individuals can both claim general respect for law and at the same time deflect or neutralise its particular claims on their conduct. This is where adjacent disciplines and methods—criminology, sociology, anthropology, ethnography—may have something to offer to our understanding of current developments in the practice and laws of war and security. So this chapter can be seen as one response to the call a few years ago for criminology to enter the burgeoning field of international criminal justice.[5] It is not, however, an original theoretical contribution, but rather an attempt to apply some existing conceptual ideas to a particular dimension of the recent wars on terror.

On one hand, for many the most troubling aspect of the GWOT was the Bush administration's legal and practical erosion of the Geneva protections for captured combatants.[6] On the other hand, the implications

---

[2] Numerous academic conferences, journal articles and books have been devoted to the question of whether new rules are needed and if so what shape they should take. For two useful examples see the edited collections D Wippman and M Evangelista (eds), *New Wars, New Laws? Applying the Laws of War in 21st Century Conflicts* (New York, Transnational Publishers, 2005) and A Lang and A Beattie (eds), *War, Torture and Terrorism—Rethinking the Rules of International Security* (London, Routledge, 2009). Also see the UN High Level Panel on Threats, Challenges and Change, *A more secure world: our shared responsibility*, UN GAOR, 59th sess, Agenda Item 55, UN Doc A/59/565 (2 December 2004).

[3] I Loader, 'The Cultural Lives of Security and Rights' in B Goold and L Lazarus (eds), *Security and Human Rights* (Oxford, Hart Publishing, 2007).

[4] Ibid.

[5] P Roberts and N McMillan, 'For Criminology in International Criminal Justice' (2003) 1 *Journal of International Criminal Justice* 315.

[6] For excellent analyses see J Goldsmith, *The Terror Presidency—Law and Judgment inside the Bush Administration* (New York, WW Norton and Company, 2009); J Meyer, *The Dark Side—the inside story of how the war on terror turned into a war on American ideals* (Melbourne, Scribe, 2008); P Sands, *Torture Team—Uncovering War Crimes in the Land of the Free* (London, Penguin, 2009).

for humanitarian law protections of civilians and civilian life in Iraq, Afghanistan and elsewhere against the destructive consequences of war received far less critical attention, at least until recently. The oversight may seem strange given there is no general dispute over the fundamental status or meaning of the principle of civilian immunity under the laws of war. There is also no doubt in a general sense that these military interventions have had manifold destructive consequences for civilian life (albeit there is much dispute in some quarters as to the details). Perhaps it is just that the experience of war in the twentieth century has habituated us to the fact that, notwithstanding the injunctions of humanitarian law, the principal victims of modern warfare will be civilians. This of course is a reason for holding to a rule of strict necessity in relation to the use of military force. At the same time, it may be a lesson in the capacity of war to anaesthetise the moral senses. What is intolerable at other times, becomes anodyne, matter-of-fact, in times of war.

Today's wars against terror beg the question. Terrorists are rightly condemned for indiscriminate attacks on civilian life. What therefore are we to make of a war on terrorism, which showed cheap regard for civilian life? The question is even more salient when it is considered that these were wars of choice waged under extended justifications claiming in part a humanitarian mandate: to protect civilians against tyrants and terrorists, to spread democracy and so on. It is this issue of civilian casualties in the war on terror that I want to consider. My principal concern is with the discourses of denial and neutralisation that have operated to submerge the issue even as public and academic analysis and criticism of so many other aspects of the war proliferated.

I. WAR, LAW AND CIVILIANS

The laws of war authorise certain categories of persons, namely combatants, to lawfully engage in the deliberate mass killing of each other in the name of military necessity. The decision to wage a war on global terrorism was thus instrumental in enlarging the scope for recourse to lethal force by the US and its allies under both international and domestic law. Of course the historical construction of a legal space in which lethal force is permissible was also designed to confine the destructive human consequences of war.

A fundamental principle of international humanitarian law enunciated in the Geneva Conventions, and also widely accepted as codifying international customary law and practice in relation to war, is the principle of discrimination (or civilian immunity):

> In order to ensure respect for and protection of the civilian population and civilian objects, the Parties to the conflict shall at all times distinguish between the civilian

population and combatants and between civilian objects and military objectives and accordingly shall direct their operations only against military objectives.[7]

Furthermore, 'it is prohibited to attack, destroy … or render useless objects indispensable to the survival of the civilian population'.[8] Armed conflicts are to be undertaken by way of confronting and defeating the military forces of the enemy, not by attacking the society of the enemy, including its civilian population, social and physical infrastructure and political, economic and cultural institutions.

The principle does not afford absolute protection for civilian life, for people and infrastructure may be harmed as the unintended collateral consequence of an attack on legitimate military targets: for example, if they are in the vicinity of a military target or are targeted or struck in error. There are requirements that precautions be taken in the preparation and execution of a military attack to avoid and minimise harm to civilians. The use of military force is also subject to the principle of proportionality. Any harm caused to civilians cannot be disproportionate to the military objective involved. The problem is that the template of war provides a licence to dismiss the many tragic, destructive, unpredictable, messy consequences as regrettable though unavoidable. But, to reiterate, these are reasons for choosing *not* to go to war in the first place unless it is absolutely necessary. The terrible consequences of war for civilians is a 'known unknown', to coin a phrase, and should figure prominently in any decision to go to war where there are political alternatives to that course. It should not serve to cloak or excuse those horrors where they may have been avoided.

An entrenched and uncontentious legal principle, the idea of civilian immunity encounters manifold interpretive complexities and ambiguities in its legal details: in wars fought by and amongst civilians, who qualifies as a protected civilian and how do we determine what 'military objective' means? Questions such as these arise even before the 'fog of war' descends on their application in practice.

II. CIVILIAN CASUALTIES IN THE GWOT

The issue of civilian casualties in the wars in Afghanistan and Iraq was not a prominent public issue until relatively recently. Yet in certain restricted, mainly humanitarian, quarters where it has been a major concern the precise

---

[7] Protocol Additional to the Geneva Conventions of 12 August 1949, and relating to the Protection of Victims of International Armed Conflicts (Protocol I), opened for signature 8 June 1977, 1125 UNTS 3 (entered into force 7 December 1979) Article 48.
[8] Ibid Article 54.

scale of civilian deaths has been hotly disputed.[9] It is not my intention to enter this debate about the numbers. Statistics have their uses but also their limitations. A preoccupation with civilian deaths, for example, can lead us to overlook the significance of less easily quantifiable factors, including those concerned with serious non-fatal injuries (a multiple of those actually killed), orphaned children, displaced persons, mental trauma, and the impact on economic life, housing, public health, education, water, electricity supplies, and so on. The GWOT was declared by George Bush to protect the American 'way of life' from terrorist threats, a sentiment echoed by other political leaders like Tony Blair and John Howard. Perhaps therefore its consequences for the 'way of life' of others should not be completely overlooked. Cold hard statistics can also have a dehumanising and de-sensitising effect, the opposite of what is intended; it was Joseph Stalin after all who reputedly quipped that the death of one person is a tragedy, the death of thousands a mere statistic.

Yet, some bald and telling contrasts emerge from an examination of the statistics of violent mortality in the GWOT. We know that almost 3,000 people died in the attacks on the Twin Towers and the Pentagon on September 11. According to the US State Department's annual reports on *Patterns of Global Terrorism* the numbers killed in acts of international terrorism in the following two years were 725 and 625 respectively.[10] As of mid-2011 Coalition combatants killed in Iraq numbered almost 4,800, those killed in Afghanistan 2,700.[11]

Intense controversy surrounds efforts to measure the number of civilian deaths from violence in Iraq caused as a direct or indirect consequence of the military intervention. Survey studies by members of the School of Public Health at John Hopkins University put the total number of post invasion deaths, sometimes referred to as 'excess deaths', at over 650,000 up to July 2006, with just over 600,000 of these being attributed to violence.[12] This figure included Iraqi combatants as well as civilians. At the other end of the spectrum passive surveillance methods, most notably used in the work of the NGO Iraq Body Count, put the number of documented civilian deaths as of September 2011 in the range of 102,000 to 112,000.[13] It acknowledges

[9] See M Karagiozakis, 'Counting excess civilian casualties of the Iraq War: Science or Politics?' (2009) *Journal of Humanitarian Assistance* reliefweb.int/node/368452; P Reynolds, 'Huge gaps between Iraq death estimates', *BBC News Analysis*, 20 October 2006.

[10] US Department of State, *Patterns of Global Terrorism 2002*; *Patterns of Global Terrorism 2003*. After much controversy over the accuracy of these reports this manner of reporting by the State Department was abandoned in 2004.

[11] See the US Department of Defense website for these statistics: www.defense.gov/news/casualty.pdf. Also see the website www.iCasualties.org.

[12] G Burnham, S Doocy, E Dzeng, R Lafta and L Roberts, *The Human Cost of the War in Iraq—A Mortality Study, 2002–2006* (Massachusetts Institute of Technology, 2006).

[13] The Iraq Body Count (IBC) database is based on media reports (which are cross checked for verification) and mortuary and other official records where available.

that their numbers are likely to undercount mortality due to the conflict. In 2006, at the height of the violence, the Iraq Study Group reported that 3,000 Iraqi civilians were being killed every month. The Study Group also quoted UN estimates putting the number of refugees who had fled the country at 1.8 million and the number of internally displaced persons at 1.6 million.[14]

The war in Afghanistan has been conducted in two phases. In October 2001 the US invaded and drove the Taliban out of the country or underground within a matter of weeks. Little official or public attention was given to civilian casualties. One US academic, Marc Herold, sought to redress this. Basing his counts on global press reports, he estimated conservatively that over 3,700 civilians were killed in the first two months after the invasion, rising to 5,000 by the middle of 2002.[15] The second phase occurred with the Taliban resurgence after 2006 when attention shifted back to the conflict in Afghanistan. Concern over civilian casualties mounted as the numbers increased from an estimate of under 1,000 in 2006 to over 1,600 in 2007 and over 2,000 in 2008.[16] In its mid-year report for 2011 the UN Assistance Mission in Afghanistan reported 1,462 civilians killed in the first six months of the year, an increase of 15 per cent on the same period in 2010.[17] Eighty per cent of deaths in 2011 were attributed to anti-government forces. Air strikes were the main cause of civilian deaths attributed to pro-government forces, all of which were inflicted by the International Security Assistance Force.[18] Despite widespread criticism and apparent efforts to protect against them, deaths from air strikes continue to be regular occurrences.

Confining attention to Iraq only, and taking the conservative IBC figure for documented deaths, there is a staggering disproportion between civilian casualties and coalition combatant casualties (of more than 20 to one). This rather mocks the cherished status accorded the principle of civilian immunity in international humanitarian law. It is no answer to blame the terrorists. Terrorist attacks by al-Qaeda and its affiliates, vicious and indiscriminate though they have been, accounted for only a small proportion of the deaths in Iraq. Nor does it suffice to simply blame it on sectarian

---

[14] *The Iraq Study Group Report* (Washington, December 2006) 10.

[15] G Alcorn, 'Civilian deaths no cause for concern', *Sydney Morning Herald*, 12–13 January 2002, 14.

[16] See Human Rights Watch, *'Troops in Contact'—Airstrikes and Civilian Deaths in Afghanistan* (New York, September 2008); D Filkins, 'Afghan Civilian Deaths Rose 40 per cent in 2008', *New York Times*, 19 February 2009, quoting unpublished UN data.

[17] United Nations Assistance Mission in Afghanistan, *Afghanistan—Midyear Report 2011—Protection of Civilians in Armed Conflict, 2011*, July 2011, 1.

[18] Ibid. In relation to data on civilian deaths in Afghanistan due to US and Nato air strikes, also see Human Rights Watch, *'Troops in Contact'* (2008); and A Rashid, *Descent into Chaos—the world's most unstable region and the threat to global security* (London, Penguin, 2008) 96–98, 106, 147.

and communal conflict. Although this was undoubtedly the largest direct contributor to excess mortality, that violence was directly triggered by the invasion and the wholesale collapse in security it produced.[19] The contradiction is heightened by the fact that the GWOT is crucially defined by the civilian immunity principle. It is the contempt for civilian life that defines the terrorist enemy. How did coalition nations therefore respond to the terrible impact on civilians of wars they elected to fight in the name of upholding the value of civilian life? The answer is that in large part their response was one of denial, but as I will attempt to show, denial is no simple or one-dimensional reaction to unwanted events or information.

III. FROM 'TECHNIQUES OF NEUTRALIZATION' TO DISCOURSES OF DENIAL

In the 1950s and 1960s two criminologists, David Matza and Gresham Sykes, challenged the then dominant view within the sociology of crime and deviance that the roots of juvenile delinquency lay in oppositional deviant subcultures that rejected, and indeed inverted, the norms of law and respectable values. Rather, they suggested (following the realist jurist, Morris Cohen) that 'one of the most fascinating problems about human behaviour is why men violate the laws in which they believe'. They deployed the concept of 'techniques of neutralization' to analyse the problem,[20] to show how the motives and values of juvenile delinquents commonly draw on a portfolio of available *rationalisations* that permit an offender to commit a particular offence *without* rejecting the conventional moral values embodied in the law he or she has violated. The key is that all normative systems are flexible, negotiable, relative to context, circumstance, and so on. (This, of course, is reflected in the structure of the criminal law itself: requirements to prove intent and capacity, to negative exculpatory conditions like self-defence and necessity and so forth.) Matza and Sykes suggested that much delinquency was 'based on what is essentially an unrecognized extension of defences to crimes' and that these defences, justifications or rationalisations are operative both before and after the fact of deviant acts. Delinquent acts are committed, not as a bald rejection of legal rules, but by way of an

---

[19] This is widely accepted and confirmed by the work of IBC: see M Hicks, H Dardagan, F Serdan, P Bagnall, J Sloboda and M Spagat, 'The Weapons that Kill Civilians—Deaths of Children and Noncombatants in Iraq, 2003–2008' (2009) *New England Journal of Medicine* 1585. However, the IBC evidence shows that whilst US air strikes were far from being the principal cause of death in Iraq they were (unsurprisingly) much more lethal and indiscriminate in their impact.

[20] D Matza and G Sykes, 'Techniques of Neutralization: A Theory of Delinquency' (1957) 22 *American Sociological Review* 664.

appeal to some extended version of one or other of an array of conventional legal and moral justifications and excuses.[21]

More recently, in *States of Denial—Knowing about Atrocities and Suffering*,[22] Stan Cohen examined strategies of denial used by officials and perpetrators in relation to state political violence and atrocities, that is, the strategies, accounts, rationalisations used to sustain certain modes of violence, to mask it, justify it, rationalise it. Cohen was surprised to find that the strategies of neutralisation and denial familiar amongst delinquents were also common in the political/ideological context with which he was concerned.

Sykes and Matza had identified five commonplace techniques of neutralisation, what they described as:

— denial of responsibility—'it was an accident', 'I didn't know what I was doing'
— denial of injury—'no-one got hurt', 'it's covered by insurance'
— denial of the victim—'he had it coming to him', 'they started it'
— condemnation of the condemners—'you're all hypocrites', 'it's no worse than what you do', 'you don't understand'
— the appeal to higher loyalties—'I couldn't let my mates down', 'we were just protecting our turf'

To these Cohen added two more of particular salience to an understanding of political violence:

— denial of knowledge—'we didn't know what was going on', 'according to our intelligence it was a bomb-making factory, not a hospital'
— moral indifference—'we did the right and necessary thing'

All but the last of these strategies—moral indifference—involves general acceptance of the relevant normative code whilst seeking to exempt the particular situation at hand. Interestingly, an examination of Osama bin Laden's statements to the world and interviews with western journalists reveals a similar logic. In seeking to justify violent Jihad, being a defensive war in Islam, he stressed at every opportunity that his attacks were a reaction to western aggression and attempts to control the Arab and Muslim world. He frequently referred to the wanton killing of innocent civilians by America and Israel, including the deaths of some hundreds of thousands of Iraqi children as a result of western sanctions in the 1990s and massacres of Palestinian refugees in Lebanon by the Israeli Defence Forces. He also cited the bombing of Hiroshima and Nagasaki as evidence that the US shows little regard for innocent life. His reply to western outrage at terrorist

---

[21] Ibid.
[22] S Cohen, *States of Denial—Knowing about Atrocities and Suffering* (Cambridge, Polity, 2001).

attacks on civilians was that 'Your innocent are not less innocent than ours'.[23]

Three things at least are important to emphasise in relation to strategies of denial and neutralisation. First, they are not individual and idiosyncratic in nature, mere personal beliefs, or states of mind. Rather they draw on widely available, socially approved vocabularies, beliefs and rationalisations that resonate in the wider society. They are 'cultural constructs', not personal belief systems. In this respect they not only pave the way for individuals to engage in certain behaviours, but are also implicated in the processes and narratives through which these behaviours are invested with meaning in legal and other public settings and discourses.[24] Secondly, they are not merely after-the-fact excuses. Techniques for denying or rationalising action enter into the conditions that make the action possible.[25] Thirdly, when we move to the context of political or state action these strategies are liable to merge with larger political and cultural narratives ('protecting our people', 'defending civilised values'), that is, the sorts of habits of mind that George Orwell called nationalistic.[26]

In what follows, the focus on modes of denial in the GWOT is selective and uneven. I will not consider all of them and my primary focus will be on how they operate in relation to the issue of civilian casualties.

IV. DISCOURSES OF DENIAL IN THE GWOT

A. Denying Knowledge

Denying knowledge of terrible events is not confined to outright or literal denial of the 'nothing happened' variety. In addition to literal factual denial Cohen pointed to two other general types of knowledge denial:

— 'interpretive denial'—'something happened but it's not what you think', 'it's not torture'
— 'implicatory denial'—'our actions were legally justified', 'it was the isolated action of a few rotten apples'

---

[23] See B Lawrence (ed), *Messages to the World—the Statements of Osama bin Laden* (London, Verso, 2005) xix.

[24] This is central to Clifford Geertz's idea that 'law is local knowledge, not placeless principle': 'Local Knowledge: Fact and Law in Comparative Context' in C Geertz, *Local Knowledge* (London, Fontana Press, 1993) 218, 181.

[25] Training people to kill or torture is centrally concerned with neutralising psychological restraints against killing or inflicting suffering: see D Grossman, *On Killing—the Psychological Cost of Learning to Kill in War and Society* (New York, Back Bay Books, 1996).

[26] G Orwell, 'Notes on Nationalism' in *The Penguin Essays of George Orwell* (Harmondsworth, Penguin, 1984).

Denial can also exploit inevitable uncertainty concerning what happened, what Cohen refers to as 'the twilight between knowing and not knowing'.[27] There is no sharp line between knowing and not knowing something, even in the most favourable of conditions, let alone in the 'fog of war'. The 'whole texture of facts in which we spend our daily life' is, as Hannah Arendt observed, 'vulnerable'. 'Facts need testimony to be remembered and trustworthy witnesses to be established in order to find a secure dwelling place in the domain of human affairs.'[28] If this is true for everyday life it is more obviously so in the context of political action, like wars and armed conflicts, undertaken across a global canvas and in extreme conditions that are generally not conducive to gathering reliable testimonies.[29]

It is interesting that in the immediate aftermath of the fall of Saddam Hussein, senior US officials (like US Secretary of State Colin Powell and the US administrator in Iraq, Paul Bremer) confidently claimed success in the campaign, referring not only to the rapid defeat of Saddam but also the 'low' civilian casualties incurred.[30] Putting to one side the question of what 'low' means here, it is noteworthy that public figures saw no difficulty in making an assessment. Otherwise the universal strategy amongst US, UK and Australian government officials, before and since, was to claim that the prevailing conditions made it impossible to fully and accurately account for civilian deaths. This was presented (illogically) as a reason for making no effort to record civilian casualties at all. Conditions of war not only make precise knowledge of civilian impacts difficult, they also facilitate adoption of a policy of actively avoiding knowing. Typical is the response of the UK minister of defence in 2003:

> We are satisfied that the coalition did everything possible to avoid unnecessary casualties. We do not, therefore, propose to undertake a formal review of Iraqi casualties sustained from 19 March to 1 May.[31]

[27] Cohen, above n 22, 80.

[28] H Arendt, 'Lying in Politics' in *Crises of the Republic* (Harmondsworth, Penguin, 1973) 11.

[29] Orwell commented on this issue in the 1940s: 'Indifference to objective truth is encouraged by the sealing-off of one part of the world from another, which makes it harder and harder to discover what is actually happening ... The calamities that are constantly being reported—battles, massacres, famines, revolutions—tend to inspire in the average person a feeling of unreality. One has no way of verifying the facts, one is not even fully certain that they have happened, and one is always presented with totally different interpretations from different sources ... The general uncertainty as to what is really happening makes it easier to cling to lunatic beliefs. Since nothing is ever quite proved or disproved, the most unmistakable fact can be impudently denied.': G Orwell, 'Notes on Nationalism' (1984 (1945)) 306, 313–15.

[30] J Sloboda and H Dardagan, 'Civilian deaths in "noble" Iraq mission pass 10,000', Iraq Body Count, Comment and Analysis, 7 February 2004, 5, www.iraqbodycount.org/analysis/beyond/ten-thousand/.

[31] Quoted in above n 6. On similar responses by Australian officials see A Ramsey, 'All for the sum total of nothing', *Sydney Morning Herald*, 19–20 February 2005, 41.

The minister's statement is interesting as an exemplar of a sort of magical thinking in which a conclusion can be stated ('we don't inflict unnecessary civilian casualties') before consideration of any evidence that might, or might not, verify it and in order to dispense with the need for the evidence.

The 'war on terror' began with air strikes in Afghanistan on 7 October 2001. It quickly became apparent to independent observers that these strikes were killing many civilians, numbering in the thousands by early 2002. But as Ian Traynor in *The Guardian* observed at the time, no-one was counting.[32] The available evidence, patchy as it sometimes is, suggests the pattern continued in Afghanistan and was replicated on a far graver scale in Iraq as a consequence of the wholesale breakdown of security caused by the invasion. Most of the news media colluded in the official indifference. Australian journalist, Gay Alcorn, quoted a US Fox News commentator: '"Civilian casualties are not news. The fact is that they accompany wars."'[33] This is not to say that incidents involving civilian casualties are not reported, but reportage has been overwhelmingly matter-of-fact in its attitude and coverage. And only exceptionally have western media raised the larger questions of responsibility and policy involved, despite the scale of the casualties caused, directly and indirectly, by the invasions of Iraq and Afghanistan. Until recently it was left almost entirely to non-government organisations, to local authorities in Iraq and Afghanistan and to a handful of journalists and commentators to raise these issues.[34] Yet, if serious about preventing or minimising harm to civilians and complying with international humanitarian law, western governments would treat monitoring and knowledge of civilian impacts as vital to planning, policy and accountability in relation to military intervention. As the authors of an IBC report observed:

> It seems clear ... that to protect civilians from indiscriminate harm, as required by international humanitarian law (including the Geneva Conventions), military and civilian policies should prohibit aerial bombing in civilian areas unless it can be demonstrated—by monitoring of civilian casualties, for example—that civilians are being protected.[35]

Their point concerning air strikes, and the more general concern with civilian casualties, was belatedly reflected in US military strategy in Iraq and Afghanistan. As the strategic implications of hostility to the western military

---

[32] I Traynor, 'Afghans still dying as air strikes go on. But no one is counting', *Guardian Weekly,* 14–20 February 2002, 1.

[33] G Alcorn, 'Civilian deaths no cause for concern', *Sydney Morning Herald*, 12–13 January 2002, 14.

[34] See the discussion under section II of this chapter.

[35] See M Hicks, H Dardagan, F Serdan, P Bagnall, J Sloboda and M Spagat, 'The Weapons that Kill Civilians—Deaths of Children and Noncombatants in Iraq, 2003–2008' (2009) *New England Journal of Medicine* 1585, 1587.

presence were recognised, greater priority was accorded to protecting the population and reducing risks to civilians.[36] Yet, an unavoidable tension arises from the politics of wars fought from choice and aims of intervening states being not the traditional ones of defending against an existential threat, defeating an enemy state, or conquering territory in the national interest, but protecting civilian populations at risk, removing rogue regimes and tyrants or destroying terrorist enclaves. Claiming a humanitarian mandate is intended to confer legitimacy in the international community, but an over-riding consideration in sustaining such interventions is domestic political support at home. And this is generally more influenced by their own combatant casualties than civilian impacts in the theatres of conflict. Thus risk-averse, 'economy of force' methods are attractive and widely adopted—air strikes, use of special forces and reliance on local irregulars (like warlords and the Northern Alliance in Afghanistan). These invariably increase the risks and harms, direct and indirect, to civilian populations.[37]

B. Denying Responsibility

i. Denying Intent

The laws of war prohibit the targeting of civilians but allow that civilians may be incidentally and unintentionally harmed in the course of pursuing legitimate military objectives. The concept of intent here is strict and narrow and does not encompass what criminal lawyers sometimes refer to as oblique or knowledge intent, which arises where an offender knows that death or serious injury is the almost certain or probable consequence of their conduct but claims it is not the intended consequence. Military commanders and combatants may know or intend that civilians will die in this sense without violating the laws of war, so long as it can be said that the military action was not excessive (ie that the harm to civilians was not disproportionate to the military objective in question and could not have been avoided or reduced by pursuing an alternative military strategy) and that reasonable precautions were taken to minimise civilian harm.

---

[36] On Iraq see T Ricks, *The Gamble—General Petraeus and the Untold Story of the American Surge in Iraq 2006–2008* (Camberwell, Allen Lane, 2009). In Afghanistan the commander of the International Security Assistance Force (ISAF) and US forces, General Stanley McChrystal, issued a directive in mid-2009 restricting use of airpower in residential areas and ISAF also introduced a mechanism for tracking civilian casualties. These steps were welcomed but their effectiveness questioned. Other sources of risk to civilians, such as the location of military bases in populated areas, were not addressed: see generally United Nations Assistance Mission in Afghanistan, *Afghanistan—Annual Report on Protection of Civilians in Armed Conflict, 2009* (2010) 17, 23.

[37] Human Rights Watch, above n 16; United Nations Assistance Mission in Afghanistan, ibid.

These distinctions have proved to be flexible and manipulable in practice, especially given the conditions of uncertain knowledge that pertain in war and the effective control that the military exercises over the facts on the ground. The idea that dreadful things inevitably happen in war also contributes to a climate of impunity. Deniability is therefore facilitated on a number of levels. Moreover, political and technological developments in the conduct of war have seen these already fluid constraints progressively eroded over the course of the twentieth century, along with the perhaps more immediate restraints imposed by human psychological inhibitions against killing.[38] Modern technological means of warfare (particularly aerial bombing) allow for denial that civilians are being targeted at the same time as they are being killed and injured in large numbers. Where loss of innocent life due to military action has to be officially acknowledged the usual strategy is to deny the intention to kill or harm civilians ('all efforts are taken to minimise civilian casualties') and to express regret.

In October 2001 a hospital inside a military compound in the Afghan city of Herat was destroyed in a US bombing raid leading to an unknown number of casualties. A Pentagon spokeswoman announced that preliminary investigations indicated 'the weapons guidance system malfunctioned'. She was quoted: 'As we always say, we regret any loss of civilian life ... We take great care in our targeting process to avoid civilian casualties.' She also acknowledged that two 500 pound bombs had missed their targets and hit residential areas near Kabul.[39]

The example shows the ease with which the concern with human consequences and the morality of killing can be submerged in a discourse conducted in the sanitised, technical vocabulary of 'system malfunction', 'targeting process errors' and the like.[40] The role of technology and bureaucratic organisation dilutes responsibility almost to the point where denial is unnecessary because human agency has been magically erased from the process. As Philip Caputo observed of the 'war ethos', it is 'a matter of

---

[38] J Glover, *Humanity—a Moral History of the Twentieth Century* (London, Pimlico, 2001) 64–68; H Strachan, 'Strategic Bombing and the Question of Civilian Casualties up to 1945' in P Addison and JA Crang (eds), *Firestorm—the Bombing of Dresden 1945* (London, Pimlico, 2006) 1.

[39] 'U.N. says hospital hit in Herat', *CNN*, 23 October 2001.

[40] This also obscures the fact that 'smart bombs' ('precision guided munitions') are not always that smart. And if bombs are dropped on civilian areas there is a considerable risk—and the certainty on some occasions—of death on a large scale: G Eason, 'Why bombing can go wrong', *BBC News Online*, 16 October 2001. Human Rights Watch has been consistently critical of the responses of US military authorities to incidents involving civilian casualties, including denial and understatement of civilian casualties, rejection of the results of other investigations, refusal to investigate, refusal to publish the results of investigation and so on: see Human Rights Watch, above n 16; Human Rights Watch, 'Afghanistan: US Investigation of Airstrike Deaths "Deeply Flawed"' (Press Release, 15 January 2009).

distance and technology. You could never go wrong if you killed people at long range and with sophisticated weapons.'[41]

ii. Blaming Others

Responsibility may also be denied by displacing it onto others. It is clear that at no time during the conflict in Iraq did outside fighters or terrorists constitute more than a fraction of those involved in violence against the US and its allies or Iraqi civilians. The insurgency was overwhelmingly home grown and, in significant part, a product of the invasion itself and blunders in US military strategy.[42] Yet, many times the label 'terrorist' was used so indiscriminately as to suggest that it was all orchestrated and directed by al-Qaeda. This not only legitimated military invasion, occupation and indiscriminate incarceration and brutality directed at Iraqi civilians in places like Abu Ghraib, but allowed the Coalition to abnegate responsibility in relation to the breakdown of order and security in the post invasion phase. If it was all the fault of terrorists pouring over Iraqi borders or orchestrating violence from afar, the chaos could not be imputed to the well documented failures of the US-led military campaign.

The recurrent claim in these conflicts, also echoed in the Israeli/ Palestinian context, that innocents die because the enemy uses civilians as human shields or embeds itself in civilian communities is a further strategy for denying responsibility by displacing it. Whilst the evidence of insurgent contempt for civilian life is abundant,[43] the claim can become a reflex response to civilian casualties that is easy to invoke and hard to dispute.[44] In any case, military forces are not relieved of the responsibility to safeguard against killing non-combatants simply because it is difficult to differentiate them from the enemy. Moreover, the United Nations Assistance Mission in Afghanistan criticised US and NATO forces in Afghanistan for locating their own military bases in populated areas, thereby endangering civilians.[45]

---

[41] *A Rumour of War*, quoted in Z Bauman, *Modernity and the Holocaust* (Cambridge, Polity Press, 1989) 25.

[42] See T Ricks, *Fiasco—the American Military Adventure in Iraq* (London, Allen Lane, 2006).

[43] Human Rights Watch, *The Human Cost: The Consequences of Insurgent Attacks in Afghanistan* (15 April 2007) www.hrw.org/en/node/10984; United Nations Assistance Mission in Afghanistan, above n 36, 2.

[44] See for an example of this USCentcom, Unclassified Executive Summary, *US Central Command Investigation into Civilian Casualties in Farah Province, Afghanistan on 4 May 2009*, 13. Also see Human Rights Watch, 'Afghanistan: US Investigation of Airstrike Deaths "Deeply Flawed"' (2009), in which the US is accused of repeating such claims without evidence.

[45] United Nations Assistance Mission in Afghanistan, above n 36, 19.

C. Denial of Injury/Denial of the Victim

i. Introduction

Violence and suffering inflicted on others can also be suppressed and rationalised by denying or minimising the injury involved and/or neutralising claims to victim status. These two strategies are often closely related and I will consider them together. Adversaries in contemporary ethno-national conflicts frequently selectively trawl through history in order to re-position themselves as righteous avengers, to indict their enemies as the true villains and to justify their own atrocities. But denial of injury and denial of the victim are not so straightforward in conflicts like those in Afghanistan, Iraq and Israel/Palestine where those exercising military force (at least in the case of the two former conflicts) partly justify their actions on humanitarian grounds, as saving other peoples from the tyranny of Saddam Hussein or the Taliban. How is it possible to simultaneously invoke, and deny, the suffering and humanity of ordinary civilians in these conflicts?

People may be stripped of any claim to be victims and any regard for their suffering by active efforts to *dehumanise* them, by, for example, consigning them to some despised outsider group: terrorists, extremists, fanatics, 'the worst of the worst'. Where the conflict is such that it is difficult to distinguish combatants and non-combatants, dehumanising rhetoric is bound to have a spill-over effect, perhaps to whole populations. This is what happened on the ground in Iraq where military sweeps gathered up large numbers of ordinary Iraqis and dumped them in prisons like Abu Ghraib to be interrogated and abused.[46] Something similar occurred, and continues to occur, in Afghanistan.[47] However, a subtler and more pervasive pattern of denial can also operate alongside such active dehumanisation.

Central to this is the normalisation of sites of conflict—Iraq, Afghanistan, the Palestinian territories—as places where violence is endemic and life cheap, whilst distancing western intervention from any role and responsibility in producing and perpetuating this. (This works closely with the denial of knowledge and responsibility. Where violence is endemic it is not possible to know exactly what happened or to allocate responsibility.) Places and people appear, or are depicted, as irredeemably *other* and alien. This is achieved by omission—the dead remain numberless and nameless—and by recruiting images of chaos on the ground as evidence that these places are extruded from civilised culture, however lamentable this may be.

---

[46] Many of the Iraqis who were the subject of the humiliation and abuse depicted in the Abu Ghraib photos, having initially been vaguely suspected of terrorism, rape and the like, were subsequently found to be innocent of any wrongdoing: P Gourevitch and E Morris, *Standard Operating Procedure—a War Story* (London, Picador, 2008).

[47] L Hajjar, 'Bagram, Obama's Gitmo' (2011) *Middle East Report*, 260.

As Sykes and Matza observed, denial of the victims (and their suffering) can stem from a 'weakened' 'awareness of the victim's existence' where 'the victim is physically absent, unknown, or a vague abstraction'.[48] Distance from these conflicts, which is social and cultural as well as physical, creates a moral and emotional gap, eroding the capacity to identify and sympathise with victims in a way that, for example, was triggered by the 11 September attacks and the Bali and London bombings. The character of this form of denial is cast into relief by contrasting it with the manner in which victims of terrorist violence are typically represented.

ii. Victims of Terrorism: Normal Life, Pathological Violence

Accounts of terrorist violence are invariably highly personalised and sentimentalised. The dead are named, their lives recounted and honoured, the grief of families and communities given wide coverage and increasingly the victims are even memorialised in a manner akin to national heroes or war dead. When the death toll from 11 September was still being finalised more than two years after the attacks, the *New York Times* observed:

> The change in the number ... reflects the best in human nature, city officials say, as personified by investigators so intent on determining *the true and sacred number of the dead* that they properly took their time, even if it meant that a few fraudulent names, or the names of the living, were sprinkled among those of the many dead. Better that, they reasoned, than to exclude the name of *one true victim*. [Emphasis added.] [49]

In the aftermath of the Bali bombings, Australia's national broadsheet, *The Australian*, ran a 'Life Cut Short' series on the 88 Australians who were killed. Such responses are nothing less than appropriate but the sacredness of western lives, the preciousness of 'our security' and 'our' right to 'live without fear'[50] is in utter contrast to the easy way in which mass death and destruction in *other* places are passed over as being of scant interest or simply a sad fact of life.

The narratives in western media accounts of terrorist violence also typically tend towards a hyper-normalisation of the victims and settings

---

[48] They add: 'Internalized norms and anticipations of the reactions of others must somehow be activated, if they are to serve as guides for behaviour; and it is possible that a diminished awareness of the victim plays an important part in determining whether or not this process is set in motion.'

[49] Quoted in J Sloboda and H Dardagan, 'Civilian deaths in "noble" Iraq mission pass 10,000', Iraq Body Count, Comment and Analysis, 7 February 2004, 13, www.iraqbodycount.org/analysis/beyond/ten-thousand/.

[50] This was something of a mantra of Tony Blair, used amongst other places in his letter to then Home Secretary, John Reid, in which the Prime Minister mooted plans to roll back the Human Rights Act: N Temko and and J Doward, 'Revealed: Blair attack on human rights law', *The Observer*, 14 May 2006.

of the violence. Wanton terrorist slaughter occurs against the backdrop of normality and innocence: ordinary, unsuspecting people going about their mundane routines and tasks in familiar everyday settings—at work, on public transport, at leisure. In the last days of 2008, in the midst of the Israeli military campaign in Gaza, an Israeli mother of young children was killed by a rocket fired by Gaza militants as she drove home from her local gym. Her funeral was the subject of a long press article in an Australian newspaper which described the impact on the community and the galvanising impact on Israeli military action.[51] She was one of 20 Israelis killed by Gaza rockets since 2000. The Israeli ambassador in Australia later described 'the terrifying plight of the people' in these southern Israeli towns.[52] Israel's Prime Minister threatened a 'harsh' and 'disproportionate' response to rocket fire or shooting from Gaza, saying that the government 'will not be drawn into a war of incessant shooting on the southern border, which would deprive the residents of the south of a *normal life*' (emphasis added). The same article quoting the Prime Minister reported that four rockets and four mortar shells had been fired into the south on the previous day, adding that one 'reportedly landed near a kindergarten'.[53]

In some instances of terrorist attacks the backdrop of normality has had a different dimension—that of western tourists holidaying in global resorts (Bali, Kenya, Egypt). In the case of the 2002 Bali bombing 88 Australians died. In the aftermath unknowing observers of the media and political response could have been forgiven for thinking that Bali was *in* Australia, with Australia being widely represented as *the* target of the terrorists. The mental geography involved is of course highly selective. Bali's actual geographical and political context, that of a complex, fractious, poor and repressive society, was largely jettisoned in favour of seeing the place as essentially a tourist haven for Australians.[54]

These images of the people and places targeted by terrorists can be contrasted with representations of the settings in which western military intervention has been undertaken in recent times.

---

[51] I Kershner, 'Resolve amid the tears at funeral of Israeli mother' *Sydney Morning Herald*, 1 January 2009, 10.

[52] So described by Yuval Rotem, Israel's ambassador to Australia in an oped piece: Y Rotem, 'Voices missing from Gaza debate', *Sydney Morning Herald*, 4 February 2009.

[53] J Lyons, 'Olmert threatens "harsh" response', *The Australian*, 3 February 2009, 9. I should stress that I am not suggesting that it is anything other than appropriate to publicly acknowledge and report the tragic death of individuals and lament the terrible surrounding circumstances and public trauma. The issue however is why this privilege is not owed to all innocent civilians and communities affected by violent conflict and whether the right of some to a 'normal life' is being used to justify the recourse to organised violence which denies that right to others and, at the same time, seeks to make that denial itself appear normal and legitimate.

[54] As Gary Younge observed at the time the idea that it is more than usually heinous for someone to die on holiday in such circumstances is 'ludicrous': 'No refuge from reality', *Guardian Weekly*, 26 December 2002–1 January 2003, 9.

iii. Victims of Military Force: Wretched Life, Normalised Violence

In the representations of military interventions we rarely find such scenes of normality, of innocent mundane daily life. Sometimes, in the imagery generated by satellite-based coverage and advanced weapons technology, for example, these places are not even represented as three dimensional, but as 'verticalised', 'cartographic', spaces devoid of civilians,[55] a gaze, which allows bomber crews (and others) to maintain the illusion that civilians are not targeted. At ground level, they more often appear as irredeemably *other* and *alien*: as torn apart by violence and conflict, debased and abject.

Western interest having refocused on Afghanistan after September 11, 2001, it was not uncommon for commentators to recall that country's recent past history of invasion, occupation and civil war and observe that it had been driven 'back to the stone age'. There were abundant images and dire statistics on life expectancy and the like to confirm the impression that this was a wretched, hellish place. Much of this commentary probably had as its purpose, if it had a purpose beyond mere reportage, to encourage sympathy for the ordinary people of the country, especially when it was juxtaposed with the brutality of the Taliban.

But the distancing devices in such reportage can produce a number of other unintended effects. One is to submerge the particular historical and contemporary lines of force that connect the most alien and de-civilised of places to the outside world, in particular to foreign military and political interventions present and past. Similarly, images of the Palestinian territories generally fail to—because they cannot—project backdrops of normality recognisable to a western audience. Most Palestinians live in refugee camps, whether in the West Bank, Gaza or other Middle Eastern countries. Resorts and holiday towns are not a feature of Gaza or the West Bank. These are conditions produced by dispossession and maintained by an elaborate and repressive regime of military, policing and town planning controls administered by the Israeli state. They are not 'normal' conditions, for Palestinians or for anyone. To depict them naturalistically through the abundant visible signs of disorder and wretchedness and without conveying the history and political context of a conflict that is centrally about land and space is to obscure the roots of Palestinian resistance and can instead make violence appear as just another symptom of degenerate Palestinian life in which distinctions between 'ordinary Palestinians', civilian victims and 'terrorists' is clouded.

A second effect stems from the tendency for representations of place and setting to be mixed up with images of the people who inhabit them and the interpretation of events that occur in them. The above story of the Israeli

---

[55] S Graham, 'Cities and the "War on Terror"' in M Sorkin (ed), *Indefensible Space—the Architecture of the National Insecurity State* (London, Routledge, 2008) 11.

mother killed by a terrorist rocket provides immediate points of identification for western readers and observers that bring this victim and others like her within their orbit of understanding and sympathy, but at the same time concealing important differences in context. Israel is not by the standards of most nation states 'normal': it is one of the most abnormally militarised societies in the world, which is not incidental to its military occupation of the neighbouring Palestinian territories over the last 40 years and the raining down of Palestinian rockets on southern Israel. In the eight years during which these rockets killed 20 Israelis, the Israeli security forces killed more than 3,000 Palestinians in Gaza, most of them civilians.

If, as David Sibley[56] argues, 'group images and place images combine to create landscapes of exclusion', the discursive strategies that distance places, that partition them as Other, that alienate them from western civilised sensibilities, can also serve to distance the people who inhabit them, as marginal people belonging to abject places, thus loosening their claims on our concern and sympathy, on our recognition of them as victims of violence. This demarcation of 'same' and 'other', 'us' and 'them', creates a mental wall around the suffering of some and masks what it has in common with all victims of violence. It eases the way to the use of military violence by displacing attention from its human consequences to its deployment according to rational criteria of defence and necessity. The death and destruction it inflicts is in the same move masked and sanitised by recourse to terms like 'collateral damage'.

V. ABU GHRAIB AND THE QUESTION OF TORTURE: DENIAL AND ITS LIMITS

[I]n modern war, what is most shocking is a poor guide to what is most harmful. Technology has created forms of cold violence which should disturb us far more than the beast of rage in man. The great military atrocities now use bombs or missiles. The decisions are taken coldly, far away.[57]

It is interesting that the events in Abu Ghraib prison in 2003 and the question of torture, rather than civilian deaths, came to dominate the controversies surrounding the GWOT. These issues raise questions concerning not only official denial but wider cultures of denial. Was it the case that *we* did not know about such practices, that they were kept secret and denied outright until the Abu Ghraib photos were published? As Mark Danner points out, 'in our recent politics, "secret" has become an oddly complex word.'[58] As early as 2002 and

---

[56] D Sibley, *Geographies of Exclusion* (London, Routledge, 1995) 14.
[57] Glover, above n 38, 64.
[58] M Danner, 'US Torture: Voices from the Black Sites', *New York Review of Books*, 9 April 2009.

early-2003 there were media reports of 'secret' interrogation centres, practices like sleep deprivation and withholding of food and 'US officials overseeing interrogations in countries with dubious human rights records'.[59] Soon after 11 September 2001, Cofer Black, head of the CIA Counterterrorism Centre, told the Senate Intelligence Committee that 'After 9/11 the gloves come off.' Torture was therefore if anything an open secret, located somewhere in a space between official denying and not denying, public knowing and not knowing, prompting the question of who exactly was in denial, how far denial reached and whether this was a case only of official denial or whether it involved a wider culture of denial.

The saga of the US Justice Department torture memos shows that an interpretive denial strategy was integral to executive planning in the GWOT from the outset.[60] It illustrated many of the specific features of interpretive denial, including recourse to euphemism, code, sanitised language and technical idiom—for example, 'alternative set of procedures', 'enhanced interrogation techniques', 'stress positions', 'sleep adjustment', 'force multipliers', etc—to disguise the reality of the practices involved. Verbs, doing words (involving doing awful things to people), were replaced by nouns that referenced discrete clinical-sounding procedures which bear no resemblance to what was done to detainees.[61]

What shattered the veneer of denial was the public circulation of the Abu Ghraib photos. Their handling was also a case study in the cycle of denial. A Red Cross report in October 2003, distributed only to US authorities (as is the conventional practice), disclosed ill-treatment of prisoners, some of which was tantamount to torture. It elicited a literal denial.[62] When the photos were initially handed over to senior army officers there was a concerted effort to cover up and contain the issue.[63] Later public circulation of the photos graphically depicting abuse and humiliation was, in the time honoured fashion, attributed to a handful of 'bad apples', several of whom were prosecuted and jailed. The internal inquiries were confined to low level military police (ie the jailers). More senior officers, and in particular military intelligence (the actual interrogators), were protected despite evidence of their own abuses (including killing suspects) and their critical role in nurturing the general climate of brutality. The small number of prosecutions and other disciplinary measures taken were confined to some of the

---

[59] J Maley, 'Torture and terror', *Sydney Morning Herald*, 10 March 2003; also see Danner, 'US Torture: Voices from the Black Sites' (2009) who tracks the early reports in the US media.

[60] M Danner, *Torture and Truth—America, Abu Ghraib and the War on Terror* (London, Granta Books, 2004); Sands, above n 6; Goldsmith, above n 6.

[61] For long extracts from some of the 'high value' detainees's testimonies to the Red Cross see Danner, above n 58.

[62] Gourevitch and Morris, above n 46, 169–71.

[63] Ibid 247–55.

soldiers who appeared in the photos that were publicly circulated (none of them above the rank of sergeant). The expose was itself an exercise in denial. Growing public evidence of the systemic nature of the ill-treatment of prisoners saw denial slide into the interpretive mode. Detainees were subject to 'enhanced interrogation techniques', not torture: *'we* don't torture'. In more recent defences of these practices, including those of former vice-president Cheney, the interpretive denial is maintained, but the claim of justification is emphasised: the interrogations yielded high-level intelligence that allowed attacks to be pre-empted.

It is important to ask the further question of why the photos had such an impact, why these images (a few in particular) came to define the war for so many and became iconic in relation to its morally discreditable nature. The behaviour, vile as it was, pales by comparison with the mass civilian deaths caused in air strikes or during the US army's siege of Fallujah or the torture inflicted on many prisoners as an integral feature of individualised interrogation plans. Also, the images that exercised the most power over the popular imagination were far from depicting the worst of the behaviour captured even in the Abu Ghraib photographs.[64]

In truth, the impact probably had little to do with the objective scale of the harms involved or the culpability of the individuals. It had everything to do with their visual content and power. Some worried at their effect on popular opinion in the Muslim and Arab world, but doubtless they came as little more than confirmation of existing views and experiences. As Jock Young suggested, they exploded western, not Muslim, illusions. They shook the stark binary—central to strategies of denial—between the irrational, grisly, carnal methods of the terrorists and the rational, professional and limited use of force by western military and security forces.[65] The photos revealed that the urge to gratuitously humiliate, torment, wound and kill, supposed to define the moral gulf separating terrorist barbarism from western civilised values and methods, was not after all the prerogative of one side in this violent conflict.

VI. CONCLUDING COMMENTS: LAW AND DENIAL

Abu Ghraib may carry other important lessons. Stan Cohen makes the point that denial strategies, with their reliance on euphemism, technical jargon and other linguistic assaults on meaning, operate to depict 'a wholly non-pictorial world', quoting Orwell that such language is '"needed if

---

[64] Ibid 180–84.
[65] J Young, *The Vertigo of Late Modernity* (London, Sage, 2007) 160–61.

one wants to name things without calling up mental pictures of them"'.[66] The Abu Ghraib photos cut through the strategies of interpretive denial. But, they did so, not because they revealed some unvarnished truth, or in any way dispensed with the need for interpretation. On the contrary, their power stemmed from the proliferation of interpretations and 'mental pictures' they engendered: from their stimulation of the imagination.[67] This is why they crashed through the Orwellian pall of bland, obscurantist, anaesthetising rhetoric and denial.

This is pertinent to a further point made by Cohen. He questioned the growing role of legalism in international responses to mass atrocity because he saw it as peculiarly amenable to strategies of interpretive denial. Legalism encourages protracted, intricate, highly technical textual commentary and dispute over the meaning of particular words and events. It is conducted in a wholly non-pictorial discourse which invariably yields opaque versions of reality. It may therefore be no coincidence that the GWOT, more than most wars, has been a lawyers' war and a war mired in legalism.[68] It is an interesting question whether this experience bears out Cohen's scepticism as to the limits of law as an instrument for controlling organised violence.

At the least this experience is a reminder that legal discourse and legal constructions of violence and lethal force do not operate in some autonomous realm. They have 'cultural lives',[69] which require understanding, and particularly require understanding by those who want to use the law to create a less violent world.

---

[66] Cohen, above n 22, 107–08; G Orwell, 'Politics and the English Language' in *Why I Write* (London, Penguin, 2004 (1946)) 115.

[67] Although Gourevitch and Morris observe in regard to the Abu Ghraib photos that 'Photography is too frank to allow for the notion of suffering as noble or ennobling' the essential point of their account was to provide a context to these events, a context that was belied by their public reception as somehow delivering some set of undeniable truths: Gourevitch and Morris, above n 46, 182–83.

[68] For an idea of the extent of lawyers' involvement (and also other professionals, like behavioural scientists and doctors) in planning, justifying and implementing techniques against detainees that were found to constitute torture see the recently declassified version of the Report of the Committee on Armed Services, United States Senate, *Inquiry into the Treatment of Detainees in U.S.Custody*, November 2008. The central role of senior lawyers in the Bush administration is also a key theme in Sands, above n 6 and J Meyer, *The Dark Side—the inside story of how the war on terror turned into a war on American ideals* (Melbourne, Scribe, 2008).

[69] See I Loader, 'The Cultural Lives of Security and Rights' in B Goold and L Lazarus (eds), *Security and Human Rights* (Oxford, Hart Publishing, 2007).

Part II

Legal Frameworks for Shooting to Kill

6

Shooting to Kill Innocents: Necessity, Self-Defence and Duress in the Commonwealth Criminal Code

IAN LEADER-ELLIOTT

THE AUSTRALIAN MODEL Criminal Code is a template for reform of federal, state and territorial criminal law. Chapter 2 of the Code declares the 'General Principles of Criminal Responsibility'.[1] The Principles are an adaptation of provisions from the UK Draft Criminal Code[2] and the American Law Institute's Model Penal Code.[3] The ensuing chapters of the Model Criminal Code provide a comprehensive coverage of offences against the person and other major criminal offences. The General Principles were enacted by the Commonwealth Government, with few changes, by the Criminal Code Act 1995, in a schedule to that Act, entitled 'The Criminal Code'.[4] Enactment of most of the substantive chapters of the Model Criminal Code followed. The Code has continued to evolve and has grown to formidable proportions. (I will refer to it as the 'Commonwealth Code', when necessary, to distinguish it from other codes.) State and territorial implementation of the Model Criminal Code has been less wholehearted. Most have refrained from enacting the General Principles. There is, however, substantial support across the jurisdictions for the Code scheme of offences against the person. They are rich in distinctions between levels of comparative severity of injury and fault requirements for liability.[5] Intentional, reckless and negligent wrongdoing are distinguished. This

---

[1] Model Criminal Code, ch 2—*General Principles of Criminal Responsibility*, Final Report (Canberra, Australian Government Printing Service, 1992).

[2] *A Criminal Code for England and Wales* (Law Commission No 177, 189).

[3] Model Penal Code, Proposed Official Draft (Philadelphia, 1962).

[4] Criminal Code Act 1995 (Cth) (Criminal Code).

[5] See generally, I Leader-Elliott, 'Faultlines Between Guilt and Punishment in Australia's Model Criminal Code' in B McSherry, A Norrie and S Bronitt (eds), *Regulating Deviance*, Onati International Series in Law and Society (Oxford, Hart Publishing, 2009) 261.

dissection of the varieties of fault provides the framework for an articulate system of offences graded by the severity of their penalties and, implicitly, by their degree of wrongfulness. The distinctions among varieties of fault and culpability are not matched, however, by a corresponding level of articulate discrimination among the defences. The three defences that will be discussed in this chapter—self-defence, extraordinary emergency (necessity) and duress—have an all or nothing character; they lack the capacity to register differences in degrees of wrongdoing, making no provision for partial defences that would reduce a serious offence to a less serious offence, rather than resulting in outright acquittal. The distinction between defences that justify and defences that excuse goes unrecognised. Necessity, self-defence and duress are approaching merger by way of an undifferentiated principle of 'reasonable response'.[6]

The trend towards a merger of necessity, self-defence and duress, and the absence of any provision for partial defences are my primary concerns in this chapter. Though these defences apply generally to all Commonwealth offences, the discussion will be confined to murder and manslaughter. These offences have potentially important applications in Commonwealth law when Australian citizens or residents are killed as a consequence of conduct beyond Australian borders[7] and when UN or associated personnel are killed.[8] It can be expected that cases in which the defences have application, whether of murder, manslaughter or other offences against the person, will involve on occasion the use of force by members of Australian defence forces or other persons in the service of the Commonwealth.

The Criminal Code definition of murder is limited, in compliance with the correspondence principle,[9] to cases in which death is caused intentionally or results from conduct that the defendant knew to involve a substantial risk of death.[10] The definition of manslaughter is similarly restrictive: liability is limited to death resulting from conduct that was intended to cause serious harm or known to involve a substantial risk of serious harm.[11] No provision has been made for offences of negligent homicide or causing serious injury, though there are templates for these offences in the Model Criminal Code.[12]

---

[6] See Appendix at the end of this chapter for text.

[7] Criminal Code, ch 5—*The Security of the Commonwealth*, Part 5.4—*Harming Australians*.

[8] Criminal Code, ch 4—*The Integrity and Security of the International Community and Foreign Governments*, div 71—*Offences Against United Nations and Associated Personnel*.

[9] See AP Simester and GR Sullivan, *Criminal Law: Theory and Doctrine*, 3rd edn (Oxford, Hart Publishing, 2007) 186–91.

[10] Criminal Code, s 71.2 (*Murder of a UN or associated person*); s 115.1 (*Murder of an Australian citizen or resident of Australia*).

[11] Criminal Code, s 71.3 (*Manslaughter of a UN or associated person*); s 115.2 (*Manslaughter of an Australian citizen or resident of Australia*).

[12] Model Criminal Code, ch 5—*Fatal Offences Against the Person*, Discussion Paper (Canberra, Australian Government Printing Service, 1998) 144; Model Criminal Code, ch 5—*Non-Fatal Offences Against the Person*, Report (Canberra, Australian Government Printing Service, 1998) 38; s 5.1.16 (*Negligently causing serious harm*).

The near merger of the defences will be discussed first. Two hypotheticals in which innocent victims are shot by state officials in circumstances of necessity will provide the basis for discussion. That discussion will be followed by a comparison between the structure of defences in the Commonwealth Code and the US Model Penal Code, where a strongly marked distinction between justification and excuses is linked to the provision of partial defences that can reduce the offence committed to one of lesser wrongdoing. Duress will play a comparatively minor role in the discussion until the concluding section of the chapter.

The more general point to be made is that Criminal Code defences fail to articulate principles that should guide courts when offences are committed in order to avert threatened harm. The object of codifying general principles of responsibility is to displace common law; these provisions fail to provide an articulate alternative to the common law. That is a serious failing in a Code that is likely, in practice, to have application to a significant proportion of cases involving the use of force by officials.

Borrowing a metaphor from Peter Westen and James Mangiafico, the object of the discussion is to explore the necessity for distinctions among the three defences in the 'metric by which evils are measured' when a person is faced with a choice between suffering a harm and committing an offence.[13] Westen and Mangiafico's central contention—that duress is a justification—can be ignored for present purposes. Their analysis is valuable because they insist on the significance of differences in exculpatory context that depend on whether a choice of evils takes the form of a plea of necessity, self-defence or duress. Human threats are different from natural threats and self-regarding or self-preferential responses to threatened harm are distinguishable from responses to threats of harm to others, when legal or moral responsibility is in issue.

There are, of course, areas where the defences will overlap in their applications and a defendant can choose from a suite of possibilities. A Commonwealth employee who is threatened with death unless she hands over some item of Commonwealth property to a robber will be justified or excused for doing so by any one or more of the defences of necessity, self-defence and duress: acquittals are neither labelled nor graded in terms of their comparative moral worth.[14] Distinctions between the defences only matter in cases that lie beyond the area of their overlapping applications. The different metrics of responsibility will reveal potential variations in three paradigms of intentional killing where each defence has a distinctive and exclusive application. These paradigms provide the framework for the

---

[13] P Westen and J Mangiafico, 'The Criminal Defence of Duress: A Justification, not an Excuse—and Why it Matters' (2003) 6 *Buffalo Criminal Law Review* 833, 923–24; see also at 894, 895.

[14] Since Commonwealth offences of this kind will usually require proof of dishonesty as an element of the offence, necessity and duress will also have a bearing on proof of the offence.

discussion that follows. In each of them, a harm is threatened and there is no practicable alternative to the use of lethal force if the threatened harm is to be averted. First, self-defence: the defendant, who is faced with an unlawful threat of harm from V, an aggressor, responds with lethal force. The defendant's response is 'reasonably proportionate' to the threatened harm. Necessity: the defendant uses lethal force and kills V, an innocent who is not an aggressor. The death of V is the 'lesser harm or evil'; many lives, let us suppose, are at stake. Duress: the defendant uses lethal force and kills V, an innocent who was not an aggressor, in order to avert a threat of harm to D from X. V's death is not a lesser harm or evil but D's 'will is overborne' by the threatened harm. In each of these paradigms the 'metric by which evils are measured' is reasonable proportionality; the references to lesser harm or evil and the overborne will are conventional. For the moment, each of these terms is a placeholder for potential distinctions in the criteria for measuring responsibility in situations of necessity, self-defence and duress.

Rather than merging existing categories, we may need more variety and more discrimination in the forms of justification and excuse than the existing three generic defences permit.[15]

I. SHOOTING INNOCENTS: NECESSITY AND SELF-DEFENCE

The Code is remarkable for its insouciant abandonment of common law limits on the defences of necessity and duress and their extension to exculpate intentional killers from responsibility for murder.[16] The principles expounded in *R v Dudley & Stephens*[17] were overturned, so that it is possible that killing a cabin boy might now be justified by necessity if there was sufficient certainty that a greater number of lives might be saved. The significance of that particular change in established law should not be underestimated. Under common law, Dudley and Stephens had no

---

[15] There are grounds for distinction among 'duress of circumstances'; duress resulting from a human threat coupled with a demand and duress resulting from a human threat that is *not* coupled with a demand. See Westen and Mangiafico, above n 13, 940–44. See M Dubber, *Criminal Law: Model Penal Code* (New York, Foundation Press, 2002) 252, on variants in legislative formulations of the defence of duress. See also, P Robinson, *Structure and Function in Criminal Law* (Oxford, Clarendon Press, 1997) 147–48, 218, 228, 238–39, distinguishing between defences of justification: self-defence and mistake as to justification, with distinct forms of verdict for each defence.

[16] A note on terminology is appropriate at this point. In the Criminal Code, an 'offence' is constituted by its 'physical elements' and 'fault elements'. Once the offence is established, defences can be considered. If there is no defence or a defence is not established, the defendant is 'responsible' for the offence.

[17] *R v Dudley & Stephens* (1884) 14 QBD 273.

defence but they did not hang or suffer any significant punishment for murdering the cabin boy: they were pardoned. If the legal process in the case is considered as an entirety, the judgment of Lord Coleridge CJ stands for the proposition that the common law cannot encompass a trial by jury of the necessity for a choice of evils, much less duress, when responsibility for murder is in issue. It was a supplementary and exceptional exercise of the royal prerogative that saved Dudley and Stephens from the normal processes of criminal justice. The Criminal Code provisions on necessity and duress extend the processes of jury trial to include the possibility of an acquittal for an intentional killing of innocents. That change is, in its own way, a salutary extension of the rule of law and limitation of executive power. However, the failure to mark any distinction between necessity and duress, when liability for murder is in issue, is a cause for concern. That problem can be put aside for the moment.

These extensions of necessity and duress were not the only departures from common law in the Criminal Code. In its present form, 'self-defence' is a misnomer. The plea of self-defence extends beyond defence of self to include an altruistic intervention to defend another person. It extends to defence of property belonging to anyone. The defence is available whether the threat was real or misapprehended. Unlike necessity and duress, there is no requirement that a mistaken perception of threatened harm be reasonable: D may have a complete defence though lethal force was used in response to an unreasonable and mistaken perception of a threat to D or another person.[18]

The significance of these changes is masked by the bland generality of the provisions, the substantial area of their common applications and the use of the same 'reasonable response' criterion for exculpation in each of the defences. The table that follows paraphrases the defences and emphasises the common elements in their structure. Several distinctions that have no immediate relevance have been omitted.[19]

---

[18] Common law requires reasonable belief in the existence of a threat. That requirement is commonly diluted, however, by further refinements of scholarship. Compare the accounts given in S Yeo, *Compulsion in the Criminal Law* (Sydney, Law Book Company, 1990) 218; and in P Fairall and S Yeo, *Criminal Defences in Australia*, 4th edn (Chatswood, NSW, LexisNexis Butterworths, 2005) 174, where a compromise position is taken: 'It is not what a reasonable person *would* have believed, but what the accused might *reasonably* have believed in the circumstances.' (Original italics.) The authors add that 'transitory characteristics such as intoxication or deluded beliefs are relevant'.

[19] As, eg, the rule that reliance on duress is precluded if the defendant was associated in a criminal enterprise with the person who made the threat and the rules that there can be no reliance on self-defence against conduct that is known to be lawful and that deadly force cannot be used in self-defence when property is threatened.

COMMONWEALTH *CRIMINAL CODE*: 10.2 DURESS; 10.3 SUDDEN OR
EXTRAORDINARY EMERGENCY; 10.3 SELF-DEFENCE

Self Defence	Extraordinary Emergency [Necessity]	Duress
1. Belief in a threat to person or property	1. Reasonable belief in sudden or extraordinary emergency	1. Reasonable belief in threat by a person
2. Belief offence is necessary to defend person or property	2. Reasonable belief offence is necessary to avoid emergency	2. Reasonable belief offence is necessary to avoid threat
3. Commission of the offence is a reasonable response to the perceived threat	3. Commission of the offence is a reasonable response to the emergency	3. Commission of the offence is a reasonable response to the threat

The Code provisions are consistent in the direction of their evolution with
Christopher Clarkson's argument that self-defence and duress are merely
'sub-species of a broader necessity defence' that should be telescoped into 'a
new single defence: necessary action'.[20] Clarkson concludes that an omni-
bus defence of this nature would simplify the law. An inclusive necessity
defence would:

> focus on the true issue that unites the present defences: whether, given the pres-
> sure/crisis, etc., facing the defendant, the response, taking into account the con-
> text and all the circumstances, was a reasonable and proportionate reaction to
> that danger.[21]

If that is a desirable objective, it is to the credit of the authors of the
Australian Code that the provisions dealing with the defences are so far
advanced towards its achievement. The distinctions between the defences
are residual in character and their interrelationship is so lacking in coherence that merger might seem to be an appropriate final step to remove the
remaining anomalies.[22]

The near obliteration of distinctions among necessity, self-defence and
duress in the Commonwealth Criminal Code is all the more apparent if one
compares the corresponding defences in the US Model Penal Code, where
necessity and self-defence are characterised as justifications and duress is

---

[20] C Clarkson, 'Necessary Action: A New Defence' (2004) *Criminal Law Review* 81, 82.

[21] Ibid 95. See also L Alexander, 'A Unified Excuse of Pre-emptive Self Protection' (1999)
74 *Notre Dame Law Review* 1475.

[22] See S Bronitt and B McSherry, *Principles of Criminal Law*, 2nd edn (Sydney, Thomson
Lawbook, Co, 2005) 338.

excluded from Article 3 *General Principles of Justification* and relegated, it seems, to the category of an excuse.[23] Necessity in the Model Penal Code justifies the commission of an offence when an offender chooses the 'lesser harm or evil'.[24] There is no comparable requirement in the Commonwealth Code, which merely requires a 'reasonable response'. Justification and excuse are not distinguished. The relationship between necessity and duress is inarticulate. Nor, for that matter, are there any criteria, explicit or implicit, for differentiation among the bars to criminal responsibility listed in the General Principles: 'excuses', 'justifications', 'exceptions', 'exemptions' and 'qualifications'.[25] Excuses count equally with justifications as 'lawful authority' for conduct that would otherwise be punishable as an offence.[26] There appears to be no instance in Commonwealth law of a statutory provision that characterises a defence to criminal liability as a 'justification'.[27] There are, it is true, many instances of offences that permit reliance on 'reasonable excuse' as an answer, but no distinction between justification and excuse appears to have been intended. The 'reasonable excuse' provision, in most if not all of its applications, is merely a convenient device for qualifying an over-inclusive prohibition with a flexible exception of indeterminate application: the defendant is excused from compliance with the law if there is a 'reasonable excuse' for the conduct.

Unlike the Model Penal Code, the Commonwealth Code establishes no order of priority among the defences of necessity, self-defence and duress. Necessity in the Model Penal Code is a residual defence in the sense that it is a plea of last resort. Justification on the ground that D chose the lesser evil has no application if the legislature has provided a specific exception or defence dealing with the situation.[28] The Commonwealth Code specifies

---

[23] The Model Penal Code (1962) places s 2.09 *Duress* in Article 2. *General Principles of Liability* while the various defences involving defence of self or property are placed in Article 3 *General Principles of Justification*, together with necessity—s 3.02 *Justification Generally—Choice of Evils*. See Robinson, above n 15, ch 5.

[24] Model Penal Code, above n 3, s 3.02—*Justification Generally: Choice of Evils*.

[25] These are all classified together as matters that go to responsibility, rather than offence definition. The defendant accordingly bears the evidential burden: 13.3 *Evidential burden of proof—defence*, ss (2). Model Criminal Code, Chapter 2, *General Principles of Criminal Responsibility*, above n 1, 67, suggests that the defence of 'sudden or extraordinary emergency' and, by implication, duress and self-defence, were conceived as excuses rather than justifications.

[26] Ibid s 10.5—*Lawful authority*: 'A person is not criminally responsible for an offence if the conduct constituting the offence is justified or excused under a law.' Reference to 'law' in the Code is to be taken as a reference to a Commonwealth statute or statutory instrument: see the *Criminal Code Schedule*, Dictionary.

[27] See, in particular, the provisions of the Australian Federal Police Act 1979 (Cth), Part II, *Constitution, functions and powers of the Australian Federal Police* and the various powers conferred on members of the Defence Force in the Defence Act 1903 (Cth), Part IIIAAA *Utilisation of Defence Force to protect Commonwealth interests and States and self-governing Territories*.

[28] Model Penal Code, above n 3, s 3.02—*Justification Generally: Choice of Evils*, ss (1)(b). But see s 2.09—*Duress*, ss (4), which permits D to rely on a defence of necessity though the circumstances might also amount to a defence of duress. The exclusionary operation of s

no rules of pre-emptive application among the defences.[29] Consider, for example, the Code provisions on self-defence, which include defence of property. The defence 'does not apply' if lethal force is used.[30] That invites the inference that the defence of necessity, arising from 'sudden or extraordinary emergency' *will* apply in appropriate circumstances to exculpate a person who uses lethal force in defence of property. When self-defence ceases to have application, necessity will fill the gap.[31] That may or may not have been the intended effect of the provisions on self-defence and necessity. The text is indeterminate on the point. If that inference is granted, one might go on to speculate that the use of lethal force in defence of property might sometimes be justified, in circumstances of exceptional necessity, depending on the significance of the property, but never *excused* by duress. But that speculation would require distinctions in terms of justification and excuse, among the provisions on necessity, duress and self-defence that are indiscernible in their existing versions. The same criterion for exculpation is used in all three defences: criminal responsibility is defeated if the defendant's conduct was a 'reasonable response' to the threatened harm.[32] None of the provisions specifies a requirement of *proportionate* response though there are variously formulated requirements of reasonable necessity.[33] The Code provides no clear indication whether courts are to revive or invent common law distinctions between the defences or proceed on the assumption that the legislature intended to eliminate distinctions in pursuit of an integrated defence of necessary action.

Could the well established theoretical distinction between justification and excuse be beneficial to Australian criminal law? The philosophical and jurisprudential literature on the differences between justification and excuse is extensive and continues to expand. With a couple of notable exceptions,

---

3.02(1)(b) is problematic in its applications. See the discussion in an extended footnote in L Alexander, 'Lesser Evils: A Closer Look at The Paradigmatic Justification' (2005) 24 *Law and Philosophy* 611, 640–41.

[29] Criminal Code, s 10.5—*Lawful authority*.

[30] Ibid s 10.4—*Self defence*, ss (3) 'This section does not apply if the person uses force that involves the intentional infliction of death or really serious injury: (a) to protect property'.

[31] *Cf* S Bronitt and D Stephens, 'Legislative Note: '"Flying under the Radar"—the Use of Lethal Force Against Hijacked Aircraft: Recent Australian Developments' (2007) 7 *Oxford University Commonwealth Law Journal* 265, 274, who take the view that the prohibition on the use of lethal force in defence of property in s 10.4—*Self Defence* pre-empts recourse to necessity.

[32] There may be circumstances in which s 10.3—*Sudden or extraordinary emergency* might extend to situations in which there was no 'threatened harm'. For the purposes of comparison with self-defence and duress, however, this possibility can be ignored.

[33] In the Criminal Code s 10.2—*Duress*, there must be no 'reasonable way that the threat can be rendered ineffective'; in s 10.3—*Sudden or extraordinary emergency*, D must act in the reasonable belief that commission of the offence in question is 'the only reasonable way to deal with the emergency' and in s 10.4—*Self Defence*, D must act in the belief 'that the conduct is necessary'.

however, Australian theorists have ignored this distinction.[34] Few if any plausible applications have been discovered or proposed in Australian common law or legislation. There is a difference, as Paul Robinson remarks, between taking an interest in philosophy 'for what it can do to improve law and being interested in philosophy for its own sake'.[35] In this chapter I will follow Robinson's lead and adopt the pragmatic stance that philosophy is subordinate to legislative policy.[36] Consistent with that commitment, I will argue that distinctions should be drawn between defences that justify and defences that excuse. The conventional line of demarcation is between duress, which is said to excuse an offence, and necessity and self-defence, which are said to be justifications. I will save my few remarks on duress as an excuse till the conclusion. My main concern is what I take to be a latent difference between necessity and self-defence. The distinction between these defences that I will propose is not a simple dichotomy. Necessity, I suggest, can be characterised as a defence that justifies (or warrants) the commission of the offence in question on the ground that it was the right or appropriate thing to have done, or one of several possible right or appropriate things to have done, in the circumstances. It is conduct that can be endorsed from the standpoint of a reasonable, impartial observer who is representative of the citizenry in whose name, we may say, a prosecution will be conducted, if that is necessary.[37] Conduct can be endorsed as a right thing to have done in the circumstances though it is apparent, ex post, that the defendant did not choose the lesser evil and that the outcome was catastrophic.[38] The demanding requirement that commission of the offence was the right or

[34] Among them, E Colvin, 'Exculpatory Defences in Criminal Law' (1990) 10 *OJLS* 381 and S Yeo, above n 18. But see P Fairall and S Yeo, above n 18, 2: 'The distinction between justifications and excuses has little practical relevance to Australian criminal law'. On the absence of need for the distinction see also: S Bronitt and B McSherry, above n 22, 299–300, 338.

[35] P Robinson, 'Justification Defences in Situations of Unavoidable Uncertainty: A Reply to Professor Ferzan' (2005) 24 *Law and Philosophy* 775, 781–82. See also, K Greenawalt, 'Distinguishing Justifications from Excuses' (1986) 49 *Law and Contemporary Problems* 89, on the limited expressive possibilities of the criminal law. Greenawalt's conclusion is tinged with regret at 108: 'A scholar may well be able to develop a comprehensive distinction between legal justification and legal excuse, but he should not expect the necessarily crude materials of statutes and opinions to endorse that distinction.'

[36] Robinson, above n 35, 782: 'the theorising is important only for what it tells us about proper formulation'.

[37] I draw here on RA Duff, *Answering for Crime* (Oxford, Hart Publishing, 2007) 53: 'As against the classical positivist, the liberal republican claim is ... that we are criminally responsible not to a separate sovereign, but to ourselves ... we are responsible not to the whole world of moral agents, but to our fellow citizens'. Duff notes that the US practice, in some states, of conducting prosecutions in the name of 'The People' can be taken as an expression of that normatively impartial stance in passing judgment on allegations of criminality.

[38] There is another controversy over justification and excuse and exculpation that will not be discussed where the defendant did 'the right deed for the wrong reasons'. The battle lines were drawn long ago: see G Fletcher, 'The Right Deed for the Wrong Reasons: A Reply to Mr. Robinson' (1975) 23 *UCLA Law Review* 293.

appropriate thing to have done ex ante is not, I will argue, a requirement for a successful plea of self-defence.

The criterion that I have proposed for justifiable necessity is similar to the 'lesser of two evils' formulation in the US Model Penal Code, which makes justification depend on the question whether 'the harm or evil sought to be avoided ... is greater than that sought to be prevented by the law defining the offence'.[39] I will treat these criteria as equivalents in this chapter. There is similarity, too, in the fact that the Model Penal Code defence of necessity is available on an ex ante determination of the lesser harm or evil, since what is 'sought' by the defendant's conduct need not be achieved. There is, indeed, no reasonable alternative, since many judgements of consequential harms and benefits are necessarily provisional. It is implicit in the Model Penal Code formulation of the defence that the determination of the lesser harm or evil is made from the position of an impartial and reasonable observer. There are obvious ambiguities, of course, in the Model Penal Code requirement that the defendant choose the lesser 'harm or evil'. The metrics for quantifying and comparing 'harms' with 'harms', 'evils' with 'evils' let alone 'harms' with 'evils',[40] are uncertain, to say the least.[41] But some such balancing process is inevitable when it is necessary to determine whether commission of an offence involving an intentional harm or evil was a right thing to do in the circumstances.

Self-defence, I will argue, is different. It is a rights based defence that requires recourse to a different metric of responsibility than necessity. When responsibility for causing death or injury is in question, self-defence extends beyond justification to excuse conduct that is neither a right nor an appropriate thing to do, where D may well have chosen the greater 'harm or evil' from the standpoint of a reasonable, impartial observer. That contention conflicts with the general tendency, particularly among US theorists, to characterise self-defence as a justification. So, for example, the Model Penal Code places self-defence in Article 3 *General Principles of Justification* and subsumes self-defence under the general principle that a justification requires the defendant to have chosen the lesser harm or evil.

The potential distinctions between necessity and self-defence that the Commonwealth Code failed to draw can be illustrated with the aid of two hypotheticals each of which involves the fatal shooting of an innocent victim by state officials in order to avoid a terrorist attack. In the first, the victim is a putative aggressor killed at a military checkpoint. The second victim is a hostage, taken by a terrorist as a human shield.

---

[39] *Model Penal Code*, above n 3, s 3.02—*Justification Generally: Choice of Evils.*

[40] Presumably the Model Penal Code uses 'or' in the inclusive mode, equivalent to 'and/or'.

[41] See RF Schopp, *Justification Defences and Just Convictions* (Cambridge, Cambridge University Press, 1998) 77: reference to 'harm' suggests a utilitarian calculation, whilst 'evil' may be taken to require a deontological metric.

A. A Checkpoint Shooting: Necessity and Self-Defence Compared

The scenario is meant as a generic instance in which the officers immediately concerned,[42] and their superiors, may avoid criminal responsibility[43] for the intentional killing of an innocent.

> There is a state of emergency where many lives are at risk from terrorist attack. There is credible intelligence of a planned assassination of a visiting dignitary or his associates during a public ceremony, by terrorists who plan to use a car bomb. Authorities establish a perimeter with checkpoints at which all vehicles passing through are searched before they are allowed to proceed. Officers at the checkpoint are instructed that vehicles that do not stop are to be warned by flashing lights and warning shots in succession, at marked distances from the checkpoint. There is a warning line, a danger line and a kill line. If a vehicle fails to stop despite warning shots, and passes the kill line, the officers are instructed to use lethal force. It is known by the authorities and by the officers at the checkpoint that innocents may fail to heed the warning lights and warning shots. The conduct of driver and vehicle is taken, however, as a sign sufficient to warrant the use of lethal force. The driver, Victor, of a vehicle carrying two passengers is shot by Officer Donald at the checkpoint, after ignoring warning shots and warning lights and continuing beyond the kill line. In hindsight, it is clear that Victor and his passengers were not terrorists at all.[44]

More complex scenarios can be imagined, but there are advantages in stark simplicity. The criminal responsibility of the authorities responsible for the operation, which may be very different from that of the perpetrators,

---

[42] The Defence Act 1983 (Cth), Part IIIAAA permits the ADF to be called out for service in Australia against perceived threats of 'domestic violence'. The legislation is discussed in M Head, 'Calling Out the Troops—Disturbing Trends and Unanswered Questions' (2005) 28 *University of New South Wales Law Journal* 179; M Head, *Calling Out the Troops: The Australian Military and Civil Unrest: the Legal and Constitutional Issues* (Annandale NSW, Federation Press, 2009). The powers conferred on ADF personnel, when called out, include the protection of places, persons and critical infrastructure. Section 51T—*Use of reasonable and necessary force* permits the use of lethal force in circumstances where the member, in exercising one of the preceding powers believes, on reasonable grounds, that such force is necessary to protect life or prevent serious injury to persons or to protect 'designated critical infrastructure'. *Cf* provisions in the Australian Federal Police Act 1979 (Cth) conferring similar powers on AFP personnel who are declared 'protective service officers'. *Cf* also Bronitt and Stephens, above n 31.

[43] In this chapter, terminology follows the conventions established in Chapter 2 of the Commonwealth Criminal Code: 'offences' are constituted by their 'physical' and 'fault' 'elements'. Defences defeat criminal 'responsibility'; a person is 'responsible' for a criminal offence and convicted of that offence when its elements are proved and defences negated. So far as 'responsibility' is concerned, that terminology conflicts with an emergent convention in UK criminal law theory, where reliance on an excuse or justification implies an acceptance of 'responsibility' but a denial of 'liability' for the offence. See, eg, Duff, above n 37, ch 1.

[44] The hypothetical is loosely based on the checkpoint shooting of an Italian intelligence officer, Nicola Calipari, at a US checkpoint near Baghdad on Friday, 4 March 2005. Reported in RJ Smith and AS Tyson, 'Shootings by U.S at Iraq Checkpoints Questioned', *The Washington Post*, 7 March 2005, A01.

will not be discussed. I will be concerned in this chapter with the criminal responsibility of the officer who fired the fatal shot.

Several elements in this hypothetical will be significant in the discussion that follows. Though Donald intended to kill the driver of the car,[45] there can be no suggestion that he 'intended to kill an innocent man'. On the contrary, the death of an innocent served no purpose and it was likely to imperil the authorities' efforts to maintain security. Nor is this a case in which Donald acted on a mistaken perception that Victor was an aggressor. Though one might say, in a loose sense, that Victor was 'shot by mistake', it is quite apparent that lethal force was not used because Donald believed Victor to be a terrorist driving a car bomb. Donald, who is an experienced and level headed officer, is admirably clear in his account of what happened. He was not mistaken in that sense at all: he was well aware that Victor might be an unwitting innocent. Victor was shot because he *might have been* a terrorist. The conduct of his vehicle was taken as a sign, in accordance with Donald's instructions, that the occupants might be involved in a terrorist operation. In this quite precise sense, the checkpoint officers were instructed to take pre-emptive action against possible threats. The officers had no fear for their own safety; Donald killed Victor in order to protect others. Conduct that was not in itself threatening was to be taken as the sign or symptom of a threat.[46]

It is arguable that shooting Victor was justifiable even though he was innocent of any involvement in terrorism for Donald's action was the right thing to do, ex ante. We may wish to distinguish, however, between lethal force that is justified and lethal force that is warranted[47] where both are encompassed in the defence of necessity. In the checkpoint shooting the officer was *warranted* in using lethal force because he read the signs aright and followed instructions that he had every reason to believe were reasonable in the circumstances. Had the car contained a bomb or other indubitable evidence that the occupants were bent on terrorism, his use of lethal force

---

[45] This characterisation of the officer's intention might encounter dissent from some, at least of those who rely on the principle of double effect to justify the use of lethal force in self-defence. See, eg, the discussion in S Uniacke, *Permissible Killing* (Cambridge, Cambridge University Press, 1994) ch 4, and her conclusions on intention at 128–30; 184. See also, KK Ferzan, 'Beyond Intention' (2008) 29 *Cardozo Law Review* 1147, 1183.

[46] Compare the account of the shooting of Daniel McCann, Sean Savage and Mairead Farrell in *McCann and Others v United Kingdom* Series A no 324 (1995) 21 ECHR 97, where the Court emphasised the expertise of the officers involved in reading the signs of intended terrorist action. Critical distance is necessary when dealing with claims to expert knowledge of the signs that justify pre-emptive use of force. See G Fletcher, *With Justice for Some* (New York, Addison-Wesley, 1995) 47, 'One man's twitch, it seems, is another man's threat'. Discussed at 45–48, 230–32.

[47] Duff, above n 37, 275–76. See also, Greenawalt, above n 35, 91: 'When something is fully justified, it is warranted. A justified belief is a belief based on good grounds; a justified action is morally appropriate action. When something is fully excused, it is not warranted, but the person involved is not blameworthy.'

would have been justified. The difference between a warranted and justified killing, in these circumstances, is a matter only of the difference between ex ante expectations and ex post reality.[48] That does not mean that the difference is insignificant. If the victim turns out to be an innocent, the shooting is a matter for profound regret. Apology, reparations and reconsideration of checkpoint procedures are appropriate. There is, however, no basis for others to blame the officer who fired the fatal shot. He may require counselling, reassurance against remorse and, perhaps, a move or promotion to a less stressful position.

Since the difference between warrant and justification depends on outcome, there will be cases where the question whether lethal force was justified rather than warranted may never be resolved, for the anticipated outcome may never be known; we may be no wiser ex post than were the officers who had to make a judgement ex ante. Ignorance on that score may be more likely when force is pre-emptive and based on the signs or symptoms of a threat, rather than the threat itself.

The checkpoint scenario is radically simplified, offering no alternatives if action is to be taken to avert the peril.[49] In more complex situations, when lethal force is warranted, there may be more room for strategic choice. Regardless of outcome, resort to lethal force will be warranted if that was a reasonable choice among acceptable alternatives. If, that is to say, the officer did one of the right things to do in the circumstances. The use of lethal force, which would have been praiseworthy and a ground for commendation, if the victim had indeed been a terrorist, is merely acceptable, as an appropriate response that had a dreadful outcome. I will refer to judgements of this nature, when conduct is warranted or justified ex ante, as judgements made from the 'impartial stance'.[50] The agent acts in a representative role, in the sense that the agent has done what was expected of him or her by the community as a right thing to do in the circumstances. That is true, whether the agent acts as an officer fulfilling a function assigned by the state or acts as a private citizen. There are very significant differences, of course, between the roles of officers and citizens qua citizens—officers are permitted a far more extended range of pre-emptive action against threatened harm than private citizens[51] and they are equipped with far more deadly weapons than

---

[48] The distinction that one might draw between circumstances that were unknown but knowable ex ante and contingencies that were both unknown and unknowable ex ante appears to be without moral significance. See Greenawalt, above n 35, 94.

[49] Compare the criticism of the course of action in *McCann and Others v United Kingdom* Series A no 324 (1995) 21 ECHR 97.

[50] References to the adoption of an 'impartial stance' or the standard of the 'impartial observer' are derived from the recurring figure of the 'impartial spectator' in A Smith, *The Theory of Moral Sentiments*, DD Raphael and AL Macfie (eds), 6th edn (Oxford, Oxford University Press, 1976).

[51] See discussion in W Kaufman, 'Self-Defense, Imminence, and the Battered Woman' (2007) 10 *New Criminal Law Review* 342. There is a sense in which all self-defensive

private citizens can be expected to command.[52] Since my central concern are the general provisions of the Code, which apply to officials and private citizens alike, I will save my brief assessment on this important distinction for my concluding remarks.

It will be apparent from the preceding account that warrant and justification are based on an evaluative standard of reasonable apprehension of the circumstances that call for action and a reasonable, competent and normatively acceptable response to those circumstances. Donald, my protagonist, has an incompetent, negative counterpart in John Gardner's exploration of excuses, where he considers a similar scenario. Gardner's checkpoint killer is a panicky or hot headed raw recruit, who falls short of any reasonable or acceptable standard for the performance of his duty.[53] He would be denied a defence of necessity under the Commonwealth Code and convicted of murder. Donald's actions on the other hand, when considered from the impartial stance, were appropriate in the circumstances. That would not be enough, in Gardner's eyes, to *justify* his act of shooting Victor. He would take the view that Donald's use of lethal force is no more than excusable simply because, ex post, it is apparent that Victor's death was completely unnecessary.[54] A similarly restrictive view of justification is taken, for divergent reasons, by George Fletcher,[55] Paul Robinson,[56] Heidi Hurd,[57] and Larry Alexander.[58] Others, such as Kent Greenawalt,[59] Peter Westen, and James Mangiafico[60] for example, would argue that Donald was justified in his use of lethal force. In this chapter I have taken a middle path[61] by distinguishing between a justified and warranted shooting. Both count, however, as instances of necessity in the Commonwealth Code and Model Penal Code.

Necessity exculpates Donald, but what is to be done with Gardner's incompetent raw recruit whose act of killing an innocent was neither warranted nor justified? Suppose he misunderstood his instructions, fired the

---

responses are pre-emptive, since the future cannot be known with certainty. KK Ferzan, 'Justifying Self Defence' (2005) 24 *Law and Philosophy* 612 and Robinson, above n 35, 775. See also, Alexander, above n 21, 1476–79.

[52] P Kennison and A Loumansky, 'Shoot to Kill—understanding the police use of force in combating suicide terrorism' (2007) 47 *Crime Law and Social Change* 151.

[53] J Gardner, *Offences and Defences* (Oxford, Oxford University Press, 2007) 124–25. Gardner's scenario is 'loosely based' on *R v Clegg* [1995] 1 AC 482.

[54] Gardner, above n 53, 258–61.

[55] G Fletcher, *Rethinking Criminal Law* (Oxford, Oxford University Press, 2000) 762–68.

[56] Robinson, above n 15, 95–96; Robinson, above n 35, 775.

[57] H Hurd, 'Justification and Excuse, Wrongdoing and Culpability' (1999) 74 *Notre Dame Law Review* 1551.

[58] Alexander, above n 21, 1483–86.

[59] Greenawalt, above n 35, 102–03.

[60] Westen and Mangiafico, above n 13, 865–68, 914, 920–21.

[61] *Cf* Uniacke, above n 45, 16–17, distinguishing between 'agent perspectival' and 'objective' justifications.

fatal shot in the mistaken belief that he was complying with his instructions, and killed an innocent who had not in reality passed beyond the warning shot zone. This was a factual mistake about the circumstances that would warrant a fatal shot. The mistake, let us say, was utterly unreasonable. The orders were quite clear to everyone else. Moral distinctions between justification and excuse are of little help here for moral blameworthiness has no structures corresponding to the law's articulate system of distinct offences graded by degrees of wrongfulness. If we are to preserve the distinction in culpability between murder and manslaughter, a conviction for murder may seem to be unnecessarily severe as a sanction for a sincere but incompetent offender who got the facts wrong.

That reflection on degrees of wrongfulness suggests the need for a partial defence of necessity that would avoid what is, arguably, an inappropriate verdict of murder. There is another answer, however, to the problem of the incompetent checkpoint shooter. Nothing in the Commonwealth Code precludes the possibility of a complete acquittal of an utterly incompetent albeit sincerely mistaken officer on the ground not of necessity but of 'self-defence'. Fear for his own safety is not a requirement. Self-defence extends to the protection of others and self-defence, unlike necessity, can be based on a completely unreasonable perception of a threatened harm. Nor is there any order of priority among the Code defences that might exclude reliance on self-defence. This oscillation between the possibilities of outright exculpation and conviction for murder, depending on the characterisation of the case as one of necessity or self-defence, undercuts any requirement that the officer's resort to lethal force be justified or warranted.

There are several ways in which that discrepancy in terms of outcome could be resolved. Perhaps self-defence should be confined, like necessity, to circumstances in which the defendant's perception of a threatened harm was reasonable. That would be consistent at least with the merger thesis. If conviction for murder is taken to be too severe a sanction when self-defence is based on an unreasonable apprehension of danger, a partial defence would permit a sentence tailored to the degree of the defendant's responsibility. That would be consistent with the suggestion made earlier, that the defence of necessity might be similarly divided between a complete and partial version of the defence. But consideration of the possible introduction of partial defences can be deferred for the moment. There is a more fundamental objection to the existing formulation of necessity and self-defence and their reliance on the same requirement of a 'reasonable response' as a measure of responsibility.

The paradigm case of self-defence involves a threat to the defendant by an aggressor that cannot be averted unless force is used. At common law the question that arises in such a case is whether the defendant's response was 'reasonably proportionate' to the threatened harm. The Code requirement of a 'reasonable response' to the threatened harm was meant to embody that requirement.[62] In the checkpoint shooting, where Donald was not threatened, I have suggested that the defence of necessity is only open if shooting Victor was warranted ex ante as the right thing to do, as the lesser harm or evil. That constraint is not present when fatal force is used in self-defence. Reasonable proportionality and choice of the lesser harm or evil are different metrics of criminal responsibility. There is a distinction between the impartial stance required in necessity where the actor must choose the lesser harm or evil and what I will call the 'agential stance'[63] of a defendant who claims to have used reasonably proportionate force in self-defence. Of course there will be occasions when self-defence is warranted or justified as the right thing to do or the lesser harm or evil. If V is about to kill D it is obviously justifiable for D to respond by cutting off V's arm, if that is the only way for D to repel the attack and avoid being killed. But self-defence extends beyond warrant or justification to excuse conduct that was not a right thing to do in the circumstances, when considered from the impartial stance. I will refer to this possible application of the self-defence as an 'excuse'. It might equally well be called 'permission'. In responding to a threat of harm the defendant is excused from compliance with the law against the use of force though the self-defensive response was neither the right thing to do nor the lesser harm or evil.

There is, I suggest, a fundamental tension between a plea of self-defence, which recognises the right of each person to protect their own physical integrity and personal autonomy and the consequentialist metric of necessity. That tension is expressed in the difference between proportionality determined from the agential stance and choice of the lesser harm or evil determined from the stance of the impartial observer. I can delineate the area of self-defence that lies beyond warrant or justification by drawing on a striking rhetorical figure in an essay by Kremnitzer and Ghanayim on proportionality in self-defence.[64] Their argument for a proportionality limit—diametrically opposed to the suggestion that I have made—is based on their characterisation of self-defence as both a defence of the autonomy of the person who responds to the attack and a defence of the exercise of a delegated power. They characterise the person who acts in self-defence as a 'substitute policeman', whose right to use force to repel an attack on their autonomy is derived from the power and authority of the state to protect the legal order. They argue that the right to use force in self-defence is correspondingly limited: 'it would not be proper for the scope of an

---

[62] Model Criminal Code, ch 2, above n 1, 69: a defensive response must be 'objectively proportionate' to the threat.

[63] *Cf* Uniacke, above n 45, 15–23, on 'agent perspectival' justification.

[64] M Kremnitzer and K Ghanayim, 'Proportionality and the Aggressor's Culpability in Self Defence' (2004) 39 *Tulsa Law Review* 875.

individual's right of self defence to exceed that of the state.'[65] If Kremnitzer and Ghanayim are right about this, there is indeed no impediment to the merger of self-defence and necessity; each use of lethal force in self-defence would have to be warranted ex ante from the standpoint of the impartial observer. That may, indeed, have been the assumption of the authors of the Model Penal Code when self-defence was characterised as a justification.

To speak of a *right* of self-defence is to make an implicit claim that the right may be exercised in circumstances where the defendant does not act as a substitute police officer and does not choose what would count as the lesser harm or evil from the impartial stance. Considered in this way, self-defence is an original or natural right in potential conflict with the state's interest in maintaining a legal order or preservation of the common good.[66] Permission to resort to reasonably proportionate force in marginal cases is inherently challenging in its applications. One might hope that everyone now accepts that a wife is not criminally responsible if she kills her abusive husband if that is the only practicable way of avoiding his threat of forcible rape. That is a quite recent change in mores: until late in the twentieth century common law courts refused to recognise that a wife could be the victim of rape by her husband. It is less certain whether legal theorists, courts or jurors would accept that a wife is not criminally responsible if she kills an abusive husband if that is the only practicable way of avoiding his threat to discipline her by locking her in a cramped cupboard overnight.[67] Citizens vary in their appreciation of how far they are entitled to go in defence of their own rights and interests. The value that I place on my autonomy and physical integrity, relative to that of a perceived aggressor, is very likely to exceed its value from the standpoint of an impartial observer who is concerned with the minimisation of consequential harms. The same impartial observer is likely to require me to accept a more serious risk of loss of autonomy and a more serious physical injury than I would accept, before conceding that it would be right for me—that I would be justified—in a

---

[65] Ibid 899.

[66] Some theorists express the conflict as a clash of sovereignties. See R Schopp, drawing on Joel Feinberg, who argues that the right of self defence, in a liberal society, is an expression of 'personal sovereignty': Schopp, above n 41, 68–71, 75; J Feinberg, *Harm to Self* (Oxford, Oxford University Press, 1990) 57–62. Self-defence lies at the disputed border between the sovereignty of the individual and the sovereignty of the legal order of which the individual is a member; *cf* Kremnitzer and Ghanayim, above n 64, 87–88, for whom there can be no clash of sovereignties.

[67] Theorists vary on the margins of tolerance for differential evaluations of threatened harm. For detailed consideration, see G Fletcher's monograph on the trial of B Goetz for shooting four putative assailants, *A Crime of Self Defence* (New York, Free Press, 1988). In ch 2 at 37, Fletcher remarks: 'The more Troy Canty, Barry Allen, James Ramseur, and Darrell Cabey come into focus as human beings worthy of our compassion, the more we might expect Goetz to have taken some risks that he could exit the confrontation on the train without inflicting the human costs that he did.' Compare KK Ferzan, above n 51, 744, 'Once the triggering conditions are satisfied, any likelihood of harm should be sufficient for self defence'.

resort to lethal force. In Fletcher's illustrative formulation of an 'autonomy based theory of self defence', a person faced with an unlawful attack 'is entitled to use whatever force is necessary to repel the attack' for Right should never yield to Wrong.[68] But no legal system sets so high a valuation on the right to protect personal autonomy. There is certainly a point beyond which an innocent victim's resort to lethal force cannot be excused even if there is no other way of avoiding violation or injury. Glanville Williams was both blunt and correct in expressing his view that, 'there are some insults and hurts that one must suffer rather than use extreme force.'[69] That is not to say, however, that the victim of an unlawful attack must adopt the impartial stance when measuring her response to an unlawful attack.[70]

The clearest case of a limiting rule is found in legislation, like the Commonwealth Code, which bars resort to lethal force in defence of property.[71] When defence of the person is in issue, however, the limits are less certain. The Code provides no guidance beyond the requirement of a 'reasonable response'. The point at which Australian common law requires an individual who is under attack to retreat, appease, or submit to violation of their autonomy or physical integrity, rather than resort to lethal force, is the subject of divergent judicial and textual opinion. It may be that the right is as extensive as the High Court said it was in 1958, when it declared that resort to lethal force is permissible when that is the only way to avoid a threat to 'life or safety ... from injury, violation, indecent or insulting usage'.[72] That descending scale of wrongfulness, from threats to life to threats of indecent or insulting usage, may be taken to suggest that Australian common law places a particularly high value on personal

---

[68] See G Fletcher and L Chiesa, 'Self-Defense and the Psychotic Aggressor' in P Robinson, KK Ferzan, S Garvey (eds), *Criminal Law Conversations* (Oxford, Oxford University Press, 2009) 365, 369.

[69] G Williams, *Textbook of Criminal Law*, 2nd edn (London, Stevens, 1983) 504; *cf* G Fletcher, *The Grammar of Criminal Law*, vol I (Oxford, Oxford University Press, 2007) 140–41, 252–53, on the conflict between a 'deontological theory of self-defence' and the limit imposed by a requirement of proportionality or by a principle that excessive self defence is an 'abuse of rights'.

[70] That is not to say that individuals who are threatened with attack should not calculate, if they have sufficient time and presence of mind to do so, the likely consequences of killing their assailant.

[71] Criminal Code, s 10.4—*Self Defence*, ss (3). Common law limits on the use of force to defend property are less clearly defined. Fairall and Yeo, above n 18, 169–70: '[I]t is surprisingly uncertain as to how far the common law privileges the forcible defence of property or reality. There is no support for an unbridled right of property defence, although some support for the permission to use reasonable force.' See also: *R v McKay* [1957] VR 560. Discussed in N Morris, 'The Slain Chicken Thief' (1958) 2 *Sydney Law Review* 414; *R v Martin (Anthony)* [2002] 1 CAR 27.

[72] *R v Howe* (1958) 100 CLR 448, 460. Discussed in I Leader-Elliott, 'Battered But Not Beaten: Women Who Kill in Self Defence' (1993) 15 *Sydney Law Review* 403, 442. More recent case law has failed to resolve uncertainty on the issue. See Fairall and Yeo, above n 18, 178, who content themselves with the statement: 'Self defence may be raised in respect of threats falling short of an apprehension of death or grievous bodily harm'.

autonomy—a suggestion not, perhaps, borne out by subsequent common law authorities.[73] The unresolved tension is apparent if one compares the liberality of that common law criterion with recent conflicting criteria in state legislation on the question. In Victoria, statute law permits resort to lethal force only if there is a threat of death or really serious injury.[74] In South Australia, on the other hand, the legislature has gone further than most in giving individuals explicit permission to resort to *dis*proportionate force when attacked in their own home.[75] That extended form of the defence will certainly include some cases where an official would not be warranted in using deadly force and an impartial observer would consider that the defendant's action was neither a lesser harm or evil nor the right thing to do in the circumstances.

Consideration of the differences between necessity and self-defence so far suggest that defence of others and defence of self should be distinguished. When Officer Donald shoots Victor, it would be inappropriate to determine his criminal responsibility by reference to the requirement of reasonable proportionality that governs self-defence. There is no question here of an exercise of a personal right. Responsibility should be measured by the more demanding metric of necessity where exculpation requires a choice of the lesser harm or evil determined from the impartial stance. When a person exercises a right of self-defence against an aggressor, however, that constraint should have no application. The difference between the two measures is probably unquantifiable though it would be possible, in theory, to specify the limits beyond which a defendant must suffer a threatened harm, rather than resort to lethal force in self-defence.[76] In practice, the question whether D's response was unreasonably disproportionate can be determined by a jury on the merits of the particular situation.

If it is accepted that the measures of responsibility are different in necessity and self-defence, it is necessary to specify a borderline between the defences. Necessity will justify or warrant intentionally killing a person in defence of others, defence of self or defence of property, if the victim was

[73] See the discussion in Yeo, above n 18, 107–11, on the drift from justification to excuse in the Australian common law on self defence and dilution of the requirement of proportionality.
[74] Crimes Act 1958 (Vic), as amended by the Crimes (Homicide) Act 2005 (Vic) s 9AC *Murder*—'*self defence*'. The effect of the prohibition is moderated by s 9AD—*Defensive homicide*, which permits conviction of a lesser homicide.
[75] Criminal Law Consolidation Act 1935 (SA), s 15C—*Requirement of reasonable proportionality not to apply in case of an innocent defence against a home invasion.*
[76] *Cf* the procedure envisaged by S Scheffler, *The Rejection of Consequentialism: A Philosophical Investigation of the Considerations Underlying Rival Moral Conceptions* (Oxford, Clarendon Press, 1982) 20: '[A] plausible agent-centred prerogative would allow each agent to assign a certain proportionately greater weight to his own interests than to the interests of other people. It would then allow the agent to promote the non-optimal outcome of his own choosing, provided only that the degree of its inferiority to each of the superior outcomes he could instead promote in no case exceeded, by more than the specified proportion, the degree of sacrifice necessary for him to promote the superior outcome.'

killed in circumstances where a reasonable and impartial observer would conclude that this was the lesser harm.[77] I have advanced the view that self-defence is more limited in its application. It will not excuse a person who kills intentionally to defend property and it has no application to altruistic interventions to protect strangers from harm. Common law accepted that self-defence did extend to cases where the defendant used force to protect a close family member and some such provision for that naturally extended sense of self would be necessary. Any dividing line between defence of the extended self and altruistic intervention on behalf of another will be arbitrary in marginal applications. That is no objection to a distinction if the purpose it serves is sufficiently important.

The scope of necessity, with its more demanding metric of responsibility and the relationship between necessity and self-defence can be tested with another hypothetical, in which the 'utilitarianism of extremity' would justify or warrant an official shooting an innocent hostage, who constitutes no threat to the official or anyone else.

B. Justification and Warrant: Shooting the Innocent Shield

In the checkpoint killing, the occupants of the car were potential terrorists. The fatal shot was warranted because the occupants represented a credible threat to others. It was a case where the officer who shot the innocent driver avoided criminal responsibility because the driver's conduct was taken to be an adequate indication of threatened aggression that warranted lethal force. Suppose the time frame of the original terrorism scenario is extended, so that this time the person shot is neither an aggressor nor a suspected aggressor, but a person who is known by the officer to be an innocent bystander who represents no threat at all.[78]

> There was credible intelligence that the terrorists had passed the checkpoint undetected and a car bomb was parked somewhere in the city centre. The public ceremony where the putative assassination was to take place was still some days away. Three suspects, two men and a woman, Vera, had been indentified. They had the relaxed demeanour of tourists and they strolled the colonnades and plazas of the city, mingling with shoppers and holidaymakers. Undercover officers, David and Albert kept them under surveillance. There was credible intelligence that any of the three suspects could be carrying a remote control device that could be used to detonate a car bomb. Any of the three might have been armed. It was

---

[77] It is possible in such a case that D kills in circumstances where there is justification or warrant for doing so if only D had been aware of it and acted for that reason. The problems arising where D does 'the right deed for the wrong reason' can be ignored for present purposes.

[78] Scenario adapted from *McCann and Others v United Kingdom* Series A no 324 (1995) 21 ECHR 97.

anticipated that the putative car bomb would be detonated ahead of time, to cause as many civilian deaths as possible, if the terrorists were detected during the days preceding the public ceremony. Vera separated from the two men and David followed her. Then, by complete coincidence a police car, with its siren wailing, entered the plaza. Vera turned and stared at David and apparently realised that he had been following her. David drew his handgun. Vera seized an elderly woman called Valerie and, using her as a shield, backed into a shop doorway. David says that she had one arm under Valerie's chin and seemed to be fumbling with her shoulder bag with her other hand. He fired three shots each of which inflicted fatal wounds on Valerie and, passing through her body, killed Vera as well.

Vera was not armed and she carried no remote control device. It now appears that there was no car bomb in the city centre. Though it was confirmed that the three suspects were terrorists, their plot was less advanced than the authorities believed to be the case. A car carrying explosives was intercepted at the checkpoint, on the day following the shooting and the threatened attack never eventuated.

The circumstances in which Valerie was shot were such that a reasonable and impartial observer would conclude that the threat was real and David's action in shooting her in order to kill Vera was the only way in which the putative threat of detonation of a car bomb could be averted.

Scenarios involving 'innocent shields of threats'[79] are much discussed in the literature. Larry Alexander argues that the innocent shield is no less a threat than others in the cast of 'innocent aggressors' who figure in these discussions—the child who points a cocked and loaded gun at D; the psychotic killer who joins D in the elevator and the human missile shot from a cannon or falling from a cliff, whose trajectory will prove fatal to D unless interrupted with a blast from D's disintegrating ray gun.[80] For Alexander this is, accordingly, a case to be brought within an extended excuse of self-defence, akin to duress. It is apparent on reflection, however, that Alexander's position is insupportable. It is quite true that there are cases of blameless aggression when self-defence will justify or excuse the use of lethal force to avert a threatened harm by the blameless aggressor, but

---

[79] R Nozick, *Anarchy, State and Utopia* (Oxford, Basil Blackwell, 1974) 35 is usually cited as the original source for subsequent discussion of shooting the innocent human shield.

[80] Alexander, above n 21, 1482–83: 'I have criticised the attempts to distinguish between innocent aggressors ... and innocent shields and bystanders on the other. All are by hypothesis non culpable. All endanger others, either by being the instruments of harm or by protecting those instruments. I cannot find any convincing explanation for why the differences among them should be morally or legally material.' On the case of the human projectile, see JJ Thomson, *The Realm of Rights* (Harvard, Harvard University Press, 1990) 369–70. Even if one accepts that the constraint against taking innocent life is not absolute, there is no reason to accept the view that there are not morally significant degrees of innocence. There is a continuum in which the moral horror of taking innocent life requires ever more catastrophic alternative outcomes to justify doing so. As, eg: (a) blameless aggressor; (b) terrorist's hostage; (c) terrorist's human shield; (c) innocent bystander; (d) terrorist's child held as hostage by a state official.

these do not extend to include shooting Valerie, the innocent shield. The reason for this is of some significance. Valerie is not a *physical* impediment to shooting the terrorist Vera.[81] David's modern, high powered handgun is quite adequate to kill both victims. The impediment to killing Vera lies solely in the fact that she is shielded by Valerie's right, as an innocent bystander who became a hostage, not to be sacrificed for the sake of others, elsewhere in the city, who would be killed if a car bomb was detonated.[82] There is a point, however, where Valerie's rights will be overridden and she *will*, as an innocent shield, be sacrificed—if the stakes are sufficiently high. But that is not because Valerie is a threat. The fact that she has a right to life cannot be reconfigured as a form of innocent aggression against anyone. Nor is it possible to blink the fact that the use of lethal force on Valerie was intentional.[83] In exceptional circumstances, however, the principle of necessity will sometimes permit the sacrifice of innocent bystanders. This is what Michael Walzer would call the 'utilitarianism of extremity' in which necessity may justify action that overrides Valerie's right to life.[84] There is a point at which consequences do count, beyond which even the life of an innocent bystander will be sacrificed to avert an appalling outcome.[85] There is implicit acknowledgement of that possibility in the Model Penal Code formulation of the defence of necessity, which envisages the possibility that there will be occasions when a choice must be made between evil actions and harmful outcomes.[86] The Commonwealth Criminal Code must also envisage such a possibility, since the defence of necessity, is supplementary to the extended plea of self-defence in section 10.4. To repeat the point made earlier, the Code departs from common law and accepts that such a case can be brought within the scope of trial by jury, rather than resolved by an exercise of executive discretion.

[81] *Cf* Larry Alexander's example, ibid, 'suppose someone is firing at me from a crowded section of a stadium. I can take him out with a hand grenade, but only by killing several bystanders as well.'

[82] In similar fashion the merely suspected terrorist, who must be presumed innocent, is her own hostage—clothed in the presumed innocence of a law abiding citizen—until the critical point when suspicion hardens into reasonable grounds for intervention.

[83] See, eg, Ferzan, above n 45, 1182 on the 'inseparable effects' of intended actions: when one has full knowledge of the facts, one would have to be irrational to think that one could separate one action from the other'—as objects of D's intentions.

[84] M Walzer, *Just and Unjust Wars*, 3rd edn (New York, Basic Books, 1977) 231. In his discussion of the morality of war and lethal action against 'innocent shields' at 173–74, Walzer suggests a possible distinction between the case where an enemy seizes innocents for use as a shield and the case where the enemy takes advantage of the shield provided by innocents going about the everyday business of their lives. In the first case, responsibility for the death is more readily deflected to the enemy.

[85] See, eg, T Nagel, *Mortal Questions* (Cambridge, Cambridge University Press, 1979) ch 5, 53.

[86] See ibid 62, on the idea of a 'deontological threshold' beyond which the prospect of catastrophic harm outweighs the evil involved in the violation of V's rights.

The difference between the metrics of reasonable proportionality and choice of the lesser harm or evil can be brought into focus if one converts the all too credible scenario that I have sketched to the more familiar form of thought experiment in which Valerie, the innocent shield, unexpectedly produces a revolver and shoots David before he can shoot her. Suppose, for the sake of the hypothetical, that it is impossible for Valerie to use her revolver against Vera, her captor. There is a variety of suggested philosophical resolutions of the dilemma involved in such a conflict between a justification and a right.[87] I doubt, however, that it would make any sense for the criminal law to attempt any *philosophical* resolution to this dilemma. It seems better to begin with a consideration of possible solutions and resolutions that might be found within the resources of the criminal law. The starting point of such an enquiry is worth a moment's reflection. The Criminal Code overturned *R v Dudley & Stephens*[88] by permitting necessity to justify or excuse murder. As a consequence David is no longer guilty of murder—the common law result—if shooting Valerie is justified or warranted on the ground of necessity. In the conventional vocabulary established by the Criminal Code, it follows that David acts *lawfully* if he shoots Valerie and his act of doing so is 'justified or excused'.[89] The same conventional vocabulary has the consequence that Valerie acts *unlawfully* if she impedes David's attempt to kill her. And if she is aware of the circumstances that induce David to try to kill her and kills him in order to save her own life, she must be convicted of murder for she has, in that case, no right of self-defence under the Code.[90] If that is accepted, it is a startling consequence of the reversal of *R v Dudley & Stephenson* in the Criminal Code.

It was a salutary reform to bring the question whether *David's* conduct was justifiable or warranted within the purview of the criminal trial if he

---

[87] On the problem of ranking different kinds of justification in order of priority, see Alexander, above n 21, 1499–505; V Bergelson, 'Rights, Wrongs and Comparative Justifications' (2007) 28 *Cardozo Law Review* 2481, 2501–03; Ferzan, above n 51, 747–49.

[88] (1884) 14 QBD 273. See Fairall and Yeo, above n 18, 109–10; Bronitt and McSherry, above n 22, 329–32. In each of these texts there are cautiously guarded suggestions that the common law might envisage such a defence. Both texts suggest that cases of separating conjoined twins, when one is certain to die, may have overturned *R v Dudley & Stephens*. See *Re A (children) (conjoined twins: surgical separation)* [2001] 2 WLR 480. The cases are, however, readily distinguishable: the twins' case can be rationalised, and was rationalised, as an instance of innocent aggression. That rationalisation was not available in *R v Dudley & Stephens*.

[89] Criminal Code, s 10.5—*Lawful Authority*. The implications of this careless reference to 'justification or excuse', when D uses force to repel the use of force by an aggressor who is *excused* rather than justified, raises problems that will have to be faced sometime, but not now. Nor is it necessary, for present purposes, to pursue the point that David was mistaken about the threat when he killed Valerie and Vera. The fact that he was mistaken about the car bomb threat might be taken to affect Valerie's criminal responsibility, even if she shared his belief that Vera was about to detonate a car bomb elsewhere in the city. For one among many discussions of the issues involved, see Robinson, above n 15, 104–24.

[90] Criminal Code, s10.4—*Self defence*, ss (4).

kills Valerie in order to save the lives of some sufficiently large number of others imperilled by Vera. It is far from clear, however that it should follow that *Valerie*, who would have been entitled to defend herself at common law, must now be convicted of murder. The criminal law is a practical discipline, not a system of logic. One might conclude that there is simply no need for consistency when the utilitarianism of extremity conflicts with Valerie's right of self-defence. This is a human tragedy in which innocence is pitted against innocence. Acquitting Valerie of murder on the ground that she was defending herself need not entail the conclusion that David would have been without justification or warrant for killing her had he acted first.[91] I will assume, however, for the purposes of the ensuing discussion that Valerie cannot rely on self-defence if she knew that David was acting lawfully.

In reality, proof that Valerie was aware of the reasons for David's attempt to kill her would be exceedingly difficult. Valerie's reliance on self-defence will fail only if the prosecution can prove that she was aware of all the circumstances that warranted David's attempt to kill her. It is almost certainly a case of mutual mistake about the facts. Let us suppose, however, that the prosecution can prove that Valerie and David were not mutually mistaken: it is a case in which Valerie shot David because she chose to place her own survival above the loss of many lives if Vera was permitted to detonate the putative bomb.

The discussion so far has oscillated between the possibilities that David or Valerie, or both of them, might be convicted of murder or gain a complete acquittal of murder. Those are not the only outcomes that might be found in a criminal code that is designed to grade offences and penalties by the degree of wrongdoing involved. The possibility that the Code might provide a partial defence that would reduce murder to manslaughter, mentioned earlier in the hypothetical case of the incompetent checkpoint officer, awaits consideration.

That possibility cannot benefit Valerie however, for she was not mistaken about the facts. If she was in error at all, it was a moral and legal error to choose to save her own life at the putative cost of many lives. It is possible, however, that she might argue the case for a complete acquittal, not on the ground of self-defence, but on the ground of duress. That possibility arises as a consequence of the near merger of the defences in the Criminal Code and the very substantial overlap in their applications.[92] She was faced with

---

[91] On the tragic dimension of the clash between 'agent-neutral' and 'agent-relative' ethical principles, see T Nagel, *The View from Nowhere* (Oxford, Oxford University Press, 1986) 182–88.

[92] Criminal Code, s 10.2—*Duress*. The conduct of a terrorist who seizes V as a human shield against lawful force by D can be said to be a *threat*—albeit indirect—to V. The Criminal Code defence of duress does not require a demand coupled with the necessary threat.

a threat of death and, in the terminology of the Code, the possibility that shooting David could count as a 'reasonable response' should be considered by a jury. The paradigm case of duress, in which it has independent application, is one in which the defendant has no plea of self-defence and acts without warrant or justification, choosing the greater rather than the lesser harm or evil. If Valerie's act of shooting David is not within the letter of Code formulation of duress, it is within its spirit. If one isolates the distinctive effect of the defence of duress in this way, however, it must be open to question whether duress should ever amount to more than a partial defence to murder.

Before dealing with that possibility, it is necessary to discuss partial defences that are based on unreasonable errors about the facts of the case. In the innocent hostage hypothetical, David and his superiors were mistaken about the threat and David was, in consequence, mistaken about the need to shoot Valerie. In the hypothetical, the mistake was reasonable in the circumstances. Suppose, however, that the mistake by David or his superiors[93] was a consequence of a completely unreasonable assessment of the facts. On that assumption it is necessary to consider whether a conviction for murder is an appropriate sanction for their conduct.

II. FAULT ELEMENTS: OFFENCES, DEFENCES AND PARTIAL DEFENCES

One of the purposes of the general part of a criminal code is to establish the conventions that will guide legislatures when framing offences and courts when they must interpret legislative intentions. The Commonwealth Code adopts a useful convention that requires a sharp distinction between the definition of the elements of an offence and its potential defences, when legislation is formulated. Useful though it is, that conventional distinction between the elements that constitute the offence and its potential defences has obscured understanding of the structure of criminal responsibility and obscured, in particular, recognition of the possibility that defences might be partial rather than complete. A mere drafting convention has been given unwarranted normative significance. A similar tendency is apparent in the common law where, however, the distinction between offence and defence is far more flexible, when flexibility is necessary.[94] As a consequence, the Code's articulate grading of the offences against the person by reference to the

---

[93] See Criminal Code, s 11.3—*Innocent agency*: There is no theoretical impediment to the conviction of David's superiors of a criminal homicide committed via an innocent agent.

[94] Characteristic common law oscillation on the offence/defence distinction is apparent in the relationship between *DPP v Morgan* [1976] AC 182 and *Beckford v R* [1988] 1 AC 130, when the principle relating to mistake as to an element of the offence of rape was imported into the law of self-defence. See AP Simester, 'Mistakes in Defence' (1992) 12 *OJLS* 295.

fault of the offender is not paralleled by equivalent nicety in discriminating between varieties of fault when their defences are in issue.

The absence of gradation for fault in relation to the defences was apparent in the earlier discussion of checkpoint shootings by Donald and his incompetent counterpart. A defendant who kills intentionally has a defence of necessity if the offence was committed pursuant to a reasonable belief in circumstances of necessity. If the belief was not reasonable, the Code would have it that the defendant must be convicted of murder. There is no apparent reason why an unreasonable mistake about facts that would justify the defendant's conduct should provide the basis for a murder conviction. When self-defence is in issue, the anomaly is reversed: an unreasonable belief is sufficient for a complete acquittal. There is no apparent reason for either anomaly beyond the assumption, embodied in the definitional structure of the Code, that fault elements have no application to defences.

The US Model Penal Code does not draw so stark a distinction between the consequences of reasonable and unreasonable mistakes about threats. Necessity, self-defence and other defences in Article 3 *General Principles of Justification* are all based on the defendant's belief, whether reasonable or unreasonable, that force was necessary to avert harm. The justification defences are qualified, however, if the prosecution can prove fault in relation to the defendant's misapprehension about the circumstantial basis of the defence. The provisions on fault in the defence of necessity, which are paralleled in the other justification defences,[95] illustrate the nature of the qualification.

> When the actor was reckless or negligent in bringing about the situation requiring a choice of harms or evils or in appraising the necessity for his conduct, the justification afforded by [necessity] is unavailable in a prosecution for any offence for which recklessness or negligence, as the case may be, suffices to establish culpability.

The effect of the scheme, when lethal force is in issue, is set out below in tabular form. A similar table could be drawn for self-defence. Fault elements have been paraphrased and some issues in the implementation of the scheme have been footnoted. The important thing, for present purposes, is to illustrate the ways in which considerations of justification and excuse have been subordinated to the necessities of legislation that ranks the offences in degrees of wrongdoing and presumptive penalties by reference to the fault of the offender.

---

[95] Model Penal Code, above n 3, s 302(2).

IMPERFECT OR QUALIFIED 'CHOICE OF EVILS' DEFENCES:
MODEL PENAL CODE SECTION 3.02

Defences Graded by Negligence & Recklessness	Outcome
1. D should have been aware of risk of error but D's conduct did not involve a gross deviation from the standard of care of a reasonable person in D's situation.	Acquit—civil liability possible
2. D should have been aware of risk of error and D's conduct involved a gross deviation from the standard of care of a reasonable person in D's situation.	s 210.4: Negligent homicide
3. D disregarded a known risk of error in circumstances where that disregard involved a gross deviation from the standard of care of a reasonable person in D's situation.[96]	s 210.3: Manslaughter (fault element: recklessness)
4. D made no error as to the nature of the threat, but did not choose the lesser harm or evil. [97]	s 210.2: Murder (fault element: purpose or knowledge)

In the Model Penal Code, the threshold of criminal liability for an intentional homicide is not determined by the question whether the defendant's conduct was *justified* or *warranted* by necessity or self-defence. It is determined by the fault requirements for the offence: the threshold of liability for the least serious of the criminal homicides requires proof of a *gross* deviation from the standard of a reasonable person. D's conduct must fall well below any standard of justification or warrant before conviction of an unlawful homicide would be appropriate.[98] The more significant point, however, is the gradation of criminal responsibility among the three varieties of wrongful homicide. A person who is mistaken about the existence or nature of a threatened harm or evil, or who misjudges the means to avert it, will not be convicted of murder, even if their mistake or misjudgement was

---

[96] As L Alexander points out, there are problems in applying the qualification for recklessness in s 3.09(2): see above n 28, 624–26.

[97] *Cf* Westen and Mangiafico, above n 13, 883–88, who argue that justification should extend to include the choice of an *equivalent* harm or evil.

[98] If that is the best that can be said of the defendant's conduct, it can hardly amount to an instance of a right or permissible thing to do in the circumstances ex ante. It is conduct that the criminal law is prepared to tolerate. See, to the same effect, Robinson, above n 15, 116, 228, who distinguishes the justification defences from mistaken justification defences, which he categorises as 'excuses'.

unreasonable. Responsibility for one of the lesser homicides will only be imposed if recklessness or negligence can be established. Justification is relevant in this sense—that it is the only appropriate guide to action when D is faced with a choice of evils, but failure to meet that demanding standard does not necessarily result in conviction.

At this point the distinction between David and Valerie, remarked earlier, becomes apparent. David was mistaken about the facts and that mistake would provide him with a complete or partial defence to murder, in a Code that did not dispense with fault requirements when a defence of justified or warranted conduct was in issue. Valerie, if she was mistaken at all, was mistaken about the law that required her to take no retaliatory action, when faced with David's justifiable threat to shoot her. Complete or partial defences based on a mistake about facts will not help her.[99] Duress may excuse her, for the Criminal Code removed the common law bar to duress as a defence to murder.[100] I have suggested, however, that this equation of duress and necessity as complete defences to murder may be yet another indefensible anomaly resulting from the near merger of the defences. If Valerie is denied an acquittal on the ground of self-defence, perhaps she should have no more than a partial defence of duress.

III. DURESS: EQUIVOCATION AND 'REASONABLE RESPONSES'

The defence of duress is defined with the same loose inclusiveness as the other Code defences. Duress is available when commission of an offence is a 'reasonable response' to avert a threatened harm. The threat must be made by another person, but it need not be an unlawful threat and the threat need not be directed at the defendant: it may not be directed at anyone at all. There appears to be no requirement that the threat be coupled with a demand; it is sufficient that the defendant has a reasonable belief that the threat will be carried out 'unless the offence is committed'. Unlike self-defence, duress will excuse conduct that involved an intentional harm or wrong to an innocent who was no threat to anyone. Unlike necessity, it is available to a defendant who chose the greater harm or evil in full knowledge of the circumstances.

---

[99] See Dubber, above n 15, 201: 'This crucial limitation was meant to keep the necessity defence from justifying defendants like the one who "genuinely believes that the life of another is less valuable than his own financial security"' [Citing the American Law Institute's official commentaries on the Code, *Model Penal Code and Commentaries* (Philadelphia, Official Draft and Revised Comments 1980–85)].

[100] Fairall and Yeo, above n 18, 140. Fairall and Yeo note that Australian common law is unsettled on the question whether an accomplice might rely on duress to escape conviction for murder. Legislatures have reversed common law in some jurisdictions: see, eg, Crimes Act 1958 (Vic) s 9AG *Duress*.

The appearance of a common spine of principle in the requirement of a reasonable response to threatened harm in duress and necessity is an illusion. In their commentary on the Code, the Model Criminal Code Officers Committee characterised the defence of duress as a concession to defendants whose 'free will is overborne'.[101] The ambiguity inherent in their requirement of a 'reasonable response' is immediately apparent. The Committee equivocated on the question whether the defendant is excused because the response is reasonable or excused because it would not be reasonable for a court to expect the defendant to have resisted the threat. The commentary suggests that the Committee simply failed to perceive the distinction between conduct that is a reasonable response to threats and the conduct of a person whose will is overborne so that they are no longer capable of a reasonable response.[102]

I have suggested that there may be cases where the killing of an innocent might be justified by the utilitarianism of extremity. But that is the province of necessity, where D's response is reasonable—justified or warranted—because D chose the lesser harm or evil. There is no question here about inadequacy of will power. Duress is meant to supplement the defences of necessity and self-defence: it has its paradigmatic application in cases where the defendant was overborne and committed an offence in full awareness that their conduct was not justifiable in the circumstances.

Duress remains the most problematic of the general defences, when an innocent is killed intentionally and the case is not one in which the utilitarianism of extremity could warrant or justify the act. The best argument for permitting duress to excuse the defendant in such a case is that fairness precludes criminal responsibility if the threat would have driven any reasonable law-abiding citizen to commit the same offence.[103] That is the basis for the common law criterion which asks whether a person of ordinary firmness of mind might have yielded to the threat in the way that the defendant did.[104] The argument in favour of permitting duress to excuse when the defendant

---

[101] Model Criminal Code, above n 1, ch 2, 66: 'Where free will is overborne by duress, the nature of the offence [committed] is not relevant'.

[102] Ibid: the failure of the Model Criminal Code Officers Committee to perceive the distinction is apparent from their citation of S Yeo, 'Private Defences, Duress and Necessity' (1991) 15 *Criminal Law Journal* 139. In that paper, and in Yeo, above n 18, 249, Yeo characterises duress as an excuse based on a demand coupled with a threat that the person 'could not reasonably be expected to resist'.

[103] See, eg, K Huigens, 'Duress Is Not a Justification' (2004) 1 *Ohio State Journal of Criminal Law* 1, 10–11.

[104] Fairall and Yeo, above n 18, 143. The authors remark that Australian courts are divided on the question whether the test should refer to merely possible or to expected responses of the person of ordinary firmness of mind. *Cf* Duff, above n 37, 288: Duress is available where the 'defendant did not display a lack of those modest levels of courage, self control and commitment to the values that the criminal law protects, that citizens can properly demand of each other on pain of public condemnation for failure'.

has violated the rights of an innocent by causing serious injury or death is far from conclusive. We may say that some offences are simply inexcusable, whatever the pressure that induced the defendant to act.[105] The alternative suggested earlier is that duress involving a threatened harm to the defendant or a close family member, which a person of ordinary moral temper could not reasonably be expected to resist, might be no more than a partial defence to murder and other serious offences against the person. If the case cannot be brought within the ambit of the complete or partial defences of necessity or of self-defence a supplementary defence of duress should not provide more than a partial defence to murder or, perhaps, other serious offences against the person.

IV. CONCLUSION

I began by remarking the insouciance with which the codifiers abandoned common law limits on the defences of necessity and duress and extended the defences to exculpate murder. That was not the only departure from common law. Unreasonable perception of a threat or danger is sufficient foundation for exculpation on the ground of self-defence, which was extended beyond defence to self to include an altruistic intervention to defend another from attack. The significance of these changes is masked by the bland generality of the provisions, the substantial areas of their common application and the use of the same 'reasonable response' criterion for exculpation in each of the defences.

The scenarios on killing innocents, in circumstances where resort to deadly force reaches the uncertain margins of acceptability, were meant to sharpen moral intuitions that should inform the structure of the criminal defences and require distinctions to be drawn in their applications and criteria for measuring criminal responsibility. When responsibility for murder is in issue, I have suggested that the line of cleavage runs between defence of self and defence of others, which is the province of necessity. The agential stance that informs the plea of self-defence is only appropriate when a defendant used lethal force in defence of their own physical integrity or personal autonomy or that of a close relative. Necessity, which extends so far as to exculpate

---

[105] Duff, above n 37, 289, fn 95. Duff suggests, however, that murder is not such an offence. No examples are given of offences that could not be excused by duress. Compare Lord Coleridge CJ in *R v Dudley & Stephens* (1884) 14 QBD 273 at 281: 'We are often compelled to set up standards we cannot reach ourselves'. See Schopp, above n 41, 145–51, proposing a practice of imposing a 'purely vindicating conviction' that would be followed by complete mitigation when sentence was determined. That would require a separate form of verdict, following a successful, mitigating plea of duress. Coercion of the will by threats is a matter of degree and it is only in extreme cases, marked by some articulate standard, that a complete mitigation of penalty would be appropriate.

a defendant for killing an innocent person who is known to pose no threat to anyone, is subject to more stringent constraints. Lethal force must be justified or warranted, in the sense that it was acceptable as a right thing to do in the circumstances ex ante.[106] When innocents are not involved, I have argued that exculpation for the use of lethal force in defence of others should still be determined from the objective stance. Kremnitzer and Ghanayim equated the criminal responsibility of a person who uses force for self-protection with that of a 'substitute policeman' who acts to preserve an existing legal order. That is appropriate when force is used to avert a threat to others. It is not appropriate to self-defence in its literal sense. On first impression it may appear strange that the constraints on altruistic action, when a person undertakes the defence of others, are more stringent than the constraints on defence of oneself. Memories of Kitty Genovese might suggest that the criminal law should encourage intervention. At the margins, however, altruism has its own characteristic set of vices, ranging from officious intermeddling and beyond to the sacrifice of individuals to avoid purely speculative harms or indiscriminate vigilantism.[107]

The difference between defence of self and defence of others reflects a distinction, familiar in its various guises in torts and criminal law, between private and public necessity. Public necessity is utilitarian in structure, and subject to deontological side constraints. Private necessity is deontological in structure and subject to the overriding demands of utilitarian concern for the public good. That distinction between private and public necessity is expressed in institutional differences in the law relating to lethal force by authorised officials and citizens without official status. The occasions when it can be argued that killing in defence of others was warranted or excused by necessity in circumstances of sudden or extraordinary emergency will not be frequent and when they do occur, they are likely to involve the use of lethal force by officials. In the checkpoint shooting, lethal force was pre-emptive and used in circumstances where it was not positively known that the victim was an innocent. So long as civil order is maintained, citizens are unlikely to be faced with choices of this order. Citizens must seek official help, if at all possible. Resort to lethal force is unlawful, unless the threatened harm is imminent. Restraints against pre-emptive force are far

---

[106] *Cf* the argument, almost diametrically opposed to the tenor of this chapter, in Bronitt and Stephens, above n 31, 269, that defence of necessity when innocent lives are taken is at best 'excusatory': 'A psychological state of emergency may "excuse" wrongful action, but would also send a clear message that the deliberate taking of life cannot be justified through a process which weighs the relative importance or value of some human lives against others.' Presumably the authors would take the same view when the calculation is made on the basis of numbers of lives sacrificed. The issue is much discussed in the philosophical literature. See, eg, M Otsuka, 'Killing the Innocent in Self Defence' (1994) 23 *Philosophy and Public Affairs* (1994) 74 and the ensuing debate.

[107] See, eg, *Nemer v Holloway* (2003) 87 SASR 147.

less stringent in their application to officials.[108] In the second scenario, where the officers believed that detonation of the car bomb was imminent, Valerie, who was seized by Vera as a shield, was known to be a hapless innocent. She was killed because David believed that many lives were potentially at stake, if the putative car bomb were to be detonated. It is certainly arguable that the utilitarianism of extremity might warrant or justify such a killing. George Christie contends that only officials could rely on the defence of necessity to justify the killing of an innocent non-aggressor:

> Public officials are charged with promoting the common good. They not only exercise the authority to decide that some people should be sacrificed to save a larger number of others, but also exercise a vastly more important authority, namely the authority to decide that some lives are more important than others ... . But the power to decide that one person's life is socially more important than another's is forbidden to private individuals.[109]

Short of a breakdown in civil order, it is highly unlikely that citizens will find themselves in situations where they have the opportunity, let alone the capacity, to test Christie's conclusion.

The argument that necessity will only exculpate a defendant whose conduct is warranted or justified ex ante from the objective stance, sets a demanding standard for compliance. That is appropriate, one might say, for a defence that will extend to exculpate a defendant for an intentional use of lethal force in a pre-emptive strike against a person who may be innocent or who is known to be innocent. It does not follow, however, that a conviction for murder is the appropriate sanction for conduct that fails to reach that demanding standard. A partial or qualified defence that will reduce murder to manslaughter would provide a fairer reflection of the moral blameworthiness of an offender whose conduct fell short of a reasonable response in the circumstances. Labelling an offender as a murderer is a significant and damning condemnation, even if the penalty for the offence is no longer one of mandatory life imprisonment. It is arguable that John Gardner's incompetent hot-head who gets the facts wrong and kills without warrant or justification should have the benefit of a partial defence that

---

[108] Criminal Code, s 10.4—*Self defence* has no specific requirement of imminence. The requirements of belief that force is necessary, coupled with the requirement that the response to the threat be reasonable differentiate officials and citizens. In an ordered society citizens must seek official help, rather than engage in pre-emptive strikes.

[109] GC Christie, 'In Defence of Necessity Considered from the Legal and Moral Points of View' (1999) 48 *Duke Law Journal* 975, 1028–29.

[110] A number of Australian jurisdictions make provision for a partial or qualified defence of self-defence. See, eg, Criminal Law Consolidation Act 1935 (SA) s 15 *Self defence*, ss (2) and s 15A *Defence of property*, ss (2); Crimes Act 1958 (Vic) s 9AD *Defensive homicide*. When self-defence is determined from the agential stance, as it is in South Australia, it may seem that the primary purpose of the partial defence is to cut off the possibility that D might gain an unmerited and complete acquittal.

would reduce murder to a lesser offence.[110] In this respect, the defence of necessity in the Australian Code is unnecessarily rigid. Self-defence, by comparison, is unnecessarily indulgent in permitting a complete acquittal when the defendant makes an utterly unreasonable assessment of the facts or the necessity for lethal force.

Duress is the outlier in this structure, for the offender who was subjected to duress does not seek to exercise a right of self-preservation against an aggressor and consciously chooses a greater harm or evil rather than a lesser. If duress is ever to excuse the taking of innocent life it could only be on the ground that it would be unjust to expect the defendant to have shown the resilience of a saint or hero when faced with the threat that induced the offence.[111] The rule of law considerations that permit necessity to justify murder have far less purchase when duress is concerned. One thing, however, is clear. The Criminal Code reliance on the same requirement of a 'reasonable response' to threatened harm, whether the case is one of necessity, self-defence, or duress, prevents any attempt to construct a coherent relationship among the defences and subverts the particular limits to which each is subject.

[111] Duff, above n 37, 289.

Appendix

Commonwealth *Criminal Code*—Chapter 2: *General Principles of Criminal Responsibility*, Extracts from Part 2.3: *Circumstances in which there is no criminal responsibility.*

10.2 Duress

(1)   A person is not criminally responsible for an offence if he or she carries out the conduct constituting the offence under duress.
(2)   A person carries out conduct under duress if and only if he or she reasonably believes that:
    (a)   a threat has been made that will be carried out unless an offence is committed; and
    (b)   there is no reasonable way that the threat can be rendered ineffective; and
    (c)   the conduct is a reasonable response to the threat.
(3)   This section does not apply if the threat is made by or on behalf of a person with whom the person under duress is voluntarily associating for the purpose of carrying out conduct of the kind actually carried out.

10.3 Sudden or extraordinary emergency

(1)   A person is not criminally responsible for an offence if he or she carries out the conduct constituting the offence in response to circumstances of sudden or extraordinary emergency.
(2)   This section applies if and only if the person carrying out the conduct reasonably believes that:
    (a)   circumstances of sudden or extraordinary emergency exist; and
    (b)   committing the offence is the only reasonable way to deal with the emergency; and
    (c)   the conduct is a reasonable response to the emergency.

10.4 Self-defence

(1)   A person is not criminally responsible for an offence if he or she carries out the conduct constituting the offence in self-defence.
(2)   A person carries out conduct in self-defence if and only if he or she believes the conduct is necessary:
    (a)   to defend himself or herself or another person; or
    (b)   to prevent or terminate the unlawful imprisonment of himself or herself or another person; or

(c)　to protect property from unlawful appropriation, destruction, damage or interference; or

(d)　to prevent criminal trespass to any land or premises; or

(e)　to remove from any land or premises a person who is committing criminal trespass;

and the conduct is a reasonable response in the circumstances as he or she perceives them.

(3)　This section does not apply if the person uses force that involves the intentional infliction of death or really serious injury:

(a)　to protect property; or

(b)　to prevent criminal trespass; or

(c)　to remove a person who is committing criminal trespass.

(4)　This section does not apply if:

(a)　the person is responding to lawful conduct; and

(b)　he or she knew that the conduct was lawful.

However, conduct is not lawful merely because the person carrying it out is not criminally responsible for it.

10.5 Lawful authority

A person is not criminally responsible for an offence if the conduct constituting the offence is justified or excused by or under a law.

7

Regulating Reasonable Force: Policing in the Shadows of the Law

SIMON BRONITT AND MIRIAM GANI[*]

I. INTRODUCING POLICE USE OF FORCE: LEGAL BLACKHOLE OR BLINDSPOT?

THIS CHAPTER EXAMINES the law governing the use of force by police officers in the execution of their duties.[1] This is a significant enquiry since the right to use of force is regarded as a defining characteristic of policing.[2] It also raises important questions about the legitimacy and legal accountability of state-sanctioned violence. Such questions bear on a key aspect of the rule of law, namely, that public officials should be subject to the ordinary laws of the land and that private citizens should be able to challenge the legality of the conduct of these officials through the criminal and civil courts.

While the proposition that police officers ought to be subject to the ordinary law of the land is uncontroversial, litigation contesting the legality of police use of force is rare. There are several reasons for this. First, instituting legal action against the police (individual officers and/or police organisations) presents enormous difficulties for private citizens. Police defendants are invariably supported by their employers and/or police unions who typically underwrite the costs of legal representation. By contrast, aggrieved citizens bear the burden of legal costs in their pursuit of justice, which

[*] The authors would like to thank Professor Geoff Alpert for his helpful comments on an earlier draft, and Lucy Schyff and Prita Jobling for their able assistance in preparing the tables and other research tasks.

[1] The issue arises most commonly when police use force in the course of making an arrest of a person suspected of or caught in the commission of an offence. This is not the only circumstance, however, where police may be lawfully permitted to use force against citizens. For example, in the field of public order, the common law duty of the police 'to keep the peace' empowers constables to use necessary and reasonable force to suppress or prevent a breach of the peace: see S Bronitt and B McSherry, *Principles of Criminal Law*, 3rd edn (Sydney, Thomson Reuters, 2010) ch 13.

[2] Scholars have argued that the power to use force (legitimately or illegitimately) is the key defining characteristic of policing, see eg E Bittner, *The functions of police in modern society* (Washington, US Printing Office, 1970).

potentially include, in cases where legal action is unsuccessful, the costs incurred by the police defendants. This disadvantage is compounded for individuals most likely to experience abuse of power at the hands of the police (the homeless, mentally ill and young persons, for example) who are least able to resource legal action.[3] These structural obstacles do not diminish even in the most serious of cases, namely, where force used by police results in death. Domestic legal rules governing standing (which determine who can institute legal proceedings in any matter) restrict plaintiffs to immediate family members or others 'materially affected' by police wrongdoing.[4] Even then, litigants with legal standing to pursue an action are not always well positioned, motivated or adequately resourced to proceed against the police. Private prosecution against the police remains available, theoretically at least, though the resources needed to mount this type of proceeding remain beyond the reach of most people.[5]

Despite the obstacles in bringing legal action against the police, misuse of force by officers is not completely beyond the reach of the law. In the cases involving death in police custody, the circumstances surrounding police use of force will be subject to an independent examination by the coroner.[6] The coronial inquiry places a forensic spotlight on the conduct of officers involved, permitting a careful examination of the nature and seriousness of the threats faced by the officers, and whether or not the response conformed to or

---

[3] That said, there have been a number of recent cases in Australia where police were prosecuted for assaults arising from excessive use of force. An example is *Rowe v Kemper* [2008] QCA 175, where the accused, an elderly homeless man, was subjected to significant use of force in the course of resisting an arrest for breach of a move-on direction. This direction was later found to be unlawful by the Supreme Court of Queensland. The accused received damages from Queensland Police, and a private prosecution for assault was successfully instituted against one of police officers. See B Murphy, 'Rowe v Kemper [2008] QCA 175' (2008) 32(6) *Criminal Law Journal* 38. The decision received prominent media coverage, and was a significant focus of the review by the Queensland's Crime and Misconduct Commission (CMC): see CMC, *Police move-on powers: A CMC review of their use,* Report (2010).

[4] The domestic rules of standing may hamper public interest litigation or administrative review. See, eg, *McCann and others v United Kingdom* (1997) Series A no 324, 21 EHRR 97 where the families of suspected IRA bombers who were killed by the SAS in Gibraltar brought a legal challenge on the deceased's behalf alleging that the action of state officials had violated the suspect's right to life. The European Court of Human Rights noted that the breach of the right to life under Article 2(2) requires an effective remedy and thus necessitated an independent and public official investigation in which the family of the deceased could participate effectively.

[5] The Director of Public Prosecutions has the power to intervene and discontinue such action for insufficiency of evidence, or because the private action has been instituted for an improper purpose or that discontinuation is otherwise in the 'public interest': see, eg, *Prosecution Policy of the Commonwealth: Guidelines for the making of decisions in the prosecution* (2008), 4.7–4.13, www.cdpp.gov.au/Publications/ProsecutionPolicy/ProsecutionPolicy.pdf.

[6] In Australia, deaths in police custody are monitored by the federally funded Australian Institute of Criminology: www.aic.gov.au. The definition of death in custody is broad and includes where a person dies in the course of arrest or while seeking to evade capture. The data show that while, overall, deaths in police custody have declined over the past decade, deaths as a result of police sieges or pursuits have increased: www.aic.gov.au/en/publications/current%20series/mr/1-20/10.aspx.

deviated from official training standards, policy or procedures. Importantly, coronial processes identify and generate material that may be used as evidence in subsequent legal proceedings.

Beyond this vital fact-finding role, coronial processes in Australia are increasingly performing a reform function since coroners have the power to attach recommendations to their verdicts on the cause of death that have implications for police training, policy and practice. Although inquests are strictly inquisitorial exercises and do not determine the legal liability of the police officers involved, coronial verdicts have significant legal effects— they can either vindicate the legitimacy and reasonableness of police conduct, or, in cases where police behaviour is subject to adverse findings, lead to internal disciplinary proceedings or in serious cases, lead Crown prosecutors to lay charges against police. (To highlight the key role of the coroner in such cases, the chapter includes a case study of a recent inquest in Victoria examining the police shooting of a mentally disturbed teenager, Tyler Cassidy.)

Legal action against the police is not limited to the pursuit of civil or criminal law remedies. Individuals also have access to a range of administrative remedies to pursue allegations of misuse of force against the police. Administrative remedies take several forms: individuals may pursue a complaint internally, through the ethics and professional standards units of the police agencies themselves, or externally, through oversight bodies such as the Ombudsman or independent police complaint commissions.[7] There is also the general right under administrative law to institute judicial review of police action, though courts have been notoriously reluctant to interfere with operational decision-making except in the most egregious cases.[8]

In light of these obstacles to seeking legal recourse through tort, criminal law or administrative review it is unsurprising that some aggrieved citizens are resorting to social media to spotlight directly alleged instances of police misconduct. Aided by the proliferation of video-recording devices

---

[7] Eg, complaints by members of the public about the Australian Federal Police (AFP) are dealt with under Part V of the *Australian Federal Police Act 1979* (Cth). These complaints are subject to inspection and review by the Office of the Commonwealth Ombudsman. The Ombudsman, over successive reports, has been critical of the delays and defensive approach to individual complaints adopted by the AFP. A recent report notes that, between 2007 and 2010, not one of the complaints by members of the public about excessive use of force had been substantiated. This lack of substantiation is striking bearing in mind that over this three-year period, there were 80 complaints from members of the public: see *Annual Report on the Commonwealth Ombudsman's activities under Part V of the Australian Federal Police Act 1979—for the period 1 July 2010 to 30 June 2011* (November 2011) www.ombudsman.gov. au/files/activities_under_part_v_05.pdf.pdf. Complaints about excessive force are classified as 'serious misconduct' under the legislation.

[8] The common law doctrine of constabulary independence confers on police a wide margin of appreciation in how officers discharge their duties, with which courts are most reluctant to interfere. As a result this area of law is doctrinally undeveloped: see S Bronitt and P Stenning, 'Understanding discretion in modern policing' (2011) 35(6) *Criminal Law Journal* 319.

(integrated into mobile phones or CCTV systems), incriminating images of police misconduct are being swiftly disseminated through new media such as YouTube and other Internet sites.[9] This phenomenon has been described by Canadian scholar, Steve Mann, as 'sousveillance', which denotes those forms of surveillance exercised from below (by citizens) rather than from above (by the state and public officials such as the police).[10] This 'new visibility' of policing increases public transparency of officer conduct in both public and private settings. Advances in technology not only enable citizen sousveillance of police, but the images recorded may provide crucial evidence in subsequent legal and/or disciplinary proceedings against police.[11] Furthermore, the use of POV (point-of-view) surveillance technologies by uniformed police, which is being widely trialled by police in Australia and elsewhere, is ostensibly used to gather (incriminating) evidence against offenders or persons of interest and provide material for rebutting accusations of professional misconduct or police illegality. An unintended and collateral effect is that POV technology sometimes works against the police using the technology. For example, in one recent case, recording from a dashboard mounted video camera in a police vehicle proved crucial in the prosecution of two senior constables who used excessive force by kicking and using batons to subdue a 'hoon' driver and his passenger in country Victoria.[12]

The existence of these structural impediments to bringing legal proceedings to test the legality and limits of police powers has two significant outcomes: (i) it produces a deficit in police accountability for use of force, and (ii) it leads to the doctrinal under-development of the law governing police use of force. However, the dearth of 'test case' litigation does not mean that the

---

[9] At the time of writing, allegations of police brutality in the arrest of a person for public nuisance in Queensland is receiving wide media coverage. CCTV footage of the incident, which occurred in a police station, was obtained by *The Courier-Mail* pursuant to a freedom of information request. Posted on the newspaper's website, the video clip went 'viral'. The person alleging excessive force had already made a complaint to the Queensland Police, triggering an internal investigation by the Ethical Standards Command. Since gaining wider publicity through the media, the investigation has been joined by the Queensland Crime and Misconduct Commission: 'Raw Police CCTV', *The Courier-Mail*, 16 February 2011, 4–5, video.couriermail.com.au/2196973875/Raw-Police-CCTV.

[10] The concept of sousveillance is explored in A Goldsmith, 'Policing's New Visibility' (2010) 50 *British Journal of Criminology* 914.

[11] A former Queensland Police officer was recently sentenced to nine months' imprisonment for a violent assault on three people in his custody at the time of the offence. A YouTube video had been posted showing the officer punching 23-year-old Timothy Steele in the head and forcing a high-powered fire hose into his mouth. The footage also showed the officer slamming Renee Toms, then 21, to the floor of the watchhouse before pulling her by the hair, lifting her off the ground: 'Former Qld cop jailed over bashings', *AAP General News Wire*, 11 October 2010.

[12] One officer was found guilty of intentionally causing injury and unlawful assault on the two men and received a 12-month supervised community-based order as well as being required to perform 60 hours of unpaid community service. The other had pleaded guilty to intentionally causing injury and was put on a 12-month community-based order, without conviction: M Buttler and A Dowsley, 'Police busted bashing hoon driver in Mansfield', *Herald Sun* (15 December 2011).

law, whether statute law or common law, is irrelevant to modern policing practice. As concluded in other 'law in policing' studies, the law governing police use of force is best viewed as a 'toolkit' of legal norms that enables—rather than a 'rulebook' that constrains—police behaviour.[13]

In relation to police use of force, the regulatory environment is shaped not only by 'hard law' found in the case law and legislation, but also by 'soft law' norms such as administrative directives, policy and guidelines. While the latter are not strictly sources of law, constituting merely the administrative operationalisation of the relevant legal norms and best practice standards, research suggests that these sources of 'soft law' often play a more prominent role in constituting the working rules governing officer behaviour than do the applicable common law or statutory rules. An important function of this research is to reveal and explore the nature and effect of the divergence between the legal rules on the one hand, and police policy and practice on the other.

Beyond illuminating the complexity of this gap between the 'law in books' and the 'law in action', our research exposes the wide blanket of legal protection conferred on police who use force—officers need neither evade nor subvert the relevant legal rules, but rather simply apply those rules, framing offenders' behaviours and officers' responses in light of the specific police powers available to them or the doctrines of self-defence, necessity or lawful authority. Whilst the rhetoric of the law, as reflected in judicial decisions, statutes and administrative directives, advocates restraint in the use of force (often expressed as 'minimum force'), in practice, police officers possess a wide margin of discretion in determining when and how much force is used against suspects.[14]

The aim of this chapter then is twofold: first, to shed light on the relevant legal rules, administrative directives, policies and practices governing police use of force; and second, to reveal how the interplay between these legal and non-legal policing norms both constructs and regulates the use of reasonable force by police.

II. CONSTRUCTING REASONABLE FORCE

Administrative directives in Australia indicate that an officer should not use excessive force in the performance of his or her duty.[15] For example, the Operational Procedures Manual (OPM) of the Queensland Police Service

---

[13] See generally D Dixon, *Law in Policing: Legal Regulation and Police Practices* (Oxford, Oxford University Press, 1997) examining the relationship between law and police interviewing practice.

[14] For an essay reviewing discretion, see Bronitt and Stenning, above n 8.

[15] See D Baker, 'Police confirmation of use of force in Australia: 'To be or not to be?" (2009) 52 *Crime, Law and Social Change* 139.

(QPS) indicates that any use of force by an officer must be 'authorised, justified, reasonable, proportionate, appropriate, legally defensible and tactically sound and effective'.[16] A significant factor that shapes police decision-making is the 'use of force model' that officers are taught during initial training. In Australia, police are trained in the situational tactical options model, first taught to Victorian Police in 1994, which has since been incorporated into the *National Guidelines for Incident Management, Conflict Resolution, and Use of Force*.[17] The model, which the police ministers of all Australian jurisdictions undertook to implement in 1998, is reproduced below.[18]

As a senior Australian Federal Police officer responsible for policing in the Australian Capital Territory noted, this model is based on a 'use of force continuum', which operates in a non-linear fashion by allowing officers to respond to particular circumstances and conditions.[19] As explained by that

[16] QPS, *Operational Procedures Manual* (Queensland Police Service, 2002) discussed Criminal Justice Commission, *Reported use of force by Queensland Police: Findings from the 1999 Queensland Defendants Survey* (2000) 3.

[17] The 1998 version of the Guidelines, which were developed by the Australian Centre for Policing Research, is available at anzpaa.org.au/anzpire/acpr-publications. For a discussion of the history and shortcomings of this model, see D Nicholson, 'Use of Force Models: Comprehension or Confusion?' available at www.articlesbase.com/self-defense-articles/use-of-force-models-comprehension-or-confusion-956580.html.

[18] *National Guidelines* (2004) app B, 25. The explanation given for preferring situational or tactical options models, such as the above, to linear, incremental models is explained on p 10: 'Situational models conceptualise the range of tactical options in a circular format in which the tactical options are randomly arranged. Such models are integrated and holistic in that they do not emphasise one option over another. Further, there is no entry point into the model and no indication of a linear progression in levels of force, thereby encouraging officers to consider all tactical options throughout the duration of the incident. Accordingly, some models feature a police officer in the middle of the circle to emphasise that officers can directly select any of the options at anytime. This highlights the need for continual assessment and re-assessment of the incident and the appropriate response. In this way, both escalation and de-escalation of incidents are emphasised for use where appropriate. Finally, situational models highlight the importance of maintaining (throughout the incident), first, the safety of officers and members of the public and, second, tactical communication.'

[19] This summary is taken from the evidence of AFP Assistant Commissioner, Audrey Fagan, to the Legislative Assembly for the Australian Capital Territory Standing Committee on Legal Affairs (Reference: Police Powers Of Crowd Control) *Hansard Transcript of Evidence* (Canberra, 23 September 2005).
    The continuum starts with the premise of verbal communication. That involves eye contact, looking for body signals and asking the person to comply when the officer chooses to exercise his or her powers lawfully, obviously. The continuum then has a range of responses. That goes from soft hands, where we will place a hand on them to effect an arrest if that person isn't complying, through to lethal force, being the final power available as far as crime prevention, preservation of life, et cetera, are concerned. The oleoresin capsicum spray, or OC spray, is well within that continuum. The continuum is not linear, it depends on conditions, as the minister raised. Similarly, the Taser X26, which is only deployed to our specialist response and security team, is part of that continuum. We think about it in the context of the situation, both for preventing injury to the person who may be being arrested—that is probably the easiest way to think about it—and to our officers. That's the prime driver. If you move up the scale in escalating the use of force response, it doesn't diminish the others. There will be a continuation of verbal command, and they will be asked to comply. That gives you an overall view of how we work through that. As I said, there's

officer, it is premised on verbal communication and is designed to de-escalate potential conflict situations and to resolve incidents without force deployment. It stresses the use of minimum force but contemplates that the use of lethal force may be reasonable and necessary. Under this model, then, use of force decision-making rests on the assessment and management of risk. This is predicated on the individual officer making rational calculations in relation to (i) the nature and gravity of the perceived threat, and (ii) the appropriate response. The model is general in its application, focussed on improving the *processes* of decision-making regardless of particular context (for example, applicable whether or not the subject is drug affected or mentally ill).

Recent research conducted in the United States by Alpert and Rojek casts doubt on the value of using this type of Rational Choice Model (RCM) to guide or improve police decision-making relating to the use of force.[20] Based on presumed static and stable environments, the authors point out that the RCM fails to recognise the contextual, uncertain and 'split-second' nature of police decisions to use force. Rather than adopt the RCM, Alpert and Rojek advocate a different model for understanding police decision-making called the Naturalistic Decision-making Model (NDM).[21] As the authors note, NDM is an increasingly accepted model for understanding and guiding decision-making in a wide range of domains, including military, aviation and healthcare settings.[22] NDM avoids the linear and sequential nature of decision-making of rational choice models, instead, as the authors note, favouring responses based on 'interpretation, knowledge and experience'.[23]

Compliance with police training, preferred decision-making models or relevant directives cannot provide complete legal assurance for officers making decisions to use force. It is well established that police directives, although often having a statutory foundation and expressed in mandatory terms, are not the same as legal rules. Indeed, administrative directives cannot fetter the individual officer's discretion, which must be exercised independently and in a manner that is free from external pressures. The Supreme Court of Canada has recently underscored that police directives do not alter the independent nature of the discretion of the officer not to proceed with an investigation: 'It should be pointed out that these [administrative] directives do not have the force of law. They therefore cannot alter

---

an annual recertification that takes them through that continuum of force that all sworn members are required to do.

[20] See generally, G Alpert and R Durham, *Understanding Police Use of Force: Officers, Suspects and Reciprocity* (New York, Cambridge University Press, 2004).

[21] G Alpert and J Rojek, 'Frontline Police Officer Assessments of Risks and Decision Making During Encounters with Offenders' (2011) *CEPS Briefing Paper*, Issue 5.

[22] For a general overview of the various domains and potential applications of NDM, see C Zsambok and G Klein, *Naturalistic decision making* (New Jersey, Routledge, 1997).

[23] Ibid.

the scope of a discretion that is founded in the common law or a statute'.[24] That said, directives can be considered relevant to determining the reasonableness of any police response, which will be an important consideration in the context of police use of force.

What then are these legal requirements? As noted above, the use of force by police is premised on notions of necessity and reasonableness and filtered through the prism of proportionality. Accordingly, although the precise language used may differ, the common law, legislation and administrative directives all coalesce around the idea of 'reasonable force' which involves consideration of the necessity, reasonableness and proportionality of police action. Before further examining the concept of 'reasonable force' in the modern law, we will provide some historical context on how the law and notions of 'reasonableness', particularly in relation to the use of lethal force, have evolved over time.

III. HISTORICAL PERSPECTIVES ON USE OF FORCE: KILLING OUTLAWS AND QUELLING RIOTS

The permissive stance of the law towards the use of lethal force against 'fleeing felons' and 'unruly mobs' has a long historical pedigree. Before the advent of a disciplined professional police force, the common law authorised a broad spectrum of lawful force, including lethal force, to apprehend felons and suppress breaches of the peace. At its most extreme, the medieval doctrine of outlawry allowed felons to be cast outside the 'pale' (that is, the protection) of the common law, legitimating the pre-emptive use of lethal force against any person formally declared 'outlaw'.[25] The significance of this pre-emptive legal doctrine declined with the advent of modern police forces, though in the colonial context, a form of outlawry was revived in the latter half of the nineteenth century to combat elusive bushrangers including the infamous Ned Kelly.[26]

---

[24] *Beaudry v The Queen* [2007] 1 SCR 190 (Sup Ct Can), discussed in Bronitt and Stenning, above n 8, 327.

[25] The origins were related to the fact that there was no efficient means of compelling the attendance of parties or enforcing their orders before the courts, as legal historians Pollock and Maitland noted: 'Outlawry is the last weapon of ancient law, but one that it must often use ... it is the sentence of death pronounced by a community which has no police constables or professional hangmen. To pursue the outlaw and knock him on the head is the duty of every law-abiding man': F Pollock and F Maitland, *The History of English Law*, 2nd edn (London, Cambridge University Press, 1923) 43, noting that the process was derived from the Danish period of English law.

[26] As Greg Woods has noted, what is interesting about the colonial 'shoot to kill' power is that it was more draconian than English law and practice; the Felons Apprehension Act 1865 (NSW) did not require pursuers to issue a warning or challenge before the use of lethal force. The law further disabled any legitimate retaliation from the outlaw, denying to the accused

A similar history applies to the common law governing breach of the peace. Both common law and statute authorise citizens and police alike to take a wide range of action, including use of force, to prevent and suppress disorder.[27] The most notorious and draconian power in this field was the British Riot Act of 1715, which was transposed into the Australian colonies. This power enabled the magistracy to call out the local militia to assist in restoring order.[28] Justices or magistrates 'read the Riot Act' to the crowd, issuing a proclamation directing those assembled to disperse immediately. Failure to disperse authorised the use of force, including lethal force, to restore order.[29] The Act made it an offence for persons to remain assembled after the proclamation had been read and provided extensive immunities to those using force to disperse unlawful assemblies. By the nineteenth century, conferring wide law enforcement immunities (through outlawry or the Riot Act) had fallen into disfavour, and these laws were either repealed or fell into desuetude.

The advent of professional, paid and disciplined police in early nineteenth-century Britain and exported to her colonies heralded significant changes to the system of criminal justice. To overcome the deep national distrust of a standing army in Britain, the architects of the 'new police' promoted the model of an unarmed force (with the constable as 'citizen in uniform') that stood in stark contrast to the paramilitary policing models common in continental Europe. As reflected in Sir Robert Peel's Nine Principles, policing rested upon the consent of the governed, rather than coercion.[30] One of Peel's Principles entreated constables: '[t]o use physical force only when the exercise of persuasion, advice and warning is found to be insufficient to obtain public co-operation to an extent necessary to secure observance of law or to restore order, and to use only the minimum degree of physical force which is necessary on any particular occasion for achieving a police objective'.[31]

---

claims of self-defence against pursuers: GD Woods, *A History of Criminal Law in New South Wales—The Colonial Period 1788–1900* (Sydney, Federation Press, 2002) 203–06.

[27] See Bronitt and McSherry, above n 1, ch 13, which provides a review of the common law and statutory powers to prevent a breach of the peace in the UK and Australia.

[28] The Riot Act 1715 (UK) was received into the Australian colonies and most Australian jurisdictions continue to retain the provisions relating to proclamation and the wide immunities for those who disperse riotous assemblies. It should be noted that the Riot Act 1715 (UK) was abolished in England in 1973 but equivalent statutory provisions have survived in most Australian jurisdictions: Bronitt and McSherry, above n 1, 867. See generally, A Hiller, *Public Order and the Law* (Sydney, Law Book Company, 1983) 77–85.

[29] Bronitt and McSherry, above n 1, 867.

[30] Although there is uncertainty about the provenance and Peel's authorship of the Nine Principles, many of these principles (independence, policing by consent, etc) have shaped the way modern policing has developed in Britain and elsewhere. See Bronitt and Stenning, above n 8, 323.

[31] Bronitt and Stenning, above n 8, 331 (Principle 6). A version of Peel's principles is extracted in Crime and Misconduct Commission, *Police Move-on Powers: A CMC Review of their Use* (2010) app 3, www.cmc.qld.gov.au/asp/index.asp.

This idealised narrative of the policing mandate in the nineteenth century (which was received into Australia) is misleading for two reasons. First, although presented as 'citizens in uniform', police officers were equipped with a range of coercive powers and immunities not otherwise available to ordinary citizens. Existing common law powers were soon supplemented with new statutory powers to keep the peace and exercise surveillance over suspect populations, and ultimately to investigate crime.[32] So, police authority on the street in the nineteenth century was bolstered by Police Acts, and a wide range of summary offences making it an offence to assault, hinder or resist police acting in the course of their duties. Secondly, when exported to colonies like Australia and Canada, the British model of policing never conformed to the ideal type of unarmed force of 'citizens in uniform'. The Border and Mounted Police of Australia and Canada, drawing heavily on military garrisons for senior ranks and constables, established a paramilitary model for policing on the frontier.[33] Obviously, the hostile conditions in frontier societies provided greater opportunity for the deployment of armed police with the capability to use lethal force to uphold law and order and British authority as required.

IV. MELDING 'SOFT LAW', 'HARD LAW' AND POLICE USE OF FORCE

Turning from this brief historical digression to the modern context, the use of force is simultaneously both a routine and an extraordinary aspect of contemporary policing. Threatening a person with arrest, with the inherent implication of using (lawful) force unless the person submits to police authority, is a common stratagem used by police officers to induce citizen compliance.[34] At the other end of the spectrum, there are those cases, albeit rare, where officers resort to using lethal force against a suspect. In high profile cases involving suspected terrorists, police action may provoke grave unease about the existence of official or unofficial 'shoot to kill' policies and practices. While routine cases rarely attract public attention, situations may escalate quickly and become deadly. As noted in our

---

[32] See generally, M Finnane, *Police and Government: Histories of Policing in Australia* (Melbourne, Oxford University Press, 1994).

[33] In the 1820s, in response to fears about attacks by Aborigines and increased threats from bushrangers, the Mounted Police of NSW was formed 'for temporary purposes from the regiments in the colony, despite express reluctance to employ the military for civil purposes': D Neal, *The Rule of Law in a Penal Colony* (Melbourne, Cambridge University Press, 1991) 150–51. The mounted police retained military pay, status and uniform.

[34] Such strategies may be counterproductive. As social psychological research on procedural justice reveals, the unfair exercise of police powers leads to 'alienation, defiance, and non-cooperation' of citizens: see L Hinds and K Murphy, 'Public Satisfaction With Police: Using Procedural Justice to Improve Police Legitimacy' (2007) 40(1) *Australian and New Zealand Journal of Criminology* 27.

introduction, without a firm legal foundation justifying the use of force, such cases impact adversely on the perceived legitimacy and levels of trust of police within the community.

The law plays an important role in legitimising force and assuaging community concern about arming general duties police. In regulatory terms, however, it is not merely 'hard law' (in the form of common law or legislation) that governs police practice. As noted above, a variety of 'soft law' shapes the regulatory context governing police use of force in Australia and elsewhere. At the international level, relevant 'soft law' instruments were developed by the United Nations (UN) including the general principles in the *Code of Conduct for Law Enforcement Officials 1979* (UN Code). Article 3 of the UN Code states that police officers 'may use force only when strictly necessary and to the extent required for the performance of their duty'.[35] This idea was further elaborated in the UN's *Basic Principles on the Use of Force and Firearms by Law Enforcement Officials* (UN Principles),[36] Principle 9 of which states:

> Law enforcement officials shall not use firearms against persons except in self-defence or defence of others against the imminent threat of death or serious injury, to prevent the perpetration of a particularly serious crime involving grave threat to life, to arrest a person presenting such a danger and resisting their authority, or to prevent his or her escape, and only when less extreme means are insufficient to achieve these objectives. In any event, intentional lethal use of firearms may only be made when strictly unavoidable in order to protect life.

While it is important not to overstate the impact of international 'soft law' norms on domestic policing generally,[37] the UN Code and Principles exerted some influence on the national guidelines relating to use of force and firearms in Australia. For example, the UN Principles were expressly identified as a model for the National Guidelines on the Use of Force in Australia,[38] which in turn provided the template for federal, state and territory police policies.[39]

---

[35] *Code of Conduct for law enforcement officials*, GA Res 34/169, UN GAOR, 34th sess, 106th plen mtg, UN Doc A/RES.34/169 (17 December 1979).

[36] Adopted by the Eighth United Nations Congress on the Prevention of Crime and the Treatment of Offenders, Havana, Cuba, 27 August–7 September 1990, extracted in National Police Research Unit, *National Guidelines Compendium—Police Use of Force, Deployment of Police in High Risk Situations, Deployment of Police Negotiators—Report No 123* (Police Commissioners' Policy Advisory Group, 1992).

[37] J Kleinig, *The Ethics of Policing* (Cambridge, Cambridge University Press, 1996) devotes only one paragraph to the UN Code, concluding that 'in the member states it has never achieved the acceptance that was sought for it': at 237.

[38] National Police Research Unit, above n 36, 4: noting that the National Guidelines were modelled on the UN Principles.

[39] M Tuckey, *National Guidelines for Incident Management, Conflict Resolution and Use of Force: 2004* (Australasian Centre for Policing Research, 2004). These are operationalised in local jurisdictions through Police Commissioner's Directives or Orders: see, eg, *AFP Commissioner's Order No 3: Use of Force*. The power to make such orders is conferred by s 38 of the Australian Federal Police Act 1979 (Cth). Under s 37(1) of the Act, the Commissioner has 'the general administration of, and the control of the operations of, the Australian Federal Police'.

These various guidelines, while not 'hard law', play a significant role in determining what constitutes reasonable force in a particular situation. As we shall see, the modern law regulating police use of force in some jurisdictions demands compliance with strict procedural requirements of the type previously required by outlawry, including the duty to call on a person being apprehended to surrender before using force where reasonably practicable. In other jurisdictions, the duty to call on a person to surrender, while no longer a strict legal requirement, may nevertheless bear on the question of the reasonableness of the officer's decision to use force.

On rare occasions, the complex relationship between sources of hard and soft law may be revealed through coronial inquests into fatal shootings by police. One such case involved Tyler Cassidy, a mentally disturbed 15-year-old boy, who died from a gunshot to the chest at the hands of four police officers in Victoria in December 2008. Police had been called to a shopping centre after Tyler had stolen two large knives from a store and had moved through the shopping centre and out into a car park threatening people with the knives and demanding that the police be called 'or people would die'.[40] The findings of the state coroner emphasised the speed with which the incident occurred (73 seconds from the time that officers engaged with Tyler to the time that the ambulance was called after Tyler had been shot).[41] In that brief time, the officers issued verbal commands to Tyler to drop the knives, sprayed him with Oleoresin Capsicum (OC) foam spray when he refused, chased him across a park before he stopped and pointed the knives at them, foamed him again and issued further commands to drop the knives or 'he would be shot'.[42] The police officers stated that Tyler responded by saying 'I'm going to kill you' and 'you're going to have to shoot me' and then advanced towards one of the officers. That officer then fired a warning shot followed by two shots at Tyler's legs, which did not halt the boy advancing with a knife in each hand. Two of the other officers also fired at this stage and, finally 'fearing for his life and having exhausted all other non-lethal options, [the first officer] fired three shots directly at Tyler's chest area as Tyler walked towards him'.[43]

The shooting was the subject of a coronial inquest, the findings of which were published almost three years later in November 2011. The coroner found that the police had fired at Tyler in self-defence.[44] Given this finding, no prosecution of the officers ensued. Although appearing to vindicate the officers involved, it should be recalled that a coronial inquest is a process of inquisitorial fact-finding to determine the circumstances surrounding the

---

[40] Coroners Court of Victoria, Finding—Inquest into the Death of Tyler Cassidy, State Coroner Judge Coate (Melbourne, 23 November 2011) [461]; www.coronerscourt.vic.gov.au/home/case+findings/coroners2+-+findings+-+inquest+into+the+death+of+tyler+cassidy.

[41] Ibid [19].

[42] Ibid [13].

[43] Ibid [18].

[44] Ibid [461].

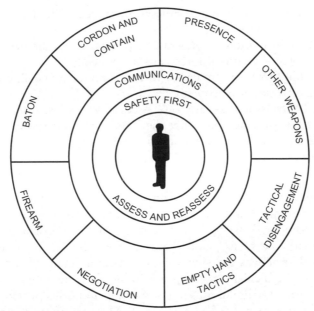

Figure 1: General structure of a situational tactical options model (from the *National Minimum Guidelines for incident Management, Conflict Resolution and Use of Force, 1998, p. 10*).

particular death.[45] It serves a different function from a criminal trial, where the prosecution ordinarily subjects any claims of self-defence to rigorous scrutiny under cross-examination.

'Soft law' sources loomed large in the coronial inquest into Tyler's death. The inquiry by state coroner, Judge Coate, extended to an examination of police policies, procedures and training, and, particularly, whether the officers had acted in accordance with their training. The coroner reviewed the Operational Safety and Tactics Training which all Victorian police are required to attend twice yearly and which included Operational Safety Principles (OSPs) that were contained in the Victoria Police Manual. The OSPs, which were integrated into the National Guidelines (see Figure 1 above), include the following 10 principles:

1   **Safety first**—the safety of police, the public and offenders or suspects is paramount;
2   **Risk assessment**—is to be applied to all incidents and operations;
3   **Take charge**—exercise effective command and control;
4   **Planned response**—take every opportunity to convert an unplanned response into a planned operation;

---

[45] The officers involved were granted to leave to appear as 'interested parties', along with the Chief Commissioner of Police, and the mother of the deceased.

5   **Cordon and containment**—unless impractical, adopt a 'cordon and containment' approach;

6   **Avoid confrontation**—a violent confrontation is to be avoided;

7   **Avoid force**—the use of force is to be avoided;

8   **Minimum force**—where use of force cannot be avoided, only use the minimum amount reasonably necessary;

9   **Forced entry searches**—are to be used only as a last resort;

10 **Resources**—it is accepted that the 'safety first' principle may require the deployment of more resources, more complex planning and more time to complete.

As the coroner found, the officers attending the incident involving Tyler had been told by their Acting Sergeant to 'cordon and contain' and 'wait for the canine unit'[46] as they were getting out of their vehicle. However, the officer who fired the fatal shot testified that this instruction, though consistent with the OSPs, soon 'became irrelevant' when Tyler showed the officers that he was carrying knives.[47] After a detailed examination of each stage of the incident, the coroner found that 'the members involved responded within the limitations of the training and skills provided to them by Victoria Police as at December 2008'.[48] Most significantly, the coroner acknowledged that there had been improvements to police training since the incident, and also identified that there was 'an immediate and urgent need for Victoria Police to focus its training to members on developing the ability to recognise and manage vulnerable young people such as Tyler'.[49] That said, in the ultimate analysis the coroner was satisfied that when 'the three police members fired at Tyler, it was at a time that [one of the officers] was in immediate and perilous danger of serious injury or death'.[50]

As this tragic case reveals, the law provides a wide margin of discretion on how police may respond to threats. It appears that even derogations from the directions of a senior officer and standard operational procedures and principles, will not necessarily render decisions to use force, including lethal force, 'unreasonable'. It is clear from cases such as this, that the reasonableness of police decisions to deploy force is examined contextually, focussing on both *objective* factors (external to the officer) and *subjective* factors (internal to the officer) to determine whether the force used was necessary and reasonable. In the next section, we will further examine the law governing these key concepts in the context of powers to make an

---

[46] Ibid [288].
[47] Ibid [140].
[48] Ibid [463].
[49] Ibid [465].
[50] Ibid [461].

arrest, one of the most common situations where police may encounter suspect resistance and be required to use force.[51]

V. MAKING ARRESTS: AUTHORISING NECESSARY AND REASONABLE FORCE

The legal rules governing arrest are an amalgam of common law and statute.[52] Unlike the substantive criminal law in most jurisdictions in Australia, the law in relation to police powers is not codified.[53] As there is no national or model code of police powers, legislation differs from jurisdiction to jurisdiction.[54] Although differently expressed, all jurisdictions permit the use of necessary and reasonable force to assist in law enforcement. Statutory powers for each Australian jurisdiction are set out in summary form in Table A below. As an example, in Australia's most populous state, New South Wales, section 230 of the Law Enforcement (Powers and Responsibilities) Act 2002 (NSW) sets out the general powers of police to use force lawfully, while section 231 specifies the powers of police to use force in the context of making an arrest. Both provisions allow police to 'use such force as is reasonably necessary' to exercise the relevant function, to make the arrest or to prevent the escape of the person after arrest. Recent case law confirmed that section 231 sets the limits of lawful arrest in that jurisdiction:

> That provision, it seems to me, sets the scope and defines the parameters of the 'duty' that the officers were performing. If they exceeded the use of 'such

---

[51] In addition to authorising use of force to make an arrest, legislation confers on police specific powers to use force. These typically include inter alia powers to enter onto property/ premises to prevent crime and disorder; to protect property; to execute warrants and other court orders; to conduct forensic testing (including the forcible taking blood or tissue samples); to prevent suicide; and to suppress riots and disorder.

[52] Notwithstanding that the Criminal Code Act 1995 (Cth) ousted common law criminal offences, the common law powers of arrest (from which the police power to use force flows) remain intact. See discussion in the Issues Paper Prepared for the Clarke Inquiry Public Forum: 'Too Safe or Too Sorry'—A forum on the effect of the relevant laws as they applied to the case of Dr Haneef (December 2008) 3 (as well as submissions to that forum). The recent NSW case of DPP v Armstrong [2010] NSWSC 885 emphasises that statutory powers of arrest sit alongside rather than abrogate common law powers.

[53] The influence of codification on the development of Australian criminal law is reviewed in S Bronitt, 'The Criminal Law of Australia' in M Dubber and K Heller (eds), The Handbook of Comparative Criminal Law (California, Stanford University Press, 2010).

[54] Eg, in New South Wales, the Law Enforcement (Powers and Responsibilities) Act 2002 (NSW) sets out the general powers of police, including the powers to use force in the context of making an arrest. Section 230 provides: 'It is lawful for a police officer exercising a function under this Act or any other Act or law in relation to an individual or a thing, and anyone helping the police officer to use such force as is reasonably necessary to exercise the function.' Section 231 provides: 'A police officer or other person who exercises a power to arrest another person may use such force as is reasonably necessary to make the arrest or to prevent the escape of the person after arrest.'

force as is reasonably necessary to make the arrest' then they were not acting in the execution of their duty.[55]

Statutory formulations in relation to the lawful use of force are articulated in broad and general terms, supplementing rather than abrogating the pre-existing common law.[56] The common law allows any person making an arrest to use 'whatever force is "reasonable" in the circumstances'.[57] Early cases articulated the legal test in terms of a 'reasonable man' standard, a concept borrowed from criminal law and tort law. As a leading case in Victoria noted, 'reasonable force' is a highly contextual concept in that it requires consideration of the objective reasonableness of the subjective belief held as to the necessity of the intervention in question, and of whether the degree of force used was such that an objective hypothetical person would consider proportionate to those circumstances:

> When a felony is committed in the presence of a member of the public, he may use reasonable force to apprehend the offender or for the prevention of the felony. What is reasonable depends upon two factors. He is entitled to use such a degree of force as in the circumstances he reasonably believes to be necessary to effect his purpose, provided that the means adopted by him are such as a reasonable man placed as he was placed would not consider to be disproportionate to the evil to be prevented (i.e. the commission of a felony or the escape of the felon).[58]

As Tables A and B illustrate, modern statutes have reformulated the 'reasonable man' test in gender-neutral terms. They also provide more detailed guidance on the parameters (and inherent limits) of necessary and reasonable force to be used during arrest or in preventing an escape after arrest. In the federal context, for example, the power to use force to arrest a person for an offence is contained in section 3ZC of the Crimes Act 1914 (Cth). Sub-section 3ZC(1) section provides:

> (1) A person must not, in the course of arresting another person for an offence, use more force, or subject the other person to greater indignity, than is necessary and reasonable to make the arrest or to prevent the escape of the other person after the arrest.[59]

Demanding that arrest involve no more force or greater indignity than is necessary and reasonable in the circumstances is consistent with the

---

[55] *R v Murray* [2008] NSWDC 226 (Unreported Judgment).

[56] The recent NSW case of *DPP v Armstrong* [2010] NSWSC 885 emphasises that statutory powers of arrest operate concurrently with pre-existing common law powers.

[57] *Woodley v Boyd* [2001] NSWCA 35, [37] per Heydon JA (Davies and Foster AJJA concurring) citing *Wiltshire v Barrett* [1966] 1 QB 312, 326, 331.

[58] *R v Turner* [1962] VR 30, 36.

[59] This provision is mirrored in relation to protective services officers in s 14B(1) of the Australian Federal Police Act 1979 (Cth). Protective services officers are AFP members who are appointed to protect Commonwealth places and interests (including airports) in Australia and overseas and to assist in international peacekeeping operations.

Table A: General Powers Governing Use for Force

	Cth	ACT	NSW	NT	Qld	SA	Tas	Vic	WA
	Crimes Act 1914 subs3ZC(1)	*Crimes Act 1900* subs221(1)	*Law Enforcement (Powers and Responsibilities) Act 2002* s231	*Criminal Code Act* s27	*Police Powers and Responsibilities Act 2000* subs615(1)	NO **STATUTORY POWERS** **COMMON LAW APPLIES**	*Criminal Code Act 1924* subs26(1)	*Crimes Act 1958* s462A	*Criminal Code Act Compilation Act 1913* s231
Authorised person	a person	person	police officer or other person who exercises a power to arrest	any person (not explicitly stated)	police officer, and anyone helping the police officer	–	any person	a person	a person, and any person lawfully assisting him
Mental state	–	–	–	does not intend to cause death or serious harm	–	–	–	believes on reasonable grounds it is necessary	–
Circumstance	in the course of arresting a person for an offence	in the course of arresting another	to make the arrest or to prevent the escape of	to lawfully execute any sentence, process or	attempting to exercise a power under this or any other	–	the person is justified or protected	to effect or assist in effecting the lawful arrest of	the person is engaged in the lawful execution of

(Continued)

Table A: (*Continued*)

	Cth	ACT	NSW	NT	Qld	SA	Tas	Vic	WA
		person for an offence	the person after arrest	warrant or make any arrest	Act against an individual		in the execution of any sentence, process, or warrant, or in making an arrest	a person committing or suspected of committing any offence	any sentence, process, or warrant, or in making any arrest
Extent of powers	must not use more force, or subject the other person to greater indignity, than is *necessary and reasonable* to make the arrest or to prevent the escape of the other person after the arrest	shall not use more force, or subject the other person to greater indignity, than is *necessary and reasonable* to make the arrest or to prevent the escape of the other person after the arrest	may use such force as is *reasonably necessary*	the application of force is justified provided it is *not unnecessary* force, and it is not such as is likely to cause death or serious harm	it is lawful to use *reasonably* necessary force to exercise the power	–	it is lawful to use such force as may be *reasonably necessary* to overcome any force used in resisting such execution or arrest	may use such force *not disproportionate* to the objective (to prevent the commission, continuance or completion of an indictable offence)	lawful to use such force as may be *reasonably necessary* to overcome any force used in resisting such execution or arrest

Table B: Specific Police Powers Governing Use of Force

	Cth	ACT	NSW	NT	Qld	SA	Tas	Vic	WA
	Crimes Act 1914 subs3ZC(2)	*Crimes Act 1900* subs221(2)	–	*Criminal Code Act* s28	*Police Powers and Responsibilities Act 2000* s616	–	*Criminal Code Act 1924* s30	–	*Criminal Code Act Compilation Act 1913* ss233, 235
Authorised person	a constable	police officer	–	police officer	police officer	–	police officer, and any person lawfully assisting	–	a police officer or a person assisting
Mental state	*believes on reasonable grounds* that it is necessary to protect life or prevent serious injury or that the person cannot be apprehended in any other manner	*believes on reasonable grounds* that it is necessary to protect life or prevent serious injury or that the person cannot be apprehended in any other manner	–	*reasonably believes* that the person may commit an offence punishable by life imprisonment	*reasonably suspects* the person has, is or will commit an offence of life imprisonment	–	the person is *suspected on reasonable grounds* of having committed a specified crime (treason, piracy, murder, rape, arson, burglary, endangering life)	–	the person is *reasonably suspected of* having committed an offence punishable with life imprisonment
Circumstance	in the course of arresting a person for an offence	in the course of arresting a person for an offence	–	when lawfully attempting to arrest (or assist) a person who may commit an	a person has, is or will commit an offence of life imprisonment; or has	–	when lawfully arresting a person, with or without warrant, and the	–	a person is being lawfully arrested for an offence of life imprisonment and attempts to

(Continued)

Table B: *(Continued)*

	Cth	ACT	NSW	NT	Qld	SA	Tas	Vic	WA
				offence punishable with life imprisonment & has taken flight	committed it and attempted to escape		person sought to be arrested takes to flight in order to avoid arrest		avoid arrest; or has been arrested for an offence punishable by more than 14 years
Safeguards	if attempting to escape arrest by fleeing—the person has, if practicable, been called on to surrender	if attempting to escape arrest by fleeing—the person has, if practicable, been called on to surrender	–	has been called upon to surrender and has been allowed a reasonable opportunity to do so	the police officer must, if practicable, first call on the person to stop doing the act	–	the person has been called upon to surrender	–	the person is called on to surrender
Extent of powers	may do anything that is likely to cause the death of, or grievous bodily harm to, the person	may do anything that is likely to cause the death of, or grievous bodily harm to, the person	–	the application of force that will or is likely to kill or cause serious harm is justified provided it is *not unnecessary* force	the police officer may use force likely to cause grievous bodily harm to a person or the person's death	–	it is lawful to use such force (which is intended or is likely to cause death or grievous bodily harm) as may be *reasonably necessary* to prevent escape	–	it is lawful to use such force (which is intended or is likely to cause death or grievous bodily harm) as may be *reasonably necessary* to prevent escape

common law's traditional commitment to protecting personal liberty.[60] Like the powers available under the common law, this provision does not distinguish between arrest by a police officer or another person purporting to make a 'citizen's arrest'.[61]

In sub-section 3ZC(2) the Crimes Act 1914 (Cth) does, however, impose further requirements, applying only to police, that qualify the concept of necessary and reasonable force:

> (2) Without limiting the operation of subsection (1), a constable must not, in the course of arresting a person for an offence:
>
> (a) do anything that is likely to cause the death of, or grievous bodily harm to, the person unless the constable believes on reasonable grounds that doing that thing is necessary to protect life or to prevent serious injury to another person (including the constable); or
>
> (b) if the person is attempting to escape arrest by fleeing—do such a thing unless:
>
> (i) the constable believes on reasonable grounds that doing that thing is necessary to protect life or to prevent serious injury to another person (including the constable); and
>
> (ii) the person has, if practicable, been called on to surrender and the constable believes on reasonable grounds that the person cannot be apprehended in any other manner.[62]

Thus, the decision to use force likely to cause death or grievous bodily harm is justified only where the constable has a belief, based on reasonable grounds, that it is necessary to protect life or to prevent serious injury. By implication, the use of deadly force merely to protect or recover property or prevent a trespass, however significant or valuable, is not justified.

The requirement contained in sub-section 3ZC(2) is consistent with both the test for and the limits of self-defence under federal criminal law (which includes defence of others).[63] Most significantly, self-defence does not apply

---

[60] This is also reflected in the directive that arrest is a measure of last resort and the statutory requirement placed on police to give consideration of alternatives to arrest such as proceeding by way of summons: *Donaldson v Broomby* [1982] 40 ALR 525. On the varied ways in which the common law upholds human dignity in the absence of any entrenched constitutional right, see S Bronitt, 'The Common Law and Human Dignity' in J Brohmer (ed), *The German Constitution Turns 60: Basic Law and Commonwealth Constitution—German and Australian Perspectives* (Frankfurt Am Main, Peter Lang, 2011) 77–88.

[61] Although 'citizen's arrest' is widely and colloquially used to describe the powers of arrest by persons who are not sworn police officers, the term is misleading as there is no requirement that the arrestor be a citizen of the particular jurisdiction in which the arrest is made.

[62] Again, this sub-paragraph is mirrored by s 14B(2) of the Australian Federal Police Act 1979 (Cth) in respect of protective services officers.

[63] The self-defence provision, s 10.4 of the Criminal Code Act 1995 (Cth) provides:

> (1) A person is not criminally responsible for an offence if he or she carries out the conduct constituting the offence in self-defence.
>
> (2) A person carries out conduct in self-defence if and only if he or she believes the conduct is necessary:
>
> (a) to defend himself or herself or another person; or

where the person uses force intending to inflict death or really serious injury for the purpose of protecting property; or preventing criminal trespass; or removing a person who is committing criminal trespass. Echoing earlier powers to deal with declared outlaws and fleeing felons, sub-section 3ZC(2) imposes a further procedural limitation on using deadly force, namely, that the person evading arrest by fleeing 'has, if practicable, been called on to surrender and the constable believes on reasonable grounds that the person cannot be apprehended in any other manner'.

As noted above, the 'law in books' (that states arrest is a measure of 'last resort' and that constables should use 'minimum force') does not necessarily conform to the 'law in action'.[64] In some cases, the circumstances leading up to the use of deadly force may have been induced by the police officer—a phenomenon that has been termed 'officer-created jeopardy' in the United States.[65] Whether or not this police practice is intentional, reckless or merely negligent, Australian courts have repeatedly observed that overuse of arrest for minor public order crimes, such as offensive language, invariably escalates the incident and provokes violent resistance to the arresting officers. As the Supreme Court of New South Wales noted in one high profile case in 2002:

> Arrest is an additional punishment involving deprivation of freedom and frequently ignominy and fear. The consequences of the employment of the power of arrest unnecessarily and inappropriately and instead of issuing a summons are often

    (b)   to prevent or terminate the unlawful imprisonment of himself or herself or another person; or
    (c)   to protect property from unlawful appropriation, destruction, damage or interference; or
    (d)   to prevent criminal trespass to any land or premises; or
    (e)   to remove from any land or premises a person who is committing criminal trespass;
  and the conduct is a reasonable response in the circumstances as he or she perceives them.
  (3) This section does not apply if the person uses force that involves the intentional infliction of death or really serious injury:
    (a)   to protect property; or
    (b)   to prevent criminal trespass; or
    (c)   to remove a person who is committing criminal trespass.
  (4) This section does not apply if:
    (a)   the person is responding to lawful conduct; and
    (b)   he or she knew that the conduct was lawful.
However, conduct is not lawful merely because the person carrying it out is not criminally responsible for it.

[64] This principle finds expression in statutory, common law or 'soft law' sources such as Police Instructions.

[65] J Ederheimer (ed), *Critical Issues in Policing: Strategies for Resolving Conflict and Minimizing Use of Force* (Police Executive Research Forum, 2007) 88, which noted: '[s]ometimes officers create scenarios that permit the justifiable use of force, but if the officer had handled the situation with different tactics, he [or she] could have avoided an escalation of the confrontation'.

anger on the part of the person arrested and an escalation of the situation leading to the person resisting arrest and assaulting the police.[66]

This is particularly of concern in relation to the policing of Aboriginal communities, and the continuing failure of police to use non-coercive alternatives to arrest for minor offences, which provokes suspect resistance to police authority and, sadly, contributes to the historically high rates of Aboriginal deaths in custody in Australia.[67]

VI. GENERAL DEFENCES: INHERENT RIGHTS OF SELF-DEFENCE AVAILABLE TO POLICE

In addition to the common law and statutory powers of arrest discussed above, where an officer has used force, general criminal law defences may provide further legal justification or excuse for police action. Foremost amongst these is self-defence (which includes defence of others), but other defences, such as necessity, duress, sudden and extraordinary emergency, or lawful authority or excuse, may also apply.[68]

In the federal context, the relevant defences are found in Chapter 2 of the Criminal Code Act 1995 (Cth) (Criminal Code).[69] The lawful authority or excuse defence in the Criminal Code is as follows: 'A person is not criminally responsible for an offence if the conduct constituting the offence is justified or excused by or under a law'.[70] The defence is intended to interact with other statutory provisions, including the power of arrest in the Crimes Act 1914 (Cth), discussed above. As noted in the Explanatory Memorandum, where a 'law enforcement officer is authorized by law to physically restrain a person and does so within the scope of his or her authority, then the officer cannot be charged for harming that person'. Conversely, the defence does not apply 'if there is no clear justification or excuse provided for by or under another law of the Commonwealth'.[71] Accordingly, the defence will only be applicable to police officers who are acting in accordance with their legal powers of arrest or some other statutory power authorising use of force.

---

[66] *DPP v Carr* [2002] NSWSC 194 at [35], discussed in C Feerick, 'Policing Indigenous Australians: Arrest as a Method of Oppression' (2004) 29(4) *Alternative Law Journal* 188 and K Adams, 'A Commentary on DPP v Carr' (2003) 27 *Criminal Law Journal* 278.

[67] See S Bottomley and S Bronitt, *Law in Context* (Sydney, Federation Press, 2012) ch 4.

[68] See S Bronitt, 'Balancing Security and Liberty: Critical Perspectives on Terrorism Law Reform' in M Gani and P Mathew (eds), *Fresh Perspectives on the 'War on Terror'* (Canberra, ANU press, 2008) 79.

[69] Note that these general defences are contained in Chapter 2 of the Criminal Code Act 1995 (Cth), which applies to all Commonwealth offences (see s 2.2).

[70] Criminal Code, s 10.5.

[71] Criminal Code Amendment (Theft, Fraud, Bribery and Related Offices) Bill 1999, Explanatory Memorandum, [11].

We now turn to some of these 'extraordinary' powers to use force inserted into the Criminal Code available to AFP when executing special powers recently enacted to prevent and investigate terrorism.

VII. POLICE USE OF FORCE IN THE WAR OF TERROR: SHOOT TO KILL POWERS IN AUSTRALIA?

In the wake of 9/11, the Anti-Terrorism Act (No 2) 2005 (Cth) inserted a preventative detention regime into the Criminal Code. Under Division 105, AFP members can seek (and in the case of an initial 24-hour order, senior AFP members can make) detention orders.[72] To obtain an order, where a terrorist act is imminent,[73] the AFP member seeking the order must be satisfied that there is reasonable suspicion ('reasonable grounds to suspect') that the person will engage in a terrorist act, possesses something connected with preparation for or engagement in a terrorist act or has done an act in preparation for or planning a terrorist act. The AFP member must also be satisfied that making the order 'would substantially assist in preventing a terrorist act occurring' and that detaining the suspect is reasonably necessary to achieve that end.[74]

Enforcement of preventative detention orders rests on AFP members. Accordingly, section 105.19(2) of the Criminal Code (Cth) sets out the power to use force in taking people into preventative detention in the following terms:

> A police officer, in taking a person into custody under and in detaining a person under a preventative detention order, has the same powers and obligations as the police officer would have if the police officer were arresting the person, or detaining the person, for an offence.

Much controversy surrounded this expansion of AFP powers. The Anti-Terrorism Bill 2005 (Cth) was drafted in the wake of the London bombings in July 2005 following discussion with state and territory premiers and chief ministers at the Council of Australian Governments (COAG) in September 2005.[75] At that meeting, premiers and chief ministers had agreed to support the 'strengthening'[76] of anti-terrorism legislation including the creation of

---

[72] See the definition of 'issuing authority' in s 100.1 of the Criminal Code.

[73] Section 105.4(5), which requires the attack be one that is imminent and expected to occur within 14 days.

[74] Section 105.4(4)(a), (b) and (c). These provisions state that where a terrorist act has occurred in the past 28 days, the AFP member must be 'satisfied' that the detention order is necessary to preserve evidence of or relating to a terrorist act and that the detention is reasonably necessary to achieve that end.

[75] See the communiqué of the Council of Australian Governments' Special Meeting on Counter-Terrorism 27 September 2005 (Canberra, 27 September 2005) www.coag.gov.au/coag_meeting_outcomes/2005-09-27/index.cfm.

[76] Ibid.

a preventative detention and control order regime. However, the Bill in its original form was not made public but was circulated 'draft-in-confidence' to the premiers and chief ministers. Jon Stanhope, Chief Minister of the ACT, was so concerned about its contents that he released the draft to the public on his website as well as seeking advice on the human rights implications of the Bill from prominent lawyers.[77]

One of the most criticised provisions[78] was proposed section 105.23, headed 'Use of Force'. This proposed section was drafted in the same terms as section 3ZU of the Crimes Act 1914 (Cth) (discussed above) but extended the powers of AFP officers to use force (including lethal force) against a person, subject to an order, in the course of taking that person into custody, detaining the person or preventing the person from fleeing custody.[79] ACT Chief Minister Stanhope was not alone amongst the state and territory leaders in voicing concerns about what became known as the 'shoot-to-kill' provision, which, they stated, had not been divulged or discussed at the September COAG meeting.[80]

---

[77] See A Byrnes, H Charlesworth and G McKinnon, *Advice to Jon Stanhope re Human Rights Implications of the Anti-Terrorism Bill 2005*. See also submissions by Lex Lasry QC and Kate Eastman.

[78] Byrnes, Charlesworth and McKinnon, ibid. See also, 'Shoot-to-kill open to abuse: Law Society', *The Age* (19 October 2005) which quotes NSW Law Society President, John McIntyre as decrying the fact that lethal force could be used against someone 'being reasonably suspected of committing of an offence. If the [police] are armed with one of these [orders] ... and if this person attempts to flee the arrest, he can be shot and fatally shot,' Mr McIntyre said. 'The police might knock on the door and [the person] might leg it out the back door without even being told why the police are there, and under these provisions they can be called on to stop and if they don't stop, they can be shot.'

[79] The original proposed s 105.23 was as follows:
105.23 Use of force
(1) An AFP member must not, in the course of taking a person into custody or detaining a person under a preventative detention order, use more force, or subject the person to greater indignity, than is necessary and reasonable:
(a) to take the person into custody; or
(b) to prevent the escape of the person after being taken into custody.
(2) An AFP member must not, in the course of taking a person into custody or detaining a person under a preventative detention order:
(a) do anything that is likely to cause the death of, or grievous bodily harm to, the person unless the AFP member believes on reasonable grounds that doing that thing is necessary to protect life or to prevent serious injury to another person (including the AFP member); or
(b) if the person is attempting to escape being taken into custody by fleeing—do such a thing unless:
(i) the AFP member believes on reasonable grounds that doing that thing is necessary to protect life or to prevent serious injury to another person (including the AFP member); and
(ii) the person has, if practicable, been called on to surrender and the AFP member believes on reasonable grounds that the person cannot be apprehended in any other manner.
(3) Subsection (2) does not limit subsection (1).

[80] See, eg, A Clennell and L Dodson, 'States draw the line at shoot-to-kill laws', *Sydney Morning Herald* (21 October 2005) www.smh.com.au/news/national/states-draw-the-line-

As conceded in Attorney-General's Department Submissions to the Senate Legal and Constitutional Affairs Committee on the Anti-Terrorism Bill (No 2) 2005, the hostile reception from some of the premiers and chief ministers was instrumental in the decision to redraft the provision.[81] The effect of redrafting is that AFP members are empowered to use force in the same way and to the same extent, in relation to people they are seeking to bring into custody under a preventative detention order, as they were previously empowered to use only in relation to arrests under section 3ZC of the Crimes Act 1914 (Cth). As the Explanatory Memorandum states, in relation to police officers from other jurisdictions, it means that:

> [E]ach individual police officer is subject to his or her usual rules and proce-
> dures in relation to arrests ... State and Territory powers vary. This provision is
> designed to ensure police are able to use those powers in relation to which they
> have received training and are experienced and familiar.[82]

Given the furore over the original in-confidence draft Bill, which, the NSW Law Society president, John McIntyre said would take away an individual's 'fundamental freedoms',[83] it is debatable whether the final version of the provision, section 105.19(2), does much to allay those fears of civil libertarians. The police remain empowered to use force against a person subject to a preventative detention order, even though that person need not be suspected of involvement, directly or indirectly, in acts of terrorism!

VIII. CONCLUSION

Police officers enjoy a relatively privileged position within the legal system when they make a decision to use force. As repeat players in our criminal justice system, who 'know the rules' and 'how the system works',[84] officers

---

at-shoottokill-laws/2005/10/20/1129775902652.html. They state 'Nearly all the other state premiers yesterday joined Mr Iemma in opposing the shoot-to-kill powers in the proposed federal laws. Victoria's Steve Bracks, Queensland's Peter Beattie, South Australia's Mike Rann and Western Australia's Geoff Gallop all said they were not part of the agreement struck with Mr Howard'.

[81] G McDonald, Assistant Secretary, Security Law Branch, Security and Critical Infrastructure Division, Attorney-General's Department, Witness at the Senate Legal and Constitutional Legislation Committee Hearing (*Hansard*, 14 November 2005) 4: 'I guess the main gripe from the state governments was that they did not want their police to be bound by the same standards as the Commonwealth Federal Police, and in the end it was agreed that each police force would use their own standard, and you will find that reflected in section 105.19 on page 57 of the bill.'

[82] Explanatory Memorandum, Anti-Terrorism Bill (No 2) 2005, 50.

[83] Above n 78.

[84] The concept of 'repeat player' was advanced in a seminal article by M Galanter, 'Why the "Haves" Come Out Ahead: Speculations on the Limits of Social Change' (1974) 9 *Law and Society Review* 95.

are able to characterise both their own behaviour (and that of suspects) so that it conforms to the legal limits of their powers and provides a persuasive legal justification for using force. The accountability deficit relating to the use of force by police means that 'hard law' is seldom tested or developed by the courts. By contrast, this margin of appreciation is less prominent where private individuals rather than police officers make a decision to use force; in such cases, the legality of private action in aid of law enforcement is likely to be carefully scrutinised by police and prosecutors and may be ultimately tested before the courts.

The limits of police power are established by 'hard law' concepts such as reasonable/necessary force and proportionality, as well as the general defences of self-defence, necessity and lawful authority. The law's conception of what constitutes 'reasonable force' in the context of arrest, or other exercises of police power, defers in large measure to the discretion of the individual officer, which will in turn be shaped by police training, policy and procedure. Adherence to 'soft law' governing police use of force (in particular administrative directives and situational tactical options models) may be sufficient to ensure no legal action is taken against police officers. Yet, departures from these norms will not necessarily render that officer's conduct unreasonable or unlawful, as was pointed out by Judge Coate in the Tyler Cassidy inquest.

At present, police officers are rarely prosecuted in relation to use of force incidents in Australia. It will be interesting to see whether the trend toward enhanced citizen 'sousveillance' of police uses of force will change this accountability deficit in the future.

8

When Shooting to Kill is Authorised by the State: A Feminist Analysis

KYLIE WESTON-SCHEUBER[1]

I. INTRODUCTION

MOST CRIMINAL LAW scholarship focuses on the process of trial and its outcome as the pinnacle of the criminal justice process. However, in the last couple of decades a number of commentators have drawn attention to the importance of the process that occurs outside the court-room—decisions made about whether to investigate, the process of evidence gathering, and the exercise of prosecutorial discretion in deciding to proceed with prosecution, or whether to accept a plea-bargain.[2] These 'external' areas of the criminal justice process, despite often lacking a formal process for recording outcomes in the way that courts record their decision-making, operate by their own formal and informal systems of rules and procedures.

Many feminist legal scholars have drawn attention to inequalities within the law in relation to legal defences such as self-defence and provocation, and their unavailability to women who kill their partners following a history of violence against them.[3] These analyses have tended to focus on inequality as it exists once a matter goes to trial—whether defences of self-defence and provocation are available as a question of law, and how a history of domestic violence is treated in sentencing women for murder or manslaughter. Less attention has been paid to the decision-making process

---

[1] The views of the author are her own and are not the views of the Office of the Australian Capital Territory (ACT) Director of Public Prosecutions nor do they in any way inform or reflect the policies of processes of that Office.

[2] D McBarnet, *Conviction: Law, the State and the Construction of Justice* (London, McMillan Press, 1983); M McConville, A Sanders and R Leng, *The Case for the Prosecution* (London, Routledge, 1991); D Dixon, *Law in Policing* (Oxford, Clarendon Press, 1997).

[3] E Sheehy, J Stubbs and J Tolmie, 'Defending Battered Women on Trial: the Battered Woman Syndrome and its Limitations' (1992) 16 *Criminal Law Journal* 369; J Tolmie, 'Provocation or Self-Defence for Battered Women who Kill?' in S Yeo, *Partial Excuses to Murder* (Sydney, Federation Press, 1991) 61–82.

that occurs prior to a matter coming to court—namely the decision to charge and proceed with prosecution in the first place.

In this chapter, I seek to further the scholarship in relation to self-defence and its application to women who kill their abusers by critiquing the decision-making that determines whether a matter proceeds to court or not. In doing so, I draw upon Adrian Howe's feminist critique of Foucault's work and examine the role that discourse plays in constructing truth, especially the truth as it relates to women.[4]

Utilising Howe's methodology, I compare the decisions that are made about women who kill following a history of violence with the law's treatment of police officers who shoot to kill in self-defence or in the execution of duty. In choosing police shootings as a point of comparison, I acknowledge that it may also be useful to compare other types of self-defence killing (such as in response to an unprovoked attack in a bar). However, I use police shootings as a point of comparison with self-defence killings in the context of a history of abuse because each represents a 'category' of killing within which certain patterns of behaviour can be identified. Thus these two 'types' of killing usefully illustrate the ways in which discursive patterns within a particular 'category' of case reflect power relations at work.

In the first section of this chapter, I examine the differential treatment in the Australian justice system of women who kill in self-defence in the context of a history of domestic violence,[5] and police officers who take lethal action when confronted with a dangerous attack. In the case of abused women who kill in circumstances suggestive of self-defence, the usual course of events is that a prosecution is commenced, and the accused may raise self-defence or the partial defence of provocation before the court.[6] On the other hand, where police have used lethal force in defence of themselves or others, or to effect arrest, it is uncommon for any prosecution to take place. Thus two different categories of lethal action taken in self-defence follow two different paths through the criminal justice process.

In the second section, I examine the processes by which legal discourse constructs the key players in these self-defence scenarios in ways that reflect

---

[4] A Howe, *Sex, Violence and Crime: Foucault and the 'Man' Question* (New York, Routledge-Cavendish, 2008).

[5] In Australia there is no single accepted definition of 'domestic violence'. However, a recent Australian Government report notes that domestic violence is abuse of a person (usually a woman) by her intimate partner, and involves an ongoing pattern of behaviour aimed at controlling her through fear, and may include economic, social, verbal, psychological and sexual abuse: Australian Government, *Time for Action: The National Council's Plan for Australia to Reduce Violence Against Women and Children, 2009–2021*, The National Council to Reduce Violence against Women and their Children (March 2009) 186.

[6] Although I acknowledge that the term 'abused woman' is problematic, I use it in preference to the term 'battered woman' because of the connotations involving 'battered woman syndrome' which are also problematic, as discussed below.

common assumptions about both law enforcement and women. Reliance on these common assumptions both provides legitimacy for, and perpetuates, the criminal justice system's differential treatment of violence. Delving into these processes reveals the way in which battered women who kill in self-defence are constructed as criminals, while the police officer who shoots in self-defence is constructed as having acted with justification.

I describe my analysis as 'feminist' because it focuses on women's treatment qua women, and because it draws attention to the role that gendered assumptions play in decisions made within and outside the criminal justice process.[7]

II. THE DIFFERENTIAL TREATMENT OF SELF-DEFENCE RESPONSES

Australian law, and the English common law in which it has its roots, have long recognised a defence for those who kill while defending themselves or others.[8] At common law, self-defence incorporates both subjective and objective components: the person acting in self-defence must have believed their conduct to be necessary in defence of themselves or another (subjective), and there must have been a reasonable basis for that belief (objective).[9] The laws of all Australian states and territories, while not homogenous, incorporate some combination of these elements.[10]

Prior to arriving at the stage where a matter comes before a court and the law of self-defence potentially comes into play, various important decisions, both formal and informal, are made that determine whether or not the matter will ever proceed through the legal system. These decisions are part of a process whereby cases are 'constructed' through the collection of evidence and determinations about what to charge. Cases that are not to proceed in this way are effectively excluded.[11]

---

[7] Generally see K Bartlett, 'Feminist Legal Methods' (1990) 103 *Harvard Law Review* 829.

[8] For an examination of the law of self-defence in the Australian context, see S Bronitt and B McSherry, *Principles of Criminal Law*, 3rd edn (Pyrmont, Lawbook Company, 2010) ch 6.

[9] *Zecevic v DPP (Vic)* (1987) 162 CLR 645.

[10] Bronitt and McSherry, above n 8, 334–37. Victoria adopts the common law test set out in *Zecevic* for offences other than homicide. In the ACT, NSW and NT and at Commonwealth level, the accused must have believed that the force was necessary, while in Queensland force must be reasonably necessary, or necessary in addition to the requirement of a belief in the necessity of force. In South Australia, the accused must genuinely believe the force to be necessary and reasonable, and the conduct must be reasonably proportionate to the threat in the circumstances as the accused believed them to be. For self-defence provisions see Criminal Code Act 1995 (Cth) s 10.4; Criminal Code Act 2002 (ACT) s 42; Crimes Act 1900 (NSW) s 418; Criminal Code Act 1983 (NT) ss 29, 43BD; Criminal Code Act 1899 (Qld) s 271; Criminal Law Consolidation Act 1935 (SA) s 15; Criminal Code Act 1924 (Tas) s 46; Crimes Act 1958 (Vic) ss 9AC, 9AD, 9AE (for homicide offences); Criminal Code Act Compilation Act 1913 (WA) s 248.

[11] McConville, Sanders and Leng, above n 2.

Criminal charges are usually laid by police officers, after which an independent determination is made by the relevant Director of Public Prosecutions (DPP) to carry on or discontinue prosecution.[12] However, prior to the DPP's consideration of a matter, it is usually referred by an investigating agency (usually police), as DPPs do not carry out investigations themselves. Certain types of killing, including deaths occurring in police custody, are subject to coronial inquest.[13] If the coroner forms the view that there is a prima facie case of an indictable offence causing death, he or she usually refers the matter to the relevant DPP.[14] In some states and territories, the coroner is also entitled to make a finding that a shooting was justified.[15] Police shootings, therefore, will be kept out of the criminal justice system unless a coroner rules that the shooting is unjustified or finds that there is evidence that an indictable offence has been committed.

It is impossible to analyse what proportion of women who kill in the context of a history of abuse are ultimately prosecuted. There is little publicly available data recording crimes that are not investigated, or that are investigated, but do not proceed to prosecution.[16] Killings by civilians, whether in self-defence or not, are rarely the subject of coronial inquiry (unless the person responsible for the homicide goes on to kill themselves).[17] However, what I have endeavoured to do in the following section is to interrogate the recorded facts of those matters that *have* proceeded to

---

[12] See the various state and territory prosecution policies, available at: www.dpp.act.gov.au/policy.htm (ACT); www.odpp.nsw.gov.au/Guidelines/Guidelines.html (NSW); www.nt.gov.au/justice/dpp/html/guidelines.html (Northern Territory); www.justice.qld.gov.au/files/CourtsAndTribunals/Directors_Prosecution_Guidelines.pdf (Queensland); www.dpp.sa.gov.au/03/ppg.php?s=03 (South Australia); www.crownlaw.tas.gov.au/dpp/prosecution_guidelines (Tasmania); www.opp.vic.gov.au/ (Victoria); www.dpp.wa.gov.au/content/statement_prosecution_policy2005.pdf (Western Australia).

[13] Coroners Act 1997 (ACT) s 13(1)(k); Coroners Act 1980 (NSW) ss 13A and 14B; Coroners Act 1993 (NT) s 15(1)(a); Coroners Act 2003 (Qld), ss 8, 10, 11(2); Coroners Act 2003 (SA) s 21; Coroners Act 1995 (Tas) ss 3 and 21; Coroners Act 1985 (Vic) ss 3 and 15(2); Coroners Act 1996 (WA) ss 3 and 19.

[14] Coroners Act 1997 (ACT) s 58; Coroners Act 1980 (NSW) s 19; Coroners Act 1993 (NT) s 35; Coroners Act 2003 (Qld) s 48(2)(a); Coroners Act 1995 (Tas) s 30; Coroners Act 1985 (Vic) s 21; Coroners Act 1996 (WA) s 27.

[15] State Coroner's Office (NSW Attorney General's Department) (2006), *Report by the NSW State Coroner into Deaths in Custody/Police Operations*, 88. cf the coroner's role in Victoria: *Khan v Keown & West* [2001] VSCA 137 (Unreported, Ormiston, Phillips and Batt JJA, 6 September 2001) per Phillips JA at [15] suggesting that it is beyond the scope of the coroner's role to determine whether killing is 'justified'. This is also the position in SA: *Geoffrey Nicholls* (Unreported, SA Coroner's Office, 29 October 2003).

[16] In *R v Metropolitan Police Commissioner; ex parte Blackburn* [1968] 2 QB 118, it was accepted that police officers possess a wide discretion in exercising their duties, which will not ordinarily be reviewable. The discretion was affirmed in *Hinchliffe v Commissioner of Police of the AFP*, unreported, V78/2000, 2 May 2001, 10 December 2001 (Federal Court).

[17] *Sonya Mercer and Darren Batchelor* (2004) TASCD 57 (12 February 2004); *Michelle Morcom and Jamie Venn* (2004) TASCD 55 (12 February 2004); *Andrea Wrathall and Stephen Pugh* (2007) TASCD 360 (2 November 2007); cf *Jodie Palipuaminni* [2006] NTMC 083 (23 October 2006) and *Anne Chantel Millar* [2005] NTMC 056 (2 September 2005).

prosecution, and compare the facts in those matters with those outlined in coronial decisions relating to police shootings. By identifying similar features between the two types of cases, I am then able to explore the way in which differential constructions of the 'facts' of these cases serve to justify the different outcomes.

A. Shoot to Kill in the Law Enforcement Context

Australia has a significant history of police shootings executed in the line of duty. Prosecutions of police for any crime (even fatal shootings) are rare,[18] and those that have proceeded have been largely unsuccessful.[19] A similar pattern has been observed in the United Kingdom.[20] This is consistent with the historical common law principle that a police officer who killed an escaping thief, or an outlaw resisting arrest, could rely on a legal justification for doing so and would not be prosecuted.[21]

Since 1990 the Australian Institute of Criminology has collected data relating to deaths in 'police custody', which include shootings during incidents in which police are involved and particularly shootings by police 'in self-defence' when they are attacked following a call-out to an incident.[22] Between 1990 and 2006, 82 people were shot and killed by police in Australia, varying between two and six each year after a peak in 1994. Ninety per cent of fatal police shootings for this period were classified as 'justifiable homicide', with one shooting in 2000 categorised as unlawful homicide and one in 2002 as accidental homicide.[23] 'Justifiable homicide'

---

[18] I Freckelton, 'Legal Regulation of the Police Culture of Violence: Rhetoric, Remedies and Redress' in T Coady, S James, S Miller and M O'Keefe (eds), *Violence and Police Culture* (Melbourne, Melbourne University Press, 2000) 140–81, 148–49. Cases of police prosecutions I discovered in my research included *Bedek v Brown* [2000] FCA 880 (Unreported, Gallop, Whitlam and Madgwick JJ, 26 July 2000) (defendant acquitted on direction of judge of attempted murder and attempted infliction of grievous bodily harm); *Hill v Richman* [2001] TASSC 148 (Unreported, Evans J, 20 December 2001) (appeal by officer allowed against convictions on assault); *Lukatela v Birch* [2008] ACTSC 99 (Unreported, Rares J, 30 September 2008) (officer pleaded guilty to unlawfully administering injurious substance).

[19] N O'Loughlin and P Billing, 'Positive Police Culture: Correcting Perceptions' in Coady, James, Miller and O'Keefe), ibid 63–84, 75–76; B Bongiorno, 'A DPP's Approach: Some Problems in the Prosecution of Police Officers' in D Moore and R Wetternall (eds), *Keeping the Peace: Police Accountability and Oversight* (Canberra, University of Canberra, 1994).

[20] J McCulloch and V Sentas, 'The Killing of Jean Charles de Menezes: Hyper-Militarism in the Neoliberal Economic Free Fire Zone' (2006) 33(4) *Social Justice* 92–106, 95.

[21] J Horder, *Provocation and Responsibility* (Oxford, Clarendon Press, 1992) 6–7.

[22] V Dalton, 'Police Shootings 1990–1997' *Trends and Issues in Criminal Justice*, No 89 (Australian Institute of Criminology, June 1998) 2.

[23] J Joudo and J Curnow, *Deaths in Custody in Australia: National Deaths in Custody Program Annual Report 2006* (Australian Institute of Criminology, Research and Public Policy Series No 85, 2008) 77–81. Six shootings were classified as 'other'. Although p 103 of the Report indicates that the unlawful homicide by police shooting occurred in NSW, it does not appear in the NSW State Coroner's Report for any of the years for which reports are publicly available.

is defined as a homicide occurring under circumstances authorised by law, for example a prison officer acting in self-defence.[24] Since a referral to the relevant prosecuting agency does not follow a finding that shooting was justified, it appears that nobody was prosecuted in relation to these 'justifiable homicides'.

B. Responding to Battered Women who Use Lethal Force

In contrast to the treatment of police who kill in the execution of duty, traditionally, the law has not looked favourably upon women who kill their abusers.[25] Until the late nineteenth century, the law provided that a woman was the property of her husband, and her legal identity upon marriage became subsumed within his.[26] Women who killed their husbands were not considered responsible simply for murder but for petit treason; killing the master was a crime secondary only to killing the king and was punishable by burning at the stake.[27] Neither self-defence nor provocation was available to those charged with petit treason.[28]

After 1828 when petit treason was abolished in the United Kingdom and the applicable charge changed to murder,[29] provocation continued to be inaccessible because the circumstances of women's actions frequently did not fit within the paradigm conduct for 'sudden loss of self-control', the requirement of a 'sudden response' or proportionality between the perceived threat and the force used in response.[30]

Feminist agitation eventually produced some recognition of the gendered nature of provocation.[31] However, a more significant problem, as feminists have frequently pointed out, is that many women who kill violent abusers should be able to rely on self-defence, rather than the partial defence of

---

[24] Ibid 25.

[25] See Sheehy et al, above n 3.

[26] RB Siegel, '"The Rule of Love": Wife Beating as Prerogative and Privacy' (1995) 105 *Yale Law Journal* 2117, 2122.

[27] J Greene, 'A Provocation Defence for Battered Women who Kill?' (1989) 12 *Adelaide Law Review* 145. In the US context see E Schneider, *Battered Women and Feminist Lawmaking* (New Haven, Yale University Press, 2000) 112–15. See the case of Elizabeth Herring, 8 September 1773, The Proceedings of the Old Bailey Ref: t17730908-6.

[28] P Alldridge, *Relocating Criminal Law* (Aldershot, Ashgate/Dartmouth, 2000) 91.

[29] Ibid.

[30] Greene, above n 27; S de Pasquale 'Provocation and the Homosexual Advance Defence: The Deployment of Culture as a Defence Strategy' (2002) 26 *Melbourne University Law Review* 110, 122–23; N Cheyne and S Dennison, 'An Examination of a Potential Reform to the Provocation Defence: The Impact of Gender of the Defendant and the Suddenness Requirement' (2005) 12(2) *Psychiatry, Psychology and the Law* 388–400; Bronitt and McSherry, above n 8, 314–15.

[31] *R v Chhay* (1994) 72 A Crim R 1 per Gleeson CJ at 11.

provocation.[32] Despite some positive developments,[33] the requirements of self-defence, like the requirements of provocation, are plagued by patriarchal meanings and a lack of understanding of women's experiences.[34]

One of the traditional requirements of self-defence (as for provocation) was the immediacy of the threat to which the accused was responding.[35] This had the effect of making it difficult for women to rely on self-defence where there was a lapse of time, even short, between the making of the threat or the assault and the response.[36] Other requirements that females accused of murder have had difficulty in meeting include the exhaustion of all avenues of peaceful resolution (including a duty to retreat); the necessity and proportionality requirements, and the stipulation that an accused's perception of danger of death or grievous bodily harm be reasonable.[37]

Despite the existence of some isolated examples of decisions not to prosecute,[38] as noted above, it is not possible to say what proportion of cases where women kill their abusers ultimately proceed to prosecution. However, it is possible to identify cases that have proceeded to prosecution despite circumstances strongly indicative that the woman was acting in self-defence. In a comprehensive study of spousal homicide cases between 1980 and 2000, Rebecca Bradfield noted that women who killed abusive

[32] See, eg, Sheehy et al, above n 3; J Tolmie, above n 3; G Coss, 'Provocative Reforms: A Comparative critique' (2006) 30(3) *Criminal Law Journal* 138.

[33] Eg, in *Secretary* (1996) 107 NTR 1, the Court of Appeal of the Northern Territory found (by majority) that a man who inflicted violence before going to sleep and threatened to inflict further violence when he woke up had an 'actual and apparent present ability to carry out the threat'; his violence constituted a 'continuing assault' on the accused.

[34] See Sheehy et al, above n 3; E Schneider, above n 27, 116. For examples of cases where the accused was convicted of manslaughter on the basis of provocation in circumstances suggestive of self-defence see *R v Hill* (1981) 3 A Crim R 397; *Bogunovich* (1985) 16 A Crim R 456; *R v Collingburn* (1985) 18 A Crim R 294; *Bradley* (Unreported, VSC, Coldrey J, 14 December 1994); *R v Kennedy* [2000] NSWSC 109 (Unreported, Barr J, 1 March 2000).

[35] See *R v Collingburn* (1985) 18 A Crim R 294, where a direction that an 'immediate threat' was required rather than 'imminent danger' was held not to be a misdirection. Imminence is no longer a technical requirement of self-defence following *Zecevic* (1987) 162 CLR 645.

[36] J Stubbs and J Tolmie, 'Battered woman syndrome in Australia: a challenge to gender bias in the law?' in J Stubbs (ed), *Women, Male Violence and the Law* (Sydney, Australia Institute of Criminology, 1994) 195–96. Stubbs and Tolmie outline cases in which self-defence was accepted in respect of pre-emptive defensive actions: see J Stubbs and J Tolmie, 'Falling Short of the Challenge? A Comparative Assessment of the Australian use of Expert Evidence on the Battered Woman Syndrome' (1999) 23 *Melbourne University Law Review* 709, 733–36.

[37] Sheehy, Stubbs and Tolmie, above n 3; Western Australian Law Reform Commission (WALRC), *Review of the Law of Homicide: Final Report* (2007) 292–95.

[38] Two examples are cited in K Polk, *When Men Kill: Scenarios of Masculine Violence* (Cambridge, Cambridge University Press, 1994) 161. The case of Sherrie Lee Seakins is reported in G Alcorn, 'No Trial after Woman Kills Violent Husband', *The Sydney Morning Herald*, 14 September 1993, 1 (cited in Stubbs and Tolmie, 'Falling Short', above n 36, 720). At least one barrister has suggested that prosecutors have traditionally felt that they must prosecute such matters: S Ross, 'Battered wife syndrome and the role of lawyers' (1998) 72(11) *Law Institute Journal* 39–40.

husbands were often convicted of manslaughter on the basis of provocation or lack of intention to kill or cause grievous bodily harm, in circumstances suggesting that they were acting in self-defence (and therefore should arguably have been entitled to a full acquittal).[39] In 65 out of 76 cases studied where women killed their male partners, there was a history of abuse by the 'victim' against the accused.[40] Women relied on self-defence in only one-third of these cases and more than 70 per cent of women who had suffered a history of abuse were convicted of manslaughter.[41]

Although these women were often given lenient sentences, Bradfield's analysis suggested that this occurred generally as a result of compassion or sympathy exercised as an aspect of 'mercy' meted out by the sentencing judge, rather than a recognition of the real danger faced by the accused and the legitimacy of their responses.[42] In those manslaughter cases where a non-custodial sentence was imposed, the extreme violence was generally de-emphasised in sentencing reasons in preference for a focus on the pathology of the accused.[43]

I examined cases reported between 2000 and 2008 in which women were sentenced for manslaughter or murder for the killing of their partners which involved a history of violence committed by the deceased against the accused.[44] In four of 17 reported cases, it was apparent on the face of the sentencing judgment that the accused had a strong self-defence argument available to her. These four cases were *Denney*,[45] *Gazdovic*,[46] *Melrose*[47] and *Russell*.[48] In *Denney* the offender was convicted of manslaughter at trial after the Crown rejected an earlier plea of guilty to manslaughter. In the other three cases, the accused pleaded guilty to manslaughter.

In *Denney*,[49] the offender killed her husband following a lengthy history of physical, financial and emotional abuse. On the day of the killing, she had been raped by the deceased just prior to the killing and killed him in fear for her life. She hid the body and evaded detection for 10 years. She was sentenced to three years' imprisonment fully suspended.

---

[39] R Bradfield, 'The Treatment of Women who Kill their Violent Partners within the Australian Criminal Justice System' (PhD Thesis, University of Tasmania, July 2002) 124–29.

[40] Ibid 22.

[41] Ibid 195–96; see also WALRC, above n 37, 271.

[42] Bradfield, above n 39, 337–44.

[43] Ibid 365–70.

[44] I searched for cases through Casebase using the search terms ['domestic violence' and manslaughter]; ['domestic violence' and murder] and ['battered woman syndrome']. I also reviewed relevant cases that were included on Lexis Nexis weekly updates and all relevant cases reported on the NSW Public Defenders' website. The search was restricted to cases from 2000 onwards, as Bradfield's research covered cases between 1980 and 2000.

[45] *R v Denney* [2000] VSC 323 (Unreported, Coldrey J, 4 August 2000).

[46] *R v Gazdovic* [2002] VSC 588 (Unreported, Teague J, 20 December 2002).

[47] *R v Melrose* [2001] NSWSC 847 (Unreported, McClellan J, 31 August 2001).

[48] *R v Russell* [2006] NSWSC 722 (Unreported, Newman AJ, 21 July 2006).

[49] *R v Denney* [2000] VSC 323 (Unreported, Coldrey J, 4 August 2000).

In *Gazdovic*,[50] after a lengthy history of physical and emotional abuse, the offender killed her husband immediately after he had threatened to kill her and had picked up an axe that he kept in the house. Justice Teague noted that the offender had only 'marginally failed to judge to a nicety' when to cease her actions in self-defence and noted, 'I cannot think of a homicide case where the level of moral culpability could be rated as low as here.'[51] The Crown did not ask for a custodial sentence and Gazdovic was sentenced to a two-year good behaviour bond.

In *Melrose*,[52] the Crown accepted a plea of guilty to manslaughter on the basis of an unlawful and dangerous act. There was a long history of physical abuse and of the deceased following the offender when she attempted to leave the relationship. On the evening in question, the deceased and the offender had gone out and the deceased had physically attacked the offender, who went home and armed herself with a knife. When the deceased returned home and physically and verbally abused her, she stabbed him once, fatally, in the shoulder. Melrose was sentenced to a good behaviour order for four years with conditions in relation to psychiatric treatment.

In *Russell*,[53] Cherie Russell was sentenced to a head sentence of six years with a non-parole period of three years for the manslaughter of her partner Jeffrey Cook. She was originally charged with murder. Russell and Cook had been in a de facto relationship characterised by violence, especially when Cook was drunk. On 18 May 2005, an argument broke out while the two were drinking. The evidence was that Cook hit Russell once and then threatened to 'kill her stone dead'. She picked up a knife and he challenged her to stab him, which she did. He died of blood loss.

Russell had had a car accident in 2001 which had left her with brain damage. She had a very low IQ and poor memory skills. There was a history of violence against her, with the police attending on a number of occasions in 2004, as well as violence against her by previous partners. There was also a history of serious violence by Cook against former partners and he was noted by the police as a 'high risk' domestic violence offender.

My aim in examining these cases is not to question whether or not the facts as presented in coronial or court decisions reflect the 'truth'. Foucault's work exposed the fallacy of relying on any concept of truth independent of the discursive context in which knowledge is constructed.[54] Rather I examine the different ways in which truth is constructed in these two categories of cases. In doing so, I argue that whether or not a person is prosecuted

---

[50] *R v Gazdovic* [2002] VSC 588 (Unreported, Teague J, 20 December 2002).
[51] Ibid [9].
[52] *R v Melrose* [2001] NSWSC 847 (Unreported, McClellan J, 31 August 2001).
[53] *R v Russell* [2006] NSWSC 722 (Unreported, Newman AJ, 21 July 2006).
[54] Howe, above n 4, 99–103.

is based on the differential construction of 'the facts', which draws upon common understandings and assumptions about particular types of violence and the people who use violence. These discursive mechanisms both reflect and perpetuate structural and procedural differences in the way that different types of killings are treated.

III. HOW SELF-DEFENCE RESPONSES ARE CONSTRUCTED WITHIN LEGAL PROCESSES

A key strategy utilised by Howe, following on from Foucault, is the exercise of attempting to separate the processes of knowledge construction from the hegemonic forces that control their operation; this is done not by seeking the 'truth' (which is impossible to find) but by problematising commonly-accepted truths.[55] I am not attempting to describe the 'real facts' in the types of violence I consider in this chapter, but to conceptualise the violence in terms of 'linguistic facts'—that is, as violence that is produced within a context of cultural productions and references.[56] I have attempted to follow Howe's example by calling into question the characterisation of killings as 'justified' or 'unjustified' within the legal context and critically examining the processes by which these characterisations are arrived at.

Within the sources outlined above, I identified general trends or patterns in the treatment of different self-defence responses within the Australian legal system. These differences reflect the different structural processes through which particular homicides are constructed as justified or not justified. When police kill, their actions are constructed within the system as 'justified' while abused women who kill are generally prosecuted, constructing their actions as (at least potentially) criminal.

Foucault argued that discourse both reflects and creates relationships of power.[57] In this way, I suggest first that differential constructions of the facts in these two types of cases *reflect* structural and procedural differences in how these cases are treated. In a coronial inquest, the purpose of the coroner's findings is to explain why the actions of the police officer responsible for the death of the victim were justifiable so that there is an explanation for why the 'usual' process of criminal prosecution for a person identified as having killed another human being is not followed. By contrast, when a judge provides reasons for the sentence in relation to a woman who kills her abuser, the criminal justice process has already been engaged and is

---

[55] Ibid 27–32.

[56] S Marcus, 'Fighting Bodies, Fighting Words' in J Butler and J Scott (eds), *Feminists Theorise the Political* (New York, Routledge, 2002) 385–403, discussed in Howe, above n 4, 171–75.

[57] Howe, above n 4, 27–32.

drawing to its logical conclusion—that of measuring the seriousness of the offence that has already been proved either by way of a jury verdict or a guilty plea. Thus the differential truth constructions reflect these different procedural avenues for dealing with certain types of killing, but at the same time they support and reinforce the process by providing a justification for the differential treatment. If police officers are usually justified in killing suspects, then it is right that they not be exposed to criminal prosecution. Conversely, if abused women are constructed as acting vengefully rather than in self-defence, it is only fair that they be subjected to criminal justice.

Reg Graycar and Rosemary Hunter have written about the common understandings and assumptions that operate concerning women and domestic violence in the legal system.[58] Just as judicial decision-making reflects judges' 'knowledge' about people's (and in particular women's) lives, decisions made outside the judicial system (eg the decision to prosecute) also reflect knowledge of 'ordinary human experience' that does not necessarily represent the experiences of women.[59] Common understandings about domestic violence include that it is a product of 'relationship conflict'; that violence can be stopped by separation; that women are (at least partly) responsible for violence against them; and that both parties are responsible for domestic violence.[60] These common understandings bear upon decisions that are made about whether or not a woman who kills her abusive partner should be prosecuted.

By contrast, police officers benefit from a perception that any lethal force they use must have been justified, due to the danger they face in their ordinary duties.[61] The state has a monopoly on the use of legitimate force,[62] and as the agents of the state, police carry the mark of state legitimacy in respect of their actions, regardless of the motivations of the individual officers involved.[63] This common conception of the police officer as protector of the community is reflected in the construction of the police officer as 'simply doing her or his job' in the coronial process.

---

[58] R Graycar, 'The Gender of Judgments: an Introduction in M Thornton (ed), *Public and Private: Feminist Legal Debates* (Melbourne, Oxford University Press, 1995) 262–82; R Hunter, 'Narratives of Domestic Violence' (2006) 28(4) *Sydney Law Review* 733.

[59] K Mack and S Roach Anleu, 'Resolution without Trial, Evidence Law and the Construction of the Sexual Assault Victim' in M Childs and L Ellison, *Feminist Perspectives on Evidence* (London, Cavendish Publishing, 2000) 127–48.

[60] Hunter, above n 58.

[61] AJ Goldsmith, 'An Impotent Conceit: Law, Culture and the Regulation of Police Violence' in T Coady, S James, S Miller and M O'Keefe, above n 18, 109–39, especially 109–14, 125–27.

[62] G Fletcher, *Rethinking Criminal Law* (Boston, Little, Brown and Company, 1978), 867–68. For monopolisation of the use of legitimate force as a criterion for statehood see M Weber, *The Theory of Social and Economic Organisation*, trans Talcott Parsons (Glencoe, Illinois, The Free Press, 1947) 156.

[63] Fletcher notes that historically—within the common law—justifications were linked with governmental conduct: see ibid 773–75.

To understand how these common assumptions operate in practice, I examine three common aspects of the two categories of cases. The coronial and sentencing decisions examined illustrate how these factors are treated in different ways depending on the category of case, and operate to construct the killing as justified or not, depending on the category it falls within. Broadly, these factors are as follows:

— Legal discourse differentially constructs the 'danger' that those who kill in self-defence are responding to: while police who shoot in self-defence are described as facing a 'real threat', the threat posed by abusers to the women who kill them is minimised or ignored;
— Police are generally constructed as 'witnesses of truth' while a woman's credibility as a witness is influenced by stereotypes of women as untruthful and by the degree to which the accused conforms to the image of the 'ideal victim'; and
— The availability of other options for women who kill provides an outlet for explaining why their conduct was not justified, while for police who kill, the availability of alternatives to lethal shooting does not preclude their conduct being presented as justified.

A. The Existence of a 'Real Threat'

The way in which the danger faced by the person who acts with lethal violence is constructed is integral to whether or not her or his actions will ultimately be characterised as justified. In the police shooting cases, time after time coroners paint a picture of police acting under pressure and in difficult circumstances, attempting to manage threats posed by dangerous, and sometimes irrational, persons to their own and the public's safety. On the other hand, in the 'battered women' cases, there is frequently little attempt to explore the challenges and dangers of the abusive relationship for the woman, and a downplaying of the threat to personal safety often involved in such relationships.

In all but one of the coronial cases examined, the coroner made reference either to the nature of the threat faced by police or to the fact that the shooting was justified in the circumstances.[64] In three cases, coroners made reference to it being 'unfair' to judge the police officer's actions without

---

[64] Eg, a 'difficult and terrifying situation' and 'difficult and dangerous situation' (*Thomas Waite, Mieng Huynh, James Jacobs, James Gear* (Qld Coroners' Court, 17 March 2008)). The exception was the Northern Territory case *Robert Jongman* [2007] NTMC 080 (Unreported, 3 December 2007), discussed in more detail below. For an interesting example of two very different judicial constructions of police conduct as 'justified' or 'not justified' see *Khan v West* (2002) 131 A Crim R 111 and *Khan v West* (Unreported, VSC, Hampel J, 11 September 1997).

consideration of the threat faced, or stated that 'no fair-minded person' could deny that the officer was acting in self-defence.[65] The recourse to concepts of fairness is a discursive mechanism that has the effect of placing the issue of self-defence beyond any challenge or dispute.

The requirement of self-defence that there be 'reasonable grounds' for a belief that defensive force is necessary suggests that the belief of the person who kills in self-defence must be rooted in the objectively discernible circumstances surrounding the act. However, despite the fact that there was no firearm possessed by the victim in 23 police shootings in Victoria between 1981 and May 1998, and no weapon at all in five of them,[66] no police were prosecuted in relation to these shootings.[67] It appears that the urgency of situations faced by police is sufficient to ground an objective belief in the necessity of use of force even in circumstances where no serious danger exists in reality.

There can be little doubt that the tension and fear felt by those who are faced with a perceived threat to their personal safety is real, nor that a response often needs to be taken quickly and with little time for reflection. A district inspector in the Victorian Police with 25 years' experience interviewed during research carried out in the 1990s stated:[68]

> It's adrenalin and I can tell you now having been involved in a number of shooting inquiries that it's amazing that if one person lets a gun off, everyone will let a gun off. And if you ask them later about how many shots they've fired and they'll say two. And the gun will be empty and they just have no idea in that adrenalin situation. And unless you've been in that situation ... that is an incredible situation to be in. When you experience that situation it is very easy to clinically say that they must have consciously thought about it and hit.

In relation to the shooting of Jean Charles de Menezes at Stockwell Tube Station in London in July 2005, the authors of the Independent Police Commission report into the shooting emphasised the need to take into account the logistical difficulties involved:

> Any assessment of the strategy adopted, how it was applied that morning and how individuals performed and reacted must be measured against the background. There is always a danger of assessing judgements with the benefit of

---

[65] State Coroner's Office (NSW Attorney General's Department) (2005) (shooting by CS); *Daniel Cory Rhodes* (Qld Coroners' Court, 24 March 2006); *Malcolm Bell* (Qld Coroners' Court, 26 May 2006).

[66] J McCulloch, *Blue Army: Paramilitary Policing in Australia* (Melbourne, Melbourne University Press, 2000) 103.

[67] The only prosecutions of police in Victoria for shootings during this period were against those responsible for the shootings of Graeme Jensen and Gary Abdullah: J McCulloch, Personal Communication (on file with author), 10 August 2009. In both cases the victim was alleged to have pointed a firearm at police prior to being shot.

[68] I Warren and S James, 'The Police Use of Force: Context and Constraints' in T Coady, S James, S Miller and M O'Keefe, above n 18, 32–62, 57.

hindsight and with the precious luxury of time for a measured consideration of possible options. That the Metropolitan Police force was facing operational problems never before encountered is plain and the constant pressures placed on individuals, over a period of more than two weeks, has been recognised.[69]

Yet in cases involving women who kill their abusive partners, the process by which cases are constructed in court often makes it difficult for the accused to present the 'tensions' involved in an abusive relationship in a meaningful way. Although a history of abuse is relevant and admissible,[70] the way the Crown constructs its case and the rules of evidence mean that abusive relationships are often broken down into a series of discrete incidents, depriving them of their meaning.[71] As investigatorial and prosecutorial decision-making is made with the ultimate end of a criminal prosecution in mind, it is inevitable that these same constructive mechanisms also come into play at the pre-prosecution stage.

In each of the four domestic homicide cases outlined above, the facts were constructed in such a way as to minimise the danger to the accused, cast doubt upon her version of events, or balance the harm caused by the 'victim' by mention of his 'redeeming qualities'. For example, in *Denney*, where the accused shot her husband who had assaulted and raped her, threatened to kill her and prevented her from seeing friends and family, Coldrey J stated:[72]

> It should not be concluded from what I say that John Denney lacked any redeeming features. The evidence before the court is of a hard worker, a man who generally got on well with his work mates and a father who related well to his children. Indeed, somewhat paradoxically, you told the investigating police that you loved John, but you did not like the things that he did.

In other words, John Denney's actions may not always have been meritorious, but that did not make him a person who deserved to die.

Another discursive tool sometimes used to minimise the threat of harm faced by women in situations of domestic violence is to describe the situation as one of 'matrimonial discord' or 'domestic discord'.[73] In this way, what might otherwise be described as real and tangible harm justifying a

---

[69] Independent Police Complaints Commission (IPCC) (2007) *Stockwell One: Investigation into the Shooting of Jean Charles de Menezes at Stockwell Underground Station on 22 July 2005*, Independent Police Complaints Commission [20.2].

[70] *Zecevic v DPP (Vic)* (1987) 162 CLR 645, 662, 663, 672, 673. See also *R v Besim (no. 1)* [2004] VSC 168 (Unreported, Redlich J, 17 February 2004) where evidence of abuse by the victim against his previous partner was admitted in relation to the self-defence argument by the female accused.

[71] Bradfield, above n 39, 253–63.

[72] *R v Denney* [2000] VSC 323 (Unreported, Coldrey J, 4 August 2000) [16].

[73] *R v Bogunovich* (1985) 16 A Crim R 456; *Whalen* (Unreported, NSWCCA, Lee J, 5 April 1991); *R v Vandersee* [2000] NSWSC 916 (Unreported, James J, 18 September 2000); *R v Melrose* [2001] NSWSC 847 (Unreported, McClellan J, 31 August 2001); *R v Russell* [2006] NSWSC 722 (Unreported, Newman AJ, 21 July 2006); *R v Gojanovic (No 2)* [2007] VSCA 153 (Unreported, Ashley and Kellam JJA and Kaye AJA, 14 August 2007).

self-defence response is repackaged as the significantly less harmful 'domestic discord', the result of which is that a lethal response is interpreted as excessive or disproportionate.

B. The Construction of the 'Victim'

Integral to the construction of cases in coronial and criminal courts is the identity of the 'narrator'—the person who claims to have been the 'victim' of an attack and to have responded in self-defence. While it appears that police witnesses are generally accepted in coronial inquests as witnesses of truth, the same cannot be said for women who kill their abusers. Despite research demonstrating that many police are prepared to lie to protect their colleagues,[74] police were generally accepted as witnesses of truth in the coronial cases examined, even in circumstances where their version of events was inconsistent with other evidence.[75]

When it comes to women claiming self-defence, the law has traditionally been reluctant to rely on the uncorroborated testimony of a single woman,[76] based on the cherished male assumption that women have a tendency to lie.[77] More than 20 years ago, an NSW Parliamentarian made the following remark:

> Judges have commonly warned juries against the dangers of conviction of rape on the uncorroborated evidence of a woman. That there might be a rule of law

---

[74] McCulloch, above n 66, 21–22; Goldsmith, above n 61, 121–23. The Stockwell One report found that, although none of the 17 civilian witnesses heard police shout 'Police' prior to the shooting of de Menezes, all eight police reported either shouting it or hearing it shouted: IPCC, above n 69, [13.2].

[75] The de Menezes case is an example: *Death of Jean-Charles de Menezes: Ruling by Coroner as to what verdicts available to the jury,* 24 November 2008 and supplementary ruling 8 December 2008, Transcript of jury verdict, 12 December 2008, stockwellinquest. org.uk/hearing_transcripts/index.htm (viewed 13 December 2008 but note: site no longer available as at 12 November 2011). A jury handed down an 'open verdict' (the only verdict available to them apart from lawful killing) and found (unanimously) that the operative had not shouted 'Armed police' and de Menezes had not advanced on the operative as per police evidence. Coronial cases where police evidence was accepted despite inconsistency with other evidence are the Victorian case of *Whyte (Gary Whyte,* Record of Investigation into Death (Unreported, Victorian Coroner's Court, 21 January 2005)) and the Queensland cases of *Waite* and *Gear (Thomas Waite, Mieng Huynh, James Jacobs, James Gear* (Queensland Coroners' Court, 17 March 2008)).

[76] Until 1981, there was a common law rule requiring the judge to direct the jury about the dangers of acting on the uncorroborated evidence of a sexual assault victim: NSW Government, *Heroines of Fortitude: the experience of women in court as victims of sexual assault* (Department for Women, NSW, 1996) 183.

[77] S Brownmiller, *Against Our Will: Men, Women and Rape* (London, Secker and Warburg, 1975) 369. In an NSW study, 84% of sexual assault complainants were asked questions about whether they were lying or making up the story: Van de Zandt, P, 'Heroines of Fortitude' in P Easteal (ed), *Balancing the Scales: Rape, Law Reform and Australian Culture* (Sydney, Federation Press, 1998) 127–42, 130. See, eg, the well-known comment of Salmond LJ in *R v Manning; R v Henry* (1968) 53 Cr App Rep 150 at 153 that, 'human experience has shown that in these courts girls and women do sometimes tell an entirely false story which is very easy to fabricate ... for all sorts of reasons ... and sometimes for no reason at all.'

or practice to this effect is unacceptable. No doubt members of the police force would be justifiably upset if Parliament were to legislate a warning against the dangers of convicting on the uncorroborated evidence of a police officer.[78]

Perhaps this historical reluctance factors into the decision-making process in determining whether or not the accused faced a real threat of danger. In situations where women kill their abusers, it will usually take place behind closed doors and out of public sight, meaning that the only witness to the killing and the preceding violence will often be the 'accused' herself. A history of violence may have been actively concealed from other parties, meaning that there is no corroboration of the woman's version of events.[79] In two of the 'domestic homicide' cases studied, the courts made reference to the fact that the deceased was not available to give his version of events,[80] however there was no similar reference made in any of the coronial cases involving shootings by police officers, and the absence of corroboration of police evidence did not prevent police actions being declared justified.[81]

Even where courts have been prepared to allow women to rely on self-defence in abuse cases, they have typically been reluctant to rely on the testimony of the woman herself, preferring instead to rely on expert testimony in relation to 'battered woman syndrome' or other mental impairment that the woman suffered from at the time.[82] In such circumstances, the woman in question may be exonerated, but it will be on the basis that she was suffering from the mental defect of 'learned helplessness' rather than because she was responding in a rational and comprehensible way to a real threat.

The victim who is killed is also constructed differently within the two types of cases. In cases involving women who kill their abusers, courts still commonly focus on the harm caused by the killing and the consequences of the accused's actions in taking a human life.[83] The quote from *Denney* above indicates the court's emphasis on the 'redeeming qualities' of the victim, despite his violent past. Although the doctrine of coverture, in which the legal identity of a woman was subsumed within that of her husband

---

[78] New South Wales, *Parliamentary Debates*, Legislative Assembly, 18 March 1981, 4773 (FJ Walker) (Second Reading of the Crimes (Sexual Assault) Bill).

[79] Sheehy et al, above n 3, 374.

[80] *Osland* (1998) 197 CLR 316 [209], [239]; *R v Denney* [2000] VSC 323 (Unreported, Coldrey J, 4 August 2000) [3].

[81] Eg, there were no independent witnesses referred to by the Coroner in relation to the shooting of AC: State Coroner's Office (NSW Attorney-General's Department), *Report by the NSW State Coroner into Deaths in Custody/Police Operations*, 2001.

[82] A Scully, 'Expert Distractions: Women who Kill, their Syndromes and Disorders' in M Childs and L Ellison, *Feminist Perspectives on Evidence* (London, Cavendish Publishing, 2000) 191–209.

[83] For reference to the seriousness of the taking of human life in self-defence cases see *Osland v The Queen* (1998) 197 CLR 316, [210]; *R v Vandersee* [2000] NSWSC 916 (Unreported, James J, 18 September 2000); *R v Melrose* [2001] NSWSC 847 (Unreported, McClellan J, 31 August 2001); *R v Trevenna* [2003] NSWSC 463 (Unreported, Buddin J, 29 May 2003); *R v Russell* [2006] NSWSC 722 (Unreported, Newman AJ, 21 July 2006).

upon marriage, was abolished in the United Kingdom and United States in the late nineteenth century, the law has continued well into the twentieth century to reinforce the concept that a woman's position within the marriage relationship is secondary to her husband's.[84] Thus a woman who kills her partner is constructed within the law as killing her superior in the marriage relationship.

In contrast, in police shootings, the emphasis is not on the police's actions or the fact that human life has been taken but often on the bad character of the victim. Through media reports, based largely on information provided by police, and at times misleading, the victim is constructed as deserving of her or his fate.[85] Many of the coronial reports studied made reference to the victim's criminal history, although it was not immediately relevant to the shooting. In one case, the coroner noted that the deceased had the words 'COPS SUCK' tattooed across his fingers and had recently showed a reckless disregard for the life of a person he had assaulted; police knew that and had every reason to fear for their lives when he pointed a weapon at them.[86] The construction of the victim as the 'bad guy' in police shootings reinforces the conclusion that police were justified in shooting him.

C. The Availability of Other Options

The final aspect for consideration that illustrates the differential factual construction in these cases relates to the availability of options other than lethal force.

In the police shooting cases, the requirement that self-defence be reasonably necessary is apparently not interpreted to require that the perpetrator have no other option before using lethal force. In most of the Victorian cases referred to above, coronial findings indicated that police had, by the operational choices they made, effectively placed themselves in a position

---

[84] J Rawls, *A Theory of Justice* (Oxford, Oxford University Press, 1972) 128 (for an example in legal theory of assuming the secondary position of the wife); C Smart, *The Ties that Bind: Law, Marriage and the Reproduction of Patriarchal Relations* (London, Routledge and Kegan Paul, 1984) ch 2; M Thornton, *The Liberal Promise* (Oxford, Oxford University Press, 1990) 71 (evidenced by the continued practice of women taking their husbands' surnames); I Marcus, 'Reframing "Domestic Violence": Terrorism in the Home' in M Fineman and R Mykitiuk (eds), *The Public Nature of Private Violence* (New York, Routledge, 1994) 11–35, 19–21; Siegel above n 26, 2122. C Pateman, *The Sexual Contract* (Stanford, Stanford University Press, 1988) 39–55 notes that most social contract theorists believed in the natural subjection of women to men.

[85] J McCulloch, 'Behind the Headlines: how does the media portray fatal shootings by the police' (1997) 22(3) *Alternative Law Journal* 133–37; J McCulloch, 'Blue Murder: press coverage of fatal police shootings' (1996) 29 *Australia and New Zealand Journal of Criminology* 102–20.

[86] *Coronial Inquest into the shooting of Edward Wilson*, Queensland Coroner's Court, 13 November 2008, [6.2]–[6.3].

where they had little option but to use lethal force.[87] However, charges were laid in relation to only two of these incidents, and ultimately charges against seven of the 11 officers involved were dropped; the three that went to trial resulted in acquittals.[88] These were the first prosecutions for police shootings in Australia.[89]

In my analysis of available coronial reports relating to police shootings,[90] of 25 reported inquiries into police shootings, there were 12 cases in which police had made errors of judgement,[91] the coroner found that the operation should have been conducted differently,[92] or there was evidence

[87] See letter from David Neal (Commissioner, LRC Victoria) to John Thwaites, 24 October 1988, cited in McCulloch, above n 66, 111. In an inquest into seven police shootings occurring between 1990 and 1994, the coroner found that in six of seven cases police had been exposed at least partly by their own actions to a person with a gun requiring them to make split-second decisions: Freckelton, above n 18, 164.

[88] The eleventh police officer committed suicide before the matter came to trial. These were the prosecutions of police for the shootings of Graeme Jensen and Gary Abdallah, detailed in McCulloch, above n 66.

[89] J McCulloch, Personal Communication (on file with author), 10 August 2009.

[90] My examination consisted of reviewing all coronial reports published on Australian coronial websites. Websites visited containing coronial cases are as follows:

www.courts.act.gov.au/magistrates/page/view/597/title/selected-findings (ACT—reviewed all cases on 'Selected findings' page);

www.lawlink.nsw.gov.au/lawlink/coroners_court/ll_coroners.nsf/pages/coroners_deathsincustody (NSW—reviewed all cases referred to in annual reports);

www.nt.gov.au/justice/courtsupp/coroner/inquestlist.shtml (NT—reviewed all 'Inquest findings'); www.courts.qld.gov.au/1680.htm (Qld—reviewed all cases on 'Findings' page); www.courts.sa.gov.au/courts/coroner/findings/index.html (SA—searched all coronial findings for 'shot'—five of 38 hits related to police shootings); www.magistratescourt.tas.gov.au/divisions/coronial/findings_alpha_listing (Tas—reviewed all 'Decisions'); www.coronerscourt.vic.gov.au/wps/wcm/connect/justlib/Coroners+Court/Home/Case+Findings/ (Vic—reports now published on current website);

www.coronerscourt.wa.gov.au/I/inquest_findings.aspx?uid=9349-4756-3915-2531 (WA—findings available by written request).

[91] State Coroner's Office, 2001, above n 81 (shooting of 'AC'); State Coroner's Office, 2006, above n 15 (shooting of Thuong Lam); Robert Jongman [2007] NTMC 080 (3 December 2007). See also the discussion of the police shooting of Joshua Yap and Chee Ming Tsen, Gerhard Alfred Sader and Arthur James Nelson in J Silvester, A Rule and O Davies, The Silent War: Behind the police killings that shook Australia, (Melbourne, Floradale Productions, 1995) chs 2, 8, 10. In relation to the shooting of Roni Levi, both officers involved had used drugs in the months leading up to the shooting, and there were hearsay reports of their having used drugs in the hours prior to the shooting: Police Integrity Commission, Report to Parliament: Operation Saigon, (NSW, Police Integrity Commission, June 2001) 52, 57, 61, 65. In a study of police shootings in the US, officers in a significant number of cases admitted that the victim did not constitute an imminent threat at the time of the shooting: W Geller, 'Police and Deadly Force: A Look at the Empirical Literature' in F Elliston and M Feldberg (eds) Moral Issues in Police Work (Totowa, Rowman and Allanheld, 1985) 197–236, 205.

[92] Luke Donaghey (Unreported, SA Coroners' Court, 15 September 2000); State Coroner's Office, 2001, above n 81 (shooting of 'AC'); State Coroner's Office (NSW Attorney-General's Department) (2002) case no 382/2001 (shooting of 'JH') (indicates if finding not made by a jury it is likely the coroner would have been critical of police conduct); Gary Whyte, Record of Investigation into Death (Unreported, Victorian Coroner's Court, 21 January 2005). See the discussion of the shooting of Jedd Malcolm Houghton in Silvester et al, above n 91, ch 11.

inconsistent with police versions of events.[93] Yet, in only two cases was the police officer referred for prosecution; in one of the two cases the indictment was quashed due to a procedural defect and disciplinary charges were also subsequently dropped against him.[94] In the other, the magistrate discharged the officer at committal.[95]

In the cases involving women who kill their abusive partners, however, the reasonableness requirement will often require them to demonstrate that no other option (including retreat from the home) was available to them.[96] Judges and juries may make decisions based on common assumptions about women's behaviour—particularly the idea that they could and should have left a violent relationship[97]—but this fails to recognise the practical realities that mean these 'alternative options' are effectively unavailable to many women.[98]

In one NSW coronial case, the coroner took into account, in ruling that the shooting was justified, that police had been hindered by the failure of commanding officers to provide back-up and support, which they had a 'right to expect'.[99] To take this into account is in keeping with the theme of allowing the reasonableness of response to be considered against the broader context in which a defendant's actions occur.[100] However, the willingness to consider context in relation to reasonableness does not always translate to the situation of women who kill their abusive partners.[101] The fact that police could or should have been called to respond to the violent behaviour of the victim rather than the perpetrator 'taking the law into her own hands' may be held against her[102] notwithstanding evidence that police

---

[93] *Warren I'Anson* (Unreported, ACT Coroner's Court, 26 February 1999); State Coroner's Office, 2002, ibid, case no 258/2000 (shooting of RS); *Grant Wanganeen* (Unreported, SA Coroner's Court, 9 October 2002); *Daniel Cory Rhodes* (Queensland Coroners' Court, 24 March 2006); *Thomas Waite, Mieng Huynh, James Jacobs, James Gear* (Queensland Coroners' Court, 17 March 2008) (Waite and Gear).

[94] *Coronial Inquest into the Death of Robert Jongman* [2007] NTMC 080 (3 December 2007).

[95] *Record of Investigation into Death, Gary Whyte* (Vic Coroners' Court, 21 January 2005).

[96] See J Stubbs and J Tolmie, 'Feminisms, Self-Defence, and Battered Women: A response to Hubble's "Straw Feminist"' (1998) 10(1) *Current Issues in Criminal Justice* 73, 79–80.

[97] Sheehy et al, above n 3, 375.

[98] M Mahoney, 'Legal Images of Battered Women: Redefining the Issue of Separation' (1991) 90(1) *Michigan Law Review* 1.

[99] State Coroner's Office, 2001, above n 81 (shooting of 'AC').

[100] This was the approach endorsed in *Zecevic* (1987) 162 CLR 645, 662, 663, 672, 673.

[101] See *Sheppard* (Unreported, SCSA, 26 August 1992) where on a plea of guilty to manslaughter Bollen J applauded the accused for not seeking to rely on a violent attack just prior to her stabbing the victim 'to make up a story to support an idea of self-defence': cited in Bradfield, n 39, 208. Bradfield found no cases where self-defence was successfully relied upon absent a context of immediate confrontational situation or uttering of a threat: 211.

[102] See S Miller, 'Shootings by Police in Victoria: the Ethical Issues' in Coady et al, above n 18, 205–18, 205 for the idea that in contemporary society the police should be the first port of call. cf *R v Kontinnen* (Unreported, 30 March 1992, Supreme Court SA, Legoe J) 53.

have systematically failed to respond effectively to domestic violence.[103] It is certainly no bar to prosecution that in a particular case police have been called previously, but have been unsuccessful in stopping the 'victim's' violent behaviour.[104]

IV. CONCLUSION

It is not my objective to argue that all instances of women who kill their abusers are straight-forward cases of self-defence and that all police shootings are unjustified. Instances where people shoot to kill are many and varied, and will range from killings that are justified in self-defence to those that are motivated by revenge, aggression, reckless impulse, or some other factor. What the theory of case construction teaches us is that whether or not killings are justified is not simply a case of sifting through the objective facts; rather cases are constructed as justified or not through a complex process of decision-making.

By comparing shoot to kill cases involving police officers on the one hand and abused women on the other, I have identified discursive mechanisms at play in the construction of 'the facts' in these cases. These discursive mechanisms play an important role in constructing certain types of killings as justified and others as unjustified. Discourse both reflects and reinforces the power relations that determine that certain types of killing will be prosecuted in the criminal justice system but not others. By constructing police killings as 'justified' and killings by abused women as 'unjustified' the structural processes that routinely direct lethal killings through different avenues are reinforced. This occurs in a way that works directly to the disadvantage of abused women, who are routinely prosecuted in situations where they kill following a history of abuse.

This is not to suggest that these processes take place without exception. As noted above, there have been four instances in Australia where police have been prosecuted (at least initially) for fatal shootings, and at least one instance of a woman who killed her abusive husband not being prosecuted. However, these 'aberrant' cases do not defeat the argument that systemic forces are at play. On the contrary, the existence of inconsistencies in the system serves to strengthen it and reinforce the conception that the system

---

[103] See Stubbs and Tolmie, above n 96, 79–80, responding to Hubble's claim that the time taken to call for police assistance should be used to delimit self-help from self-defence.

[104] *R v Bogunovich* (1985) 16 A Crim R 456 (defendant convicted of manslaughter had previously sought help in vain from police, a magistrate and solicitor); *R v Kennedy* [2000] NSWSC 109 (Unreported, Barr J, 1 March 2000) (Aboriginal accused had been unable to rely on police for practical and emotional reasons). In *R v Gazdovic* [2002] VSC 588 (Unreported, Teague J, 20 December 2002), police had attended previously and confiscated the deceased's firearms; he later bought an axe which the prisoner used to kill him.

is in fact neutral and unbiased simply *because* it is able to generate these 'exceptions that prove the rule'.

Lest it be thought however, that there is no room for change given these structural and discursive patterns, it behoves us to keep in mind Foucault's notion of 'resistant discourse', which always carries the potential to undermine and ultimately fracture the dominant discourses that produce power.[105] The Victorian DPP's decision to 'buck the trend' in non-prosecution of police in the 1980s is a powerful example of resistant discourse at play. Likewise, brave decisions to *not* prosecute battered women who kill in appropriate situations may provide the catalyst for more systemic changes in the way those who kill in self-defence are treated.

---

[105] L McNay, *Foucault and Feminism: Power, Gender and the Self* (Cambridge, Polity Press, 1992) ch 4.

9

Fundamental Rights and Fundamental Difference: Comparing the Right to Human Dignity and Criminal Liability in Germany and Australia

SASKIA HUFNAGEL

I. INTRODUCTION

THIS CHAPTER EXAMINES the concept of human dignity, and the extent to which it serves as a dividing line between degrees of criminal liability in 'shoot-to-kill' and torture cases involving state officials in Australia and Germany. The actions of state officials which enliven the arguments about right to human dignity relate to a wide range of extraordinary measures authorised by the 'war on terror' including infringements of the right to life and the right not to be subject to torture and other cruel, inhuman or degrading treatment or punishment. The question whether human rights in general and the principle of human dignity in particular should be curtailed in order to facilitate the fight against terrorism will be addressed. The chapter focuses on the impact of the human dignity principle on fundamental criminal law concepts such as the legal doctrines of self-defence and necessity, since these are commonly invoked by state officials to justify or excuse their responsibility for conduct which otherwise amounts to a criminal offence. Prominent examples are the intentional use of lethal force to destroy a 'hijacked aircraft' carrying both terrorists and innocent civilians, and the 'ticking bomb' scenario, where a person is tortured in order to obtain information that prevents, or is likely to prevent, an act of terrorism.

A comparative perspective between Germany and Australia has been chosen to expose and highlight the distinct and privileged status of the right to human dignity in German law and jurisprudence, and to illustrate the differences between that system, and a system of human rights protection in Australia that neither constitutionally entrenches nor prioritises human dignity as a fundamental human right.

II. POST 9/11 CHALLENGES TO HUMAN DIGNITY

The far-reaching legal responses to terrorism following the attacks of 9/11 have led to a re-examination of the legally justifiable derogations, limits and restrictions on human rights such as the right to life,[1] human dignity,[2] and the right not to be subject to torture.[3] The balancing of these rights against each other, and the weighing of these rights against the interests of security have been widely canvassed in academic literature.[4] This process of adjustment in the legal discourse, requiring the balancing of competing human rights and interests, is not novel; indeed it has always been a feature of human rights law since there are few rights which are strictly 'absolute' (torture being an exception).[5] A further difficulty, however, emerges in German law with its constitutional elevation of the right to human dignity to the status of a 'quasi-absolute human right', that is, a right which admits only minor limitation or qualification.

The importance of Article 1 of the Grundgesetz (GG), the Basic Law for the Federal Republic of Germany (hereafter Basic Law),[6] which proclaims

---

[1] See Article 3 of the Universal Declaration of Human Rights (UDHR); Article 6(1) of the International Covenant on Civil and Political Rights (ICCPR); Article 2(1) of the European Convention on Human Rights (ECHR).

[2] See the Preamble of the Universal Declaration of Human Rights (UDHR); Preamble of the International Covenant on Civil and Political Rights (ICCPR); Preamble of the European Convention on Human Rights (ECHR) and in particular Article 1 of the German Basic Law (Grundgesetzt) 1949.

[3] Australia and Germany are signatories to the four Geneva Conventions of 1949, and their two additional protocols of 1977. Australia ratified the Convention Against Torture in 1989.

[4] See Part IV: 'Human Rights and Terrorism: Is a Trade-Off Necessary?' in A Lynch, E MacDonald and G Williams (eds), *Law and Liberty in the War on Terror* (Sydney, Federation Press, 2007) 137–64; B Golder and G Williams, 'Balancing National Security and Human Rights: Assessing the Legal Response of Common Law Nations to the Threat of Terrorism' (2006) 8 *Journal of Comparative Policy Analysis* 43; G Williams, *The Case For An Australian Bill of Rights: Freedom in the War on Terror* (Sydney, University of New South Wales Press, 2004); S Bronitt, 'Balancing Security and Liberty: Critical Perspectives on Terrorism Law Reform' in M Gani and P Mathew (eds) *Fresh Perspectives on the 'War on Terror'* (Canberra, ANU E-Press, 2008); S Bronitt, 'Constitutional Rhetoric versus Criminal Justice Realities: Unbalanced Responses to Terrorism?' (2003) 14 *Public Law Review* 76; M Gani, 'Upping the Ante in the War on Terror" in P Fawkner (ed), *A Fair Go in an Age of Terror* (Ringwood, Victoria, David Lovell Publishing, 2004); L Zedner, 'Securing Liberty in the Face of Terror: Reflections from Criminal Justice (2005) 32 *Journal of Law and Society* 507.

[5] C Gearty, *Principles of Human Rights Adjudication* (Oxford, Oxford University Press, 2004) 9–10; Security Legislation Review Committee (SLRC), *Report of the Security Legislation Review Committee* (2006) 39.

[6] Basic Law for the Federal Republic of Germany or Deutsches Grundgesetz (hereafter Basic Law or GG).

that 'Human dignity is inviolable.' is revealed in the hierarchy of rights within the constitution (being the first Article of the Basic Law). The right is not merely legal window-dressing in the Preamble or objects clause of the Basic Law. Article 1 entrenches into law a positive right with corollary remedies. From this slender legal provision, the Constitutional Court of Germany has developed a remarkable—some might even say impractical and unworkable—jurisprudence around the right to human dignity.

From the German perspective, the paramount status of the right to human dignity is a legal 'fact of life', its centrality arising from the horrific experiences of human rights infringements and abuses of state power before and during the Second World War. It is also consistent with a longer pedigree of German legal theory associated with Immanuel Kant's writings. The Kantian definition of human dignity states that 'no specific human being shall be made an object, the mere means, a mere replaceable entity of state action',[7] a proposition that has been accepted by the German courts since the 1950s and has so far resisted all attempts of scholars and politicians to limit it.

The influence of Kantian theory is most apparent in the landmark German Constitutional Court decision of 2006,[8] where the court ruled that a hijacked plane threatening to destroy an inhabited building could not be shot down. While the main reasons for this decision were based on the conflict of competences between the 'Bund' and the 'Länder',[9] the court stressed additionally that the human dignity of the innocent people on the plane could not be weighed against the human dignity of the innocent people in the building into which the plane would inevitably crash. In other words, the lives of the people on the plane could not be made the means to the state's end, namely to save the people in the building.[10] This interpretation of the right to human dignity placed formal limits on state power to apply pre-emptive force, and it underscored the state's potential responsibility for human rights infringements in executing extreme counter terrorism measures.

---

[7] See G Dürig, 'Der Grundrechtssatz von der Menschenwürde' (1956) 81 *Archiv des öffentlichen Rechts* 117, 127.

[8] German Constitutional Court Decision of 1 BvR 357/05 (2006).

[9] Under Article 35 GG the military as a federal institution can only under very specific circumstances have competence to act on the territory of the 'Länder' which was not considered in § 14 III of the German Aviation Security Act. Furthermore, § 14 III did not take into account the ministerial decision-making powers under Article 35 GG. See German Constitutional Court Decision of 1 BvR 357/05 (2006) paras 90–117.

[10] For further discussion see, eg, S Hufnagel, 'The Impact of the German Human Dignity Principle on the Right to Life and the Right not to be Subject to Torture' in J Bröhmer (ed), *The German Constitution Turns 60* (Frankfurt, Peter Lang, 2011) 55; M Bohlander, 'In Extremis—Hijacked Airplanes, 'Collateral Damage' and the Limits of Criminal Law' (2006) *Criminal Law Review* 579; K Moller, 'On Treating Persons as Ends: The German Aviation Security Act, Human Dignity, and the German Federal Constitutional Court' (2006) *Public Law* 457.

State officials are nevertheless not powerless to act. Some protection is conferred through the normal doctrines of self-defence and necessity provisions in criminal law. However, these doctrines are also influenced by the right to human dignity jurisprudence outlined above. This chapter explores the potential impact of the concept of human dignity on the criminal liability of state officials for human rights violations and whether this differs from responses available in the Australian context.

From an Australian perspective, the contours of what constitutes a lawful and proportionate measure to deal with a hijacked aircraft is shaped by a different set of legal and normative concerns. As explored elsewhere, Australian jurisprudence is marked by a strongly pragmatic and inherently utilitarian model.[11] Indeed, the German limitations which deny the right of the state and its officials to assume control in these situations where the life of innumerable human beings is threatened may seem shocking and paradoxical from an Australian perspective. Why must more people die in Germany in the name of human dignity than in those common law systems (like Australia) that lack this fundamental protection? In Australia, federal law authorises the use of lethal force pre-emptively to shoot down a hijacked aircraft. This power, contained in Part IIIAAA of the Defence Act 1903 (Cth)[12] is available to members of the Australian Defence Force (ADF), even where the terrorist threat relates only to destroying, or impairing, designated critical infrastructure—it is not essential that human lives are directly endangered.

Part IIIAAA of the Defence Act 1903 (Cth) passed into Australian law in 2006 without significant media or legislative scrutiny. By comparison, the passage of German aviation security legislation the year before, which authorised the shooting down of hijacked aircraft, triggered public outcry and a swift constitutional challenge to its validity. This difference of responses in Germany and Australia may be due to the existence of human rights provisions in the German Basic Law, which intensifies the scrutiny of proposed legislation for potential human rights violations, as well as stimulating a strong 'complaint culture' with more legal avenues for individuals and civil society organisations to make human rights challenges.[13]

---

[11] For a comparative analysis comparing the common law and German human dignity provision see S Bronitt, 'The Common Law and Human Dignity: Australian Perspectives' in Bröhmer (ed), above n 10.

[12] Explanatory Memorandum (Revised), Defence Legislation Amendment (Aid to Civilian Authorities) Bill 2006 (Cth).

[13] Article 93, s 1, no 4a GG enables individuals that are affected 'themselves, immediately and directly' to put a complaint in form of a *Verfassungsbeschwerde* ('complaint against constitutional breach') before the German Constitutional Court; see consistent jurisprudence of the German Constitutional Court at BVerfGE 1, 97 at 101; BVerfGG 109, 279 at 305 and also B Merk, '"Auch über den Wolken dürfen Gesetze nicht grenzenlos sein": Das Flugzeug als Waffe—Grenzüberschreitungen im Verfassungs- und Strafrecht' (2006) 56 *Augsburger Universitätsreden* 13.

By contrast, Australia lacks a constitutional bill of rights and thus individuals have limited scope to challenge before the courts the validity of proposed or existing legislation on general human rights grounds. Because of the supremacy of statutes over judge-made common law, valid legislation cannot be declared void simply because it violates fundamental common law values, principles or rights. That said, the courts do apply a principle of statutory interpretation that Parliament does not intend to abridge, unless expressly stated, fundamental common law rights.[14]

Human rights protection is addressed piecemeal through specific provisions and statutes at federal, state and territory level—such as section 23Q of the Crimes Act 1914 (Cth)[15] or in the field of anti-discrimination law the Racial Discrimination Act 1975 (Cth) or the Anti-Discrimination Act 1977 (NSW).[16] The only jurisdictions to enact general human rights legislation based on the ICCPR are the Australian Capital Territory (ACT) and Victoria. The ACT enacted the Human Rights Act 2004 (HRA) and Victoria has largely followed the ACT model in its Charter of Human Rights and Responsibilities Act 2006 (Vic).[17] Under this model of human rights legislation, courts are placed under a duty to interpret legislative provisions consistently with human rights, or, if this is not possible, to make a declaration of incompatibility or inconsistent interpretation. Upholding the principle of parliamentary supremacy, the courts do not have the power to invalidate legislation on the grounds of inconsistency with the enumerated human rights. Even presuming that Australia may one day introduce a federal bill of rights similar to the ACT and Victorian models, new legal measures, such as Part IIIAAA of the Defence Act, could not be declared invalid by the High Court. At best, this model would permit the court to make a declaration of incompatibility, placing the obligation on the legislature to remedy the infringement. This represents a significant difference to the German model.

This chapter offers an overview of the applicable international and domestic laws protecting human rights in relation to the 'hijacked aircraft' and 'ticking bomb' scenarios. It assesses whether, despite the existence of human rights provisions and the right to human dignity in the German Constitution, human rights are protected to a similar extent in Australia. It will be concluded that Australian statutes and common law

[14] *Coco v R* (1994) 179 CLR 427, the High Court held unanimously that the courts should not impute to the legislature an intention to interfere with fundamental rights, unless that intention is manifested by unmistakable and unambiguous language.

[15] Section 23Q states that a person in federal police custody 'must be treated with humanity and with respect for human dignity, and must not be subjected to cruel, inhuman or degrading treatment'.

[16] See also, Sex Discrimination Act 1984 (Cth); Human Rights And Equal Opportunity Commission Act 1986 (Cth); Disability Discrimination Act 1992 (Cth) and a number of related state and territory laws.

[17] See for a detailed analysis: A Byrnes, H Charlesworth and G McKinnon, *Bills of Rights in Australia: History, Politics and Law* (Sydney, University of New South Wales Press, 2009).

do sufficiently protect human rights in relation to the use of lethal force and torture. However, while the fundamental principles remain the same in the Australian context, the way in which these principles are *legally* protected differ from the German approach.

This will become even more apparent when the concepts of self-defence and necessity are discussed. These are defences that could be invoked, in both German and Australian jurisdictions, by state officials who use of lethal force or perpetrate an act of torture in order to save the lives of innocent third parties. It will be argued that the German principle of human dignity limits these defences more severely and increases exposure of German state officials (police or military) to legal liability for their actions compared with their Australian counterparts.

While the differences between the German and the Australian approach to balancing human rights against security in practice are minimal, the fact that the German legal system is based on the paramount status of human dignity does create a dividing line in relation to state officials' accountability. Neither in the Australian nor German system will a state official who shoots down a hijacked aircraft or tortures a terrorist to save innocent lives be punished severely by the criminal justice system. However, the Australian system, unlike the German system, provides for the legitimate exercise of discretion by both police and prosecutors which involves consideration of a range of 'public interest' considerations.[18] Thus state officials who shoulder that responsibility for balancing 'life against life' may never be investigated or prosecuted. Indeed, even where officials are prosecuted in Australia for intentional, reckless or criminally negligent conduct causing death (potentially constituting murder or manslaughter), they may be justified by invoking the defence of necessity under the common law or some statutory variant.[19]

By contrast, the German 'legality principle'[20] in criminal law removes discretion in relation to investigation and prosecution in all but petty crimes.[21] There are, however, special 'mitigating' circumstances that may be taken into account in the sentencing phase. A German state official who assumes the responsibility for balancing competing human rights will be subject to the full court procedure before the special 'mitigating' circumstances may be taken into account. In most cases the official will then be given a significantly reduced, or virtually no sentence. This is a clear difference to

---

[18] See S Bronitt and P Stenning, 'Understanding Discretion in Modern Policing' (2011) 35 *Criminal Law Journal* 319.

[19] See Criminal Code (Cth), s 10.3(2). The defence of sudden or extraordinary emergency is available to all offences including murder and remains available to ADF members acting under Part IIIAAA of the Defence Act 1903 (Cth), s 51WB(3).

[20] Derived from § 1 of the German Criminal Code (Deutsches Strafgesetzbuch or StGB).

[21] See, eg, J Fionda, *Public Prosecutors and Discretion: A Comparative Study* (New York, Oxford University Press, 1995) 167.

the Australian model: while the state and its officials in Germany must be held responsible for their actions before the courts, the system mitigates the strictures of the principle of legality by mitigation of the penalties.

III. THE RIGHT TO LIFE AND THE RIGHT NOT TO BE TORTURED IN AN INTERNATIONAL AND DOMESTIC CONTEXT

Human rights lawyers typically disclaim any hierarchy of rights.[22] That said, some international human rights are absolute in the sense that these rights are non-derogable and are not subject to any exceptions such as the right not to be subject to torture.[23] According to the German Basic Law the right to human dignity should be regarded as paramount. This right is not expressly included in the ECHR and ICCPR, and there is no equivalent protection in the Australian Federal[24] or State Constitution, or even in the recently enacted human rights legislation in the Australian Capital Territory or Victoria (despite being mentioned in their respective Preambles).[25] Only few other countries have included the right to human dignity in their constitution, like for example South Africa.[26]

International laws applying to both Australia and Germany in relation to torture are the Four Geneva Conventions and their Protocols and the Convention against Torture. The prohibition against torture is considered to be absolute. In international law terms it is a peremptory norm or *jus cogens*,[27] which distinguishes it from the right to life and the right to human dignity, which have not required such a standard in international law. However, the right to life is protected in several international human rights instruments and is a right that requires special care when being balanced. The key principle in relation to balancing the right to life when it comes to the use of lethal force is proportionality.[28] The right to human dignity

---

[22] See, eg, T von Boven, 'Distinguishing Criteria of Human Rights' in HJ Steiner and P Alston, *International Human Rights in Context: Law, Politics, Morals*, 2nd edn (Oxford, Oxford University Press, 2000) 154–57.

[23] Article 2(2) of the United Nations Convention Against Torture, opened for signature 10 December 1984, G.A.Res 39/46 (entered into force 26 June 1987).

[24] See Commonwealth of Australia Constitution Act 1901 www.aph.gov.au/SEnate/general/constitution/index.htm.

[25] Human Rights Act 2004 (ACT), A2004-5, Republication No 3, Effective: 2 January 2007, Republication date: 2 January 2007, Last amendment made by A2006-3 and Charter of Human Rights and Responsibilities Act 2006 (Vic) (the charter), which was passed by Parliament in July 2006.

[26] See Constitution of the Republic of South Africa 1996 (South Africa) c 2, s 10.

[27] See, eg, E de Wet, 'The Prohibition of Torture as an International Norm of Jus Cogens and its Implications for National and Customary Law' (2004) 15 *European Journal of International Law* 97.

[28] C Michaelsen, 'International Human Rights on Trial—The United Kingdom's and Australia's Legal Response to 9/11' (2003) 25 *Sydney Law Review* 275.

has at least in the German context, as noted above, reached the level of a 'quasi-absolute' human right and thus cannot be balanced according to German jurisprudence.

Differences between human rights protection of individuals become apparent in Australian and German domestic laws. While Australia does not have a human rights charter embedded in its constitution, in Germany, the protection of both, the right to life and the right not to be subject to torture, are cemented into the Basic Law. The right to life is protected by Article 2, Section 2, Sentence 1 of the Basic Law: 'Every person has the right to life and physical integrity'. In some cases, where the right to life is balanced against an equal right, the balancing prohibition of Article 1 of the Basic Law, the human dignity principle, becomes relevant in conjunction with Article 2 of the Basic Law. In relation to torture, Article 1 of the Basic Law in conjunction with Article 2, Section 2, Sentence 1, Part 2 of the Basic Law ensures the right to physical integrity, and Article 14 of the Basic Law ensures the prohibition of coercive interrogation methods. Of course these rights are also reflected in criminal laws and other statutes, like §136a of the Criminal Procedural Code (StPO)[29] which prohibits the admissibility of evidence gathered through the use of coercive interrogation methods. What needs to be emphasised in relation to both rights—life and physical integrity—is that apart from their protection through specific provisions in the Basic Law, they can also be protected through Article 1, Section 1 of the Basic Law, the right to human dignity.[30]

In Australia, various federal laws prohibit the use of coercive interrogation methods and prescribe that evidence gathered in this way is inadmissible. These are, for example, section 23Q of the Crimes Act 1914 (Cth), section 84(1) of the Evidence Act 1995 (Cth) and section 138 of the Evidence Act 1995 (Cth). It follows that torture is prohibited in both Australia and Germany and evidence obtained on the basis of illegal interrogation methods is inadmissible. The only difference is that Germany has stated this prohibition in its Basic Law rather than limiting it to legislation on criminal procedure. With regards to the 'ticking bomb' scenario, the significance of this difference between the two systems is further revealed in practice. In the 'ticking bomb' scenario, an Australian state official having threatened a person to find out information that could potentially save innocent lives may not be prosecuted.[31] In the German context, prosecuting a state official who has threatened a suspect would be mandatory, as police and prosecution have

---

[29] Deutsche Strafprozessordnung (German Criminal Procedural Law).

[30] See also S Hufnagel, 'German Perspectives on the Right to Life and Human Dignity in the War on Terror' (2008) 32 *Criminal Law Journal* 100, 101.

[31] This would, of course, depend on the circumstances. We assume that the person threatened is clearly the offender and that the death of innocent people could be averted by this action.

to adhere to the 'legality principle'[32] whereas in Australia the prosecution has discretion (not) to prosecute. In the German *Daschner* case,[33] which is comparable to a 'ticking bomb' scenario, the German state officials threatening the suspect therefore had to be prosecuted.

However, in relation to the right to life and dignity, Australian common law places some limits on claims of necessity, prohibiting the weighing of the right to life of 'the many' against 'the few'. This value is manifested in the common law position adopted in *R v Dudley and Stephens* (1884) 14 QBD 273. In this case, four sailors were shipwrecked on the high seas and following the old maritime custom of cannibalism, decided to kill and eat one of their number— the cabin boy—in order to avoid starvation. Two of the survivors were charged with the murder of the cabin boy. The Court of Queen's Bench held that necessity could not be pleaded as a defence to homicide. Lord Coleridge CJ emphasised the moral and practical difficulties in weighing competing interests involved in the defence:

> Who is to be the judge of this sort of necessity? By what measure is the comparative value of lives to be measured? Is it to be strength, or intellect, or what? It is plain that the principle leaves to him who is to profit by it to determine the necessity which will justify him in deliberately taking another's life to save his own.

Although convicted and sentenced to death, the penalty of the two survivors was later commuted to six months' imprisonment.[34]

This decision stresses the importance of the right to life in common law systems like Australia. It does not, however, confine the express legal power conferred by Parliament that permits a hijacked aircraft in Australian airspace to be shot down. The decision in *Dudley and Stephens* only refers to a person killing another human being who is not a direct threat to his or her life in order to save his or her own life. The judgment does not address the question of state action taken for saving the lives of others. While stressing the paramount value of life, the case has not been invoked in similar scenarios such as the use of lethal force to protect civilians from illegal threats in general. It can therefore not be considered the equivalent to the right to human dignity in the German context. In Germany the principle of human dignity prohibits the weighing and sacrifice of innocent lives by state actors. In Australia, no equivalent common law principle exists. In relation to human rights protections this might be an indicator for a major difference between the systems. However, it needs to be highlighted that the principle derived from *Dudley and Stephens* could be considered to go even further than the right to human dignity as it prohibits weighing the relative

---

[32] See, eg, Fionda, above n 21, 167.
[33] Decision of the Landgericht Frankfurt am Main decision Az. 5/27 Kla—7570 Js 03814/03 (2004).
[34] *R v Dudley and Stephens* (1884) 14 QBD 273, 287–88.

value of human lives even in cases where that action is necessary to save one's own life. As discussed later in this chapter, this would be likely to be excused under German criminal law.

IV. APPLICATION OF DEFENCES: SELF-DEFENCE AND NECESSITY

To examine the similarities and differences of the Australian and the German approach in relation to criminal liability of state officials, two case studies have been selected for further analysis—the 2006 decision of the German Constitutional Court relating to the shooting down of hijacked aircraft[35] and the Frankfurt District Court decision on the right not to be subject to torture.[36]

A. Case Study 1: Shooting Down Hijacked Aircraft in Germany

Passed in January 2005, § 14 III of the German Aviation Security Act[37] (*Luftsicherheitsgesetz*) provided that a hijacked plane could be shot down by the German military on German territory if it threatened to crash into an inhabited building or an otherwise populated area. The German Constitutional Court declared this section of the Act void. Apart from raising major concerns in relation to competences of the defence minister, the minister of the interior, the German Parliament, the 'Bund' and the 'Länder', the decision also discussed the limits of Article 1 (right to human dignity) and Article 2 (right to life) of the German Basic Law. While Article 2 was decided to be subject to limitations and hence the right to life could under certain circumstances be balanced against an equal right, Article 1, section 1, the right to human dignity, could not be balanced against itself. The court argued that where the right to human dignity confronted itself (viz. innocent lives against innocent lives), the state had to refrain from action. However, § 14 III of the German Aviation Security Act was declared void for a number of reasons, not exclusively because of the infringement of Article 1 of the Basic Law.[38] The court's statement on the supremacy of

---

[35] German Constitutional Court Decision BVerfG, 1 BvR 357/05 of 15/02/2006.

[36] Decision of the Landgericht Frankfurt am Main decision Az. 5/27 Kla—7570 Js 03814/03 (2004).

[37] Deutsches Luftsicherheitsgesetz of 11/01/2005, entered into force on 15/11/2005 and was triggered by the attacks of September 11 and a following 'joy-flight' incident in German airspace in 2003.

[38] § 14 III of the German Aviation Security Act violates Article 35 II 2 and III 1 of the Basic Law as German armed forces have no competence on the territory of the Länder and the decision-making process was declared unconstitutional.

Article 1 was nevertheless the trigger for extensive political and academic debate.

The court also discussed an alternative scenario: the plane being occupied only by terrorists. In those cases, it determined that there could be a balancing of rights. As the terrorists would pose a direct threat to lives of innocent people, their right to life could be balanced against the rights to life *and* human dignity of the innocent people in the building. In terms of proportionality the terrorist's right to life was considered less worthy of protection.[39] This reasoning is closely related to criminal law necessity defences in German criminal law. If there is a direct threat to a person, that person or a third party may take all reasonable and proportionate measures to avert the threat.[40] So, the right to life and human dignity of a person acting illegally can be limited. This might be the first indication that the right to human dignity even in Germany is not absolute and that there are ways to waive it.

It has to be noted that the right to human dignity according to the Kantian definition only limits the right of the *state* to use a human being as a means to its ends. As we will discuss later, a private person could be excused for shooting the plane down even if it was also occupied by civilians, provided a relative or another person close to them is in the building into which the plane threatens to crash. The criminal law provisions, like the Basic Law, therefore distinguish between state action and the actions of civilians.

The three major German criminal law defences applying in the 'hijacked aircraft' and 'ticking bomb' scenarios are §§ 32, 34 and 35 of the German Penal Code (StGB). § 32 StGB is the self-defence provision:

(1) Whoever commits an act in self-defence does not act unlawfully.
(2) Necessary defence is the defence which is required to avert an imminent unlawful attack from oneself or another.

Shooting down a hijacked aircraft cannot be justified under self-defence. For self-defence to apply, the defence has to be necessary. It is only necessary if it is required to avert an imminent and unlawful attack. As the civilians on the plane are not carrying out an unlawful attack, there is no necessary act of self-defence and the action cannot be justified under § 32 StGB. A state official could only be justified under the provision if the plane had been occupied only by terrorists. In this latter scenario the state official would be able to invoke self-defence which applies to the defence of 'oneself or another'. It therefore limits the rights to life and human dignity for the terrorists, but not the civilians and is in line with the decision of the Constitutional Court.

---

[39] German Constitutional Court Decision BVerfG, 1 BvR 357/05 of 15/02/2006, at 119–53.
[40] See § 34 of the German Penal Code (Strafgesetzbuch or StGB) Rechtfertigender Notstand (justifying necessity).

§ 34 StGB is called the 'justifying necessity' provision:

> Whoever commits an act in order to avert an imminent and not otherwise avoidable danger to the life, limb, liberty, honour, property or other legally protected interest directed against himself or another does not act unlawfully if, taking into consideration all the conflicting interests, in particular the legal ones, and the degree of danger involved, the interest protected by him significantly outweighs the interest which he harms. This rule applies only if the act is a proportionate means to avert the danger.

If it applies, all actus reus and mens rea elements of the offence will be justified and liability is extinguished. The act will not be classified as 'illegal'. In contrast to § 34 StGB, § 35 StGB is the so-called 'excusing necessity':

> (1) Whoever, faced with an imminent danger to life, limb or freedom which cannot otherwise be averted, commits an unlawful act to avert the danger from himself, a relative or person close to him, acts without guilt. This shall not apply if the perpetrator could be expected under the circumstances, in particular in cases where he himself has caused the danger or where he was in a special legal relationship with the victim, to accept the danger without resistance. The punishment may be mitigated pursuant to § 49(1), if the perpetrator was not required to assume the risk with respect to a special legal relationship.

> (2) If upon commission of the act the perpetrator mistakenly assumed that circumstances existed which would excuse him under subs (1), he will only be punished, if he could have avoided the mistake. The punishment may be mitigated pursuant to § 49(1).

This means the actus reus and mens rea elements are prima facie fulfilled and the act is 'illegal', but guilt cannot be attributed. Excusing necessity is therefore considered to be a 'weaker' type of defence than justifying necessity.

§ 34 StGB does not require that the attack involving imminent danger has to be unlawful and therefore prima facie could be invoked to justify the shooting down of a hijacked plane even where innocent civilians were on board. That said, § 34 StGB is further constrained by the principle of proportionality, which requires that the defendant has to 'take into account all the conflicting interests, in particular the legal ones, and the degree of danger involved'. Also, the interest protected by the defendant has to *significantly* outweigh the interest being harmed. The principle of proportionality means that the state (or a civilian) has to weigh all the legal rights involved. These include *per force* the right to human dignity, which as noted above cannot be balanced or traded. Thus it follows that § 34 StGB does not provide an unambiguous legal authority to shoot down a plane that is (also) occupied by innocent civilians.

The principle of proportionality is however not a requirement under § 35 StGB. Even if it were disproportionate, shooting down a plane occupied by innocent civilians could be justified if a relative or close person to the defendant was inside the building into which the plane threatens to crash.[41] It is therefore unlikely to act as a defence for a state official, but could under certain circumstances excuse a civilian (although it is unlikely that he or she would have the technical means to commit the offence).

It follows that the German criminal law provisions relating to defences reflect the Kantian interpretation of the right to human dignity and are unlikely to provide justification or excuse to a state official. State action is therefore severely limited in this scenario.

In the Australian context, state officials (members of the ADF) involved in shooting down hijacked aircraft, and acting under Part IIIAAA of the Defence Act, no longer need to rely on the common law defences of necessity or self-defence. Indeed, it is not clear that the *Dudley and Stephens* decision would in any event provide a lawful justification for intentional uses of lethal force against the hijacked aircraft, particularly in relation to force used to protect property or installations of vital importance. Since Part IIIAAA has so far not been tested in the courts, it remains to be seen whether the principles articulated in *Dudley and Stephens* may be relevant *indirectly* to the interpretation of Part IIIAAA.

A similar approach to the Australian 'sudden or emergency' defence was considered in Germany, revealing the differences between the 'law in books' and the 'law in action'. In 2007, the then German minister of defence (Franz Josef Jung) publicly stated that a hijacked plane would be shot down notwithstanding the court's ruling and that state action would be justified under the concept of 'suprastatutory state of emergency'. This political decision provoked protest among the German Airforce Pilot Association, which issued a statement that they would not follow orders in a similar scenario.[42] The concept of 'suprastatutory state of emergency' had initially been introduced by the German Imperial Court in 1927 to provide a legal basis for abortion, but had been annulled in 1949.[43] The attempt of the defence minister to revive the defence and circumvent the paramount right to human dignity can be seen as the continuation of the German attitude towards legality in the war on terrorism in the 1970s, when the executive similarly sought to justify human rights abuse under the untested legal doctrine of 'suprastatutory state of emergency'. It should be noted that the concept never found formal recognition in the German Criminal Code.

---

[41] See for a detailed discussion on § 35 StGB: M Bohlander, *Principles of German Criminal Law* (Portland, Oregon, Hart Publishing, 2009) 123–29.

[42] GP Hefty, 'Übergesetzlicher Notstand—Jenseits von Gesetz undVerfassung', *Frankfurter Allgemeine Zeitung NET* (Frankfurt, 19 November 2007); See the arguments of the pilot associations commenting on the Aviation Security Act in paras 68 and 69 of the BVerfG judgment.

[43] RGSt 61, 242. Similar in this respect to abortion: see *R v Davidson* [1969] VR 667 in S Bronitt and B McSherry, *Principles of Criminal Law*, 2nd edn (Pyrmont, New South Wales, LawBook Co, 2005) 328.

It appears then that throughout the German history of terrorism, the 'law in books' and the 'law in action' have diverged significantly, with *Realpolitik* and political pragmatism circumscribing the fundamental rights to human dignity and life. However, in cases where the right not to be subject to torture is concerned, the human dignity principle is more assertive, and German politicians have been unwilling to invoke the doctrine to legalise coercive interrogation techniques.

The reality in the criminal procedural context would look quite different again in the 'hijacked aircraft' cases. In contrast to the Australian system, the German legal system applies the 'legality principle' and therefore does not offer a margin of discretion in whether state officials involved in shooting down the plane will be subject to investigation and prosecution. Neither does the German legal system—as detailed above—offer the possibility of justification or excuse for these actions. That said, in the sentencing phase at the end of the criminal process, the special extenuating circumstances of the offence (namely the situation of immense pressure the offenders find themselves in, having to weigh up the most valuable rights of all parties involved), are legitimate factors to be taken into account in mitigating the sentence. The state officials would therefore in all likelihood receive low sentences.

Interestingly, this (German) approach of sentence mitigation mirrors that adopted in *Dudley and Stephens*.[44] Although the accused were convicted of murder and initially sentenced to death, their sentences were commuted to six months' imprisonment, which takes into account the unique circumstances under which the crime was committed. This can lead to the conclusion that the more absolute the right that needs to be balanced, the later in the criminal process the special circumstances find consideration. The common sentiment expressed in Article 1, section 1 of the German Basic Law and the common law in *Dudley and Stephens*, is that innocent life cannot be weighed against innocent life (the 'innocence' carrying with it the right to human dignity). In the case of *Dudley and Stephens* this exacting principle even required the giving up of one's own life as it could not be balanced against the life of another innocent person. As the strict application of this principle would lead to unjust outcomes for offenders (in the case of *Dudley and Stephens* capital punishment) an adjustment had to be applied in the sentencing phase (capital punishment being commuted to six months' imprisonment). The *Daschner* decision below similarly adopted this approach that combines high principle with pragmatism.

In conclusion the human dignity principle embedded in the German Basic Law is a dividing line in relation to determining the course of action in the 'hijacked aircraft' scenario. Both the German Constitutional Court and the

---

[44] *R v Dudley and Stephens* (1884) 14 QBD 273, 287–88.

common law courts applying *Dudley and Stephens* (the former focussing on the right to human dignity and the latter on the right to life), in principle prohibit the shooting down of hijacked aircraft occupied by innocent people. However, this convergence has been threatened in Australia since 2006, with Part IIIAAA of the Defence Act departing from the common law principle in *Dudley and Stephens*. A state official may legally shoot down a hijacked aircraft in Australia in accordance with Part IIIAAA. While the defence minister seeks to evoke an emergency defence in the German context, with fundamental legal principles and political reality seemingly diverging in this case, it is unlikely that he would succeed with this reasoning. However, the state official called upon to make the decision would be protected (in part) by the criminal justice system, which would likely soften the strict application of the right to human dignity in the sentencing phase.

B. Case Study 2: Ticking Bomb Scenario (Torture)

This outcome differs to some extent from the ticking bomb scenario above. In the German *Daschner* case,[45] a young boy was abducted by his tutor (Magnus Gäfgen) and hidden in a place not known to police. When police identified the suspect Gäfgen and took him in for the interview, he refused to reveal the whereabouts of the boy. Desperate to find out where the boy was being held and to save his life, the acting police president of the city of Frankfurt (Wolfgang Daschner) where the suspect was being interviewed, explored ways to extract information from Gäfgen. He concluded that the only possible way to bring the suspect to reveal the boy's whereabouts was to threaten him with the infliction of considerable physical pain that would leave no visible impact on the suspect and be supervised by a medical expert. The superintendent of the police station where Gäfgen was being interviewed (Ortwin Ennigkeit) had developed a 'multiple-step-plan' to convince the offender to reveal the information by confronting him with members of his family and appealing to his morality. However, as that plan had so far not produced any investigative successes, Daschner ordered his subordinate Ennigkeit to threaten the offender with above specified violence. After these procedures had started, the abducted boy was found dead by police. He had already been killed before Gäfgen had been taken in for the interview. Daschner was charged with 'instructing a subordinate to commit a criminal offence' and Ennigkeit was charged with 'coercion while exercising a public office' and both were consequently convicted. Both received a 'warning' and were sentenced to relatively high

[45] LG Frankfurt am Main, Urteil vom 20.12.2004, Az. 5/27 Kls - 7570 Js 203814/03 -.

fines,[46] but the execution of the sentence was subject to parole, a so-called 'warning and conditional sentence'.[47] If the offenders did not commit any further offences, they would not have to pay the fines. It has been suggested that the court chose these strikingly mild or negligible sentences, to take into account the stressful situation the officers had found themselves in. The sentences were indeed so low that the officers were not prohibited from remaining in the police service. However, Daschner resigned after the incident and left the service.

The low sentences applied here, similar to *Dudley and Stephens*, reflect the attitude of the District Court that the right to human dignity needs to be upheld, while the situation of immense pressure on the accused needs to be taken into account. The existence of an irrevocable right to human dignity prescribes that the court process is necessary to hold state officials accountable for human rights infringements, but the application of minor punishments can 'soften the blow' of subscribing to this paramount principle. The mere existence of the right to human dignity makes it mandatory to conduct court procedures and pronounce a sentence. This makes it the fundamental dividing line between German and Australian approaches to state accountability.

Daschner raised a number of defences, including self-defence and justifying necessity and he even tried to claim the 'suprastatutory state of emergency' defence.[48] The judges rejected all arguments—the difficulty with self-defence was that it requires an imminent attack and the justifying necessity defence only operates where the response is proportionate. As the defendants could have proceeded with the legal 'multiple-step-plan', the threat of physical harm was disproportionate.[49] Not only the right to physical integrity of the offender had to be weighed up against the right to life of the boy, but as torture is a breach of the right to human dignity, the human dignity of the offender had to be balanced against the human dignity of the boy. In these scenarios, as the District Court confirmed the rulings of the German Constitutional Court, a balancing of rights was not possible and the state had to refrain from action. Here the court went further than the Constitutional Court in the hijacking decision, as it did not claim that Gäfgen had lost his right to human dignity by acting illegally. The two decisions

---

[46] Daschner to 90 penalty units each valued at 120 Euros (10.800 Euros) and Ennigkeit to 60 penalty units valued at 60 Euros see at LG Frankfurt am Main, Urteil vom 20.12.2004, Az. 5/27 Kls - 7570 Js 203814/03 -; Summary of the case in German language available at www.lg-frankfurt.justiz.hessen.de/irj/servlet/prt/portal/prtroot/slimp.CMReader/HMdJ_15/LG_Frankfurt_Internet/med/acb/acb50880-b973-6411-aeb6-df144e9169fc,22222222-2222-2222-2222-222222222222,true.pdf.

[47] § 59 StGB (Verwarnung mit Strafvorbehalt).

[48] LG Frankfurt am Main, Urteil vom 20.12.2004, Az. 5/27 Kls - 7570 Js 203814/03 -.

[49] See also summary of procedures: *Schriftliche Urteilsgründe in der Strafsache gegen Wolfgang Daschner*, Pressemitteilung des LG Frankfurt vom 15. February 2005.

are difficult to reconcile. However, this outcome might be justified by the 'absolute' status of the right not to be subject to torture compared to the qualified nature of the right to life. The right to human dignity can hence be 'more or less' absolute. If combined with an absolute right, a *jus cogens*, protected by international law and carrying with it an inherent right to human dignity, such as the right not to be subject to torture, Article 1, section 1 of the Basic Law is 'more' absolute. If combined with a non-absolute right, like the right to life, that can be limited under certain circumstances like self-defence and necessity, Article 1, section 1 GG is 'less' absolute.

This is also reflected in the criminal law defences applying to it. First, self-defence is not applicable as there is no imminent attack by the abductor of the child. Justifying necessity is not applicable as the response was not proportionate. Lastly, excusing necessity would only protect the mother (close relative) threatening the offender to reveal the boy's whereabouts, but not the unrelated police officer. No defence is therefore available for state officials threatening to harm a suspect in Germany.

The Australian approach, even without taking recourse to the human dignity principle, is similar. Australian criminal and criminal procedural laws, in particular section 23Q of the Crimes Act 1914 (Cth), section 84(1) of the Evidence Act 1995 (Cth) and section 138 of the Evidence Act 1995 (Cth), prohibit the coercion of suspects during interviews. Australia, like Germany, is signatory to the four Geneva Conventions of 1949 and their Two Additional Protocols of 1977. Australia ratified the Convention Against Torture in 1989. There is therefore very limited possibility to apply criminal law defences in relation to an Australian police officer in torture cases. However, Australia's position is not as clear as the German one in relation to the deprivation of an individual's right to physical integrity as there are several decisions by higher courts in the United Kingdom—issued in relation to the Northern Ireland conflict in the 1970s—where security force operations against terrorists involving a reasonable degree of temporary hardship during detention and questioning, but not involving the application of force, were not considered to be torture or illegal coercion.[50] Should Australian courts follow the UK example, the application of torture practices cannot be excluded. The threshold in the Australian context therefore appears to be lower than in the German example. Also, unlike in Germany, police and prosecution in Australia do not have to adhere to the 'legality principle'.[51] The police and prosecution can exercise discretion whether to investigate or prosecute the police officer who violated the right and might use their discretion in cases of extreme emotional stress in favour of the accused officer.

---

[50] See also N James, 'Torture: What is it, Will it Work and Can it be Justified?' in Lynch, MacDonald and Williams, above n 4.

[51] See, eg, Fionda, above n 21, 167.

Again, it can be concluded that the principle of human dignity is the dividing line between approaches to the criminal responsibility of state officials in Germany and Australia. The common law does not offer protection as far reaching as the German Basic Law—even 'a little' torture is not allowed in the German context, while it could be under Australian common law. However, German courts do recognise the situation of extreme stress as a mitigating factor during sentencing. Like the 'hijacked aircraft' scenario, the 'law in books' and the 'law in action' differ markedly in the German context.

V. CONCLUSION

The principle of human dignity as embedded in the German Basic Law and as defined by German courts is the dividing line between the German and Australian approaches to criminal responsibility for state officials using force in counter terrorism operations. In Australia the special circumstances surrounding such operations will be considered before the trial as public interest factors relevant to the discretion to investigate or prosecute; by contrast, the principle of human dignity in the German context prescribes that these circumstances can only be taken into account at the sentencing stage. The decisions of the German courts show, however, that the level of protection accorded to the right to human dignity depends on the rights concerned and the context. The terrorists abducting a plane can be shot down, but the abductor of a child cannot be tortured. While state officials would not act illegally under the notions of necessity and self-defence if they shot down the plane only occupied by terrorists, they would not be justified or excused if the plane was also occupied by civilians. It follows that the right to human dignity is only absolute when attached to an absolute right, like the right not to be subject to torture, but not, if attached to the limitable right to life.

In the hijacked aircraft scenario human dignity is the dividing line between the German and the Australian approach. The principles prohibiting the balancing of life against life stem from different sources (Article 1 of the Basic Law in the German context and the decision in *Dudley and Stephens* in the Australian context), but they would both lead to the outcome that the plane cannot be shot down. However, it is questionable whether the limitations in *Dudley and Stephens* apply in the Australian context. The German law does not provide lawful authority for state officials to shoot the plane down, and if they did, they would have to face charges and be subject to the criminal trial process. In the Australian context, shooting the plane down is now lawful under Part IIIAAA and therefore charges cannot be laid.

In relation to the torture scenario, the principles applying—despite the existence of absolute prohibition under international law—are different.

Australia's colonial heritage becomes apparent in the common law applied to the torture scenario. A 'little' torture might be justified. The German approach here is very consistent. Even the mere threat of torture cannot be justified. The human dignity principle becomes a critical dividing line.

Despite some case law, it cannot be predicted what the German courts will decide in the future. What can be concluded is that the human dignity principle is in fact not as 'absolute' as it seems because of political and legal realities, while the common law, without having an explicit human dignity principle, could potentially afford a very similar protection to human rights through *Dudley and Stephens* and lead to very similar outcomes.

The fact that in the German system state officials must be subject to the criminal trial process before they can resume their positions—having received virtually no sentence—is a similar outcome to Australia. What difference does it make whether a state official is prosecuted and let off lightly, or not prosecuted at all? From the German perspective this makes a considerable difference. The fact that state officials must defend their actions in a public trial means that they may weigh considerations more carefully before infringing human rights provisions. In the light of Germany's past, this is an important factor that should not be underestimated.

Part III

Shooting to Kill in Context: Case Studies

10

The Fatal Police Shooting of Jean Charles de Menezes: Is Anyone Responsible?

IAN GORDON AND SEUMAS MILLER

T HIS CHAPTER EXPLORES the operational policing context and the ethical issues surrounding the fatal shooting of Jean Charles de Menezes in 2005 by members of the Metropolitan Police in London. Section I (authored by Ian Gordon) focuses on the operational context and the actual shooting incident itself, section II (authored by Seumas Miller) analyses the key issue of moral responsibility for the fatal shooting by police of an innocent person wrongly suspected of being a terrorist.

I. OPERATIONAL ISSUES

A. Background

The issuing of a firearm to a police officer does not itself, constitute a use of force; it is when a police officer makes use of a firearm,[1] for example by pointing or by firing. Use of force must be within the law as set out in:

— the common law;
— statute law, including section 3 of the Criminal Law Act 1967 and section 117 of the Police and Criminal Evidence Act 1984 ('A person may use such force as is reasonable in the circumstances in the prevention of crime, or in the effecting or assisting in the lawful arrest of offenders or suspected offenders or of persons unlawfully at large.');
— international law, in particular the European Convention on Human Rights (ECHR) is now incorporated in domestic law by the Human Rights Act 1998.

---

[1] The Manual of Guidance on Police Use of Firearms, ch 2, para 3.

Article 2.2 of the ECHR[2] outlines the conditions under which the use of force by police is permissible, namely:

— in defence of any person from unlawful violence;
— in order to effect a lawful arrest or to prevent the escape of a person lawfully detained;
— in action lawfully taken for the purpose of quelling a riot or insurrection.

The ECHR states the principles that are absolutely critical if firearms are to be used by police officers:

— *Legality*—there must be clear legal grounds for whatever action is taken by the police;
— *Proportionality*—the officer must have relevant and sufficient reasons to use force and there must be a balance between what action the police take and what they are trying to prevent occurring;
— *Necessity*—the officers must only act out of 'absolute necessity'.[3]
— *Accountability*—the police officers are accountable for their actions,[4] which will be carefully scrutinised, in any later inquiry.
— *Planning of the operation*—in particular the information gathering and planning stages will be considered as to whether opportunities for non-lethal intervention and/or no intervention occurred.[5]

The UK police service operates a common command structure at three levels for all policing operations, whether involving firearms or not. The structure has been well tested in countless operations including some of the largest operations mounted in the UK—the G8 summit in July 2005, for example. In relation to firearms operations Chapter 4, paragraph 3 of the Manual of Guidance on Police Use of Firearms defines the roles.

The 'GOLD' commander is strategic (only one 'Gold' is in the operation):

— They are in overall strategic command with responsibility and accountability for the operation.
— They are required to resource the operation.

---

[2] Convention for the Protection of Human Rights and Fundamental Freedoms, opened for signature 4 November 1950, 213 UNTS 221 (entered into force 3 September 1953) article 2(2).

[3] 'An AFO [authorised firearms officer] can only open fire when absolutely necessary and after conventional methods have been tried and failed, or must, from the nature of the circumstances be unlikely to succeed if tried.': Manual of Guidance on Police Use of Firearms, ch 2, para 3.

[4] In *McCann and Others v United Kingdom* Series A no 324 (1995) 21 ECHR 97 the Court held that where an agent of the state takes a life, in terms of Article 2(2), there must be an effective official investigation which is independent and public and in which the next of kin can participate effectively.

[5] In addition:
— information/intelligence assessment;
— competence and training of the commander and the AFO deployed;
— acceptability of their actions—human rights and risk of injury or death;
— proportionality in relation to the threat;
— the appropriateness and effectiveness of the police response.

— They chair any strategic coordinating group if the operation is a multi-agency response.
— They set, review and update the strategy—which may include some tactical parameters.

The 'SILVER' commander is tactical (there may be more than one 'Silver' in operation):

— They are responsible for developing and coordinating the tactical plan to achieve the 'Gold's' strategic intention within any tactical parameters set.
— They ensure all officers/staff are fully briefed.
— They are located to be able to maintain effective tactical command.
— They ensure that all decisions are documented in the Command Log.
— They are the pivotal link in the command chain to ensure other commanders are kept appraised of continuing developments.
— They constantly monitor the need for/use of firearms and any information change.

The 'BRONZE' commanders organise the groups of resources to carry out the tactical plan:

— They know and understand the 'Silver's' tactical plan and their role in it and ensure their staff are appropriately briefed.
— They implement the tactical plan and update the 'Silver' on developments in their area.
— They are located to be able to maintain effective tactical command in their area.

During firearms operations it is likely that 'Gold' and 'Silver' will each have a tactical firearms adviser (TFA) working alongside them. The role of the TFA is to offer tactical options and advice in relation to the use of firearms to 'Gold' and 'Silver'. However, it is not the role of the TFA to make decisions.

Officers in UK police services are most of the time unarmed, however, firearms are issued to authorised firearms officers (AFOs) under certain circumstances. Firearms are issued to AFOs when an authorising officer (generally above the rank of Inspector) approves their being carried (for operational use) whilst on patrol or for a specific firearms operation. The authorising officer must have reason to suppose that in the course of their duty, they may have to protect themselves or others from a person who:

— is in possession of a firearm, or
— has immediate access to a firearm, or
— is otherwise so dangerous that the officer's use of a firearm may be necessary.

The term 'reason to suppose' is attached to the 'threat' and authorisation to carry the weapon. There can be no justification for using a weapon based solely on the fact that firearms have been issued. The AFO is accountable for their use, in cases where the weapon is:

— pointed at another person, or
— fired at another person in self-defence or in defence of another whether or not injury or death results, or
— discharged in any other operational circumstances, including unintentional discharge.

The AFO has significant personal accountability for these actions. The ultimate responsibility for firing a weapon rests with the individual officer, who is accountable before the law.

Individual officers are accountable and responsible for all rounds they fire and must be able to justify them in the light of their legal responsibilities and powers. Their response must be proportionate to the threat they or some other person may face and they must report every discharge of a weapon, whether intentional or otherwise. The pointing of a firearm at any person may constitute an assault and must also be reported and recorded.

The test of using 'force which is no more than absolutely necessary' as set out in Article 2(2) of the ECHR, should be applied in relation to the operational discharge of any weapon.[6]

A Gold or Silver commander can authorise instances where shots *may* be fired but such authorisation will not exempt an individual AFO from their legal responsibility. No general rule is laid down and much will depend on the circumstances of individual incidents.

It may, however, be appropriate for a commander to direct that shots *will* be fired. This direction will not exempt an individual AFO from their legal responsibility and so must always be supported by appropriate and necessary information to justify the firer's actions. An example of circumstances where directed fire may be necessary would be in siege or terrorist incidents, for example, suicide bombers. An interesting aspect of a direction would be if the AFO declines to shoot based on their own assessment of the situation. The author is unaware whether this has already occurred in practice, but the use of apparently pregnant women in suicide terrorism may provoke a moral dilemma for the AFO. Such dilemmas are factored into training where equal emphasis is placed on competency in handling of firearms, tactical skills/awareness and judgement.

In an operation the AFO should identify themselves as such and give a clear warning of their intent to use firearms, with sufficient time for the warnings to be observed: unless to do so would unduly place any person at a risk of death or serious harm, or it would be clearly inappropriate or pointless in the circumstances of the incident.

---

[6] Manual of Guidance on the Police Use of Firearms, ch 5, para 2.4.

B. The Jean Charles De Menezes Shooting

Following the terrorist attacks in New York and Washington on 11 September 2001, the UK police service examined its strategy to combat the increased threat of 'suicide terrorist' bombing. A working party was formed to research the phenomenon of suicide terrorism across the world and to suggest the tactics that the police in the UK could deploy to counter this threat. Extensive work followed which involved research and visits to other countries, liaison with government departments and expert legal advice, resulting in a policy drawn up by the Association of Chief Police Officers (ACPO) and shared with all forces in the UK.

There has been a significant worldwide increase in terrorist attacks by suicide terrorist bombers and responses to the threat are not clear cut as there is no definitive profile of a suicide bomber in terms of age, sex or ethnicity. The research by the working party highlighted the problems of identifying such threats and then neutralising them. The plan 'Operation Kratos' was created as a result and encompasses a range of tactics used to defend against the threat from suicide terrorist bombers. Operation Kratos was adopted as part of the national firearms tactics in UK police forces.[7]

On 7 July 2005 suicide bombers detonated explosives in London with devastating effects. On 21 July 2005 there were further failed attempts to detonate bombs in London and suspects were identified. The following day, during a pre-planned police surveillance operation (Operation Theseus) linked to the attempted bombings, Jean Charles de Menezes was shot in the head at close range by armed police officers whilst on a train at Stockwell Underground Station. It is now known that his identity was mistaken for that of a failed suicide bomber. It was not conclusively established whether or not the armed officers gave any warning to Mr de Menezes.

The details of tactics for Kratos are contained in Part 2 of the Manual, access to which is restricted. Following the incident in London, however, the Metropolitan Police Authority (MPA) published a number of reports on the incident. One of the MPA reports[8] states:

> It is essential that the MPS have tactics available for the defence and protection of officers and the public in proximity to the threat. This is not a 'shoot to kill'

---

[7] A summary of the development of Kratos is contained in Independent Police Complaints Commission (IPCC), *Stockwell One: Investigation into the shooting of Jean Charlies de Menezes at Stockwell underground station* (February 2007) s 9, paras 9.1–9.19, 40–44 www.ipcc.gov.uk/Docments/stockwell_one.pdf.

[8] Events of July 2005—MPS response to suicide terrorism—Update Report: 8 of 23.02.06, see Metropolitan Police Authority 'September Meeting' (3 September 2007) www.mpa.gov.uk/committees/mpa/2006/060223/08.htm.

policy. The tactics are wholly consistent with Section 3 Criminal Law Act.[9] This is well articulated in the Manual.[10]

Another report includes a description of Operation Kratos:[11]

There are three separate plans under the generic title of Operation Kratos:

— Operation Andromeda is designed to deal with the spontaneous sighting by a member of the public of a suspected suicide bomber.
— Operation Beach is where there is an intelligence-led covert operation to locate and arrest persons suspected of involvement in acts of terrorism.
— Operation Clydesdale is where intelligence has been received about a suicide attack on a pre-planned event.

The aim of the operation is to: identify, locate, contain and neutralise the threat posed. The options for all three operations range from an unarmed stop of the suspect by uniformed officers, through to the deployment of armed police officers. These options involve a range of tactics that have remained confidential to avoid giving information to terrorist groups. It has become clear however that 'neutralising the threat' may involve shooting dead a suspected suicide bomber without warning.

The MPS received advice on the legality of this operational strategy and regular reviews to show the procedure remains 'fit for purpose' were recommended. The advice further emphasised the importance of reviewing the 'threat and intelligence available' for appropriateness and proportionality. A review of the national firearms policy by ACPO after the de Menezes incident concluded that it was still 'fit for purpose' under the new circumstances.[12]

So-called 'spontaneous incidents' and 'pre-planned incidents' need to be distinguished. The former generally arise from calls to police control rooms where a firearm (or what appears to be a firearm) has been seen or used during an incident. Usually—if practicable and available—an armed response vehicle (ARV) is deployed. A supervisor (not below the rank of Inspector) will decide whether to authorise the officers to arm themselves based on the information available at the time. Some forces keep the firearms in a locked container in the vehicle whilst others (including the MPS) allow their ARV officers to wear a sidearm whilst on duty. ARV personnel are employed in instances where firearms or risk of serious injury or death to a person is likely to occur. They are able to self arm and respond to that incident in line with their judgement and training.

---

[9] 'A person may use such force as is reasonable in the circumstances in the prevention of crime, or in the effecting or assisting in the lawful arrest of offenders or suspected offenders or of persons unlawfully at large.'

[10] Manual of Guidance on Police Use of Firearms, ch 2, para 3.

[11] Metropolitan Police Authority (MPA), *Suicide Terrorism Report*, No 13 (27 October 2005) www.mpa. gov.uk/committees/mpa/2005/051027/13.htm.

[12] Association of Chief Police Officers (Press release, No 28/06, 7 March 2006).

It is not always the case that an ARV will be deployed or be first at the scene. If unarmed officers are in attendance they will make an assessment of the situation and report to Control.

At the start of the operation the officer tasking the ARV officers is a Gold commander (and may also be the authorising officer). The aim for any operation involving firearms is to identify, locate, contain and neutralise the threat posed.

The circumstances in which Jean Charles de Menezes was killed were a pre-planned operation, but one which was part of an ongoing major investigation into failed 'suicide terrorist' bombings in London (Operation Theseus). The Independent Police Complaints Commission (IPCC) conducted a full investigation and the subsequent report[13] is a comprehensive narrative and analysis of what allegedly occurred.

Following the events in London on 7 July 2005, suicide terrorist bombers unsuccessfully attempted on 21 July to explode devices on three underground trains and a bus. The UK threat level for terrorism was at Level 1 'Critical'—the highest it had ever been and there was enormous pressure on the MPS to protect the public and arrest suspects. The MPS began a major operation to locate those suspects and prevent further similar acts; the Gold commander for the firearms operation (Operation Theseus 2) was Commander John McDowall. Information was received that Hussain Osman and Abdi Omar, could have been involved and a possible address at 21 Scotia Road was identified. A surveillance operation began at Scotia Road, which is a multi occupancy building. The Gold commander's strategy included:[14]

> To control the premises at SCOTIA ROAD through covert surveillance, follow any person leaving the premises until it was felt safe to challenge them and then stop them.

The Gold commander considered that an Operation Kratos situation could develop and appointed a Designated Senior Officer (DSO)—Commander Cressida Dick. He also appointed two Silver commanders, a Detective Chief Inspector for the firearms operation and a Detective Superintendent for the operations room (Room 1600) to provide a link with SO13—the MPS Anti Terrorism Branch, which provided an intelligence feed to the DSO.

'DSO'[15] was a new term to the Command terminology and, since the Stockwell incident, it has been renamed 'DSO-SILVER'. This officer is in

---

[13] IPCC, above n 7.
[14] IPCC, above n 7, 24.
[15] MPA, above n 11. Owing to the extreme nature of the risk to the public, a very robust command structure has been designed and implemented. Specially trained ACPO officers, acting as the 'Designated Senior Officer' (DSO), will command these operations. It is the DSO who will give the order to a firearms officer to shoot.

command of the tactical operation (Kratos) and, if necessary, may order a firearms officer to shoot a suspect.

When Kratos was introduced into UK policing there was some confusion as to whether the DSO was a Gold or Silver commander in a Kratos operation. That said, it is very clear from the Stockwell One Report that Commander Dick, as DSO, considered herself in command of the firearms operation with the responsibility to achieve the strategic aims set by the Gold commander. Commander Dick was trained as a DSO and had considerable experience commanding firearms operations involving life-threatening situations. She was in operational command of the firearms operation and the Silver Firearms commander was apparently working as her ground commander. Both the DSO and the Silver Firearms commander had firearms tactical advisers working with them (Trojan 80 and Trojan 84 respectively). The DSO had a loggist who recorded her verbal decisions and their rationale. The DSO transcribed them into her Decision Log, some hours later. A specialist tactical firearms team (CO19) was assigned to the operation.

As she had been given a wrong location, the DSO missed the first 25 minutes of the Gold commander's briefing to the Silver commanders and their firearms advisers. The DSO requested and was given a second briefing by the Gold commander and he later gave her a written intelligence update.

Trojan 84 initially briefed CO19; they were told about the command structure in place, that a DSO had been appointed and that they should trust the intelligence being provided. The Silver firearms commander further briefed CO19. This was a comprehensive intelligence briefing, encompassing all knowledge on incidents and including a link to the actual bombings on 7 July 2005. He described the individuals involved in the bombings as being 'deadly and determined' and 'up for it'. CO19 was told that any subject coming from the flats would be allowed to 'run' and that an interception would take place as soon as possible away from the address so as not to compromise it. These briefings were not recorded, which was justified by time constraints. CO19 was instructed to move to a holding point near Scotia Road.

The address at Scotia Road had a communal doorway. At 9.33–9.34 am, Jean Charles de Menezes came out of the doorway and was seen by surveillance officers to walk to a bus stop and board a Number 2 bus. He was kept under surveillance and remained on the bus until Brixton Road, where he got off. It appeared that he had the intention of using the underground at Brixton Station. The station was closed due to a security alert, so he walked back to the bus stop and actually boarded the bus he had left. This behaviour apparently raised a question with surveillance officers as to whether he was using anti-surveillance techniques. He travelled on the bus to a stop near Stockwell Station.

Room 1600 did not have equipment to record radio and telephone conversations coming into the room. It was occupied by about 20 people and described as 'noisy'. The inquiry report details conversation between the surveillance team members about identification of Mr de Menezes as the suspect Mr Osman.[16] There was no positive identification. The terms 'good possible likeness', 'could not positively identify' were used, with one staff member saying that he 'did not believe the person was identical to Osman'.

It is apparent from the inquiry report that this uncertainty was not made clear to the DSO and Silver firearms commanders. CO19 officers and those in Room 1600 stated that they were made aware that Mr de Menezes was acting nervously or was twitchy.[17] The Silver firearms commander, who was with CO19 at the holding point, heard on the surveillance radio that Mr de Menezes had been identified as the suspect, which was also heard by Trojan 84 and the CO19 team leader. The DSO stated that she was informed, 'it is him, the man is off the bus. They think it is him and he is very, very jumpy.' This is recorded within her loggist's notes.

As the bus was nearing the station, the officers directing the operation formed the view that he was likely to be the suspect, Hussain Osman. CO19 was directed to get behind the suspect but had to travel from the holding point.

Mr de Menezes got off the bus at Stockwell and walked towards the station. In the belief that Mr de Menezes had been positively identified as Mr Osman and, following consultation with her firearms adviser Trojan 80, the DSO decided that Mr de Menezes could not be allowed to enter the Stockwell Underground Station. The order to stop him was therefore given by the DSO. There is no evidence that the DSO gave an order to shoot Mr de Menezes.[18]

The CO19 team was not yet in place at the underground station and it was not clear who had been designated to carry out the stop order. The surveillance team members were armed but not trained for such interventions. The order was directed to them but due to the arrival of CO19 outside the station, the DSO countermanded the order and specified that CO19 should stop Mr de Menezes. By this time, however, he had gone into the station still followed by the surveillance team; CO19 ran into the station in pursuit, but they were two minutes behind Mr de Menezes.

It follows from the inquiry report[19] that all CO19 officers believed they were dealing with a person who had been identified as a suspect terrorist bomber. The firearms officers, however, had different perceptions of what was meant by the order 'to stop Mr de Menezes'. Some believed that the threat required armed intervention, others that even shooting him may

---

[16] IPCC, above n 7, paras 12.1–12.17, pp 53–57.
[17] Ibid para 12.17, p 57.
[18] Ibid para 12.37, p 61.
[19] Ibid para 12.27, p 59 and para 12.36, p 61.

be necessary to protect the public and police officers on the underground train.

Mr de Menezes boarded the train and sat in a carriage with other passengers and three members of the surveillance team. Two CO19 officers entered the carriage and a surveillance officer pointed to Mr de Menezes. Accounts differ on this point, but it is believed that Mr de Menezes stood up and faced the arriving police officers. He was grabbed around the waist by one of the nearby surveillance officers (Ivor) who believed he was about to detonate a bomb and pushed back into his seat. The CO19 officers stated that they felt they had to act immediately to prevent loss of life to the people on the train. They tackled Mr de Menezes and both fired a number of shots into his head killing him. The time between Mr de Menezes leaving Scotia Road and his death was 33 minutes.

The question arises—on the evidence available—did the officers (including the commanders) use 'force which is no more than absolutely necessary'?

The Independent Police Complaints Commission (IPCC) carried out the investigation into the shooting at Stockwell Underground Station.[20] The main issues identified in the report are:

1. This was a case of mistaken identity where the police killed an innocent man. There is nothing to suggest this mistake was the result of any deliberate act or intention to endanger life.

2. The central issue is whether the actual quality of identification by the surveillance team was properly communicated to officers in Room 1600 and the specialist firearms team CO19. The report states that the surveillance team leader expressed a level of doubt in using words to the effect that 'they believed the subject to be Osman', 'it was a good possible'; he did not communicate that some of his team did not think Mr de Menezes was the suspect Mr Osman.[21] The Incident Command Team and the tactical firearms team (CO19) all believed that a positive identification had been made.[22]

3. The strategy set by the Gold commander involved containment of 21 Scotia Road and stopping all those who left it; yet eight people left that address without being challenged, after the surveillance observation post had been set up at 6.40 am that day. The inquiry report concludes that insufficient resources had been in place at Scotia Road when Mr de Menezes left the address at 9.30 am despite surveillance having been in place since 6.40 am.

4. In particular, the specialist firearms team, CO19, was essential to implement the strategic containment and controlled stop of persons

[20] IPCC, above n 7.
[21] Ibid para 20.53, p 128.
[22] Ibid para 12.7–12.8, p 59.

leaving 21 Scotia Road. It was, however, located elsewhere. Mr de Menezes was able to travel on two buses, enter an underground station and board a train without challenge. No tactical options were in place as a contingency plan if CO19 was not in place to deal with potential suspects leaving Scotia Road. The report suggests that Mr de Menezes could have been stopped before getting on the first bus if appropriate resources had been in place.

5. No contingency plan or alternative tactical options existed to deal with a suspect leaving 31 Scotia Road before CO19 was in place.

6. No contingency plan existed to deal with a suspect travelling on public transport.

7. Radio malfunctions impacted on the quality of the radio traffic between the surveillance team members. When the CO19 officers entered the underground station, they were out of radio contact due to lack of reception underground. The lack of recording facilities for communications impacted on the later assessment of events by the IPCC investigation team.

8. The briefings of the CO19 team made it clear that they may have been facing a suicide bomber. They included a comprehensive intelligence update and the links to the actual bombings on 7 July. They were also reminded of the law in relation to the use of force. The briefings did not include the circumstances in which the Operation Kratos plan could be used. However, it was understood that action should only be taken as a matter of last resort when they were sure of the identity of the person in relation to whom the policy was to be applied.

9. The state of mind of the firearms officers is important. The Manual states[23] that the content of a briefing may directly affect the response of armed officers to any perceived threat from the subject. In each of their briefings the Silver firearms officer and Trojan 84 made a conscious effort to ensure that the CO19 officers were not 'under-briefed'. They considered that they had a duty of care towards the team to ensure they were aware of the threat facing them. The CO19 officers who fired the shots stated they believed Mr de Menezes to be a suicide bomber who was about to detonate a bomb and kill the people on the train.

10. The order 'to stop Mr. de Menezes getting on the train', had different meanings to different officers, which has to be considered in line with the state of mind of the firearms officers. At no time was this declared a Kratos incident. The report said:

Neither those in command of Operation Theseus 2 nor those on the ground assert that the shooting of Jean Charles de Menezes was the product of a formal 'Kratos

---

[23] Manual of Guidance on Police Use of Firearms, ch 4, para 7.7.

policy' decision. A direct Kratos decision is not advanced by those in Room 1600 and the two CO19 officers who shot de Menezes do not suggest that they acted on such a direct instruction.[24]

It is pertinent to repeat that at the time of this incident the UK and in particular London was at significant threat (Level 1) from further terrorist outrages. The MPS was stretched to an extent that it had never been before and the officers involved in this incident were working long tours of duty under the most stressful conditions. This information is not an excuse for the death of an innocent man; they are facts to consider when opinions are being formed and conclusions drawn.

The IPCC report went to the Crown Prosecution Service (CPS) to determine criminal liability on the part of any officer in the incident. On 17 July 2006, the CPS informed the IPCC that there was insufficient evidence to bring prosecutions against any individual officer. The CPS opened proceedings against the office of the Commissioner of Police of the Metropolis for offences under sections 3 and 33 of the Health and Safety at Work Act 1974 for failing to provide for the health, safety and welfare of Jean Charles de Menezes on 22 July 2005. The jury returned a guilty verdict and the MPS was fined £175,000 and £385,000 costs.

When the foreman of the jury delivered the verdict she added the rider, 'In reaching this verdict the jury attached no personal culpability to Commander Dick.'

When delivering the sentence the trial judge made the following comment with regard to Commander Dick, 'The jury's rider in relation to her was anticipated by me and it accords with my view of the facts. She was in charge of and controlling an extremely difficult situation. She has now that rider to depend on and in my judgement, rightly so.'

He also said:

> We heard, Commissioner, of some magnificent police work by several officers. The work of the officer codenamed 'Ivor' in grasping a suspected suicide bomber by both arms, pinning them to his side, was magnificent, and if he had been dealing with a suicide bomber, he may well have saved many lives. As it was, he risked his own life, not only by way of proximity, but because he was dressed similar to Mr. de Menezes, he was of similar complexion, and was indeed apparently for a short time understandably treated by the firearms team as an associate of the man they believed to be the bomber. It should be remembered also that he volunteered himself to make the stop before Mr. de Menezes entered the tube station.

On 12 December 2008 the inquest[25] held into the death of Mr de Menezes returned an open verdict. The jury declined to bring a verdict of lawful killing. The coroner had previously concluded that a verdict of

---

[24] IPCC, above n 7.
[25] IPPC, above n 7, para 9.14, p 43.

unlawful killing was not justified so it was unavailable to the jury. There was criticism in the media of the coroner's decision to withhold the verdict 'unlawful killing' from the jury.

The IPCC has reviewed its original decision in the light of the inquest into Mr de Menezes' death. On 2 October 2009 it reported that it would stand by its decision not to recommend disciplinary actions against the MPS officers involved in the fatal shooting of Mr de Menezes.

II. ETHICAL ANALYSIS: IS ANYONE RESPONSIBLE?

Jean Charles de Menezes was an innocent person wrongly suspected by police of being a terrorist suicide bomber who was intentionally killed by police in the belief that he was a mortal threat to the passengers in the London underground station where he was shot dead. The ethical issue to be addressed in this section concerns the individual and/or collective *moral* responsibility, if any, for the killing of an innocent person.

While the events that terminated in Mr de Menezes' death involved a number of what might at this point be referred to as mistakes or errors of judgement on the part of police (see section A), I will focus on just three: (1) the failure of the surveillance team in relation to determining whether or not Mr de Menezes was the terrorist suspect Hussain Osman and, in particular, clearly communicating to Commander Dick that Mr de Menezes was or was not Mr Osman, or that they did not know or were otherwise uncertain of their subject's identity; (2) the failure on the part of Commander Dick to see to it that Mr de Menezes was challenged and stopped at some point after leaving Scotia Road, but prior to his entering the underground railway station, that is, at a location which would not have compromised the surveillance operation at Scotia Road, and in a manner that would not have required killing him (he being at most a threat to himself, the arresting officers and, perhaps, one or two passersby); (3) the failure on the part of the two officers who shot Mr de Menezes each to provide himself with adequate grounds for believing that they were shooting dead a suicide bomber who was at the time in question a mortal threat to the train passengers; after all, the person shot dead was merely a suspected suicide bomber and one in relation to whom the firearms officers had no clear evidence that he was carrying a bomb—because the operation had not been declared by Commander Dick to be a Kratos operation and they did not at any point perceive a bomb or were otherwise provided with good evidence that the suspect was carrying a bomb. In referring to these failures as mistakes or—especially in the case of Commander Dick and the firearms officers—errors of judgement, I am not implying any specific moral failing on the part of the police; whether or not there was a moral failure is a matter to be determined. Certainly, as stated above, there was no intention to kill an innocent person; indeed, police actions were carried out with the intention to save innocent lives. Moreover, obviously the police did not foresee that an innocent life would be taken.

A related ethical issue concerns Kratos as a mode of police operations. Is Kratos an ethically sustainable operational policy? If not, then a question arises in relation to the moral responsibility of those who put the policy in place for any untoward consequences that might emanate from its application on the ground. In relation to the ethical acceptability of Kratos, suppose that the police shot dead a person under the same circumstances as they shot Mr de Menezes except that the person turned out to be Mr Osman; would their actions have been justified if, for example, Mr Osman was *not* carrying a bomb with him at the time? Mr Osman was, after all, only a suspected suicide bomber; otherwise, why was the plan to 'let him run' upon leaving Scotia Road? At no point was any good evidence provided that the person under surveillance was actually carrying a bomb. Is it therefore ethically justifiable for police to shoot dead a suspect without warning, when the suspect is in a crowded location and they have good evidence that he is a suicide bomber, but they do not know whether he has a bomb on him at the time? (By the way, this is, it seems to me, a shoot to kill policy of the sort, for example, that is used by military forces in relation to combatants.) And if shooting dead a person under these circumstances is not permissible under Kratos, because it is not permissible under the relevant criminal laws, is it, nevertheless, not likely that under Kratos police will end up shooting suspect suicide bombers under these circumstances? Indeed, on one construal of events—a construal that is admittedly at odds with the testimony of the police and not found by the coroner to be correct by the standard of being beyond reasonable doubt—this is exactly what happened in the case of the shooting of Mr de Menezes. The firearms officers, rightly or wrongly, reasonably or unreasonably, believed the situation was a de facto Kratos operation and, therefore, did not give Mr de Menezes any warning, did not afford him the opportunity to be arrested without the use of force, and for his part Mr de Menezes did not fail to comply with any instruction from the police.

A. Moral Responsibility

We first need to distinguish some different senses of responsibility. Sometimes to say that someone is responsible for an action is to say that the person had a reason, or reasons, to perform some action, then formed an intention to perform that action (or not to perform it), and finally acted (or refrained from acting) on that intention, and did so on the basis of that reason(s). Note that an important category of reasons for actions are ends, goals or purposes; an agent's reason for performing an action is often that the action realises an agent's goal. Moreover, it is assumed that in the course of all this the agent brought about or caused the action, at least in the sense that the mental state or states that constituted his reason for performing the action was causally efficacious (in the right way), and that his resulting intention was causally efficacious (in the right way).

I will dub this sense of being responsible for an action 'natural responsibility'. This sense of being responsible is relevant to the actions of the firearms officer in shooting Mr de Menezes in that they intentionally performed an action of shooting Mr de Menezes dead and did so for the reason that they believed him to be a suicide bomber.

On other occasions, what is meant by the term 'being responsible for an action' is that the person in question occupies a certain institutional role and that the occupant of that role is the person who has the institutionally determined duty to decide what is to be done in relation to certain matters and to see to it that it does happen. Thus the members of the surveillance team had the responsibility to identify Mr Osman, video record anyone leaving the premises, and communicate information in a clear and precise manner to the control room, irrespective of whether or not they did so, or even contemplated doing so. Clearly, they failed in respect of their institutional responsibility in this regard.

A third sense of 'being responsible' for an action, is a species of our second sense. If the matters in respect of which the occupant of an institutional role has an institutionally determined duty to decide what is to be done include ordering other agents to perform, or not to perform, certain actions, then the occupant of the role is responsible for those actions performed by those other agents. We say of such a person that he is responsible for the actions of other persons in virtue of being the person in authority over them. Thus, as the person in authority, Commander Dick had a responsibility to see to it that the police on the ground interdicted Mr de Menezes before he entered the underground station. Her failure in this respect was a failure to discharge her institutional responsibility as the person in authority.

The fourth sense of responsibility is in fact the sense that we are principally concerned with here, namely, moral responsibility. Roughly speaking, an agent is held to be morally responsible for an action or omission, if the agent was responsible for that action or omission in one of our first three senses of responsibility, and that action is morally significant.

An action or omission can be morally significant in a number of ways. The action or omission could be intrinsically morally wrong, as in the case of a rights violation. Or the action or omission might have moral significance by virtue of the end that it was performed to serve or the foreseen or reasonably foreseeable outcome that it actually had, for example, the killing of an innocent person, as in the case of Mr de Menezes.

We can now make the following preliminary claim concerning moral responsibility:

1. If an agent is responsible for an action or omission (or foreseen or reasonably foreseeable outcome of that action or omission) in the first, second or third sense of being responsible, and the action, omission or outcome is morally significant, then—other things being equal— the agent is morally responsible for that action, omission or outcome, and—again, other things being equal—ought to attract moral praise or blame and (possibly) punishment or reward for it.

Here the 'other things being equal' clauses are intended to be cashed in terms of capacity for morally responsible action, for example, suppose the agent was a psychopath, or in terms of exculpatory conditions either by way of justification or excuse. Thus, other things might not be equal if, for example, the agent was coerced, or there was some overriding moral justi- fication for performing what would otherwise have been a morally wrong action. Note also that contra some accounts of moral responsibility I am distinguishing this notion from that of blameworthiness/praiseworthiness.

Let us first consider the surveillance officer or officers who failed in their institutional responsibility by not clearly communicating whether or not Mr de Menezes was Mr Osman or whether they were uncertain in this regard. Given the moral stakes, that is, the possibility of loss of innocent life (whether the life of an innocent person mistakenly identified as a suicide bomber or the lives of innocent Londoners caught in a bomb blast), and the fact that the members of a surveillance team can reasonably be expected to provide clear communications in relation to their subjects, then they can be held morally responsible for their failure to provide a clear communication, albeit there might be mitigating circumstances, for example, confusion, lack of resources.

Now consider Commander Dick. Again, given the moral stakes, the exis- tence of a plan (namely, to stop any suspected suicide bomber before they got to an underground train station or similar locale) that she could reason- ably have been expected to adhere to, she can be held morally responsible for failing to see to it that Mr de Menezes was interdicted prior to going into the underground, albeit there might be mitigating circumstances.

Of course, in making these claims regarding moral responsibility for a variety of failures, I am not claiming that the surveillance team or Commander Dick is morally responsible for Mr de Menezes' death.

What of the firearms officers? The justification for killing Mr de Menezes available to the firearms officers was that they believed him to be a suicide bomber and they shot him to protect the lives of the train passengers and their own lives.

It seems clear that the coroner was correct to argue that it was not a case of unlawful killing, because it cannot be shown beyond reasonable doubt that the two officers did not believe that the man they shot was a suicide bomber who was a mortal threat to the lives of the passengers and themselves.

However, the jury in reaching an open verdict rather than a verdict of lawful killing did so on the grounds that on the balance of probabilities it was not clear that the two police officers believed that they were shooting a suicide bomber who was a deadly threat at the time of the shooting. Moreover, even if they did believe that this was the case, there remain further questions from a moral, if not a legal, perspective. This is, in part, because of the nature of individual moral responsibility when it comes to taking the life of another human being.

B. Deadly Force and Individual Moral Responsibility

Police officers need to exercise authority on a daily basis; they have institutional responsibilities in the sense explained above.

Historically, policing in the UK and Australia has made use of a distinctive notion of authority, so-called original authority. In relation to the concept of original authority, we need to distinguish compliance with laws from obedience to the directives of men and women, especially one's superiors. Thus, according to the law, an investigating officer must not prosecute a fellow police officer if the latter is self-evidently innocent. On the other hand, the investigator might be ordered to do so by his superior officer. Now, individual police officers are held to be responsible to the law as well as their superiors in the police service. However, their first responsibility is to the law. So, a police officer should disobey a directive from a superior officer that is clearly unlawful. And yet, the admittedly controversial doctrine of original authority does not end here. It implies further that there are at least some situations in which police officers have a right to disobey a superior's otherwise *lawful* command, if obeying it would prevent them from discharging their own obligations to the law.[26]

---

[26] Relevant legal cases here are the 'Blackburn cases', principally *R v Metropolitan Police Commissioner; Ex parte Blackburn* [1968] 2 QB 118, cited in K Bryett, A Harrison and J Shaw, *An Introduction to Policing: The Role and Function of Police in Australia*, vol II (Sydney, Butterworths, 1994) 43, in which Lord Denning considered the Commissioner of the London Metropolitan Police 'to be answerable to the law and to the law alone' in response to a demand for *mandamus* from a plaintiff seeking to get the courts to require police intervention, and *Fisher v Oldham Corporation* [1930] 2 KB 364, cited as above at 42, in which the court found the police service was not vicariously liable in virtue of the original authority of the office of constable. Concerning the exercise of original authority in decisions to arrest, in some jurisdictions proceeding by summons has increased significantly and officers do not possess original authority in respect of any part of the summons process. To this extent their original authority has diminished.

According to the doctrine of original authority, there are at least some actions, including the decision to arrest or not arrest (at least in some contexts) or to shoot or not shoot, which are ultimately matters for the decision of the individual officer, and decisions for which he is, or might be, individually legally liable.[27] The contexts in question are ones in which the action of arresting a given person would prevent the police officer from discharging his obligations to the law, and (in this instance) his obligation to keep the peace, in particular. If this is indeed the legal situation, then it reflects a commitment to the ethical notion of professional autonomy. Police are being held to be akin to members of professional groups such as doctors. In the case of a surgeon, for example, it is up to the surgeon— and not the surgeon's employer—to decide whether or not to operate on a patient who might suffer complications if operated on.

In some tension with this understanding of the legal situation in UK policing, I note that it was the Commissioner of the Police of the Metropolis, in his capacity as the employer, who was fined for an offence under the Health and Safety at Work Act for failing to provide for the health, safety and welfare of Mr de Menezes. At any rate, my concern is morality not legality.

Consider a situation in which police officers are confronted with passive non-compliance on the part of a criminal known to be dangerous. On the one hand, if they shoot him and he turns out to be unarmed, they might be up on a murder charge. On the other hand, they put their own lives at risk by rushing him and trying to overpower him. After all, there is reason to believe that he might be armed. Faced with this dilemma, it might seem that a third option is preferable, namely the option to let him go free. Certainly, this is an option available to ordinary members of the public when they confront armed and dangerous persons. But matters are somewhat different for the police. They have a moral and a legal duty to apprehend such persons. Failure to try to apprehend an armed and dangerous offender would amount to serious neglect of duty on their part. Indeed, if they simply allowed him to go free, and he went on to murder an innocent person, this neglect of duty might be held to be a moral failure of negligence and might also be held by a court to be criminal negligence.

Moreover, if a senior and superior officer issued an apparently lawful directive to these subordinate officers to shoot the offender on the grounds that the evidence indicated that he was probably concealing a dangerous weapon and was highly likely to use it, the subordinate police officers might

---

[27] A concept very close to original authority is sometimes referred to as a species of discretionary power, namely the concept of a discretionary decision that cannot be overridden or reversed by another official. See R Dworkin, *Taking Rights Seriously* (Cambridge, Harvard University Press, 1977) 32. Here we need to distinguish a decision that cannot as a matter of fact be overridden, eg, the use of deadly force by a lone officer in the field, and a decision that cannot be overridden as a matter of law. Only the latter can be referred to as a species of authority.

well be acting within their legal rights to refuse to do so. For they might disagree with the senior officer's judgement and hold that they might find themselves liable for wrongful killing if it turned out that the offender was unarmed.

The above-described individual civil and criminal liability of police officers, supposing it is correct, would stand in some contrast with military combatants. A civilian would in general sue the military organisation itself, rather than the soldier whose actions resulted in harm to the civilian. Moreover, presumably soldiers do not reserve a general institutional right to refuse to shoot to kill when (lawfully) ordered to do so by their commanding officers. My understanding is that in keeping with the absence of such a general right, criminal liability in relation to negligence and many categories of wrongful killing is generally sheeted home to the military officer who issued the command, rather than his subordinates who were his instrument.

Whatever the legal situation, arguably soldiers ought to reserve a moral right to refuse to shoot to kill; perhaps this is an inalienable moral right. If this is correct then it has two important implications.

First, it entails an important difference between the basis for different elements of original authority (and possibly professional autonomy). One basis derives from the nature of the relevant institution and its institutional purposes. If individual police officers have a right to refuse a lawful command by a superior to arrest someone in some circumstances then this is because, speaking generally, their possession of this right makes for a better and more effective police service. However, the second basis, as I have suggested above, is a fundamental moral right; a moral right not to be required to kill another human being, if one judges it to be wrong or otherwise unwarranted. And perhaps the professional autonomy of surgeons likewise has two different bases, one institutional, the other a fundamental moral right.

The second implication is that the above-mentioned contrast between the police and the military would be much less sharp. Soldiers, like police, have a moral right to refuse a lawful order to use lethal force. However, a distinction between the military and the police might still be able to be drawn at the institutional level in terms of, for example, the notion of presumption. The presumption might be that an individual soldier would not be the one to decide whether or not he or she would shoot to kill in cases where he or she was directed by a superior to do so (or not to do so); rather the superior would be the one to decide. In the case of police officers, this would not be the case; there would be no such presumption in favour of a superior officer. Rather the individual police officer—the shooter—would be the one to decide. The situation is further muddied by the existence of paramilitary police roles, such as police snipers.

Let us now return to our two firearms officers who shot dead Mr de Menezes.

The first point is that it was the moral responsibility of the two police officers to decide whether or not to shoot Mr de Menezes, irrespective of whether they had been ordered to do so; and, evidently, this is reflected in the law. (See section I A above on this point.) The second point is that they had not been ordered to do so; the situation had not been declared to be a Kratos operation. So, for better or worse, individual moral responsibility can in principle be sheeted home to the two firearms officers for killing an innocent person depending, of course, on the facts of the case.

What of exculpatory conditions? Their justification was that they believed that Mr de Menezes was a suicide bomber. Even supposing this to be true—and the jury did not accept that on the balance of probabilities—there remains the question of the justification for that belief. Did they have sufficient evidence to warrant that belief? It seems that they did not, especially given that good and decisive evidence is required in the case where the taking of another human life is concerned.

However, there is another important moral consideration in play here. The firearms officers had a moral obligation to protect the lives of innocent train passengers. If they had failed to shoot the suspect, and he had turned out to be Mr Osman carrying a bomb, then in all probability there would have been a far greater loss of life. This consideration has considerable moral weight and does so notwithstanding the inadequacy of the evidence for their belief (or judgement) that Mr de Menezes was Mr Osman and a mortal threat at the time. So whatever the legal situation, and whatever any past failure to satisfy themselves with regard to the identity of Mr de Menezes, at the point of decision whether or not to shoot him, the firearms officers confronted what was in effect a moral dilemma: (1) shoot dead a person they believe is highly likely to be a suicide bomber about to detonate a bomb; of course, if he turns out not to have a bomb then they will have killed an innocent person; (2) refrain from shooting him; of course, if he turns out to be a suicide bomber about to detonate a bomb then numerous innocent passengers and the police officers themselves will be killed. In these circumstances it is difficult not to view the 'other things being equal' as having application. Arguably, there was not a good and decisive reason in favour of either course of action. Rather, at the point of decision great risks attached to each of the available options; there was a moral balancing act to be performed, and a split second decision to be made. In these circumstances the firearms officers might be held to be morally responsible for the death of an innocent person, but they surely cannot be held to be morally *culpable* for what they did; they were morally responsible but not morally blameworthy.

C. Collective Moral Responsibility

Above we distinguished four senses of responsibility, including moral responsibility. Let us now consider collective moral responsibility.

As is the case with individual responsibility, we can distinguish four senses of collective responsibility. In the first instance I will do so in relation to joint actions.

Agents who perform a joint action are responsible for that action in the first sense of collective responsibility. Accordingly, to say that they are collectively responsible for the action is just to say that they performed the joint action. That is, they each had a collective end, each intentionally performed their contributory action, and each did so because each believed the other would perform his contributory action, and that therefore the collective end would be realised. So, the individual members of the surveillance team performed the joint action of surveilling Scotia Road.

It is important to note here that each agent is individually (naturally) responsible for performing his contributory action, and responsible by virtue of the fact that he intentionally performed this action, and the action was not intentionally performed by anyone else. Of course the other agents (or agent) *believe* that he is performing, or is going to perform, the contributory action in question. But mere possession of such a belief is not sufficient for the ascription of responsibility to *the believer* for performing the individual action in question. So what are the agents *collectively* (naturally) responsible for? The agents are *collectively* (naturally) responsible for the realisation of the (collective) *end* which results from their contributory actions. Consider two agents jointly killing someone in a crowded setting, one by grabbing him and holding him fast, the other by shooting him in the head. Each is individually (naturally) responsible for his own action, and the two agents are collectively (naturally) responsible for bringing it about that the person is dead, given that the actions of both were necessary.

Again, if the occupants of an institutional role (or roles) have an institutionally determined obligation to perform some joint action then those individuals are collectively responsible for its performance, in our second sense of collective responsibility. Here there is a *joint* institutional obligation to realise the collective end of the joint action in question. In addition, there is a set of derived *individual* obligations; each of the participating individuals has an individual obligation to perform his or her contributory action. (The derivation of these individual obligations relies on the fact that if everyone performs his or her contributory action then it is probable that the collective end will be realised.)

There is a third sense of collective responsibility that might be thought to correspond to the third sense of individual responsibility. The third sense of individual responsibility concerns those in authority. Suppose the members of the Cabinet of country A (consisting of the Prime Minister and his or her Cabinet ministers) or the members of the relevant police authority, collectively decide to exercise their institutionally determined right to introduce a counter terrorism measure, for example, Kratos. The Cabinet and/or the relevant police authority (say, ACPO) is then collectively responsible for this policy and, potentially, for the untoward consequences of its implementation.

There are a couple of things to keep in mind here. First, the notion of responsibility in question is, at least in the first instance, institutional—as opposed to moral—responsibility.

Second, the 'decisions' of committees, as opposed to the individual decisions of the members of committees, need to be analysed in terms of the notion of a joint institutional mechanism introduced above. So the 'decision' of the Cabinet, and also perhaps of the ACPO, can be analysed as follows. At one level each member of the Cabinet or the ACPO voted for or against Kratos. Let us assume some voted in the affirmative and others in the negative. But at another level each member of the Cabinet or ACPO (or both) agreed to abide by the outcome of the vote; each voted having as a collective end that the outcome with a majority of the votes in its favour would be realised. Accordingly, the members of the Cabinet and/or of the ACPO were jointly institutionally responsible for the policy change, that is, Cabinet and/or ACPO were collectively institutionally responsible for the change.

What of the fourth sense of collective responsibility, collective *moral* responsibility? Collective moral responsibility is a species of joint responsibility. Accordingly, each agent is individually morally responsible, but conditionally on the others being individually morally responsible. There is interdependence in respect of moral responsibility. This account of collective moral responsibility arises naturally out of the account of joint actions. It also parallels the account given of individual moral responsibility.

Thus we can make our second preliminary claim about moral responsibility:

2. If agents are collectively responsible for a joint action or omission (or the realisation of a foreseen or reasonably foreseeable outcome of that action or omission), in the first or second or third senses of collective responsibility, and if the joint action, omission or outcome is morally significant then—other things being equal—the agents are collectively morally responsible for that action, omission or outcome, and—other things being equal—ought to attract moral praise or blame, and (possibly) punishment or reward for bringing about the outcome.

As is the case with the parallel account of individual moral responsibility, there are crucial 'other things being equal' clauses to provide for the possibilities that the agents in question either lack the requisite moral capacities—and so cannot be held morally responsible—or are possessed of moral capacities but in the circumstances in question have an excuse or justification for their joint actions and omissions, and for the outcomes of such actions and omissions.

In the light of our account of collective moral responsibility, what sense can we now make of the police killing of Jean Charles de Menezes?

The first point is that, as noted already, collective moral responsibility for an outcome is consistent with individual moral responsibility for individual actions that are in part constitutive of some joint action, omission or outcome. As we have seen, the surveillance team was morally responsible for failing to clearly communicate to the control room whether or not Mr de Menezes was Mr Osman—or that they were uncertain in this regard. Moreover, Commander Dick is morally responsible for failing to see to it that Mr de Menezes was stopped prior to his entering the underground station. Finally, the two firearms officers were morally responsible for failing to provide themselves with good and decisive evidence for the proposition that Mr de Menezes was a suicide bomber and a mortal threat to the train passengers. Here I stress that these failures all had mitigating factors, especially no doubt the failures of the firearms officers.

The second point is that each of these failures was a necessary condition for the outcome, that is, the outcome that may be described as the killing of an innocent person.

This second point gives rise to the question as to whether the surveillance team, Commander Dick and the firearms officers are collectively morally responsible for that outcome, albeit none individually intended the outcome and none individually foresaw the outcome. I suggest that notwithstanding that the failure of each was a necessary condition for the outcome, this causal chain was not accompanied by a collective end (so there was no joint action or joint omission). Moreover, the members of the group did not as a group foresee the outcome; indeed, not even one of these individuals foresaw the outcome.

Could the members of the group reasonably have foreseen that the consequences of their actions would be the killing by police of an innocent person? Surely not all of them could reasonably have foreseen this outcome, for example, not the members of the surveillance team. Accordingly, the police were not collectively morally responsible for the death of an innocent person, Jean Charles de Menezes.

In section I it was mentioned that the Metropolitan Police as a corporate entity were found to have committed a criminal offence under the Health and Safety Act and fined £175,000 (plus court costs). If a criminal offence implies a moral offence, then perhaps there is some acceptably weaker notion of collective moral responsibility that might be provided to underpin the guilty verdict of the criminal court. On the other hand, the fact that the penalty is a small fine for a large organisation such as the London Metropolitan Police with a multi-billion pound budget, suggests that the notion of criminal offence in play here is an attenuated one. At any rate, for reasons of space this issue must be left for another occasion.

11

The Use of Lethal Force in Counter-Piracy Operations off Somalia

DOUGLAS GUILFOYLE AND ANDREW MURDOCH[*]

I. INTRODUCTION

A. Origins and Present Form of Piracy off Somalia

PIRATE ATTACKS IN the Gulf of Aden and off Somalia's east coast are now a familiar occurrence. In the first 11 months of 2011 there were 219 pirate attacks on vessels off Somalia, resulting in 25 successful hijackings; as at November 2011 there were nine vessels and over 200 sailors still being held for ransom.[1] There is now a significant international naval presence in the region and the Security Council has passed nine resolutions on Somali piracy. Somalia itself has been without an effective central government with control of its entire territory since civil conflict broke out in 1991. Poverty, unemployment, political instability, drought and illegal fishing have 'all contribute[d] to the rise and continuance of piracy in Somalia.'[2] Recruiting young men to act as pirates is not difficult when so many have grown up in a conflict zone and without job prospects. The internationally recognised Transitional Federal Government (TFG) has limited control only in the southern third of the country, where fighting continues. Two regions, Puntland (claiming to be a self-governing region within a federal Somalia) and Somaliland (claiming to be a secessionist state), are

---

[*] The views expressed in this article are those of the authors and do not necessarily represent those of the Royal Navy, the UK Ministry of Defence or Her Majesty's Government.

[1] House of Commons, Foreign Affairs Committee (House of Commons), *Piracy off the Coast of Somalia* (5 January 2012) www.publications.parliament.uk/pa/cm201012/cmselect/cmfaff/1318/1318.pdf, 30, 39.

[2] United Nations International Expert Group on Piracy off the Somali Coast (UN Expert Group), *Piracy off the Somali Coast: Final Report* (2008). www.imcsnet.org/imcs/docs/somalia_piracy_intl_experts_report_consolidated.pdf, 15.

effectively under separate government. Local governments appear largely unable to restrain piracy.[3]

It is commonly suggested that Somali pirates are responding to illegal fishing by foreign vessels. This paints the pirates as a de facto coast-guard levying informal taxes on foreign delinquent vessels, which may have been more or less true in the 1990s.[4] This account now appears substantially less convincing. When pirates capture foreign fishing vessels in Somali waters, typically artisanal dhows (small, open decked wooden fishing vessels with an enclosed wheelhouse) or other small craft, they do not usually hold them for ransom. Instead, they are hijacked—sometimes with crew still aboard—and used as 'mother ships' to tow pirate skiffs further out to sea to attack the higher-value targets offered by international shipping. This targeting reveals the obvious point: the scale, organisation and aggressiveness of Somali piracy has long outstripped any 'eco-pirate' origins.

Somali piracy is a form of organised crime, worth US$18–30 million in 2008 alone.[5] Pirate groups are organised principally around clan groupings, though others may be accepted to make up numbers, or 'if they have a particular [necessary] skill'.[6] Fishermen are also recruited, through rewards or bullying, to assist pirates who 'generally have little or no knowledge of the sea'.[7] Pirate tactics are increasingly uniform. As noted, pirates now operate far out to sea using mother ships, which are often hijacked fishing vessels. Pirates' preferred targets are slower, less manoeuvrable vessels which ride low in the water for ease of boarding (such as the fully laden tanker vessel, the *Sirius Star* hijacked in November 2008). It can take as little as 15 minutes from the time a vessel realises it is under attack to the point at which pirates assume control, leaving only a narrow window for military intervention that does not risk hostages' lives. The division of profits among pirate gunmen, bosses, reinvestment for 'future missions', and payoffs to government officials means 'a single armed pirate ... earn[s] anywhere from $6,000 to $10,000 for an $US 1,000,000 ransom'.[8] Some in the Somali diaspora put up operational capital and take a significant cut of the profits.[9] While gunmen at the bottom of this pyramid might not make the most money, piracy pays better than any other available occupation and

---

[3] Although Somaliland has had some success: K Menkhaus, 'The Seven Ways to Stop Piracy', *Foreign Policy* (April 2009, online edition) www.foreignpolicy.com/story/cms.php?story_id=4872.

[4] It is often suggested that early pirates were first trained by internationally financed coast-guard development programmes or were ex-Somali military.

[5] UN Expert Group, above n 2, 19.

[6] Ibid 17.

[7] Ibid.

[8] Ibid (references omitted). See also, M Harper, 'Chasing the Somali piracy money trail', *BBC News*, 24 May 2009, news.bbc.co.uk/2/hi/africa/8061535.stm.

[9] X Rice and A Hassan, 'Life is sweet in piracy capital of the world', *The Guardian*, 19 November 2008, www.guardian.co.uk/world/2008/nov/19/piracy-somalia.

the risks involved are small.[10] Somali fishing communities also benefit from pirates' conspicuous consumption and supplying captured vessels with food during long ransom negotiations.[11]

B. The International Response and Incidents Involving the Use of Lethal Force Against Pirates

On average more than 20 vessels are now active at any time in the Gulf of Aden, under an array of mission and command structures. Until recently the principal naval operation was providing an armed escort to World Food Program (WFP) vessels entering Somali ports. The more significant commitment of resources is now the military patrolling of the Internationally Recommended Transit Corridor (IRTC) described below.

In August 2008 Operation Enduring Freedom's Combined Maritime Forces (CMF)[12] first established 'a maritime security patrol area (the MPSA) in international waters off the Somali coast'.[13] This MPSA is a militarily defined area within the Gulf of Aden the exact coordinates of which are classified. It provides a common system of reference that allows states with vessels in the Gulf to 'de-conflict' and/or coordinate their activities. Running through the MPSA is an internationally recommended (and military patrolled) shipping corridor in the Gulf of Aden (the IRTC), established in August 2008 by the United Kingdom Maritime Trade Organization. As of 1 February 2009, information for mariners using the IRTC is available only through a secure website administered by the Maritime Security Centre (Horn of Africa) (MSC (HOA)), itself part of the European Union (EU) counter-piracy mission Operation Atalanta. The US, UK, Denmark and EU have concluded memoranda of understanding or (in the EU case) exchanges of letters with regional states for the transfer of captured pirates to their jurisdictions for trial. However, as of January 2012, only an arrangement between the EU and Mauritius, and separate arrangements between the UK, US, Denmark, EU and the Seychelles are still operational. Some pirates have also been taken to face trial in Puntland (Somalia), Yemen, European capitals and North America. The International Maritime Organisation (IMO) has also worked to promote a regional response: a regional Code of

---

[10] 'Pentagon looks to move battle against pirates ashore', *CNN*, 14 April 2009, edition.cnn.com/2009/POLITICS/04/14/obama.pirates/index.html.

[11] UN Expert Group, above n 2, 17–18; see also Rice and Hassan, above n 9. For a view that such support may be waning, see J Gettleman, 'For Somali Pirates, Worst Enemy May Be on Shore', *New York Times*, 8 May 2009, www.nytimes.com/2009/05/09/world/africa/09pirate.html?_r=1&emc=tnt&tntemail0=y.

[12] See US Naval Forces Central Command, www.cusnc.navy.mil.

[13] *Report of the Secretary-General on the situation in Somalia*, UN SCOR, UN Doc S/2008/709 (17 November 2008) para 55.

Conduct Concerning the Repression of Piracy was concluded in Djibouti in January 2009. Within this context there have been several notable cases in which force has been used against pirates. Some of these are discussed in further detail below. First, however, it is relevant to examine the applicable international law standards governing such operations.

II. THE GENERAL LAW OF PIRACY AND AUTHORITY TO USE FORCE IN MARITIME LAW-ENFORCEMENT OPERATIONS[14]

A. The Customary International Law of Piracy

The international law applicable to piracy is relatively straightforward, despite being bedevilled by historical confusion and a lawyerly propensity to see difficulties where few exist. The core of the customary law of piracy, as codified in treaty law, is relatively simple.[15] Piracy is defined as:[16]

(1)   'any illegal acts of violence or detention, or any act of depredation';[17]
(2)   committed for private ends;
(3)   on the high seas or in a place outside the jurisdiction of any state; and
(4)   committed by the crew or passengers of a private craft, against another vessel or persons or property aboard.

While it is not generally contentious that this *now* represents customary law, there are worse and better arguments that this definition is not, historically, a codification. The worse arguments focus on individual national decisions of the nineteenth or early twentieth century. These cases sometimes contradict the third and fourth elements above, by proclaiming acts in any state's territorial sea or aboard a single vessel may be piracy by 'the law of nations'.[18] These pronouncements should not be taken as a reliable guide to the law a century later, not least because such national decisions notoriously conflated elements of national and international offences. Better arguments

---

[14]   An earlier draft of this section appears as: D Guilfoyle, 'Counter-Piracy Law Enforcement and Human Rights' (2010) 59 *International and Comparative Law Quarterly* 141, 142–45.

[15]   1958 Geneva Convention on the High Seas, opened for signature 29 April 1958, 450 UNTS 82 (entry into force 30 September 1962) Articles 14–22 (High Seas Convention); United Nations Convention on the Law of the Sea 1982, opened for signature 10 December 1982, 1833 UNTS 3 (entry into force 14 November 1994) Articles 101–107 and 110 (UNCLOS).

[16]   High Seas Convention, Article 15; UNCLOS, Article 101.

[17]   The reference to 'any *illegal* act' has been criticised as tautological or question-begging: A Rubin, *The Law of Piracy*, 2nd edn (Newport, Rhode Island, Naval War College Press, 1998) 344; D O'Connell, *The International Law of the Sea*, IA Shearer (ed) vol 2 (Oxford: Clarendon Press, 1984) 969. It is, however, at worst superfluous and the provision's intent is clear, D Guilfoyle, *Shipping Interdiction and the Law of the Sea* (Cambridge, Cambridge University Press, 2009) 42–43. The drafting is consistent with piracy being an act of violence lacking *lawful* (ie state) authority, as discussed below.

[18]   O'Connell, ibid 966, 972.

focus on the wide range of historically contradictory case law and views of commentators and ask how any coherent rule can be extracted from such incoherent material.[19] Both arguments fail to acknowledge that the successive re-enactment of this definition in treaties and regional instruments—as well as its incorporation by reference in Security Council Resolutions—evidences the fact that states *now* accept it as codifying customary law,[20] no matter how historically unconvincing that might seem when scrutinised over the longue durée.

Once this definition is accepted, a number of points may be briefly made about its limitations. First, piracy must be committed by persons aboard one vessel against another. Internal hijackings, as occurred in the notorious 1961 *Santa Maria* or 1982 *Achille Lauro* incidents,[21] are not piracy. This presents no problem for the situation off Somalia, where the hijackers invariably attack their targets from small boats.

Second, it is commonly said that the 'private ends' requirement means politically-motivated acts cannot be piracy.[22] One of the present authors has explained at length elsewhere why he considers that the better view must be that any act of violence not sanctioned by state authority is one for private ends.[23] This is quite consistent with monopoly of states on lawful violence, as reflected in the UNCLOS definition of piracy as an 'illegal' act, which cannot be committed by government vessels unless they mutiny.[24] The correct dichotomy is thus not 'private/political' but 'private/public'. In any event, the point is of no practical relevance here. The exorbitant ransoms demanded for seized vessels by Somali pirates from private parties are clearly sought 'for private ends'.

---

[19] See, however, Rubin, above n 17, especially 331–72, and A Rubin, 'Revising the Law of Piracy' (1990–91) 21 *California Western International Law Journal* 129.

[20] *North Sea Continental Shelf Cases (Federal Republic of Germany v Denmark)* [1969] ICJ Reports 3, 41. While the Preamble to UNSCR 1838 (2008) merely provides that the relevant law includes UNCLOS, para 3 requires force only be used against pirates in accordance with international law 'as reflected in' UNCLOS. Even more directly, the Preamble to UNSCR 1848 (2008) reaffirms 'that international law, as reflected in [UNCLOS], sets out the legal framework applicable to combating piracy and armed robbery at sea, as well as other ocean activities'.

[21] See LA McCullough, 'International and Domestic Criminal Law Issues in the Achille Lauro Incident: A Functional Analysis' (1986) 36 *Naval Law Review* 53; L Green, 'The Santa Maria: Rebels or Pirates?' (1961) 7 *British Yearbook of International Law* 496.

[22] See, eg, I Brownlie, *Principles of Public International Law*, 7th edn (Oxford, Oxford University Press, 2008) 232; MN Shaw, *International Law*, 6th edn (Cambridge, Cambridge University Press, 2008) 615.

[23] D Guilfoyle, 'Piracy off Somalia: UN Security Council Resolution 1816 and IMO regional counter-piracy efforts' (2008) 57 *International and Comparative Law Quarterly* 690, 693–94, 699; Guilfoyle, above n 17, 32–42. See also M Halberstam, 'Terrorism on the High Seas: The Achille Lauro, Piracy and the IMO Convention on Maritime Safety' (1988) 82 *American Journal of International Law* 269, 278–84; *Castle John v NV Mabeco* (Belgium, Court of Cassation, 1986) 77 ILR 537, 540.

[24] UNCLOS, Articles 101–102.

Third, the most important limitation inherent in this definition is geographical and governs both the offence itself (as a matter of prescriptive jurisdiction) and the powers granted to suppress it (enforcement jurisdiction). Piracy can only be committed in international waters, being all waters beyond the territorial sea;[25] equivalent acts within the territorial sea are a matter for the criminal jurisdiction of the coastal state alone.[26] Modern practice now generally refers to offences in territorial or internal waters as 'armed robbery against ships'.[27] As regards enforcement powers, any state warship or government vessel in international waters may board a ship suspected of piracy as an exception to the otherwise exclusive jurisdiction of the flag state.[28] Where piracy is discovered the government vessel has the further powers to seize the pirate craft, arrest persons on board, and subject them to the jurisdiction of the capturing vessel's courts. Piracy also includes 'any act of voluntary participation in the operation of a ship ... with knowledge of facts making it a pirate ship', and a pirate ship is one 'intended by the persons in dominant control to be used' in a pirate attack or which has been used in such an attack and is still under the same control.[29] Thus a warship has a right of visit and inspection where it suspects a vessel to be under the control of persons intending to use it for a future pirate attack. By definition, these powers of visit and capture are granted only *in international waters* and thus do not extend to pursuing pirates from the high seas into foreign territorial waters.[30]

B. International Law and the Use of Force in Maritime Law-Enforcement Operations

UNCLOS' piracy provisions say nothing directly about the use of force. One must therefore turn to the general public international law governing the use of force in maritime law enforcement operations. The critical case is

---

[25] Including a state's 200 nm Exclusive Economic Zone (where declared), see UNCLOS, Article 58(2).

[26] [1956] II *Yearbook of the International Law Commission* 282 at (3).

[27] See, eg, *Code of Practice for the Investigation of the Crimes of Piracy and Armed Robbery Against Ships*, IMO, 22nd sess, Agenda Item 9, IMO Doc A 22/Res.922 (22 January 2002) Article 2.

[28] UNCLOS, Articles 92(1), 110.

[29] Ibid Articles 101(b), 103.

[30] Such a power has been suggested. See JW Bingham (reporter), 'Harvard Research in International Law: Draft Convention on Piracy' (1932) 26 *American Journal of International Law* Sup 739, 744, 833 (*Harvard Draft Convention and Commentary*); and *cf* authorities quoted in Z Keyuan, 'Enforcing the Law of Piracy in the South China Sea' (2000) 31 *Journal of Maritime Law and Commerce* 107, 111. However, see now Code of Conduct Concerning the Repression of Piracy and Armed Robbery against Ships in the Western Indian Ocean and the Gulf of Aden (concluded in Djibouti, 29 January 2009) Article 4(5), rejecting any such suggestion.

MV Saiga (No 2), where the International Tribunal for the Law of the Sea (ITLOS) found that in cases of 'boarding, stopping and arresting' a vessel international law:

> requires that the use of force must be avoided as far as possible and, where ... unavoidable, it must not go beyond what is reasonable and necessary in the circumstances. Considerations of humanity must apply...

> The normal practice ... is first to give an auditory or visual signal to stop, ... [then to take other action], including the firing of shots across the bows of the ship. It is only after the appropriate actions fail that the pursuing vessel may, as a last resort, use force. Even then, appropriate warning must be issued ... and all efforts should be made to ensure that life is not endangered.[31]

In reaching these conclusions ITLOS had little to draw on. It could cite only two cases: *Red Crusader* and *I'm Alone*.[32] The *I'm Alone* case concerned the deliberate sinking of a vessel to prevent its continued flight, while in *Red Crusader* 40 mm solid shot was fired into a fleeing fishing vessel. The *MV Saiga* case itself involved the deliberate firing of large calibre live rounds without warning shots into a slow-moving vessel suspected only of customs offences. Such cases may be considered relatively unhelpful because they deal with clearly *disproportionate* uses of force in order to board and stop a vessel. Perhaps as a result of this scant authority, the Tribunal went on to quote Article 22(1)(f) of the UN Fish Stocks Agreement (FSA)[33] as having further 'reaffirmed' the 'basic principle'.[34] The provision reads relevantly:

> The use of force shall be avoided except when and to the degree necessary to ensure the safety of the inspectors and where the inspectors are obstructed in the execution of their duties. The degree of force used shall not exceed that reasonably required in the circumstances.

The FSA is not an intuitive source of law for standards regarding the boarding and arrest of a vessel as it deals only with the use of force to carry out an authorised inspection *once already aboard*. It does not contemplate, for example, imminent threats to life as fishermen are not usually violent criminals. Nonetheless, the provision is consistent with ITLOS' broad conclusion that the key consideration is 'reasonableness'. A more useful reference point is Article 9 of the United Nations Basic Principles for the Use of Force

---

[31] *M/V 'Saiga' (No 2) (Saint Vincent and the Grenadines v Guinea)* ITLOS Case No 2; (1999) 38 ILM 1323, 1355 (*M/V 'Saiga' (No 2)*). The issue is also discussed in T Treves, 'Piracy, Law of the Sea, and Use of Force: Developments off the Coast of Somalia' (2009) 20 *European Journal of International Law* 399, 412–14.

[32] (1935) 3 RIAA 1609 and (1962) 35 ILR 485 respectively.

[33] The United Nations Agreement for the Implementation of the Provisions of the United Nations Convention on the Law of the Sea of 10 December 1982 relating to the Conservation and Management of Straddling Fish Stocks and Highly Migratory Fish Stocks 1995, opened for signature 4 August 1995, 2167 UNTS 88 (entered into force 11 December 2001).

[34] *M/V 'Saiga' (No 2)* 1355.

and Firearms by Law Enforcement Officials[35] (UN Basic Principles) which provides that firearms shall only be used 'in self-defense or defense of others against the imminent threat of death or serious injury, to prevent the perpetration of a particularly serious crime ... and only when less extreme means are insufficient' and that 'intentional lethal use of firearms may only be made when strictly unavoidable in order to protect life.'

In maritime police actions, then, the use of force is a last resort—to be avoided where possible and in all cases must be strictly limited to what is reasonable and necessary. While an 'appropriate warning must be issued' in the case of attempting to board a vessel, no such warning need necessarily be given, for example, when there is an imminent and overwhelming danger to human life (as in the *Maersk Alabama* hostage-rescue incident).[36] True, these standards are far from a detailed code and might be thought to have more to say about the outer limits at which the use of force becomes impermissible, rather than providing clear guidance as to when force is permitted.

However, it is far from clear whether international law should do much more than set outer limits. As argued elsewhere, the circumstances in which a government vessel is entitled to use force against foreign merchant vessels on the high seas constitute a general exception to the prohibition on the use of force in international relations.[37] The *lex specialis* of the law of the sea grants a limited positive right to use force in certain cases—including the suppression of piracy—to government vessels. Once a state is granted that exceptional right of extra-territorial law-enforcement jurisdiction, the matter will, within the limits set by international law, be regulated primarily by the national law of the enforcing state. Officers of the state conducting a counter-piracy operation should obviously, in the first instance, comply with their own national criminal law on questions of using force to prevent a crime, in defence of others or to relieve an immediate danger to human life. Attempts to suggest the laws of war might provide standards or guidance on the use of force against pirates are fundamentally unhelpful, for reasons discussed further below.

---

[35] United Nations Basic Principles for the Use of Force and Firearms by Law Enforcement Officials, Adopted by the Eighth United Nations Congress on the Prevention of Crime and the Treatment of Offenders, Havana, Cuba, 27 August to 7 September 1990, www2.ohchr.org/english/law/firearms.htm (UN Basic Principles). See also the discussion in this volume, ch 12.

[36] See 'In Rescue of Captain, Navy Kills 3 Pirates', *New York Times*, (12 April 2009) www.nytimes.com/2009/04/13/world/africa/13pirates.html.

[37] D Guilfoyle, 'Interdicting Vessels to Enforce the Common Interest: Maritime Countermeasures and the Use of Force on the High Seas' (2007) 56 *International and Comparative Law Quarterly* 69. The issue becomes rather confused in the *Guyana v Suriname* (2008) 47 ILM 164 where the Arbitral Tribunal (at para 445) suggests a clear dividing line between (non-prohibited) police uses of force and (prohibited) military uses of force based solely on the quantum or character of the force used or threatened.

III. UN SECURITY COUNCIL RESOLUTIONS 1814, 1816, 1838, 1846 AND 1851

A. The General Framework of the Counter-Piracy Resolutions

The relevant Security Council Resolutions for present purposes are 1816, 1846, 1851 (the 'territorial resolutions') as well as Resolutions 1814 (on protection of World Food Program convoys) and 1838 (on measures taken on the high seas).

Resolutions 1816, 1846 and 1851 concern actions in Somalia's territorial waters or land territory, and each contains the talismanic Chapter VII authority to use 'all necessary means' to counter piracy, language usually associated with the use of force. Resolution 1816 has been discussed in detail elsewhere and requires only brief mention here.[38] Notably, it was only to operate for an initial period of six months and so was renewed by UNSCR 1846 on 2 December 2008, UNSCR 1897 on 30 November 2009, UNSCR 1950 of 23 November 2010 and UNSCR 2020 of 22 November 2011.[39] The three 'territorial' Resolutions contain a grant of power and a procedural limitation. In broad-brush terms Resolutions 1816 and 1846 grant specific authority to 'cooperating States' to enter Somalia's territorial sea to repress piracy in a manner consistent with the international law applicable on the high seas. This might involve 'hot pursuit' of pirates into, or counter-piracy patrols within, Somalia's territorial waters. Generally speaking, this has not been the subsequent practice. Most operations against Somali pirates have occurred on the high seas, perhaps limiting these Resolutions' practical significance. UNSCR 1851 authorises 'cooperating States' to go further and engage in counter-piracy action on Somali soil.[40] To be a cooperating state under the Resolutions a state must be operating with the consent of the TFG as notified in advance to the UN Secretary General.[41] This provision makes the Resolutions, at first glance, superfluous. Chapter VII is not needed to permit consensual operations; Somalia itself is competent to authorise foreign law-enforcement action in its waters and on its soil. All the Resolutions might be thought to do is add further bureaucracy through requiring UNSG notification.

Nonetheless, the Resolutions may serve political and practical ends. Some states find it constitutionally easier to participate in foreign operations

---

[38] Guilfoyle, above n 23.

[39] The wording of operative paragraphs 7, 9 and 11 of Resolution 1816 are repeated mutatis mutandis as paragraphs 10, 11 and 14 of Resolution 1846. Subsequent Resolutions refer back to the powers granted in Resolutions 1846 and 1851.

[40] See Security Council Report, UN SCOR, 6046th mtg, UN Doc S/PV.6046, 4 (United Kingdom), 9 (United States), 27 (Germany).

[41] The approach was first used in UNSCR 1814 (2008), para 11, on protecting humanitarian shipments.

sanctioned by the United Nations. This may avoid the need for separate legislative authorisation, or constitutional difficulties arising from the use of military forces in extra-territorial law enforcement operations. Other states may doubt the TFG's ability to give authorisation in a timely fashion. Having a system for granting blanket authorisation in advance is certainly faster than negotiating arrangements ad hoc with high-ranking officials. In the rare case of a 'hot pursuit' into national waters it may simply not be possible to find someone with power to grant such authority in the time available.[42] Finally, states not recognising the TFG as a government can rely on the Resolutions, rather than direct TFG consent.[43]

The Resolutions also expressly emphasise, in a relatively standard savings clause that each was passed with Somalia's consent, each applies only to the situation off Somalia, and none serves as a precedent for customary law or modify parties' rights and obligations under UNCLOS.[44] This was necessary to appease a number of states on the Council.[45] The underlying logic is that it is the situation in Somalia, of which piracy is a symptom, which justifies Security Council action: piracy is not an inherent threat to international security and the Council has not intended to 'legislate' to change UNCLOS.

B. Provisions on the Use of Force in the Counter-Piracy Resolutions

Operation Atalanta invokes as the legal basis for its dual mission UNSCR 1814, 1816 (as discussed above) and 1838.[46] UNSCR 1814 '*calls upon* States and regional organizations, in close coordination with each other and as notified in advance to the Secretary-General, and at the request of the TFG, to take action to protect shipping involved with the transportation

---

[42] It is often not clear to governments themselves which official if any has constitutional authority to permit action within their territorial sea or aboard their flag vessel, see, eg, W Gilmore, 'Drug Trafficking at Sea: The Case of *R. v. Charrington and Others*' (2000) 49 *International and Comparative Law Quarterly* 477, 479 (only the Attorney-General of Malta was found competent to give permission sought).

[43] JG Dalton, JA Roach, and J Daley, 'Introductory Note to United Nations Security Council: Piracy and Armed Robbery at Sea—Resolutions 1816, 1846 and 1851' (2009) 48 *International Legal Materials* 129, 130. The concern does not appear to have been to overcome Somalia's (unlawful) claim of a 200 nm territorial sea as suggested in Treves, above n 31, 407.

[44] See UNSCR 1816 (2008) para 9; UNSCR 1846 (2008) para 11; UNSCR 1851 (2008) para 10.

[45] See the comments of Indonesia, Vietnam, South Africa and China in the United Nations Security Council, 'Security Council Condemns Acts of Piracy, Armed Robbery Off Somalia's Coast' (Press Release, SC/9344, 2 June 2008) www.un.org/News/Press/docs/2008/sc9344.doc.htm.

[46] Council Decision 2008/918/CFSP, 8 December 2008, Official Journal of the EU, L 330/19-L 330/20; see also 'EU NAVFOR Somalia—Legal Basis', www.consilium.europa.eu/showpage.aspx?id=1519&lang=EN.

and delivery of humanitarian aid to Somalia'.[47] UNSCR 1816 and its successor 1846 encourage states with an interest in nearby commercial maritime routes 'to increase and coordinate their efforts to deter ... piracy ... in cooperation with the TFG' and urge all states to 'render assistance to vessels threatened by or under attack by pirates or armed robbers, in accordance with relevant international law'.[48] UNSCR 1838 '[c]alls upon States whose naval vessels ... operate on the high seas ... off the coast of Somalia to use ... the necessary means, in conformity with international law, as reflected in the [UNCLOS], for the repression of acts of piracy'.[49] None of these provide an independent legal basis for the use of force. Action under UNSCR 1814 is preconditioned on the 'request of the TFG', which could—as previously discussed—be granted without a UNSCR. UNSCR 1816 is merely hortatory and provides no novel legal powers. UNSCR 1838 authorises 'necessary means', the talismanic words for granting authority to use force under Chapter VII, but only where action is taken in conformity with UNCLOS (ie is already permissible). While much invoked, these Resolutions add nothing to general international law. One must therefore turn to general international law for the applicable rule. However, a further question is whether humanitarian law is, in any sense, applicable.

UNSCR 1851 provides that cooperating states:

> may undertake all necessary measures that are appropriate in Somalia, for the purpose of suppressing acts of piracy ... at sea, pursuant to the request of the TFG, provided, however, that any measures ... shall be undertaken consistent with applicable international humanitarian and human rights law.

This authorisation to use force is subject to two limitations: the invitation of the TFG and compliance with 'applicable international humanitarian and human rights law'. The reference to international humanitarian law (IHL) is regrettably confusing. Some have interpreted it to suggest that the Resolution per se makes all of IHL applicable to counter-piracy operations in Somalia's land territory.[50] This is clearly wrong: the Resolution only refers to 'applicable' IHL; that is, law that would apply *irrespective* of the Resolution. It would be a mistake to assume that the use of military force necessarily implicates IHL. IHL is applicable only in an international or non-international armed conflict.

First, despite some classical writers' rhetoric suggesting that pirates are at war with all humankind, we cannot assume we are at war with pirates. The existence of either an international or non-international armed conflict

---

[47] Paragraph 11. See also UNSCR 1838 (2008) para 5.
[48] UNSCR 1838 (2008) paras 2, 3.
[49] Ibid para 3.
[50] E Kontorovich, 'International Legal Responses to Piracy off the Coast of Somalia' (6 February 2009) 13(2), *ASIL Insights* www.asil.org/insights090206.cfm.

is a determination of fact: 'an armed conflict exists whenever there is a resort to armed force between States or protracted armed violence between governmental authorities and organized armed groups or between such groups within a State.'[51] The term 'armed force' connotes a certain level or scale of violence required for an international armed conflict, while the term 'protracted armed violence' in relation to non-international armed conflicts requires a certain 'intensity' of violence as opposed to a strict test of duration.[52] Both tests also require an element of 'identity' to be satisfied: the actors in an international armed conflict must be states (or their actions must be attributable to states); and in a non-international armed conflict the relevant violence must be between armed bands or between such bands and government forces. Somali pirates are at best several different groups of armed bands acting without state sanction who have mounted a series of individual attacks against vessels of varying nationalities. These attacks have, on occasion, been seen off by foreign naval vessels with (on even fewer occasions) shots being exchanged occasioning loss of life. Neither the actors involved (disparate private parties and disparate military forces), nor the level of violence reached (small scale exchange of fire) could seriously justify the characterisation of an international armed conflict. Nor do the pirates satisfy the definition of those engaged in a non-international armed conflict: first, their actions are not *within* a state; second, a series of violent attacks and hostage takings committed against civilians satisfies neither the criterion of intensity nor identity.[53] On any evaluation, pirate activity seems closest to 'situations ... such as riots, [and] isolated and sporadic acts of violence' falling below the threshold for the existence of any armed conflict.[54]

Further, applying IHL would produce legal difficulties. Pirates should not—as a matter of principle—be considered combatants. If so, they could legitimately be targeted with lethal force based on their status: participants in a conflict. The international law standards governing the use of force in policing actions would certainly not permit targeting pirates with lethal force simply on the basis of status. Thus, there is a risk that invoking IHL could justify using against criminals what would otherwise be excessive force. Alternatively, if one starts from the premise that there is a conflict

---

[51] *Prosecutor v Tadic* (*Decision on the Defence Motion for Interlocutory Appeal on Jurisdiction*) (Case No IT-94-1-AR72, 2 October 1995) para 70.

[52] *Prosecutor v Ramush Haradinaj, Idriz Balaj and Lahi Brahimaj* (*Judgment*) (Case No IT-04-84-T, 3 April 2008) para 49.

[53] There is a separate issue of whether the pirates could satisfy the test of armed bands in control of territory found in Article 1(1), Protocol Additional to the Geneva Conventions of 12 August 1949, and relating to the Protection of Victims of Non-International Armed Conflicts (Additional Protocol II), 8 June 1977.

[54] Rome Statute of the International Criminal Court, opened for signature 17 July 1998, 2187 UNTS 90 (entered into force 1 July 2002) Article 1(2), Additional Protocol II; *cf* Article 8(2)(d), (f).

and pirates are civilians, this may lead to the conclusion that they may not be deliberately targeted with lethal force at sea or on land.[55] Under IHL, civilian casualties are only acceptable where proportionate to achieving a legitimate military end, or where civilians have illegally taken up arms against enemy forces which may then return fire in self-defence. The deliberate targeting of civilians *as such* is prohibited. Thus, if hostage-taking piracy is governed by IHL then either: (1) pirates are liable to be targeted with lethal force *at any time* as enemy combatants; or (2) pirates are civilians and any decision to target them directly would be illegal unless it was proportionate and incidental to securing some other legitimate military objective. Invoking IHL in counter-piracy actions only confuses the issues involved.

The Resolution may be better construed as acknowledging either the possibility that 'some Somali pirates may also be civil war insurgents'[56] or that counter-piracy operations against those supplying or equipping pirates might result in military engagement with insurgents. In either case IHL would apply as 'any international counter-piracy forces on land ... [could then be] considered forces intervening in an otherwise internal conflict at the invitation of the government.'[57]

It is national criminal law and national military rules of engagement that develop detailed rules as to when one has positive authority to use force and in what manner rather than public international law.[58] International law sets much broader minimum standards. The starting premise should be that we are dealing—in the maritime domain—with a parallel *lex specialis*: authority under customary international law to use reasonable force as a last resort to suppress piracy, capture pirates or preserve human life. Those questions will now be explored further with reference to concrete cases.

IV. THE OPERATIONAL CONTEXT

A. Military Response: Disrupt, Deter and Capture

Before the sharp spike in piratical activity in the Gulf of Aden in summer 2008, the majority of warships operating in these waters did so as part of the CMF[59] and, in particular, its longest standing Combined Task Force

---

[55] Kontorovich, above n 50.

[56] Guilfoyle, above n 17, 70.

[57] Ibid.

[58] *Cf* the comments of Justice Brennan in *Polyukovich v The Commonwealth* (1991) 172 CLR 501 [41].

[59] See US Naval Forces Central Command, above n 12, and accompanying text.

150 (CTF 150).[60] At its inception at the beginning of Operation Enduring Freedom, CTF 150 had a purely counter terrorism focus. This has gradually evolved to encompass 'Maritime Security Operations' (MSO),[61] a concept considered flexible enough to permit CMF to deploy CTF 150 warships to respond to acts of piracy.[62] In January 2009 CMF created CTF 151 with a dedicated counter-piracy mission. Until this time, and prior to NATO and EU counter-piracy missions commencing in October and December 2008 respectively, CTF 150 was at the vanguard of the military maritime response to piracy.

CMF's immediate response to the piracy surge was to increase the Gulf of Aden military presence to deter attacks. However, various factors made such a tactic unlikely to succeed: the speed of pirate attacks; the difficulty in distinguishing pirate ships from innocent fishing vessels; the vast patrol area;[63] and a limited number of warships. With CTF 150's presence having only a localised deterrence effect, CMF examined alternative military options. The powers reflected in UNCLOS appeared sufficient for warships to take enforcement action against suspected pirates and pirate vessels. However, even if international law grants certain powers, whether CMF warships could exercise them depended in practice upon the Rules of Engagement (ROE) in force.

ROE delineate inter alia the degree and manner in which force may be used. ROE comprise prohibitions as well as authorisations for military elements, such as warships, to take certain actions when judged necessary to achieve a mission's aims.[64] Force in ROE terms is generally understood to consist of the use or threat of any physical means to achieve an authorised objective, including measures such as arrest and detention or lethal force. While ROE should never authorise conduct that is prohibited by international law, there is no requirement for them to extend to the limit of what is legally permissible. ROE are also influenced by domestic law as well as operational, diplomatic and political factors, and these may result in rules that are more restrained than that which may be permitted by international law.

As CMF does not issue its own ROE, it is the ROE issued by each warship's own higher authorities that determines the tactics CMF warships could

---

[60] CTF 150's Area of Responsibility encompasses waters of the Gulf of Aden, Gulf of Oman, Red Sea and the North West quadrant of the Indian Ocean.

[61] On varying definitions of 'MSO', see the US definition at www.cusnc.navy.mil/cmf/cmf_command.html, and the UK definition at www.royalnavy.mod.uk/training-and-people/the-rn-today/joint-operations-rn-army-raf-nato/gulf/maritime-security-operations.

[62] NAVCENT (Fifth Fleet), 'Maritime Security Operations Key to Regional Stability, Security', NAVCENT, (Combined Maritime Forces Press Release, 8 October 2007) www.cusnc.navy.mil/articles/2007/207.html.

[63] The Gulf of Aden is 205,000 square miles (530,000 square km) in area.

[64] D Fleck (ed), *The Handbook of International Humanitarian Law* (Oxford, Oxford University Press, 2008) 655–56.

actually employ. In deciding whether to commence operations involving the arrest of suspected pirates for the purposes of criminal prosecution (so-called 'capture operations'), CMF had to determine whether warships under its command had appropriate ROE. While states have different approaches to interpreting ROE,[65] the arrest and detention of individuals would only be undertaken with express authorisation from appropriate national authorities. Unfortunately, the patchwork of national ROE meant individual warships were subject to different permissions and constraints.[66] Despite the existence of universal jurisdiction over piracy, it quickly became apparent that states were reluctant to permit their warships to commence 'capture operations'.

Some states had, despite IMO recommendations to the contrary,[67] enacted only limited domestic law offences of piracy, requiring a national nexus to the crime (such as the nationality of the pirate or attacked vessel, or nationality of the pirates or victims). Other states appear to require a national nexus as a matter of prosecutorial policy despite having domestic law that contains no such requirement. Further, in the summer of 2008 there were no formal arrangements in place to facilitate the transfer of suspected pirates from a CMF participating warship to another state willing to commence an investigation and prosecution. The resultant operational problems are well illustrated by a September 2008 incident involving the Danish warship *Absalon*.

As part of CTF 150 *Absalon* intervened during a piracy attack and arrested 10 suspected pirates. The suspects were detained on board the warship pending a decision by Danish authorities on their disposition. On 24 September, after being held for six days, the suspects were released on a Somali beach after Danish authorities concluded that they could not be prosecuted in Denmark owing to deficiencies in Danish law. The release of the pirates attracted some criticism and it was suggested that pirates would now regard themselves as able to operate with impunity.[68] The incident also highlighted the reluctance of some states to allow the transfer of suspected pirates from their warships to regional states for prosecution, if doing so

---

[65] Some adopt a 'permissive' interpretative approach, and failing a prohibition in the ROE, an activity is deemed to be permitted. Other militaries adopt a restricted approach to ROE and failing an express authorisation an activity is deemed to be prohibited.

[66] M Houben, 'Making Waves and Building Bridges: Dutch Experiences in the Arabian Sea' (2007) 10(1) *RUSI Defence Systems* 82 www.rusi.org/downloads/assets/Houben,_Making_Waves_and_Building_Bridges.pdf.

[67] Code of Practice for the Investigation of the Crimes of Piracy and Armed Robbery Against Ships, IMO, 22nd sess, Agenda Item 9, IMO Doc A 22/Res.922 (22 January 2002) para 3(1).

[68] M Hand, 'Danish Navy release 10 Somali pirates', *Lloyd's List*, 25 September 2008 www.lloydslist.com/ll/news/danish-navy-releases-10-somali-pirates/20017574257.htm.

would expose them to risks of the death penalty, torture or other treatment breaching human rights obligations.[69]

On 2 January 2009 a second incident, also involving the *Absalon* illustrated further legal and political complications involved in 'capture operations'. Five Somali pirates were detained following their attack on the *Samanyulo*, a Dutch-Antilles flagged cargo ship. During the attack the pirates' own vessel became unseaworthy and the pirates were rescued by the *Absalon*. The suspected pirates spent 40 days aboard the warship before agreement was reached with Dutch authorities for the suspects to be transferred to the Netherlands to stand trial. This prolonged detention attracted criticism from human rights organisations on the grounds that it was not subject to any judicial oversight.[70] Consideration of the extra-territorial application of human rights obligations during maritime law enforcement operations, however, falls outside the scope of this chapter.[71]

The lack of a clear, reliable, disposition path to facilitate the investigation and, if there is sufficient evidence, prosecution of suspected pirates resulted in the CMF commander directing that warships operating as part of CMF were not to arrest pirates until such criminal justice disposition arrangements were in place.[72] That the disposition problem was negatively affecting counter-piracy efforts was well-recognised by the international community.[73] Commanders of Operations *Allied Provider* and *Atalanta* faced the same disposition problem. States within these operations were also reluctant to permit their warships to engage in 'capture operations' without knowing in advance where the arrested pirates would be taken. The result was that any decision to arrest or detain pirates would have to be a *national* decision which required the warship to revert to national chain of command.[74] While some states were prepared to do this to detain pirates, this approach was very much the exception in 2008.[75]

---

[69] Ibid.

[70] 'Amnesty demands Dutch and Danish take care of pirates', *NRC International*, 4 February 2007 www.nrc.nl/international/article2141530.ece/Amnesty_demands_Dutch_and_Danish_take_care_of_pirates.

[71] See, eg, *Medvedeyev and Others v France*, App no 3394/03 (ECHR, 10 July 2008) para 50.

[72] See Vice Admiral W Gortney, 'DoD News Briefing with Vice Adm, Gortney from the Pentagon' (News Transcript, 15 January 2009) www.defenselink.mil/transcripts/transcript.aspx?transcriptid=4341.

[73] See, eg, UNSCR 1846, para 14.

[74] See 'NATO to resume counter piracy operation off Horn of Africa', www.snmg1.nato.int/SNMG1_ficheiros/Page4065.htm#OP10 ('Persons who have committed or are suspected of committing acts of piracy on the high seas or armed robbery in Somali territorial waters *cannot* be arrested or detained by NATO forces. In such cases the NATO vessel would revert to national control.')

[75] HMS *Cumberland* which was operating off Somalia as part of NATO's Operation Allied Provider reverted to national command in order to transfer pirates to Kenya in November 2008. See also Hand, above n 68, involving HDMS *Absalon*.

Without judicial disposition/transfer arrangements in place the tactical options available to CMF in 2008, as well as EUNAVFOR and NATO, were limited to disrupting pirates using measures falling short of 'capture'. Nonetheless, even after 'capture operations' became a reliable option for some states following the conclusion of transfer arrangements with Kenya, disruption operations remained the most common naval counter-piracy tactic for a variety of practical, operational and legal reasons.[76] Disruption operations can be divided into two broad categories—proactive and reactive. The first involves several stages: the identification of ships reasonably suspected of engaging in piracy; visiting such ships; seizing and disposing of unmanned pirate ships known as 'skiffs' (unmanned small, fast, open vessels used to commit the attack, launched from larger 'mother ships'); and seizing and disposing of arms and equipment used in committing piracy. Pirates are then released. The second type of operation involves warships or aircraft 'reacting' to merchant ships' distress calls. The aim is then to disrupt the attack, avert any threat to human life, and prevent the pirates from boarding the merchant vessel. Both categories may result in the use of force as discussed in the following case studies.

B. Case Studies: HMS *Cumberland* and INS *Tabar*

On 12 November 2008 the *Cumberland* was operating in the Gulf of Aden as part of NATO Operation Allied Provider when the master of the Panamanian registered MV *Powerful* reported he was being attacked by pirates in a 'skiff' using automatic weapons. After aggressive manoeuvring by the *Powerful* the pirates failed to board and returned to its mother ship, a nearby dhow. Having received a description of and location for the mother ship the *Cumberland* identified the dhow and, with reasonable grounds to suspect it was engaged in piracy, decided to conduct an UNCLOS Article 110 right of visit. At the time there was no indication the dhow contained anyone other than pirates. The boarding was intended as part of a 'proactive' disruption operation to prevent the dhow and skiff from conducting further attacks. Despite being part of the NATO Operation, which at the time had its own ROE,[77] the *Cumberland* conducted this incident mission in accordance with UK ROE.[78]

---

[76] 'HMS Portland intercepts pirates', *Defence News*, 3 June 2009, www.mod.uk/DefenceInternet/DefenceNews/MilitaryOperations/HmsPortlandInterceptsPirates.htm.

[77] NATO 'Counter Piracy Operations' briefing (2 April 2009) www.nato.int/issues/allied-provider/index.html.

[78] R Norton-Taylor and T Parfitt, 'British Commandos kill two pirates in stand-off', *The Guardian* (13 November 2008) www.guardian.co.uk/world/2008/nov/13/pirates-killed-gulf-aden.

The *Cumberland* approached the dhow and requested that it stop for boarding; the translated instructions were issued verbally and over VHF radio. The warship manoeuvred close to the dhow, which was being steered erratically, and used its siren and flashing lights to repeat the signal to stop. Flares and signal rockets were fired near, but not at, the dhow but it continued to head towards Somali territorial waters. The *Cumberland* then, rather inventively, went alongside the dhow and aimed a fire-hose at the dhow's wheelhouse to encourage its occupants to stop the vessel. This did not succeed. Royal Marine boarding teams were then launched in two rigid inflatable boats (RIBs) with an armed helicopter overhead providing protection. Each RIB contained several Royal Marines armed with 5.56 mm small arms and one manning a mounted 7.62 mm general purpose machine gun. The RIBs circled the dhow repeating instructions to stop and for the crew to move to the bow with their hands in the air. Fourteen individuals on board congregated on the bow as instructed, leaving two pirates in the wheelhouse. These two then, without warning, each picked up an automatic rifle—later identified as AK47 variants—previously concealed out of sight, and aimed them at one of the RIBs 20 to 30 metres away. Six Royal Marines, in both the RIBs, opened fire at the two armed pirates at the same time as shots were fired by the pirates. Despite the difficulty in firing from an RIB on the high seas[79] the incident lasted only a few seconds, ceasing when the threat from the two individuals was no longer believed to exist. The two Somali pirates in the wheelhouse were shot dead as a result.[80] The Royal Marines then boarded the dhow discovering a third individual, later identified as a Yemeni national, injured. Despite receiving emergency treatment from the *Cumberland's* doctor he died shortly afterwards from an injury sustained during the firefight.

Only after the boarding was it discovered that the fishing dhow had itself been previously captured by the Somali pirates aboard. The Yemeni crew had been held, under the use and threat of violence, while the pirates looked for merchant vessels to attack using their own skiff. The crew was told they would be released once a large merchant was successfully pirated. After an investigation into the incident by UK authorities and following diplomatic discussions, the dhow and its crew were escorted to Yemeni territorial waters and released into the protection of the Yemeni Coast-guard. Although there was no plan at this time to capture pirates, arrangements were made for the eight Somali pirates to be transferred to Kenya for investigation and prosecution;[81] their trial started in January 2009. The two

[79] ie, in firing from an unstable platform at targets aboard another unstable platform.

[80] 'Royal Navy in firefight with Somali pirates', *The Times*, 12 November 2008, /www.timesonline.co.uk/tol/news/world/africa/article5141745.ece.

[81] 'Navy hands over pirate suspects', *BBC News*, 18 November 2008, news.bbc.co.uk/1/hi/uk/7735088.stm.

deceased Somali pirates were eventually, after consultation with Somali religious leaders, buried at sea.

Less than a week later an Indian naval frigate, the INS *Tabar*, encountered the *Ekawat Nava 5*, a medium sized, steel-hulled, multi-deck fishing vessel. The Kiribati-registered fishing vessel's owner had reported it pirated, and an alert to this effect had been issued by the International Maritime Bureau (IMB) piracy reporting centre in Kuala Lumpur. This alert notified CMF and EUNAVFOR what had happened, but it appears that the *Tabar*, which was operating independently under national command did not receive this information.[82] The *Tabar's* assessment was that the *Ekawat Nava 5* was being used a pirate mother ship. An unspecified number of men were seen on deck openly displaying automatic weapons and RPG launchers, and the vessel was towing two skiffs. Unknown to the *Tabar*, most of the 16 crew members of the *Ekawat Nava 5* were tied up on board and out of sight. The *Tabar* decided to stop and board the vessel as a suspected pirate ship. Over a period of approximately 90 minutes the *Ekawat Nava 5* failed to respond to repeated instructions to heave to for boarding. The *Tabar* then fired several warning shots; the pirates responded by threatening to blow up the fishing vessel and warship.[83] At approximately 9.17 pm the pirates fired at the *Tabar*. The *Tabar* responded 'as per its ROE' by firing a medium range weapon system[84] consisting of a single turret containing two 30 mm six-barrel automatic weapons (which fire a thousand rounds a minute).[85] This resulted in a series of explosions on the *Ekawat Nava 5* and its sinking. The pirates appear to have escaped in the skiffs; one of which was later discovered abandoned. Of the fishing vessel's crew of 16, there was only one survivor. He was recovered six days later by a passing ship.

C. Operational Use of Force—Analysis and Evaluation

The case studies illustrate that during counter-piracy operations the military may well use force, including lethal force. The *Cumberland* and *Tabar* cases both illustrate an escalatory approach to using force to stop and board suspected pirate ships. The UK warship very gradually escalated its measures, firing no shots to enforce a right to board. Similarly, the *Tabar* only used non-forcible measures to encourage the suspected pirate ship to

---

[82] 'India navy defends piracy sinking', *BBC News*, 26 November 2008, news.bbc.co.uk/1/hi/world/south_asia/7749486.stm.

[83] 'Ship shot down in self-defence: Navy', *The Times of India*, 27 November 2008, timesofindia.indiatimes.com/World/Middle-East/Ship-shot-down-in-self-defenceNavy/articleshow/3761244.cms.

[84] Ibid.

[85] Details of the GSh-30k six-barrel automatic guns can be found at www.bharat-rakshak.com/NAVY/Kashtan.html.

stop, escalating eventually to the use of warning shots. Use of force to stop and board the pirate ships would have been justifiable as the next necessary measure, as envisaged in *MV Saiga (No 2)*. This use of force may also be escalated, starting with shots directed at non-critical areas, before aiming at critical areas that will disable the vessel (such as the rudder, engine-room or wheelhouse). Importantly, such force should only be used after all efforts have been taken to ensure life is not thereby endangered.

Neither warship, however, reached this stage, as the situation in both cases changed rapidly to become one of protecting life. In the *Cumberland* incident the two pirates presented an imminent threat to life. Six Royal Marines simultaneously and immediately used force in either defence of their own life (those with weapons pointed at them) or the defence of those threatened. Giving warnings would have increased the likelihood of death or grave injury. The *Tabar* incident is more difficult to assess, given the paucity of information available; it is not known how many of the pirates fired, what weapons they used, and how far away the warship was at the time. Certainly automatic or RPG fire presents a threat to life, even on board a warship, and therefore a response by the *Tabar* in self-defence, without warning, *may* have been necessary.

While the use of force to prevent loss of life was necessary in the *Cumberland* incident, and possibly the *Tabar* incident, was the level of force used reasonable? There are no indications that the use of force by the *Cumberland*'s marines was excessive, as lethal force was unavoidable given the threat, and the shots were only fired for a short period until the threat no longer existed. The *Cumberland* was armed inter alia with a 30 mm multi-barrelled gun and an array of smaller calibre weapons for close-in force protection purposes. No doubt any of these weapons could have neutralised the threat on the dhow. However, only the smallest calibre weapons carried by individuals from the warship were used; weapons designed to be used with some precision against personnel. The *Tabar* incident, however, is more troubling given the resultant, large loss of innocent life. The *Tabar*'s twin 30 mm multi-barrelled weapon system is not designed to target individuals accurately. Its purpose is to engage much larger and faster targets. In using it against the *Ekawat Nava 5* it put the lives of everyone aboard at risk irrespective of whether they were firing at the warship, posed no threat at all, or had presented a threat but no longer did so.

Principle 5 in the 1990 UN Basic Principles states that whenever the use of firearms is unavoidable, law enforcement officials shall 'minimize damage and injury, and respect and preserve human life'. Principle 11 adds that rules and regulations on the use of firearms by law enforcement officials should include guidelines ensuring firearms are used only 'in a manner likely to decrease the risk of unnecessary harm' and 'prohibit the use of those firearms and ammunition that cause unwarranted injury or present an unwarranted risk'. These Principles are intended to apply to military personnel when exercising police powers,[86] and to avoid a lacuna they should remain a useful reference point when such powers are exercised extra-territorially. The employment by the *Tabar* of its twin 30 mm multi-barrelled weapon system does not fit well within these guidelines given its calibre, rapid rate of fire and inability to engage individuals accurately. It is doubtful that such a weapon system is ever suitable for a law enforcement mission as its use will normally result in excessive force.

Warships, unlike police or coastguard vessels, are predominantly designed for armed conflict and not police actions against armed maritime criminals such as pirates. If they are to be used by states for such missions they need to be equipped with suitable weapons and manned by trained personnel, if the limits on using force in maritime law enforcement operations are to be respected. It is likely that warships will be called upon to use force, as a last resort, to stop pirate vessels to enforce a right of visit. As pirate vessels range from skiffs to steel hulled mother ships, it will be necessary for warships to be able to choose from a range of weapons in order to deliver the level of force required to achieve the lawful aim, while minimising the risk of endangering life in the process. If a warship does not possess a weapon that can disable a ship without endangering life then it should not attempt such a task.

Suitable weapons, properly manned, should also be readily available such that if force is necessary to protect life, whether one's own or others, during counter-piracy operations then only a reasonable level of force is used. It is inappropriate to be too prescriptive about what weapons may be required. In some cases owing to the number of pirates presenting an imminent threat, their weapons and lack of innocent bystanders, the use by the warship of a large calibre weapon with a high rate of fire may be reasonable. However, as the *Maersk Alabama* and *Cumberland* incidents reveal, maritime law enforcement operations against pirates will more often require the use of a more precise response to a limited threat; small calibre, accurate, weapons capable of reducing the unnecessary risk of harm to others in the vicinity who present no threat. The use of snipers in the *Maersk Alabama* episode and the Royal Marines from the *Cumberland* demonstrate how effective this capability can be.

Principle 22 of the UN Basic Principles states *inter alia* that when firearms are used in law enforcement operations:

> Governments and law enforcement agencies shall ensure that effective review process is available and that independent administrative or prosecutorial authorities are in a position to exercise jurisdiction in appropriate circumstances. In cases of

---

[86] See fn 1 to the UN Basic Principles, above n 35.

death and serious injury or other grave consequences, a detailed report shall be sent promptly to the competent authorities responsible for administrative review and judicial control.

This requirement to conduct a national review of an incident involving the use of firearms by law enforcement officials reinforces national authorities' primary role in ensuring that force has been used lawfully. Following the *Cumberland* incident, the UK Ministry of Defence emphasised that 'a post-shooting incident investigation' was being conducted.[87] Later the Royal Navy confirmed that a 'full inquiry into the circumstances around the incident has taken place' which found that 'personnel acted lawfully and in self defence'.[88] Investigating such incidents on board a warship that is required to remain in international waters to continue its mission will pose significant logistical and practical challenges. However, there is no reason why military personnel should be subjected to a review process that is ineffective or lacks independence. While the exact review procedure is a matter for the state concerned, it should be in place before an incident occurs and require the compilation of a detailed report for scrutiny by competent authorities who can take appropriate action if there is evidence that national laws or procedures may have been breached. Such authorities should be independent and free from actual or perceived bias.

If military personnel use force during counter-piracy operations resulting in death or injury, they risk national criminal proceedings if force was used in a manner contrary to national law. Commanders can mitigate this risk by issuing well-drafted ROE, appropriate weapons and training in both. ROE do, however, have limitations if poorly drafted, as, in most jurisdictions, adherence to the Rules does not, in itself, provide a defence during criminal proceedings. In *Clegg*,[89] an appeal case involving a soldier convicted of murder as a result of using excessive force while on duty, the House of Lords considered ROE issued to soldiers on a 'yellow card' entitled 'instructions for opening fire in Northern Ireland'. On a literal reading, the ROE permitted firing at a car where a person had been injured, irrespective of the seriousness of the injury. In considering whether the ROE could assist Clegg, the Lords concluded that it had no legal force, because English law does not have a general defence of superior orders.

---

[87] Royal Navy, 'HMS Cumberland Fights Piracy', 13 December 2008, www.royalnavy. mod.uk/operations-and-support/surface-fleet/type-22-frigates/hms-cumberland/news/hms-cumberland-fights-piracy.

[88] 'Pirate killings were lawful', *Western Morning News*, 20 December 2008, www. thisiswesternmorningnews.co.uk/news/PIRATE-KILLING-LAWFUL/article-562319-detail/article.html.

[89] *R v Clegg* [1995] WLR 80, 90.

V. CONCLUSION

This chapter has principally discussed the rules applicable to the most usual form of naval counter-piracy operations, 'disruption'. Authority to conduct 'disruption' operations is grounded in Article 110 UNCLOS. Right of visit is subject to the general rules outlined in the *MV Saiga* and other case law. In essence, it is a law-enforcement operation requiring a ship to be stopped and boarded. The ordinary principles governing the measures that may be taken to get on board a suspect vessel apply. Force should only be used as a last resort, and the use of force to effect a boarding will be subject to over-riding constraints such as the requirement of giving warning, using force only as a last resort, and taking measures to prevent risk to human life. However, if the vessel attempting to conduct the boarding is itself attacked or if suspect pirates threaten hostages aboard then the case becomes one of using lethal force to protect one's own life, or the lives of others. In such cases a warning should still be given unless do so would increase the risk of death or serious injury to anyone being threatened.

Serious questions as to the reasonableness of force used may arise, however, if a warship acts in self-defence (or to disrupt an actual pirate attack) with weapon-systems that are not designed to be used against individuals, as the INS *Tabar* incident illustrates. We have argued that naval vessels engaged in counter-piracy will need to be appropriately equipped and trained for their mission. This requirement extends further in the context of 'capture' operations designed to lead to subsequent prosecutions. Since the conclusion of transfer agreements with Kenya (and given the apparent willingness of Yemen, Puntland, the Seychelles and the TFG to accept such transfers) there has been an increased willingness to engage in 'capture' operations. Nonetheless, disruption operations remain the most commonly used tactic at present. Transferring suspect pirates to a regional state remains fraught with practical complexities (principally in relation to conducting evidence-gathering in a manner that will support prosecution in the receiving state and associated training) and prosecution by the capturing warship remains very much the exception.[90]

The importance of appropriate equipment, training and above all an acknowledgement that this is essentially a law-enforcement exercise is well-illustrated by the reaction to the INS *Tabar* incident. Initially the sinking of the pirate ship was praised by the head of the IMB, Mr Choong, who stated 'if all warships do this it will be a strong deterrent ... it's about time that such forceful action is taken'.[91] However, once the deaths of the fishermen became

---

[90] In practice this only occurs where national interests are directly affected, typically where flag-state nationals are taken hostage.

[91] 'India praised for sinking pirates', *BBC News*, 20 November 2008, news.bbc.co.uk/1/hi/world/south_asia/7739171.stm.

known Mr Choong described the incident 'an unfortunate tragedy'.[92] The complexity of piracy off Somalia amply demonstrates the need for clear ROE setting out the limits on the use of force: failure to do so not only has the potential to put innocent hostages in harm's way, but may also expose naval personnel to criminal prosecution under the law of their flag state.

12

Unlawful Killing with Combat Drones: A Case Study of Pakistan, 2004–2009

MARY ELLEN O'CONNELL[*]

I
N MAY 2009, the Director of the United States Central Intelligence Agency (CIA), Leon Panetta, responded directly to the growing criticism of America's use of unmanned aerial vehicles, better known as 'drones'. The US began using weaponised drones in 2001, but the criticism became heated as the US increasingly used drones to attack in the border area between Afghanistan and Pakistan.[1] These attacks resulted in the deaths of hundreds of unintended victims, including children.[2] In a public speech Panetta attempted to counter the criticism, asserting that drone attacks are 'precise' and cause only 'limited collateral damage'.[3] 'And very frankly,' he said, 'it's the only game in town in terms of confronting and trying to disrupt the al-Qaida leadership.'[4]

Counter terrorism experts David Kilcullen and Andrew Exum wrote in *The New York Times* in March 2009, however, that drones are anything but 'precise' and the numbers of civilian casualties have not been 'limited'.[5]

---

[*] With thanks for research assistance to LT Ethan McWilliams, JD and Mirakmal Niyazmatov, LLM (SJD candidate) and for suggestions from David Ackerson, Peter Bauer, David Cortright, Yuval Ginbar, and Russell Hogg. The research for this chapter was completed in 2010.

[1] For details of the CIA drone programme, see J Mayer, 'The Predator War, What are the Risks of the C.I.A.'s Covert Drone Program?', *The New Yorker*, 26 October 2009.

[2] The US does not release official data on the drone programme. A number of websites do provide data, eg, the drone database of the New America Foundation, which tracks strikes in Pakistan. See counterterrorism.newamerica.net/drones. Care must be taken with this and most sources as international legal terms of art such as 'civilian' and 'combatant' are used imprecisely. See below n 6.

[3] ML Kelly, 'Officials: Bin Laden Running Out of Space to Hide', *NPR*, 5 June 2009, NPR, www.npr.org/templates/story/story.php?storyId=104938490.

[4] Ibid.

[5] D Kilcullen and A McDonald Exum, 'Death From Above, Outrage Down Below', *New York Times*, 17 March 2009. See also Hearing of the House Armed Services Committee, *Effective Counterinsurgency: The Future of the U.S. Pakistan Military Partnership*, 23 April 2009 (Testimony of David Kilcullen).

They estimated at that time the US was causing 50 unintended deaths for each intended target.[6] Moreover, killing leaders has typically had only a short-term impact on repressing terrorist violence, while every civilian killed 'represents an alienated family, a new desire for revenge, and more recruits for a militant movement that has grown exponentially even as drone strikes have increased'.[7] In general, studies show that military force has rarely put an end to terrorist groups in comparison with law enforcement approaches and political processes.[8] With respect to Pakistan, Kilcullen and Exum argue that the use of drones against targets has alienated people from the Pakistani government and has contributed to the country's instability.[9] Pakistanis hold their government responsible for allowing the drone attacks to continue.

This chapter analyses the international law relevant to use of drones by the US to carry out attacks in Pakistan from 2004 to 2009. The US use of drones in Pakistan and elsewhere raises serious questions under the international law governing both resort to armed force as well as the law governing the conduct of armed conflict. The chapter begins with an overview of the facts with regard to drones and Pakistan; it then applies international law to these facts, concluding that in the circumstances of Pakistan between 2004 and 2009, US attacks appear to have violated fundamental law. The chapter also inquires into why America's leaders—from both political parties—have been so willing to use an unlawful and arguably counter-productive tactic.

---

[6] Kilcullen and Exum estimate that between 2006 and early 2009, 700 persons died in attacks killing 14 intended targets: Kilcullen and Exum, above n 5. Mirakmal Niyazmatov has confirmed the numbers in a check of public websites (data on file with the author). Peter Bergen and Katherine Tiedemann have found similar ratios of intended to unintended victims: 'Since 2006, our analysis indicates 82 U.S. drone attacks in Pakistan have killed between 750 and 1000 people. Among them were about 20 leaders of al Qaeda, the Taliban, and allied groups, all of whom have been killed since January 2008': P Bergen and K Tiedemann, Revenge of the Drones, *New America Foundation*, 19 October 2009 newamerica.net/publications/policy/revenge_drones.

Those who provide a lower ratio are basing their numbers on their own interpretation of who is a 'civilian' and who is not. See, eg, the *Long War Journal* which claims only '10%' of the persons killed are 'civilians'.www.longwarjournal.org/. The problem with the claim, as this chapter details, is that the US has little concrete information about victims other than the 'leaders' who have been the intended targets. It is very difficult to distinguish militants from non-militants in Western Pakistan but before the spring of 2009, there was not even an armed conflict in Pakistan. Outside of armed conflict everyone is a civilian. See below, nn 97–104 and accompanying text. Thus, the most accurate way to characterise the persons killed as a result of US drone attacks is to refer to the list of persons the US intended to kill and the numbers of those who the US did not intend to kill. See also above n 2.

[7] Ibid.

[8] See, eg, SG Jones and MC Libicki, *How Terrorist Groups End, Lessons for Countering Al Qa'Ida* (2008) available at www.rand.org/pubs/monographs/2008/RAND_MG741-1.pdf. See also below n 63 and accompanying text.

[9] Ibid.

I. DRONES IN PAKISTAN

The US Department of Defense defines an unmanned aerial vehicle (UAV) as a 'powered aerial vehicle that does not carry a human operator, ... can fly autonomously or be piloted remotely, can be expendable or recoverable, and can carry a lethal or non-lethal payload'.[10] Drones were probably invented during or right after the Second World War and were ready for use by the 1950s.[11] The first large-scale use of drones was for reconnaissance during the Vietnam War. During the 1991 Gulf War, Iraqi soldiers surrendered to an unarmed surveillance drone.[12] Drones continued to be widely used for reconnaissance during the conflicts in the Balkans in the 1990s.

Reportedly, in 2000, the US was ready to employ drones for a dramatic new use: as a launch vehicle for missiles. Reconnaissance drones found indications of Osama bin Laden's whereabouts in Afghanistan. Plans were then readied to kill him with missiles fired from a drone. The plans were not carried out, but drones with missile launch capability began to be used in early October 2001 in Afghanistan, apparently at first with the permission of the country hosting a US airbase where the drones were kept, Uzbekistan. A drone was used in November 2001 to launch a missile to kill al-Qaeda's Mohammed Atef in Afghanistan.[13]

On 3 November 2002, the US used a drone outside a combat area to fire laser-guided Hellfire missiles at a passenger vehicle traveling in a thinly populated region of Yemen. The drone was operated by CIA agents based in Djibouti. The US Air Force, at that time, operated the US's drones, but was concerned about legal issues raised by the Yemen operation, so the CIA carried out the strike. All six passengers in the vehicle were killed. US officials said one of the six men was a suspected 'lieutenant' in al-Qaeda; another was an American citizen in his early twenties.[14] In January 2003,

---

[10] The Department of Defense Dictionary of Military and Associated Terms 579, Joint Publication 1-02, 12 April 2001 (amended 17 October 2008).

[11] G Sommer et al, *The Global Unmanned Aerial Vehicle Acquisition Process: A Summary of Phase I Experience* 11 (Rand 1997); see also, PW Singer, 'Robots at War: The New Battlefield', *The Wilson Quarterly*, Winter 2009 www.wilsoncenter.org/index. cfm?fuseaction=wq.essay&essay_id=496613, 30; and PW Singer, *Wired for War: The Robotics Revolution and Conflict in the 21st Century* (New York, Penguin Press, 2009).

[12] The US's Public Broadcasting Service broadcast a television programme on the Gulf War that contained this information, www.pbs.org/wgbh/pages/frontline/gulf/weapons/drones.html.

[13] E Schmitt, 'Threats and Responses: The Battlefield; U.S. Would Use Drones to Attack Iraqi Targets', *New York Times* www.nytimes.com/2002/11/06/world/threats-responses-battlefield-us-would-use-dro ....

[14] D McManus, 'A U.S. License to Kill, a New Policy Permits the C.I.A. to Assassinate Terrorists, and Officials Say a Yemen Hit Went Perfectly. Others Worry About Next Time', *Los Angeles Times*, 11 January 200, A1; J Kelly, 'U.S. Kills Al-Qaeda Suspects in Yemen; One Planned Attack on USS Cole, Officials Say', *USA Today*, 5 November 2002, A1; JJ Lumpkin, 'Administration Says That Bush Has, in Effect, a License to Kill; Anyone Designated by the President as an Enemy Combatant, Including U.S. Citizens Can Be Killed Outright, Officials Argue', *St Louis Post-Disp.*, 4 December 2002, A12.

the United Nations Commission on Human Rights received a report on the Yemen strike from its special rapporteur on extrajudicial, summary, or arbitrary killing. The rapporteur concluded that the strike constituted 'a clear case of extrajudicial killing'.[15]

During its invasion of Iraq that began in March 2003, the US regularly used reconnaissance and attack drones.[16] The US has also used attack drones in Somalia, probably starting in late 2006 during the Ethiopian invasion when the US assisted Ethiopia in its attempt to install a new government in that volatile country. Among other actions, the US pursued fleeing terrorist suspects using helicopter gunships and attack drones. The US has continued to target and kill individuals in Somalia after Ethiopia pulled its forces out of the country.[17]

Drone attacks by the US in Pakistan began in 2004.[18] The number of attacks jumped dramatically in 2008 and continued to climb in 2009.[19]

By 2009, the US was deploying two types of combat drones: the MQ-1 or Predator and the MQ-9 or Reaper. The Reaper is similar in design and function to the Predator, but the Reaper is 'a new[er] and more heavily armed cousin of the Predator'.[20] The US is rapidly increasing its supply of

---

[15] UN Doc E/CN.4/2003/3, paras 37–39. See also Michael J Dennis, *Human Rights in 2002: The Annual Sessions of the UN Commission on Human Rights and the Economics and Social Council*, 97 *American Journal of International Law* 364, 367, fn 17 (2003). 'The United States' response to the ... Yemen allegations has been that its actions were appropriate under the international law of armed conflict and that the Commission and its special procedures have no mandate to address the matter': ibid. But see the conclusion that the Yemen strike was an unlawful action because it was military force used outside of an armed conflict. ME O'Connell, 'Ad Hoc War' in H Fishcher et al (eds), *Krisensicherung und Humanitärer Schutz— Crisis Management and Humanitarian Protection* 405 (Berlin, Berliner Wissenschafts-Verlag, 2004).

[16] BM Carney, 'Air Combat by Remote Control', 12 May 2008, *The Wall Street Journal* online.wsj.com/article/SB121055519404984109.html#printMode.

[17] S Bloomfield, 'Somalia: The World's Forgotten Catastrophe', *The Independent*, 9 February 2008, available at www.independent.co.uk/news/world/africa/somalia-the-worlds-forgotten-catastrophe-778225.html. See also *CBS News*, 'U.S. Missile Strike Hits Town in Somalia', 3 March 2008, available at www.cbsnews.com/stories/2008/03/03/world/main3898799.shtml; *Spiegel Online*, 'A Strike Against Al-Qaeda's Hornet's Nest', 1 September 2007, available at www.spiegel.de/international/0,1518,458597,00.html.

[18] Nek Muhammad Wazir was killed in a strike near Wana in Pakistan. Four people were killed along with him. It is not clear if they were Taliban fighters or not, see D Rodhe and M Khan, 'The Reach of War: Militants; Ex-Fighter for Taliban Dies in Stricke in Pakistan', *New York Times*, www.nytimes.com/2004/06/19/world/the-reach-of-war-militants-ex-fighter-for-taliban-dies-in-strike-in-pakistan.html.

[19] P Stewart and R Birsel, 'Under Obama, Drone Attacks on the Rise in Pakistan', *Reuters*, 12 October 2009 www.reuters.com/articlePrint?articleld=USN11520882. ('There have been 39 drone strikes in Pakistan since Obama took office not quite nine months ago, according to a Reuters tally of reports from Pakistani security officials, local government officials and residents. That compares with 33 strikes in the 12 months before Obama was sworn in on Jan. 20') (paragraph break omitted.) See also above n 6.

[20] C Drew, 'Drones Are Weapons of Choice in Fighting Qaeda', *New York Times*, 16 March 2009, available at www.nytimes.com/2009/03/17/business/17uav.html?_r=1&hp.

drones.[21] By 2009, it had about 100 Predators and 15 Reapers.[22] The US will soon have more unmanned than manned aerial vehicles in its arsenal. Other states and non-state actors are also acquiring drones, including Pakistan, Russia, Georgia, Brazil, China, Hamas, Iran and Israel.[23]

Before they were outfitted with missiles, drones were used primarily for reconnaissance missions. They were 'used as a cheap form of aerial reconnaissance which avoided endangering pilots' lives'.[24] After 9/11, the role of drones evolved from reconnaissance to attack vehicle. US Joint Chiefs of Staff General Richard Myers has praised the drone's capacity to remain in the air for long periods and then respond immediately when a target is detected.[25] Drone technology is rapidly evolving. At the time of writing, drones could linger for up to 24 hours at altitudes greater than 60,000 feet (18.3 km), providing real-time intelligence to commanders.[26] When a target of interest is detected, the same drone could attack it with significant force.[27]

Clearly drones have a number of advantages for the US in comparison to alternatives. First and foremost, they spare pilots' lives. 'Pilots' operate the 'unmanned' aerial vehicle with a joystick at a comfortable site far from the attack zone. Thus, even if a drone is shot down, there is no loss of human life. They are also relatively cheap and easy to manufacture. Drones cost less than manned military aircraft. In 2009, a Predator cost about $4.5 million, 30 times less than a fighter jet. Further, drones can be used for any battlefield operation: surveillance, reconnaissance, precision attacks, targeted killings, etc. As any other robot, a drone can be used to carry out dull, dirty or dangerous battlefield operations, referred to as the 'Three Ds'.[28]

Nor do drones suffer from human weaknesses. They do not get hungry, scared, shocked, or tired (although they can run low of fuel). You can use a drone whenever it is needed whereas pilots fly according to a certain schedule of flights. Predators and Reapers have been flying dozens of surveillance patrols each day in Iraq and Afghanistan and transmitting thousands of hours of video each month, some of it directly to troops on the ground.

---

[21] Ibid.

[22] Ibid.

[23] A Rodriquez, 'Pakistan Turns to Drones of Its Own', *latimes.com*, 9 October 2009. See also Philip Alston (Human Rights Council), *Report of the Special Rapporteur on extrajudicial, summary or arbitrary executions*, UN GAOR, 14th sess, Agenda Item 3, UN Doc A/HRC/14/24/Add.6 (28 May 2010) para 27 (40 states have drones).

[24] K Somerville, 'US Drones Take Combat Role', *BBC News*, 5 November 2002, available at news.bbc.co.uk/2/hi/in_depth/2404425.stm.

[25] Ibid.

[26] Ibid.

[27] In addition to the US, 'Israel is a major producer and user of military drones, using them for reconnaissance of its borders and to gather military intelligence about its Arab neighbours' military capabilities': ibid.

[28] Singer, above n 11.

If a drone is shot at during surveillance, it, of course, does not panic. Drones keep flying if they can—over mountains and other rugged terrain to reach places ground troops would have great difficulty reaching. They then have the ability to hover for hours, which conventional aircraft cannot.

Perhaps most significant for the inquiry here, drones may be operated far from the target. Attack drones in Afghanistan have been 'piloted' from as far away as Nevada.[29] According to Jane Mayer of *The New Yorker*:

> The U.S. government runs two drone programs. The military's version, which is publicly acknowledged, operates in the recognized war zones of Afghanistan and Iraq, and targets enemies of U.S. troops stationed there. As such, it is an extension of conventional warfare. The C.I.A.'s program is aimed at terror suspects around the world, including in countries where U.S. troops are not based. ... The program is classified as covert, and the intelligence agency declines to provide any information to the public about where it operates, how it selects targets, who is in charge, or how many people have been killed.[30]

The two programmes may not be as clearly separated as Mayer suggests, however. Many facts about the use of drones are classified, so it is difficult to get a full and accurate picture. Some evidence suggests a more complicated situation. In an interview with a former commander of the drone operation at Nellis Air Force Base in Nevada, it was clear that all drone operations are 'joint' operations—none is carried out by the Air Force alone. The commander said a '1000' people see the video—from 'pilots' in their trailers in Nevada and New Mexico, to intelligence analysts at Central Command (CENTCOM) headquarters in Florida, to persons in 'Japan', to 'POTUS' (the President of the US).[31] There are also persons involved located in Afghanistan, Pakistan, and elsewhere where drones are kept ready for missions. Apparently, the US now has secret airfields in Pakistan for this purpose.[32] A former assistant general counsel at the CIA, John Radsan, indicated to the author that all decisions to actually fire a missile are made by the CIA at their headquarters in Langley, Virginia.[33]

Whatever the actual organisation of the operation, one thing is clear, the use of drones in Pakistan has resulted in a large number of persons being killed along with the intended targets. Several factors suggest why this has

---

[29] P Bergman and K Tiedemann, 'The Drone War', *New Republic*, 3 June 2009, available at www.tnr.com/politics/story.html?id=b951d70b-db5e-4875-a5b9-4501e713943d&p=1.

[30] Mayer, above n 1, 37.

[31] The former commander asked that his name not appear in print despite the fact that he revealed no classified information. The interview took place by telephone on 15 September 2009. The commander's name and notes of the conversation are on file with the author.

[32] Mayer, above n 1, 38.

[33] AJ Radsan, Remarks to the author, 8 October 2009, University of Notre Dame Law School. See also R Murphy and AJ Radsan, *Due Process and Targeted Killing of Terrorists*, Working Paper No 114 (March 2009) ssrn.com/abstract=1349357.

been the case. One problem is structural. The remote pilot of a drone is relying on cameras and sensors to transmit the information he or she needs to decide on an attack. The technology is improving, but it is still difficult to be certain about targets.[34] Weather plays a role, as does the attitude of the 'pilot'. We also know there is a tendency to trust the computer in distinction to the pilot's own judgement. If the computer registers that a target has a gun that was recently fired, pilots have a tendency to defer to the computer.[35] This tendency is encouraged by the multiple decisions pilots must make every day in split seconds. It is likely to increase as pilots oversee multiple drones. So while the computer is not technically 'autonomous' in deciding to strike, that is becoming the reality.[36]

In the situation of Western Pakistan the US has little reliable on-the-ground information to confirm or discredit computer data. A media report drawing attention to problems with target identification explained: 'Somebody operating a Predator will see a bunch of vehicles and they'll say, "We know they're not ours"'. The Air Force's standard tactics have been 'to bring in other recon, like special operations teams, and try to figure out what they're seeing. But to start with, all they know is that there's movement'.[37] 'Looking through the Predator's camera is somewhat like looking through a soda straw. ... Your field of view tends to become distorted. ... [Y]ou might be able to tell a Saudi headdress from an Afghan one. They are different. But it'd be pretty hard to do.'[38]

This describes the approach that the Air Force has taken. It depends on having on-the-ground information. In Pakistan, the US has had little on-the-ground information, and what it has had has not been very reliable.[39] 'In Afghanistan and Pakistan, the local informants, who also serve as confirming witnesses for the air strikes, are notoriously unreliable.'[40] Even with the improvements in technology, reliable, ground-level information remains extremely important. Plenty of mistakes are being made:

> The first two C.I.A. air strikes of the Obama Administration took place on the morning of January 23rd—the President's third day in office. Within hours, it was clear that the morning's bombings, in Pakistan, had killed an estimated twenty people. In one strike, four Arabs, all likely affiliated with Al Qaeda, died. But in the second strike a drone targeted the wrong house, hitting the residence

---

[34] Peter Bergen and Katherine Tiedemann indicate that the number of unintended victims is declining: P Bergen and K Tiedemann, 'No Secrets in the Sky', *New York Times*, 25 April 2010 www.nytimes.com/2010/04/26/opinion/26bergen.html?_r=1.

[35] Singer, above n 11, 39–42.

[36] Ibid; see also PW Singer, 'In the Loop? Armed Robots and the Future of War', *Brookings*, 28 January 2009 www.brookings.edu/articles/2009/0128_robots_sineger.aspx.

[37] E Umansky, 'Dull Drone: Why Unmanned U.S. Aerial Vehicles Are A Hazard to Afghan Civilians', *Slate*, 13 March 2002, available at www.slate.com/id/2063105/.

[38] Ibid.

[39] Mayer, above n 1, 44.

[40] Ibid 45.

of a pro-government tribal leader six miles outside the town of Wana, in South Waziristan. The blast killed the tribal leader's entire family, including three children, one of them five years old.[41]

Another issue in drone use is the fact that strikes are carried out by joint operations. The heavy involvement of the CIA and CIA contractors in the decisions to strike may alone account for the high unintended death rate. CIA operatives are not trained in the law of armed conflict.[42] They are not bound by the Uniform Code of Military Justice to respect the laws and customs of war. This fact became abundantly clear during the revelation of US use of interrogation methods involving torture and cruel, inhuman and degrading treatment. Given the impact of that unlawful conduct it is difficult to fathom why the Obama administration is using the CIA to carry out drone attacks. Under the law of armed conflict, only lawful combatants have the right to use force during an armed conflict. Lawful combatants are the members of a state's regular armed forces. The CIA is not part of the US armed forces. They do not wear uniforms. They are not subject to the military chain of command. They are not trained in the law of war, including in the fundamental targeting principles of distinction, necessity, proportionality and humanity.[43] Rather, the CIA has a list of intended targets. They judge success by the number of persons on the list they kill.

It may also be that the US military is no longer training its members in the law of war as it once did. The former drone commander emphasised that he had never had a single day of training in the law of armed conflict in his 17 years of active duty. A currently serving Army lawyer reported he had had only three days of international law training during his specialised course at the Army JAG School in Charlottesville, Virginia in 2005. He subsequently served an 18-month tour in Baqubah, Iraq, in some of the heaviest fighting during the 'surge' period. The Naval War College may be trimming its law of armed conflict programme. These anecdotal accounts are of great concern given that the soldiers convicted of crimes at Abu Ghraib prison also reported they had had no training in the Geneva Conventions, despite the fact that the majority of Geneva Convention rules concern detention. After years in which the US has disrespected the international law on the use of force, including having a White House counsel and later Attorney

---

[41] Ibid 37.

[42] WC Banks, expert on US national security law, e-mail to the author, 28 September 2009 (on file with the author). Accord, Radsan, above n 33.

[43] See below n 44.

General call the Geneva Conventions 'quaint' and 'obsolete',[44] it should be no surprise that training of troops in this area may be suffering. Inadequate training may account for the high rate of unintended deaths even where Air Force personnel are involved in the decision to strike. It would seem to be a time when the US should be expanding its programmes in the law of armed conflict and ethics.

On the other hand, law of armed conflict scholars and ethicists are just beginning to consider the implications of the new drone technology. So far they have little to offer the military or public officials specifically about drones, although there is plenty of law to draw on as will be discussed in more detail in the next section. The remainder of this section considers some of the unique features of drones that must be taken into account as we consider the law and ethical principles that apply to this technology.

As already mentioned, drone operators work at a distance—an amazing distance—from the scene of drone attacks. The 'pilot' may be in Nevada; CIA personnel may be in Langley, Virginia at CIA headquarters; members of the military's Central Command may be in Florida, and others in Afghanistan. The operators never see with their own eyes the persons they have killed. Indeed, they have no physical contact with the place where the attacks are happening. Even a pilot of a conventional bomber or fighter jet who, like the drone pilot, sees only with the aid of a radar screen or video camera, knows he is over the place where his attack will occur. He knows he may be shot down. In the trailer in Nevada, the pilot knows she will not be attacked. She will go home to her family at the end of the day, coach a soccer game, make dinner, and help with homework.

Lieutenant Colonel Dave Grossman in his 1995 book, *On Killing*, describes factors that can overcome the average individual's resistance to killing. The most important of these factors characterise drone operations and while many also characterise high aerial bombardment from a plane, the distances for drone operators are even more remote and disconnected:

Miligram's famous studies of killing behavior in laboratory conditions (the willingness of subjects to engage in behavior that they believed was killing a fellow subject) identified three primary situation variables that influence or enable killing behavior; in this model I have called these (1) the demands of authority, (2) group

---

[44] A Gonzales, 'Memorandum for the President Re: Decision Re: Application of the Geneva Convention on Prisoners of War to the Conflict with al Qaeda and the Taliban' (25 January 2002) reprinted in KJ Greenberg and JL Dratel (eds) *The Torture Papers, The Road to Abu Ghraib* (New York, Cambridge University Press, 2005) 118.

absolution (remarkably similar to the concept of diffusion of responsibility), and (3) the distance from the victim.[45]

For Grossman, 'distance from the victim' includes various concepts of distance:

— Physical distance between the killer and the victim
— Emotional distance between the killer and the victim, including:
  — Social distance, which considers the impact of a lifetime of viewing a particular class as less than human in a culturally stratified environment;
  — Cultural distance, which includes racial and ethnic differences that permit the killer to 'dehumanise' the victim;
  — Moral distance, which takes into consideration intense belief in moral superiority and 'vengeful' actions;
  — Mechanical distance, which includes the sterile 'video game' unreality of killing through a TV screen, a thermal sight, a sniper sight, or some other kind of mechanical buffer.[46]

A 20-something Christian Air Force pilot living with her two children in suburban Las Vegas who views a monitor to locate her targets would seem to be as distant as a one can be from targets in rural, Muslim Pakistan. Television and YouTube video of drone pilots on the job reveal a set-up that looks very much like video game.[47] These factors and others likely contribute to the high death rate among unintended targets.

Even without killing, drones terrify people. They fly for hours overhead, hovering, filming, threatening to strike at any time. Residents of the Occupied Palestinian Territories report on the terror and oppression inflicted by Israeli drones.[48] With respect to Pakistan, Kilcullen and Exum have said: 'While violent extremists may be unpopular, for a frightened population they seem less ominous than a faceless enemy that wages war from afar and often kills more civilians than militants.'[49]

Between 2006 and late 2009, about 20 suspected militant leaders have reportedly been killed in Pakistan during strikes that killed between 750

---

[45] D Grossman, *On Killing: The Psychological Cost of Learning to Kill in War and Society* (New York, Back Bay Books, 1996) 187.

[46] Ibid 188–89.

[47] See, eg, CBS, *60 Minutes*, episode 29, 10 May 2009 www.cbs.com/primetime/60_minutes/video/video.php?cid=60%20Minutes/60%20Minutes%20Full%20Episodes&pid=miUvvT94XD89Z_dB12qJFU0x_u9BDLMg&category=episodes&play=true.

[48] For an account of the use of drones during the Israeli incursion in Gaza December 2008–January 2009, see C Chassay, 'Cut to Pieces: the Palestinian Family Drinking Tea in Their Courtyard', *The Guardian*, 23 March 2009 www.guardian.co.uk/world/2009/mar/23/gaza-war-crimes-drones.

[49] Kilcullen and Exum, above n 5.

and 1000 other persons.[50] In June 2009, the former US Afghan commander, General Stanley McChrystal, restricted the use of airstrikes in Afghanistan because of the high number of civilian deaths. He ordered that '[t]he restrictions … be especially tight in attacking houses and compounds where insurgents are believed to have taken cover'. McChrystal explained that 'Air power contains the seeds of our own destruction if we do not use it responsibly … .We can lose this fight.'[51] Since this order, reports of deaths among unintended victims appear to be somewhat lower in Pakistan. Whether the numbers have actually declined is difficult to confirm because the US and Pakistan have succeeded in keeping journalists out of the border region. The governments may also be controlling reports from on-the-ground contacts.[52]

Even if the numbers of persons killed are somewhat lower during particular attacks, the overall number of strikes has significantly increased. The intended targets of these attacks are in villages, in homes, in vehicles, and in general surrounded by many persons not involved in hostilities, not suspected militants, and not intended targets.[53] In August 2009, the US attacked a home where an infamous Taliban leader, Baitullah Mehsud, was staying with one of his wives and her parents. He was on the roof of the house, at night, apparently receiving an intravenous transfusion.[54] He is known to have suffered from diabetes and a kidney ailment. His uncle, a medic, was believed to be administering the treatment. His wife was with him. Missiles from a drone tore him to pieces. His wife, parents-in-law, seven men described as 'bodyguards' and one man described as a 'lieutenant' also, reportedly, died in the strike.[55] Presumably only Mehsud was an intended target. The strike killed 12 for one intended target. Jane Mayer reports that the US carried out as many as 16 attempts to kill Mehsud with drone strikes. In the conditions of the Pakistan border region, using drones to selectively target individuals has not been possible with current technology.

---

[50] Bergen and Tiedemann, above n 6; see also Kilcullen and Exum, above n 5. Jane Mayer reports that between January and October 2009, 'estimates suggest the C.I.A. attacks have killed between three hundred and twenty-six and five hundred and thirty-eight people. Critics say that many of the victims have been innocent bystanders, including children': Mayer, above n 1, 37.

[51] D Filkins, 'U.S. Tightens Airstrike Policy in Afghanistan', *New York Times*, 22 June 2009.

[52] Mayer, above n 1.

[53] See, eg, a report of a strike after McChrystal's order that hit a funeral: P Zubair Shah and S Masood, 'U.S. Drone Strike Said to Kill 60 in Pakistan', *New York Times*, 23 June 2009, www.nytimes.com/2009/06/24/world/asia/24pstan.html.

[54] Mayer, above n 1. Bergen and Tiedemann report that Mehsud was receiving a 'leg massage'. The discrepancy indicates that even the information about the intended target may not be as solid as US statements imply, above n 6.

[55] Ibid.

Despite these difficulties with drones, American leaders seem to consider them an unqualified success:

> Privately, American officials rave about the drone program. One former Bush administration official said that the drones had so crimped the militants' activities in FATA [the Federally Administered Tribal Areas of Pakistan] that they had begun discussing a move to Yemen or Somalia. Two officials familiar with the drone program point out that the number of 'spies' Al Qaeda and the Taliban have killed has risen dramatically in the past year, suggesting that the militants are turning on themselves in an effort to root out the sources of the often pinpoint intelligence that has led to what those officials describe as the deaths of half of the top militant leaders in the FATA.[56]

At time of writing, however, the militants in Pakistan are carrying out deadly attacks on a regular basis. Baitullah Mehsud's followers quickly reconstituted themselves under two new leaders. This outcome recalls the hydra—one head is cut off and several more take its place. The evidence is supporting Kilcullen's assessment that going after leaders with drones is proving counter-productive of peace and stability in Pakistan. New leaders have stepped up to take the place of the slain, and they have more than enough new recruits. Meanwhile, anti-American sentiment in Pakistan grows. During Secretary of State Clinton's visit to Pakistan in late October 2009, a woman at a town hall meeting 'characterized U.S. drone missile strikes on suspected terrorist targets in northwestern Pakistan as de facto acts of terrorism themselves'.[57]

Even if such strikes could be counted on to dissolve terrorist or militant groups in Pakistan, the US would still need to forgo them as their use is not consistent with America's legal duties, which is the topic of the next section.

II. THE LAW ON DRONES

International law, like all law, provides an alternative to force and violence in human interactions. As in all human communities, the international community uses law to restrict the right to resort to force to emergency self-defence and to those persons authorised to use force for the good of the community. States may use force in self-defence or with the authorisation of the United Nations Security Council. States are restricted from using military force outside these situations, but may resort to law enforcement measures. While all uses of force are subject to human rights principles, the use of military force is further restricted by international humanitarian law.[58]

---

[56] Bergen and Tiedemann, above n 6.

[57] A Rodriguez, 'Clinton's Pakistan Visit Reveals Widespread Distrust of U.S.', *Los Angeles Times*, 31 October 2009, latimes.com/news/nationworld/world/la-fg-clinton-pakistan1-2009-nov.01,0,1313175.story.

[58] See N Melzer, *Targeted Killing in International Law* (Oxford, Oxford University Press, 2008) 243; see also O'Connell, above n 15, 15.

The law on state use of military force is set out in the United Nations Charter, in rules of customary international law, and in general principles (collectively the '*jus ad bellum*'). The rules on resort to force were reconfirmed by a consensus of all UN members at the 2005 World Summit in New York.[59] The rules on how military force may be used during an armed conflict is found in the Hague Conventions, the Geneva Conventions and their Additional Protocols, customary international law, and, again, general principles (collectively the '*jus in bello*'). The rules on conduct of force are the subject of regular review and comment by the International Committee of the Red Cross (ICRC). Also in 2005, the ICRC published a comprehensive review of customary international humanitarian law, which had the effect of providing a handbook of international humanitarian law for the two types of armed conflicts for which there are well-developed sets of rules: international armed conflict and non-international armed conflict.[60] It is important also to emphasise that certain human rights principles apply even during an armed conflict.[61] Human rights principles are also the subject of litigation, review, and updating. The view that the world does not have up-to-date rules for responding to terrorism and other contemporary challenges is simply incorrect.[62]

In the period under review, international law contained a clear and up-to-date set of principles governing the use of force. Nevertheless, in the US, at least since the 1960s, but especially since the end of the Cold War, political leaders and academics have chafed against international law limits on the use of force.[63] Realist and other ideologies have clouded our

---

On the scope of international humanitarian law (IHL or law of armed conflict) and human rights law, see, eg, F Hampson, 'The Relationship between International Humanitarian Law and Human Rights Law from the Perspective of a Human Rights Treaty Body' (2008) 90:871 *International Review of the Red Cross* 549 and W Schabas, '*Lex Specialis*? Belt and Suspenders? The Parallel Operation of Human Rights and the Law of Armed Conflict, and the Conundrum of *Jus Ad Bellum*'(2007) 40 *Israel Law Review* 592.

[59] 2005 World Summit Outcome, UN GAOR, 60th sess, UN Doc A/60/L.1 (15 September 2005) 22–23. Today all fully sovereign states are members of the United Nations.

[60] JM Henckaerts and L Doswald-Beck (eds), *Customary International Humanitarian Law* (Cambridge, Cambridge University Press, 2005) 13.

[61] See, eg, *Legality of the Threat or Use of Nuclear Weapons*, (*Advisory Opinion of 8 July*) [1996] ICJ Rep 226, para 25: 'The Court observes that the protection of the International Covenant of Civil and Political Rights does not cease in times of war, except by operation of Article 4 of the Covenant whereby certain provisions may be derogated from in a time of national emergency.'

[62] For an author who questions the adequacy of international law, see PM Cullen, 'The Role of Targeted Killing in the Campaign Against Terror' (2008) 48 *Joint Forces Quarterly* 28.

[63] See, eg, K Anderson, 'Targeted Killing in U.S. Counterterrorism Strategy and Law', *Social Science Reseach Network* (11 May 2009) ssrn.com/abstract=1415070. Anderson describes Melzer's book, *Targeted Killing in International* Law, above n 58, as 'formidable', the 'leading treatise', and 'a marvelous work of scholarship': ibid 13, fn 58. Nevertheless, Anderson points out that Melzer's book 'gives some sense of how far American domestic political views in the centrist political spectrum are from the views of the "international law community," of which Melzer's views are representative': ibid 13.

understanding of the very limited utility of military force[64] and the very real benefits of promoting peace and non-violence through law. It is hoped that the discussion in the next section might contribute to a renewed appreciation of the international law restricting the use of force and how respect for this law is the better path.

The drone attacks in Pakistan involve significant firepower—this is not the force of the police, but of the military. In law enforcement lethal force is restricted to situations of absolute necessity; by contrast, on the battlefield making use of bombs and missiles is lawful. The drones used in Pakistan can be lawfully employed only on the battlefield. The right to resort to them must be found in the *jus ad bellum*; the way they are used must be based on the *jus in bello* and human rights.

The US provided no public statement about the legality of its drone use in Pakistan between 2004 and 2009.[65] In March 2010, the State Department Legal Adviser spoke briefly to the question.[66] This next section considers his argument and others.

III. *JUS AD BELLUM*

The most important rule on resort to force, and perhaps in all of international law, is Article 2(4) of the United Nations Charter that prohibits the

---

Anderson's own paper is an example of American political views that are removed from mainstream international law. He strongly criticises Melzer for analysing international law as it is and rejecting US positions that are not in compliance with it: ibid fn 58. Anderson apparently wants Melzer to accept that the US should have a broader right to kill. Anderson does not explain why the US should have this right. He incorporates none of the literature that demonstrates adherence to the accepted rule of law and law enforcement methods have had the best results against terrorism. He seems to assume without providing evidence that the US needs a more flexible legal regime to kill people in certain places—places that are not scenes of armed conflict hostilities, but are also not the US itself or the territory of close allies, such as the UK: ibid 29–31. For alternative views, see J Mueller, 'How Dangerous are the Taliban?', *Foreign Affairs*, (2009) www.foreignaffairs.com/print/64932; Jones and Libicki, above n 8; L Richardson, *What Terrorists Want: Understanding the Enemy, Containing the Threat* (New York, Random House, 2007); ME O'Connell, 'Enhancing the Status of Non-State Actors Through a Global War on Terror' (2005) 43 *Columbia Journal of Transnational Law* 435. For another author who believes the US should have greater rights to use military force than other states, see, J Yoo, 'Using Force' (2004) 71 *University of Chicago Law Review* 729.

[64] See on this topic, R Smith, *The Utility of Military Force, The Art of War in the Modern World* (New York, Knopf, 2007).

[65] P Alston, *Promotion and protection of all human rights, civil, political economic, social and cultural rights, including the right to development* (Report of the Special Rapporteur on extrajudicial, summary or arbitrary executions), UN GAOR, 11th sess, Agenda Item 3, UN Doc A/HRC?11/2/Add.5 (28 May 2009). See also A Mathias, 'UN Rights Investigator Warns US Drone Attacks May Violate International Law', *Jurist*, 28 October 2009 jurist.law.pitt.edu/paperchase/2009/10/un-rights-investigator-wrns-us-drone.php#at.

[66] H Hongju Koh, *The Obama Administration and International Law*, Annual Meeting ASIL, US Department of State (25 March 2010) www.state.gov/s/l/releases/remarks/139119.htm.

use of force.[67] Article 2(4) is properly interpreted as prohibiting all uses of force above a certain minimal level. Minimal uses of force such as firing a single shot across an international boundary might violate the principle of non-intervention, but is probably too minor to come within the purview of Article 2(4). The Charter contains two exceptions to this general ban on virtually all uses of force. In Chapter VII, the Security Council is given authority to act in cases of threats to the peace, breaches of the peace and acts of aggression. It may order measures to maintain or restore international peace and security, including mandating or authorizing the use of force by member states.

Chapter VII also provides in Article 51 that states may respond in self-defence 'if an armed attack occurs' until the Security Council acts. The evident restrictions in this Article have come under some pressure, especially from academics in the US.[68] The International Court of Justice (ICJ), however, has restated in several cases that the Charter means what it says. The ICJ in the 1986 *Nicaragua* case made clear that acts triggering the right to use armed force in self-defence must themselves amount to armed attacks. In *Nicaragua*, the Court held that low-level shipments of weapons did not amount to an armed attack and could not be invoked as a basis for self-defence.[69]

It is important to realise that 'self-defence' is a term of art in international law. The reference in Article 51 to self-defence is to the right of the victim state to use significant offensive military force on the territory of a state legally responsible for the attack.[70] The ICJ has made clear that the armed attack that gives rise to this right of self-defence must be an attack that involves a significant amount of force—it must be more than a mere frontier incident, such as sporadic rocket fire across a border.[71] In the *Oil Platforms* case, the ICJ said:

> Even taken cumulatively, and reserving, as already noted, the question of Iranian responsibility, these incidents do not seem to the Court to constitute an armed attack on the United States of the kind that the court, in the case concerning

---

[67] Charter of the United Nations, Article 2(4): All Members shall refrain from the threat or use of force against the territorial integrity or political independence of any state, or in any other manner inconsistent with the Purposes of the United Nations.

[68] See, eg, Yoo, above n 63.

[69] *Military and Paramilitary Activities in and against Nicaragua (Nicaragua v United States) (Merits)* [1986] ICJ 14, 195, 230 (hereafter Nicaragua).

[70] *Legal Consequences of the Construction of a Wall in the Occupied Palestinian Territory, (Advisory Opinion)* [2004] ICJ Rep 136, 215 (Judge Higgins) (hereafter Wall).

[71] The ICJ also said that when a state has been attacked with use of force too minor to trigger the Article 51 provision on self-defence, the right way to respond is with non-forceful countermeasures, such as economic sanctions. Nicaragua, above n 69, 110–11,127. States are also free, of course, to establish defences on their own territory. See Wall, above n 70.

Military and Paramilitary Activities in and against Nicaragua, qualified as a 'most grave' form of the use of force.[72]

In addition to a lawful basis in the Charter, states using force must show that force is necessary to achieve a defensive purpose. If a state can show the necessity element, it must also show that the method of force used will not result in disproportionate loss of life and destruction compared to the value of the objective. Necessity and proportionality are not expressly mentioned in the Charter, but the ICJ held in the *Nuclear Weapons* case '"there is a specific rule whereby self-defence would warrant only measures which are proportional to the armed attack and necessary to respond to it, a rule well established in customary international law". This dual condition applies equally to Article 51 of the Charter, whatever the means of force employed.'[73]

An armed response to a terrorist attack will almost never meet these parameters for the lawful exercise of self-defence. Terrorist attacks are generally treated as criminal acts because they have all the hallmarks of crimes,[74] not of armed attacks that can give rise to the right of self-defence. Terrorist attacks are usually sporadic and are rarely the responsibility of the state where the perpetrators are located. The Supreme Court of Israel found in 2006 that Israel was engaged in a 'continuous state of armed conflict' with various 'terrorist organizations' due to the 'constant, continual, and murderous waves of terrorist attacks' and the armed response to these.[75] The court described a situation that was more than crime and would seem to share important features of the textbook case on self-defence, the 1990–91 liberation of Kuwait following Iraq's invasion. After Iraq invaded, Kuwait had the right to use force in self-defence and other states could join it in collective self-defence in order to expel the invader.[76]

The Kuwait case had two aspects not found in connection with most terrorist attacks. First, no one doubted who carried out the aggression: Iraq. Second, the occupation of Kuwait created a continuing wrong that could be righted, especially since the Security Council had authorised a coalition of states to liberate Kuwait. In the case of September 11 and other terrorist attacks, the first task was evidence gathering. Solid evidence of who attacked has been a central focus of the debate among states over the right to use force in response to terrorism. Because the state must respond quickly

---

[72] *Oil Platforms (Iran v United States)* [2003] ICJ Rep 161, 191 (hereafter Oil Platforms).
[73] *Legality of the Threat or Use of Nuclear Weapons (Advisory Opinion)* [1996] ICJ 226, 245 (8 July) (hereafter Nuclear Weapons). See also Nicaragua, above n 69, 94 and Oil Platforms, above n 72, 198.
[74] O'Connell, above n 63.
[75] HCJ 769/02, *The Public Committee Against Torture in Israel v Israel* [2006] (2) IsrLR 459, 16 (14 December 2006). But see Wall, above n 70.
[76] ME O'Connell, 'Enforcing the Prohibition on the Use of Force: The U.N.'s Response to Iraq's Invasion of Kuwait'(1991) 15 *Southern Illinois University Law Journal* 453, 479–80.

to an armed attack and may even counter the attack as the offensive attack commences, states have a problem responding lawfully using military force in the case of terrorist attacks. These attacks are usually brief and do not result in an ongoing wrong such as the unlawful occupation of territory. It usually takes some time to find out who the perpetrators are and where they are. But force may not be used long after the terrorist act has ended as it loses its defensive character and becomes an unlawful reprisal.

Even where militant groups remain active along a border for a considerable period of time, their armed cross-border incursions are not considered attacks under Article 51 giving rise to the right of self-defence unless the state where the group is present is responsible for their actions. In the case of *Congo v Uganda*, Uganda sent troops into Congo after years of cross-border incursions by armed groups from Congo into Uganda. Congo, however, was not responsible for the armed groups—it did not control them. Even Congo's failure or inability to take action against the militants did not give rise to any right by Uganda to cross into Congo to attack the groups themselves:

> During the period under consideration both anti-Ugandan and anti-Zairean rebel groups operated in this [border] area. Neither Zaire nor Uganda were in a position to put an end to their activities. However, in the light of the evidence before it, the Court cannot conclude that the absence of action by Zaire's Government against the rebel groups in the border area is tantamount to 'tolerating' or 'acquiescing' in their activities. Thus, the part of Uganda's first counter-claim alleging Congolese responsibility for tolerating the rebel groups prior to May 1997 cannot be upheld.[77]

But Uganda was found to have violated Article 2(4) of the UN Charter for its attacks on Congolese territory. The ICJ did not have to decide the case of 'large-scale attacks by irregular forces'.[78] The cross-border incursions resulted in dozens of deaths, not hundreds or thousands. One could predict a different assessment of state responsibility in the case of large-scale attacks. Such an eventuality would indicate that Congo had either consented to the force or had lost control of the territory where the group was.

These are basically the rules governing the resort to force between states. The Charter does not directly regulate the resort to force within states between government forces and non-state actors or between non-state actor militant groups. This is an unfortunate gap in the law as the most common form of armed conflict today is the internal armed conflict, armed conflicts mostly within the boundaries of a single state fought by groups contending for power or to secede. The tragic conflicts in Colombia, Congo, Somalia,

---

[77] *Armed Activities on the Territory of the Congo (Congo v Uganda) (Judgment)*[2005] ICJ para 301.
[78] Ibid para 147.

Sri Lanka, Sudan, Yugoslavia and the Philippines are examples. While international law does not include an express prohibition on the use of significant military force to take power within or to break away from a state, it does contain allied principles making such conduct generally unlawful. Most states make the use of force against a government a violation of domestic law, the crime of treason, but other domestic criminal law may be relevant as well, such as the crime of murder. Also, international human rights law prohibits a government from using excessive force in responding to an armed group seeking to take power or secede. A government may only resort to military force if the use of force by an opposing armed group is significant. In other cases, international human rights law restricts governments to the use of force permissible to police in responding to violent crime.[79] If a government seeks assistance from another state or international organisation, the party providing assistance may only use that level of force that the government itself has the right to use. Those commenting on the right of the US to use drones in Pakistan often overlook this important set of legal principles governing internal armed conflict.[80] For much of the period that the US has used drones on the territory of Pakistan, there has been no armed conflict. Therefore, even express consent by Pakistan would not justify their use.

The Bush and Obama administrations have also made the argument that because the 9/11 attacks were significant and were preceded and succeeded by acts of terrorism, the US may target and kill al-Qaeda members wherever they are found.[81] As discussed above, this position ignores the law of state responsibility. However, the further argument is made that if the US has the consent of the territorial state to carry out the attacks, there is no violation of the law of state responsibility. This position ignores the law just discussed that the consenting state may not consent to the use of military force on its territory in the absence of armed conflict hostilities. Colonel Peter Cullen argues for new rules to allow the US to use military force against terrorist suspects in just such situations. He wants an expansion of the *jus in bello*

---

[79] *International Covenant on Civil and Political Rights*, UN GAOR, Supp No 16, UN Doc A/6316 (1966), Articles 4 and 6 (no arbitrary deprivation of life) 52. See also cases of the European Court of Human Rights assessing excessive force used by Russia in the Chechen conflict and Turkey in the Kurdish conflict. *Isayeva, Yusopova and Bazayeva v Russia*, nos 57947/00, 57948/00 and 57949/00, ECHR 24 February 2005. *Isayeva v Russia*, no 57950/00, ECHR 24 February 2005 (hereafter *Isayeva II*); and *Khashiyev & Akayeva v Russia*, nos 57942/00 and 57945/00, ECHR 24 February 2005. Similarly, in *Ergi v Turkey*, no 66/1997/850/1057, ECHR 28 July 1998, the ECHR considered Turkey's use of force to repress the Kurdish Worker's Party. See also Melzer, above n 58.

[80] See, eg, S Murphy, 'The International Legality of U.S. Military Cross-Border Operations from Afghanistan into Pakistan' (2009) 85 *International Law Studies* 109. Murphy discusses consent at length and raises concerns about it as a solid basis for the US use of force in Pakistan, but he fails to begin by assessing what Pakistan has the legal right to consent to: ibid 118–20.

[81] See Koh, above n 66.

to apply to the use of force by a state against non-state actors suspected of terrorist attacks and located outside the state's own territory.[82] Under current law, if terrorist suspects are located in a state other than the US, the US may offer assistance to that other state. The *jus in bello* will apply if there is an armed conflict in the state. Peacetime criminal law applies if not. Indeed, as Cullen accepts, the US is resorting only to peacetime criminal law on the territory of the US. He does not believe there is any right to kill without warning persons in the US.[83] How can there be any such right on the territory of other states that are, like the US, not experiencing hostilities on their territory?

By the spring of 2009, Pakistan's armed forces began engaging various Taliban militant groups when one group tried to take over Buner Province.[84] Pakistani forces repulsed the Taliban in fighting that plainly amounted to armed conflict.[85] Pakistan had a right to resort to major military force to respond to this type of challenge to the legitimate government of Pakistan. The government of Pakistan, however, did not request US assistance, let alone the use of drones to end the challenge to its authority in Buner. On the contrary, many US attacks have been in areas where the Pakistani government had been attempting through a variety of methods to prevent an armed conflict. The Pakistani government position until 2009 had been to seek stability through peaceful means.[86] The legal restriction on the use of military force in such situations is found in human rights law. The major human rights treaties, for example, permit derogation from the otherwise prevailing rules only in situations of emergency. Outside an emergency,

---

[82] Cullen, above n 62, 23.

[83] Ibid 27.

[84] See J Perlez, 'Taliban Seize Vital Pakistan Area Closer to the Capital', *New York Times*, 22 April 2009 www.nytimes.com/2009/04/23/world/asia/23buner.html. The situation in Pakistan is complex and changes rapidly. One observer points out that there are many groups that call themselves 'Taliban'. Some are organised armed groups; some are not. Some are sympathetic to al-Qaeda; some are not. This makes the US decision to use drones in this context all the more questionable. Remarks of M Schleich, Kroc Institute for Peace Studies, University of Notre Dame, 6 April 2009.

[85] The International Law Association's Committee on the Use of Force Initial Report defines armed conflict as:

Looking to relevant treaties—in particular IHL treaties—rules of customary international law, general principles of international law, judicial decisions and the writing of scholars, as of the drafting of this Initial Report, the Committee has found evidence of at least two characteristics with respect to all armed conflict:
1.) The existence of organized armed groups
2.) Engaged in fighting of some intensity

International Law Association, *Initial Report of the Use of Force Committee, The Meaning of Armed Conflict in International Law* (August 2008, Rio de Janeiro) www.ilahq.org. See also ME O'Connell, 'Defining Armed Conflict' (2008) 13 *Journal of Conflict and Security Law* 393.

[86] See, eg, D Cortright, '"Winning" in Afghanistan, How to Splinter the Taliban and Support Afghans', *Sojourners Magazine*, March 2009 www.sojo.net/index.cfm?action=magazine.articl e&issue=soj0903&article=winning-in-afghanistan.

a state may only take a human life when 'absolutely necessary in the defence of persons from unlawful violence'.[87]

The United Nations Basic Principles for the Use of Force and Firearms by Law Enforcement Officials (*UN Basic Principles*), which are widely adopted by police throughout the world, provide in Article 9:

> Law enforcement officials shall not use firearms against persons except in self-defense or defense of others against the imminent threat of death or serious injury, to prevent the perpetration of a particularly serious crime involving grave threat to life, to arrest a person presenting such a danger and resisting their authority, or to prevent his or her escape, and only when less extreme means are insufficient to achieve these objectives. In any event, intentional lethal use of firearms may only be made when strictly unavoidable in order to protect life.[88]

When in 2009, Pakistan resorted to major military force, the US could have joined it upon an invitation to do so. It is well known that the elected government of Pakistan is weak and that the military and the intelligence services have differing views to the president on various issues at various times. The Pakistani president has protested some strikes,[89] while the military and/or the intelligence services have reportedly assisted the US with others. Moreover, it appears the drones operating in Pakistan are located in Pakistan. This is hardly a basis, however, to found the right to use significant lethal force on a state's sovereign territory. The US has put itself in a vulnerable position. Without express, public consent of the kind the US received from Afghanistan and Iraq, Pakistan is in a position to claim the US is acting unlawfully, even bringing a future legal claim for compensation. This would be true even if there were some sort of secret consent that the US would have difficulty proving in a court or other public fora. In the 2004 *Congo v Uganda* case, Congo expressly requested military assistance from Uganda, which it gave. The ICJ, nevertheless, found that Uganda violated the *jus ad bellum* when it did not withdraw its troops from Congo following Congo's indirect signals to do so.[90] The Pakistan government's protests to date would make a good argument that it, like Congo, has withdrawn any implicit consent that might have been given.

---

[87] *McCann & Others v United Kingdom*, Series A no 324, App no 18984/91 (1995).

[88] Adopted by the Eighth United Nations Congress on the Prevention of Crime and the Treatment of Offenders, Havana, Cuba, 27 August to 7 September 1990, www.2ohchr.org/english/law/firearms.htm. It is not possible to give a warning from a drone and thus drones, like bomber aircraft, cannot lawfully be used in law enforcement. The indication from the US that it might use weaponised drones in action against pirates, a law enforcement operation (see Guilfoyle chapter, this volume), creates confusion over this point of law. See 'U.S. Deploys Drones Against Somali Pirates', *CBS News*, 24 October 2009 www.cbsnews.com/stories/2009/10/24/world/main5417885.shtml.

[89] See K DeYoung, 'U.S. Options in Pakistan Limited', *Washington Post*, 4 May 2009 www.washingtonpost.com/wp-dyn/content/article/2009/05/03/AR2009050302212_pf.html.

[90] See generally *Congo v Uganda*, above n 77.

Besides the risky legal situation the US is in, it wants Pakistan's civilian, elected government to succeed. The US needs to treat that government with respect and defer to its policies aimed at extending its authority in Pakistan. This can hardly occur as drone attacks continue in the face of the government's protests.

Equally the Security Council has not authorised attacks, and the US has no right on that basis to use drones. In the wake of the 9/11 attacks, the Security Council did find in Resolution 1368 that the attacks triggered Article 51 self-defence. The Council did not, however, authorise the use of force against any particular state. Even if it did, such action would have to comply with the principles of necessity and proportionality. Necessity in the *jus ad bellum* refers to the decision to resort to force as a last resort and that the use of major force can accomplish the purpose of defence. Apparently US drone attacks in Pakistan aim at militants who attack US troops in Afghanistan or join with al-Qaeda to plot future 9/11-type attacks in the US. One of the leading experts on counter terrorism does not believe terrorism suppression will be the result of the drone attacks. In Congressional testimony in March 2009, David Kilcullen said:

I think one of the things we could do that would send a strong message right now is we could call off the drone strikes that have been mounted in the western part of Pakistan.

I realize that they do damage to al Qaeda leadership. Since 2006 we've killed 14 senior al Qaeda leaders using drone strikes. In the same time period we've killed 700 Pakistani civilians in the same area. The drone strikes are highly unpopular.

They are deeply aggravating to the population. And they've given rise to a feeling of anger that coalesces the population around the extremists and leads to spikes of extremism well outside the parts of the country where we are mounting those attacks.

Inside the FATA [Federally Administered Tribal Areas] itself some people like the attacks because they do actually target the bad guys. But in the rest of the country there's an immense anger about them. And there's anger about them in the military and the intelligence service. I realize it might seem counterintuitive, but we need to take our foot off the necks of these people so they feel that there's a degree of trust. Saying we want to build a permanent relationship, a friendship with them whilst continuing to bomb their population from the air, even if you do it with robot drones, is something that they see through straight away.[91]

The views of Kilcullen and others raise serious questions as to whether drone strikes can be defended as accomplishing the military objective in any

---

[91] Hearing of the House Armed Services Committee, *Effective Counterinsurgency: the Future of the U.S. Pakistan Military Partnership*, 23 April 2009 (Testimony of David Kilcullen).

meaningful way.[92] Moreover, the difficulty of accomplishing the military objective is compounded by the disproportionate loss of civilian lives.[93] In Western Pakistan missile strikes are inevitably going to kill far more unintended than intended targets. Even with improvements in the technology, high numbers of civilians are going to be killed using missiles and bombs in places where no hostilities are occurring and, thus, civilians are living and working normally. In armed conflict zones, civilians will evacuate or take some precautions.[94]

The media have reported on another attempt at a legal argument to justify drone attacks: 'hot pursuit'.[95] There is, however, no right of hot pursuit on land. Even attempting to extrapolate from the hot pursuit permitted under the law of the sea, the use of drones bear almost no resemblance to that right. Hot pursuit at sea provides a narrow right of coastal state law enforcement to extend the exercise of jurisdiction when a crime is suspected in the state's territorial sea or contiguous zone. Coastal law enforcement agents may pursue a suspect on the high seas when attempting to make an arrest if the pursuit began in maritime zones where law enforcement agents have jurisdiction and the agents remain in visual contact with the suspect until the arrest.

Related to the hot pursuit argument is an argument that US commando or special operation forces may cross from Afghanistan into Pakistan to kill or capture suspected militants or terrorists using drones or other weapons.[96] There appears to be no international law authority directly on point for this view, although the author has written that the law of countermeasures might support cross-border police action where a state has failed to exercise due diligence. The argument is at its strongest in a failed state situation. However, the US does not recognise Pakistan as a failed state.

[92] See also, above n 63, but see views of CIA Director Leon Panetta, above opening paragraph of this chapter.

[93] The principle of proportionality, like necessity, has a place in the *jus ad bellum*, as well as the *jus in bello*. According to Gardam: 'The legitimate resort to force under the United Nations system is regarded by most commentators as restricted to the use of force in self-defense under Article 51 and collective security action under chapter VII of the UN Charter. The resort to force in both these situations is limited by the customary law requirement that it be proportionate to the unlawful aggression that gave rise to the right. In the law of armed conflict, the notion of proportionality is based on the fundamental principle that belligerents do not enjoy an unlimited choice of means to inflict damage on the enemy': J Gardam, 'Proportionality and Force in International Law'(1993) *American Journal of International Law* 391.

[94] The US has an obligation to take feasible precautions to protect civilians, such as providing advance warning of an attack; never attacking homes; or only attacking at night in open spaces. The author has found no evidence that the US is taking precautions in Pakistan. See below n 104 and accompanying text.

[95] J Northam, 'Airstrikes in Pakistan's Tribal Areas Legally Murky', *NPR*, 10 June 2009 www.npr.ort/templates/story/story.php?storyID=101953944 (remarks of Harvey Rishikof, professor at the National War College). See N Lubell, *Extraterritorial Use of Force Against Non-State Actors* (Oxford, Oxford University Press, 2010) 72–73.

[96] See Murphy, above n 80.

The US has urged Pakistan to make greater efforts to control lawlessness on its territory. To some extent, the US and Pakistan disagree as a matter of policy as to what steps Pakistan should take. The situation does not appear to be an example where the US may disregard Pakistan sovereignty to carry out its own police actions. Moreover, the US needs Afghanistan's consent to carry out such raids from Afghan territory. Afghanistan has not, apparently, given this consent.

The strongest conclusion to draw under the *jus ad bellum* is that there is no legal right to resort to drone attacks in Pakistan. Drone attacks are uses of military force. Pakistan is not responsible for an armed attack on the US and so there is no right to resort to military force under the law of self-defence. Pakistan has not expressly invited the US to assist it in using force. At best there have been mixed signals from Pakistan about the US strikes. Further, even with express consent, the attacks would have to be part of Pakistan's own military operations. Even then, drone attacks may well be counter-productive to the military objective of eliminating the challenge from Pakistani militants, and they have been responsible for the deaths of many unintended victims, leading to serious questions about whether they may be used consistently under the principle of proportionality.

IV. *JUS IN BELLO*

If the government of Pakistan continues to be engaged in internal armed conflict on its territory and requests US assistance, the US must still comply with strict limits on how it uses drones. Indeed, in the circumstances of Western Pakistan, using drones lawfully may be an insurmountable challenge.

In the spring of 2009, Pakistan used major military force on its territory to respond to increasing challenges to central authority. In other words, the nature of the only armed conflict in Pakistan is an internal or non-international armed conflict. In such a conflict, some IHL rules applicable in international armed conflict do not apply, but these are generally rules respecting detention. The core IHL rules respecting targeting are the same in international and non-international armed conflict. These are the rules of distinction, necessity, proportionality and humanity.[97]

One of the most important rules with regard to the conduct of armed conflict may well be the rule of distinction. Under international law, civilians may not be intentionally targeted. Only members of a state's armed forces during armed conflict or persons taking a direct part in hostilities

---

[97] Henckaerts and Doswald-Beck, above n 60, 3, 29, 46. See also Y Sandoz et al, *Commentary on the Additional Protocols of 8 June 1977 to the Geneva Conventions of 12 August 1949* (International Committee of the Red Cross, 1987) section 1389.

may be targeted. In the ICRC study of customary international humanitarian law, distinction is the first rule:

> Rule 1. The parties to the conflict must at all times distinguish between civilians and combatants. Attacks may only be directed against combatants. Attacks must not be directed against civilians.[98]

This rule is supported by a number of legal authorities, including, perhaps most importantly, Additional Protocol I of 1977 to the 1949 Geneva Conventions:

> Article 43(2) Members of the armed forces of a Party to a conflict (other than medical personnel and chaplains covered by Article 33 of the Third Convention) are combatants, that is to say, they have the right to participate directly in hostilities.

> Article 51(3) Civilians shall enjoy the protection afforded by this section, unless and for such time as they take a direct part in hostilities.[99]

Persons with a right to take direct part in hostilities are lawful combatants; those without a right to do so are unlawful combatants.[100] Having a right to participate in hostilities means that the person may not be charged with a crime for using force. CIA operatives, like the militants challenging authority in Pakistan, have no right to participate in hostilities and are unlawful combatants.[101] They may be charged with a crime.[102]

---

[98] Henckaerts and Doswald-Beck, above n 60, 3.

[99] Protocol Additional to the Geneva Conventions of 12 August 1949, and relating to the Protections of Victims of International Armed Conflicts (Protocol I) opened for signature 8 June 1977, 1125 UNTS 3 (entered into force 7 December 1979). See also Protocol Additional to the Geneva Conventions of 12 August 1949, and relating to the Protections of Victims of Non-International Armed Conflicts (Protocol II) opened for signature 8 June 1977, 1125 UNTS 609 (7 December 1978).

[100] K Dörmann, 'The legal situation of "unlawful/unprivileged combatants"' (2003) 85 *International Review of the Red Cross* 45, 46: '[U]nlawful/unprivileged combatant/belligerent' is 'understood as describing all persons taking a direct part in hostilities without being entitled to do so and who therefore cannot be classified as prisoners of war on falling into the power of the enemy.'

[101] Cullen, above n 62, 27: 'The CIA has an important role in developing the actionable intelligence that is key to success. The operations themselves, however, should be executed solely by military personnel.'

[102] Some prefer to continue to reserve the term 'combatant' for members of a state's armed forces in an international armed conflict. See, eg, J Paust, 'Responding Lawfully to Al Qaeda' (2007) 56 *Catholic University Law Review*. They use 'unprivileged belligerent' for someone with no right to engage in an international armed conflict. Frits Kalshoven remarks, 'The "unprivileged belligerent" goes back to Baxter's famous article; he was an army major (and a lawyer) at the time and his terminology came from the Hague Regulations. In the seventies, he was not using this terminology any longer, so we may all forget it. The choice is reduced to "combatant" or "civilian"!': F Kalshoven, E-mail message to the author, 1 November 2005. See R Baxter, 'So-called Unprivileged Belligerency: Spies, Guerillas, and Saboteurs' (1951) 28 *British Yearbook of International Law* 323; Dörmann, above n 100. This term may also be used respecting rebels in a non-international armed conflict. The term is, however, increasingly being abandoned. See the discussion in *A, B v Israel*, Supreme Court of Israel, sitting as the Court of Criminal Appeals (11 June 2008) (Gaza Detainee case). The court introduces a new test for combatancy: 'indirect' participation in hostilities. This is a dangerous extension not

In the case of drone attacks in Pakistan, there will generally be some question as to the identity of persons the US intends to kill with missile strikes. This is not a situation like the invasion of Iraq where US forces met large, organised units of the Iraqi Army outside Baghdad. Outside Baghdad, using drones to launch missile attacks might in fact have protected civilians from bombs dropped from aeroplanes flying at high altitudes. But can drones ever be precise enough to comply with the rule of distinction in the situation of Western Pakistan? Suspected militant leaders wear civilian clothes. Even the sophisticated cameras of a drone cannot reveal with certainty that a suspect being targeted is not a civilian. The ICRC Interpretative Guidance on Direct Participation in Hostilities points out that in just such a situation, international humanitarian law gives a presumption to civilian status:

> [I]n case of doubt as to whether a [sic] specific civilian conduct qualifies as direct participation in hostilities, it must be presumed that the general rule of civilian protection applies and that this conduct does not amount to direct participation in hostilities. The presumption of civilian protection applies, *a fortiori*, in case of doubt as to whether a person has become a member of an organized armed group belonging to a party to the conflict. Obviously, the standard of doubt applicable to targeting decisions cannot be compared to the strict standard of doubt

supported by the weight of authority. The court's decision was, however, limited to detention. The term 'combatant' in English means someone who takes part in combat. That meaning tracks the more up-to-date use adopted here. Attempts to substitute other straightforward terms, such as 'fighter' have not succeeded, in part because other languages do not reflect a distinction between 'fighters' and 'combatants'. Henckaerts and Doswald-Beck, above n 60, 13. But see M Sassòli, 'The International Legal Framework for Stability Operations: When May International Forces Attack or Detain Someone in Afghanistan?' (2009) 39 *Israel Yearbook on Human Rights* 177. Sassòli prefers the term 'fighters'. The ICRC defines 'enemy combatant' as 'a person who, either lawfully or unlawfully, engages in hostilities for the opposing side in an international armed conflict'. International Committee of the Red Cross (ICRC), Official Statement, *The Relevance of IHL in the Context of Terrorism* (21 July 2005), available at www.icrc.org/Web/Eng/siteeng0.nsf/html/terrorism-ihl-210705. However, in its 2005 study of customary international law, the ICRC found:

> Persons taking a direct part in hostilities in non-international armed conflicts are sometimes labeled 'combatants'. For example, in a resolution on respect for human rights in armed conflict adopted in 1970, the UN General Assembly speaks of 'combatants in all armed conflicts'. More recently, the term 'combatant' was used in the Cairo Declaration and Cairo Plan of Action for both types of conflicts. However, this designation is only used in its generic meaning and indicates that these persons do not enjoy the protection against attack accorded to civilians, but does not imply a right to combatant status or prisoner-of-war status, as applicable in international armed conflicts.

Henckaerts and Doswald-Beck, above n 60, 12.

In its 2009 interpretative guidance on direct participation in hostilities, the ICRC has introduced new terminology for members of non-state actor military groups: 'members of an organized armed group with a continuous combat function'. International Committee of the Red Cross, *Interpretative Guidance on the Notion of Direct Participation in Hostilities under International Humanitarian Law* (May 2009) 27 (hereafter ICRC Guidance on DPH). Somehow one suspects that this will not become the phrase of art on the battlefield. It is imperative, however, to have a clear understanding of who may be lawfully targeted and who may not. Combatants may be targeted. Civilians may not.

applicable in criminal proceedings but rather must reflect the level of certainty that can reasonably be achieved in the circumstances.[103]

Even when a drone operator is reasonably certain in the circumstances that his or her target is not a civilian, the US is obligated to 'take all feasible precautions in the choice of means and methods of attack with a view to avoiding, and in any event to minimizing, incidental loss of civilian life, injury to civilians and damage to civilian objects'.[104] Little information is available as to whether the US takes *any* precautions when carrying out drone strikes.

In addition to distinction, the US must also respect the principles of necessity, proportionality and humanity in carrying out drone attacks. 'Necessity' refers to military necessity, and the obligation that force is used only if necessary to accomplish a reasonable military objective.[105] 'Proportionality' prohibits that 'which may be expected to cause incidental loss of civilian life, injury to civilians, damage to civilian objects, or a combination thereof, which would be excessive in relation to concrete and direct military advantage anticipated'.[106] These limitations on permissible force extend to both the quantity of force used and the geographic scope of its use.

If, as discussed above, drone attacks in Pakistan are fuelling interest in fighting against the US rather than suppressing it, using drones is difficult to justify under the principle of necessity. Most serious of all, perhaps, is the disproportionate impact of drone attacks. Fifty civilians killed for one suspected combatant killed is a textbook example of a violation of the proportionality principle. Even in cases with fewer unintended victims, it makes a difference whether the victims are children, elderly people, in a home, and so on. Proportionality is not just a matter of numbers.

Another principle that provides context for all decisions in armed conflict is humanity. The principle of humanity supports decisions in favour of sparing life and avoiding destruction in close cases under either the principles of necessity or proportionality. Again, according to the ICRC Guidance, the principles of necessity and humanity are particularly important in situations such as Pakistan:

> In classic large-scale confrontations between well-equipped and organized armed forces or groups, the principles of military necessity and of humanity are unlikely

---

[103] ICRC Guidance on DPH, 75–76 (footnotes omitted).

[104] Additional Protocol I, Article 57(2)(a)(ii).

[105] WM Reisman and D Stevick, 'The Applicability of International Law Standards to United Nations Economic Sanctions Programmes' (1998) 9 *European Journal of International Law* 86, 94–95.

[106] Additional Protocol I, Article 51(5); see also Additional Protocol I, Article 35(1): 'In any armed conflict, the right of the Parties to the conflict to choose methods or means of warfare is not unlimited.'

to restrict the use of force against legitimate military targets beyond what is already required by specific provisions of IHL. The practical importance of their restraining function will increase with the ability of a party to the conflict to control the circumstances and area in which its military operations are conducted, may become decisive where armed forces operate against selected individuals in situations comparable to peacetime policing. In practice, such considerations are likely to become particularly relevant where a party to the conflict exercises effective territorial control, most notably in occupied territories and non-international armed conflicts.[107]

In the well-documented case of the attack on Baitullah Mehsud's in-laws' house in August 2009, we see the serious legal problems with the US approach.[108] Reports on the attack say that the CIA carried out the killing. CIA operatives have no legal right to participate in armed conflict killing. The reports indicate US authorities were certain that they correctly identified Mehsud. They reported they could even see that Mehsud was receiving an intravenous transfusion. The very first Geneva Convention of 1864 forbids the targeting of the sick and wounded as a basic principle of humanity. The 2005 ICRC study of customary international humanitarian law says:

> Rule 47. Attacking persons who are recognized as *hors de combat* is prohibited. A person *hors de combat* is:
>
> ...
>
> (b) anyone who is defenceless because of unconsciousness, shipwreck, wounds or sickness.[109]

Without specific medical information regarding his conditions, it is impossible to say whether or not Mehsud's illnesses rendered him 'defenceless' or '*hors de combat*'. He might have continued to give orders by cell phone. Did the US have such information? As already discussed, Mehsud was, presumably, the only intended target. He is likely to be the only target about whom the CIA had any detailed information. What did the US know of the others in the house? Reports say a wife, her parents, 'seven bodyguards' and one 'lieutenant' were also killed. Was that all? What about the uncle, identified as a 'medic'? Was anyone else in the house? Were the bodyguards and the lieutenant direct participants in hostilities? At the time of the attack, the 'bodyguards' and 'lieutenant' were not directly participating in hostilities. The ICRC Interpretative Guidance might still support targeting them if, as appears to have been the case, they were engaged in a continuous combat function. Without this sort of information, however, as the Guidance advises,

---

[107] ICRC Guidance on DPH, 80–81.

[108] For a detailed description of the strike, see Mayer, above n 1, 36.

[109] Henckaerts and Doswald-Beck, above n 60, 164; see also Geneva Convention for the Amelioration of the Condition of the Wounded and Sick in Armed Forces in the Field of 12 August 1949, Articles 3 and 12.

the US should treat individuals as civilians. In this case, 12 persons were killed in the targeting of one man hooked up to an intravenous drip.

The US has publicised the Mehsud attack, and, therefore, presumably takes the position it was lawful. Yet, the killing raises concerns about possible negative repercussions. If Pakistani forces—police or military—following law enforcement rules had attempted to arrest Mehsud and the members of his organisation, Pakistan might have had a chance of gaining information about the organisation, to conduct more arrests, to hold trials, and to promote the rule of law in the region.[110] Instead, such US strikes may well keep the cycle of violence in motion.

V. CONCLUSIONS

The US use of combat drones in Afghanistan between 2004 and 2009 appears to fall far short of meeting the international law rules governing resort to armed force and the conduct of armed force.[111] The US has used drones in Pakistan to launch significant military attacks, attacks only lawful in the course of an armed conflict. The US has not, however, restricted its attacks to situations of armed conflict. Moreover, Pakistan has neither requested US assistance in the form of drone attacks nor expressly consented to them. Pakistan's civilian authorities have protested on occasion, which is significant considering the many difficulties those authorities face. There is no Security Council authorisation for drone attacks nor does the US have a basis in the law of self-defence for attacking inside Pakistan.

Even if the US had a right to resort to combat drones in Pakistan, their use to date has conflicted with the principles governing the conduct of armed conflict. The CIA operatives involved are not lawful combatants with the combatant's privilege to kill during an armed conflict. CIA operatives are not trained in the IHL rules governing the use of force and there is evidence the rules are being violated in the context of Western Pakistan: drones kill many unintended victims for each intended one, raising questions of proportionality. Counter terrorism experts doubt the efficacy of military force to end terrorist groups, raising doubts about the necessity of drone strikes. Nor has the US apparently taken the necessary precautions to protect civilian lives. The ease of killing with drones seems to be encouraging the narrow

---

[110] Pakistani authorities arrested a number of Taliban leaders in 2010. See, eg, *BBC News*, 'Pakistan "Arrests Key Taliban Leader"', 4 March 2010 news.bbc.co.uk/2/hi/south_asia/8550725.stm.

[111] See also Alston, above n 23.

US view that military force is the only 'game in town' in response to the serious problem of terrorism.[112]

International law, by contrast, supports the position of counter terrorism experts that law enforcement methods are the proper means to employ in suppressing terrorism. Confronting the violent lawlessness that is terrorism with strict adherence to the rule of law makes common sense and moral sense.

---

[112] Lawrence Korb, a respected commentator on military affairs, predicts robotic warriors will make the US more likely to engage in war in general: 'It will make people think, "Gee, warfare is easy." Remember all the claims of a "cakewalk" in Iraq and how the Afghan model would apply? The whole idea that all it took to win a war was "three mean and a satellite phone?".... [He predicts] more punitive interventions such as the Kosovo strikes of 1999, launched without ground troops, and fewer operations like the invasion of Iraq. As unmanned systems become more prevalent, we'll become more likely to use force'. Quoted in Singer, above n 6, 44–45.

13

Corporations that Kill: Prosecuting Blackwater

DAVID KINLEY AND ODETTE MURRAY

I. INTRODUCTION

T HE DEATHS OF 17 civilian Iraqis in Baghdad's Nisour Square in
September 2007 at the hands of Blackwater (subsequently renamed
'Xe', and later renamed 'Academi') personnel was as notable for the
horrifying manner in which the 17 died as it was for revealing the abject lack
of effective regulation and accountability mechanisms for private military
corporations engaged in lethal actions. How did this circumstance come to
be? What are the dimensions of the growing phenomenon of security and
military privatisation? What ought to be the framework within which the
exercise of public power in private hands is regulated when the power in
question is in extremis? And what are the challenges in establishing such
control? This chapter addresses these questions working through the prism
of the Nisour Square massacre and its aftermath. It concludes that even if
some progress can be made through private sector initiatives, the filling of
the current regulatory lacunae must be seen as primarily a task for the states
which contract-out to private military corporations, and it is to states that
we must look to lobby for change.

II. THE INCIDENT

Around lunchtime on 16 September 2007, in Nisour Square, a busy traffic
intersection in central Baghdad, several employees of the US security firm
Blackwater travelling in a convoy of four armoured vehicles shot dead 17
civilians and wounded 20 others.[1] Blackwater was contracted by the US

---

[1] These facts and those that follow are collected from the following sources: 'Factual Proffer
in Support of Guilty Plea' dated 18 November 2009 in *USA v Jeremy P Ridgeway* (Criminal
Action No 1:08-cr-341-RMU, US District Court for the District of Columbia); S Raghavan,

State Department to provide personal security services to US diplomats and other personnel in Baghdad. The actions of the employees were allegedly unprovoked,[2] and many of the dead and injured were shot while trying to flee the scene. Investigations by ballistic experts from the US military suggest that all of the more than 100 rounds discharged came from weapons used by the Blackwater personnel.[3] There were also numerous eyewitness accounts of shots being fired by contractors in Blackwater helicopters hovering overhead. Assault rifles, machine guns, grenade launchers and pistols were all used in what was described in one report as an 'overwhelming barrage of gunfire', and in another, by an Iraqi survivor, as 'shooting like rain'. Victims were shot while sitting in slow-moving or stationary cars stuck in traffic, while trying to crawl out of cars, or while lying on the ground. In one instance a man was shot in the chest as he stood in the street with his hands in the air; in another, a mother was machine-gunned to death as she cradled her dead son in her arms screaming for help. After discharging at least 40 bullets into the car occupied by that same mother and son, one of the Blackwater guards also fired a grenade through the car window, turning the vehicle into a fireball, with the result that relatives were later only able to identify the bodies by the boy's footwear and the mother's dental bridge.

The whole incident was over in a matter of a few minutes and was witnessed by countless numbers of people in the Square itself, in the buildings that overlook it and in adjacent streets. The incident was apparently as chaotic as it was catastrophic. As the hail of bullets swept across the Square, at least one Blackwater employee appeared to be aware of the mistake being made and was heard by an Iraqi lawyer stuck in the traffic at the time (and moments later to be shot in the neck, shoulder, arm and lower back as he tried to flee) screaming 'No! No! No!' at his colleagues. Fourteen months later, a somewhat sensational factual statement as to what occurred was entered in the US District Court for the District of Columbia in support of a guilty plea to manslaughter and attempted murder by Jeremy Ridgeway,

---

'Tracing the Paths of 5 Who Died in a Storm of Gunfire', *Washington Post*, 4 October 2007, A01; J Glanz and A Rubin, 'From Errand to Fatal Shot to Hail of Fire to 17 Deaths', *New York Times*, 3 October 2007, A1; J Glanz, 'New Evidence That Guards Took No Fire', *New York Times*, 13 October 2007, 1; J Ryan and B Ross, 'Blackwater Guard in Secret Deal to Testify in Massacre Case', *ABC News*, 8 December 2008, abcnews.go.com/Blotter/FedCrimes/story?id=6417440.

[2] There are conflicting accounts of the incident. Most accounts consistently report that the incident began when Blackwater guards opened fire on a white sedan which was approaching the convoy. Initial reports by Blackwater employees claimed they had come under small arms fire. Eye-witness accounts dispute this, claiming that the Blackwater guards were the only persons who discharged weapons in the square.

[3] Note, however, that subsequent forensic investigations by the FBI were inconclusive, unable to confirm that 30-calibre bullets recovered from the scene were discharged by Blackwater firearms. See M Appuzo, 'No forensic match for ammo in Blackwater shooting', *Associated Press*, 1 April 2009.

one of the Blackwater employees involved in the incident. It stated that: (i) the convoy 'had *not* been authorized to depart from the International Zone [aka the 'Green Zone']' on the day in question, and that (ii) in any case, Ridgeway and all the other members of the Blackwater convoy were well aware that their mission in the country was 'defensive in nature' and that, under the company's operational mandate, employees were 'not permitted to engage in offensive military actions, use the military tactic known as "suppressive fire", or exercise police powers'.[4] Ridgeway further states that all employees 'understood that they were authorized to discharge their firearms' only 'in self-defense and as a last resort'.[5]

Yet, the convoy was deployed, and deployed offensively. Ostensibly, the Blackwater vehicles were responding to reports of a bomb exploding 'in the vicinity of a different Blackwater personal security detail' that was escorting a US State Department official.[6] The reported explosion had occurred about a mile away from Nisour Square. There were some subsequent reports that the Nisour Square convoy ('Raven 23 Convoy') had, in fact, first come under fire, to which the Blackwater personnel then responded. But none of the eye-witness accounts, nor indeed Ridgeway's sworn statement, backed these claims.

The incident prompted a host of diplomatic, political and legal responses and questions, the ramifications of which are still far from settled. In this chapter, we aim to draw together the principal legal dimensions of the aftermath. We do this, in part, to provide a better understanding of what has and is happening in that respect. More significantly, however, we aim through this process to expose the regulatory deficiencies in dealing with private security and military corporations when events such as those described above occur (as they inevitably do) in conflict zones. We conclude the chapter by examining the challenges that will be encountered if efforts are made to better regulate the phenomenon of large-scale privatised military and security services and by making some recommendations as to how these challenges might be overcome.

III. IRAQI AND US GOVERNMENT RESPONSES

In and of itself, the operation was an unmitigated disaster. It is a case study of spooked security personnel, escalating panic (in the ranks of both the fired upon and those pulling the trigger), and catastrophic breakdowns in discipline and communication. The dead and the injured were almost certainly innocent, and the harms they suffered were inexcusable and

---

[4] 'Factual Proffer' in *USA v Ridgeway* (2009), above n 1, paras 5, 7.
[5] Ibid para 5.
[6] Ibid.

unpardonable. But the wider implications of the incident are, perhaps, even more compelling. For a start, the affair exposed the simmering rift between private security contractors and the regular military. Many in the military resent the fact that if they had behaved in this way and with these consequences, they would be likely to be court-martialled. They are also keenly aware that, as a result of incidents like this, their own goal, to secure peace and security by trying to win the hearts and minds of the Iraqi people, becomes very much harder to achieve. At the very least, the Nisour Square massacre gave the impression, widely and loudly voiced by ordinary Iraqis as well as community leaders and government officials, of 'a cheapening of Iraqi blood'.[7] Certainly, this sentiment was widely and deeply felt. A few months after the incident, the first-named author was doing some work with a contingent of senior Iraqi officials from the nascent Iraqi Human Rights Commission as well as other Ministries and government agencies engaged in an AusAID training programme conducted in Jordan and Australia.[8] The fact that a private security firm could do such a thing—and apparently get away with it—was a source of palpable resentment, even among these admitted moderates. It added to the bitterness already engendered by years of bloodshed and oppression.

In the grand scheme of atrocities that Iraq has suffered over the past eight years (let alone the past 50 years), the Nisour Square incident may not seem that monumental. Since the invasion in 2003 alone, it has been conservatively estimated that somewhere between 100,000 and 200,000 Iraqi civilians, 4,800 foreign military personnel, and more than 1,550 contractors have lost their lives.[9] Many more have been injured. Seventeen

---

[7] Glanz, 'New Evidence That Guards Took No Fire', above n 1.

[8] See World Wide Project Management Services, 'Training Delivered to Iraq's Ministry of Human Rights' (4 December 2007) www.project.com.au/news/item/4c9a11356b5ff0398b000031.

[9] It is notoriously difficult to estimate the number of Iraqis who have died since the invasion. Iraq Body Count (www.iraqbodycount.org) calculates Iraqi *civilian* (not combatant) casualties as a result of violence (as opposed to other consequences of the invasion), based on deaths documented in news reports, morgues, hospitals, etc. On this analysis, the number of Iraqi civilians killed by the violence is between 103,261 and 112,832 as at 7 November 2011. Given that this figure is only based on documented casualties, it is considered that the 'real' death toll is probably much higher. The World Health Organization (WHO) and the Iraqi government conducted a large household survey (the Iraq Family Health Survey) which produced an estimate of 151,000 Iraqi deaths from violence between March 2003 and June 2006. See WHO, 'New study estimates 151 000 violent Iraqi deaths since 2003 invasion' (News Release, 9 January 2008) www.who.int/mediacentre/news/releases/2008/pr02/en/index.html. A study by Iraqi physicians and epidemiologists at Johns Hopkins University conducted in 2006 estimated the death toll at 655,000, of which at least 601,000 deaths resulted from violence (the rest from disease and other causes). This figure is an estimate of *all* Iraqi deaths—civilian and combatant—that would not have occurred but for the coalition invasion. See D Brown, 'Study Claims Iraq's 'Excess' Death Toll Has Reached 655,000', *Washington Post*, 11 October 2006, A12. Regarding foreign military deaths, there have been 4,801 foreign military casualties, of which 4,483 are US military personnel (as at 7 November 2011, based on US Department of Defense casualty confirmations; see icasualties.org/Iraq/index.aspx). Regarding contracted personnel deaths, figures are much harder to confirm, but one estimate is provided by the US

deaths may not seem so grave in the face of such appalling statistics. Yet, 'this incident caused an unusually unified and strong condemnation from the various elements of the Iraqi Government', as one military commentator has noted.[10] The senselessness and flagrancy of the convoy's actions, together with the indemnity enjoyed by Blackwater and all other security contractors—which was, notoriously, secured by the head of the Coalition Provisional Authority (CPA) in Iraq, Paul Bremer, on the eve of the CPA's expiration in late June 2004[11]—appears to have been especially galling. Iraqi officials immediately called for Blackwater's licence to be suspended (which was, apparently, acted upon by the Iraqi Ministry of the Interior),[12] and for the company to be immediately ordered to leave the country (which manifestly did not happen).

The Iraqi government also turned its thoughts to legislation. Six weeks later, on 30 October, a draft bill was approved by the Iraqi Cabinet to repeal CPA Order 17, and thereby remove the immunity of private security contractors in Iraq.[13] However, the Iraqi Parliament never got around to approving the legislation, and the issue has since been dealt with through the negotiation of the US–Iraq Status of Forces Agreement 2008 (SOFA).[14]

Department of Labor, which estimates that there have been 1,554 contractor casualties in Iraq to 20 September 2011, see www.dol.gov/owcp/dlhwc/dbaallnation.htm. However, note the reservations expressed by the US Government Accountability Office (GAO) about reliance on these figures—which represent compensation claims for contractor deaths—as a measure of total contractor casualties: GAO, *Contingency Contracting: DOD, State and USAID Continue to Face Challenges in Tracking Contractor Personnel and Contracts in Iraq and Afghanistan*, Report No GAO-10-1 (Washington DC, GAO, October 2009) 16–18.

[10] J Thurnher, 'Drowning in Blackwater: How Weak Accountability over Private Security Contractors Significantly Undermines Counterinsurgency Efforts' (2008) 7 *Army Lawyer* 64.

[11] Coalition Provisional Authority (CPA) Order 17 (27 June 2004), which provides in Section 4: 'Contractors shall be immune from Iraqi legal process with respect to acts performed by them pursuant to the terms and conditions of a Contract or any sub-contract thereto.' See www.iraqcoalition.org/regulations/20040627_CPAORD_17_Status_of_Coalition__Rev__ with_Annex_A.pdf.

[12] See S Tavernise, 'U.S. Contractor Banned by Iraq Over Shootings', *New York Times*, 18 September 2007, 1. It is unclear whether Blackwater's licence was actually revoked at this stage, given that the company continued to operate in the country. It may have been that the licence was revoked, but ignored by the company and the US Administration—according to the *Washington Post*, 'the [Iraqi] ministry revoked Blackwater's license in September 2007 and threatened to expel the company's employees, but US officials ignored the order and renewed the company's contract the following April.' See E Londoño and Q Mizher, 'Iraq to Deny New License To Blackwater Security Firm; U.S. Embassy's Preferred Contactor Accused of Killings', *Washington Post*, 29 January 2009, A12.

[13] See A Paley, 'Iraq Moves to Repeal Immunity for Guards', *Washington Post*, 31 October 2007, A14.

[14] The US–Iraq Status of Forces Agreement 2008 (SOFA), which provides the timetable for US troop withdrawal, as well as signalling the end of US contractor immunity, was concluded on 17 November 2008 by representatives of both the US and Iraqi governments. The SOFA provides in Article 12 that 'Iraq shall have the primary right to exercise jurisdiction over United States contractors and United States contractor employees.' However, it is not clear that the SOFA subjects all contractors to Iraqi jurisdiction; it may only cover Department

In addition, the government initiated its own inquiry into the incident, the report of which was released three weeks after the shooting. The report called for the US authorities to hand over the relevant Blackwater employees to face prosecution in Iraqi courts, and for the firm to compensate each of the seventeen victims' families (to the tune of $8 million each). This total amount, the report says, is warranted 'because Blackwater uses employees who disrespect the rights of Iraqi citizens even though they are guests in this country'.[15]

The incident also ignited an unprecedented series of official US responses. The day following the massacre, the then US Secretary of State, Condoleezza Rice, telephoned Iraqi Prime Minister Nouri al-Maliki to express regret and to pledge a swift response. Indeed, the State Department, through its embassy in Iraq, had already begun an investigation and had taken statements from the Blackwater guards. The *Washington Post,* 10 days later, reported that it had obtained a copy of a two-page contemporaneous 'spot report' prepared by the State Department's Bureau of Diplomatic Security, which detailed the events as described by the Blackwater guards.[16] It later transpired that this 'spot report' was written by a Blackwater employee.[17] There were also credible reports, subsequently confirmed,[18] that the State Department offered the guards immunity from criminal investigation in return for their statements.[19]

Some two weeks after the shooting, the Federal Bureau of Investigation (FBI) also began its own investigation. This investigation had a number of

---

of Defense (DOD) contractors, since Article 2 defines 'US contractors' and 'US contractor employees' as non-Iraqi persons or legal entities, and their employees, who supply goods, services, or security 'under a contract or subcontract with or for the United States Forces', where 'US Forces' means the 'United States Armed Forces'—that is, DOD, but not Department of State, USAID or other agencies. This is the conclusion reached in R Chuck Mason, *U.S.-Iraq Withdrawal/Status of Forces Agreement: Issues for Congressional Oversight* (Washington DC, Congressional Research Service, 13 July 2009). However, at least one government body, the Commission on Wartime Contracting, considers that the SOFA 'removed the immunity previously provided by CPA Order 17' such that 'Iraq now has primary jurisdiction over US contractors, subcontractors, and their employees.' See Commission on Wartime Contracting in Iraq and Afghanistan, *At What Cost? Contingency Contracting in Iraq and Afghanistan: Interim Report* (Arlington, CWC, June 2009) 70.

[15] J Scahill, 'Iraqis Sue Blackwater for Baghdad Killings', *The Nation*, 11 October 2007, www.thenation.com/article/iraqis-sue-blackwater-baghdad-killings.

[16] S Fainaru and S Raghavan, 'Blackwater Faced Bedlam, Embassy Finds', *Washington Post*, 28 September 2007, A1.

[17] 'Blackwater Contractor Wrote Government Report on Incident', *CNN.com*, 2 October 2007, www.edition.cnn.com/2007/WORLD/meast/10/02/blackwater.spot.report/index.html.

[18] That is, in the course of the prosecution of the five guards. This proffered immunity was in fact the basis for the indictment being dismissed. See further discussion below at n 49.

[19] See D Johnston and JM Broder, 'F.B.I. Says Guards Killed 14 Iraqis Without Cause', *New York Times*, 14 November 2007, 1, who noted that later FBI investigators, 'did not have access to statements taken from Blackwater employees, who had given statements to State Department investigators on the condition that their statements would not be used in any criminal investigation like the one being conducted by the FBI.'

peculiar features. For a start, the FBI inquiry and its final report seemed to be at odds with the US military investigations. Preliminary findings of the FBI were reported as concluding that 'at least 14 of the shootings were unjustified and violated deadly-force rules in effect for security contractors'.[20] The report added that three of the shootings may have been justified as a use of lethal force in response to an imminent threat, in contrast to an earlier military investigation of the incident that had concluded that all of the killings were unjustified and potentially criminal. One of the military investigators was later reported as saying that 'the Bureau was being generous to Blackwater in characterizing any of the killings as justifiable'.[21] Also, in what must surely count at best as a shocking lack of judgement, the FBI team sent to Baghdad to investigate the killings was originally assigned a security detail of Blackwater guards![22]

The US Congressional Committee on Oversight and Government Reform initiated a series of public hearings to examine the mission and performance of Blackwater in Iraq and Afghanistan, before which Erik Prince, CEO of Blackwater, testified, along with three State Department officials.[23] Secretary of State Condoleezza Rice also established an expert Panel on Personal Protective Services in Iraq.

Out of these initiatives, certain actions flowed. The House of Representatives passed a bill[24] to expand the Military Extraterritorial Jurisdiction Act to create ordinary (that is, non-military) federal criminal jurisdiction over the conduct of private military contractors working in proximity to a contingency operation, such as Blackwater personnel working for the State Department in Iraq. However, despite overwhelming support in the House, the bill languished in the less-sympathetic Senate. Failing to be put to a vote before the end of the session, the legislation was never enacted. In a more promising development, Condoleezza Rice's expert Panel issued an interim report with interim recommendations, some of which were immediately adopted and implemented by direction

---

[20] Ibid.

[21] Ibid.

[22] Chesterman and Lehnardt dryly note that 'following protests, the FBI announced that in order to avoid "even the appearance" of a conflict of interest their agents would be protected by US government personnel': S Chesterman and C Lehnardt (eds), *From Mercenaries to Market: The Rise and Regulation of Private Military Companies* (Oxford, Oxford University Press, 2009) preface, x.

[23] While initially convened to address the 16 September 2007 Nisour Square killings, at the request of the Justice Department and FBI who were currently investigating those events, the Oversight Committee, and those who testified, agreed not to directly address the Nisour Square incident. For the testimony given at the hearing, see: 'Blackwater USA', Hearing Before the Committee on Oversight and Government Reform, House of Representatives, 110th Congress (2 October 2007), Serial No 110–89 (Washington DC, US Government Printing Office, 2008) www.gpo.gov/fdsys/.

[24] Military Extraterritorial Jurisdiction Act Expansion and Enforcement Act of 2007, HR 2740, 110th Cong, 1st sess (2007) (not enacted).

of the Secretary of State.[25] Also, the State Department began the process of making compensation payments to the families of Iraqi victims killed in the incident.

Despite all, however, little more than six months after the incident, the US State Department renewed Blackwater's licence to provide personal security services for a further year, albeit under the new corporate name of 'Xe'.[26] In fact it was not until September 2009 that the company was officially removed from all contracts in Iraq.[27] A slew of litigation has also ensued in the US courts. Civil suits were brought against Blackwater and its CEO Erik Prince, and criminal prosecutions were mounted against a number of its employees.[28]

IV. THE PHENOMENON OF PRIVATE SOLDIERS AND THEIR CORPORATISATION

Soldiers of fortune, mercenaries, private soldiers, security personnel, contractees—whatever their label—have long been conspicuous players in armed conflicts. Their prominence, historically, may have waxed and waned, but they have always remained a presence. The practice of mercenary soldiering was common and widespread in the sixteenth century, but had virtually died out by the seventeenth century,[29] at least as a pursuit available to individuals or small groups.[30] By the twentieth century, as Jonathan Finer notes, there was approximately only one private soldier for every 500 enlisted men in the Vietnam War. However, by the Gulf War in 1991, this had grown to one in 50.[31] During the Iraq war, the total of all

---

[25] On 5 October 2007; see Department of State, Press Statement, 'Implementation of Recommendations from the Secretary of State's Report on Personal Protective Service Details' (23 October 2007) 2001–2009.state.gov/r/pa/prs/ps/2007/oct/94013.htm.

[26] This was despite the fact that, as the *Washington Post* reported, 'the Iraqi government has informed the U.S. Embassy in Baghdad that it will not issue a new operating license to Blackwater Worldwide, the embassy's primary security company … The officials said Blackwater must leave the country as soon as a joint Iraqi-U.S. committee finishes drawing up guidelines for private contractors under the security agreement.' See E Londoño and Q Mizher, 'Iraq to Deny New License To Blackwater Security Firm' (2009); and also M Tran, 'US security firm Blackwater faces expulsion from Iraq', *The Guardian*, 29 January 2009, www.guardian. co.uk/world/2009/jan/29/iraq-licence-blackwater.

[27] Though the State Department continued to use Blackwater guards in Afghanistan. See M Landler, 'Contractor to Continue Work in Iraq Temporarily', *New York Times*, 3 September 2009, 10; see also M Landler and M Mazzetti, 'U.S. Still Using Security Firm, the Former Blackwater, That It Publicly Broke With', *New York Times*, 22 August 2009, 6.

[28] Discussed below, see nn 49, 60, 61 and 65 and accompanying text.

[29] S Percy, 'Morality and Regulation' in Chesterman and Lehnardt (eds), above n 22, 12.

[30] By the seventeenth century mercenary bands increasingly tended to be state-subsidised. For discussion see J Cockayne, 'The Global Reorganization of Legitimate Violence: Military Entrepreneurs and the Private Face of International Humanitarian Law' (2006) 88 *International Review of the Red Cross* 459.

[31] J Finer, 'Holstering the Hired Guns: New Accountability Measures for Private Security Contractors' (2008) 33 *Yale Journal of International Law* 259, 259–60.

contractors (that is, those ancillary to the conflict (eg cooks and engineers), as well as those directly engaged in conflict) outnumbered US service personnel.[32]

What has been of particular significance, over the past two decades or so, is the corporatisation of this commercial enterprise. Security has become big business. Peter W Singer has stated that 'from 1994 to 2002, the US Defense Department entered into more than 3,000 contracts with US-based firms, estimated at a contract value of more than $300 billion'.[33] Given the size of the contingent of private military corporations in Iraq since 2003 (and in Afghanistan since 2001) and the longevity of their stay there, it is hardly surprising that these figures, large though they are, have leapt significantly.[34] There are many reasons for the spread of security privatisation. But at least three forces, which have combined in a sort of pincer movement on states and their regular military personnel, have been key.

---

[32] In July 2007, the *Los Angeles Times* reported that there were more than 180,000 contractors working in Iraq under US contracts, based on State and Defense Department figures it had obtained. Of these, about 10,800 were estimated to be private security contractors. The private security industry's own estimate of contractors in Iraq—working under both government and non-government contracts—was 30,000. See TC Miller, 'Contractors Outnumber Troops in Iraq', *Los Angeles Times*, 4 July 2007, articles.latimes.com/2007/jul/04/nation/na-private4; see also Finer, above n 31, 260. Even at the height of the US troop deployment following the so-called 'surge' in 2007, troop numbers never exceeded 171,000: M O'Hanlon and I Livingston, 'Iraq Index: Tracking Variables of Reconstruction & Security in Post-Saddam Iraq', 28 October 2011 (Washington DC, Brookings, 2011) 13, www.brookings.edu/iraqindex. Based on data provided by the Department of Defense, Department of State and the US Agency for International Development (USAID) to the Government Accountability Office, the total number of contractors in Iraq in the first half of fiscal year 2009 (October 2008–March 2009) was approximately 148,000, with 16,000 of those contractors providing security. See GAO, above n 9, 9–14 (taking the average of Department of Defense figures for the first two quarters of fiscal year 2009). Based on data as at 31 March 2010, the Commission on Wartime Contracting (CWC) found that the total number of Departments of Defense, State and USAID contractors in both Iraq and Afghanistan was 262,631 personnel. Experience in Iraq has shown that as US military personnel were withdrawn, the number of contractors increased. As the CWC notes, while 'the Status of Forces Agreement between the United States and Iraq mandates a specific military drawdown from Iraq, there is no similar stipulation for withdrawing US contractors'. Commission on Wartime Contracting in Iraq and Afghanistan, *Transforming Wartime Contracting: Controlling Costs, Reducing Risks: Final Report to Congress* (Arlington, CWC, August 2011) 20–21, available at www.wartimecontracting.gov.

[33] PW Singer, *Corporate Warriors: The Rise of the Privatized Military Industry* (Ithaca, Cornell University Press, 2003) 15.

[34] The Commission on Wartime Contracting in Iraq and Afghanistan, in its June 2009 report states that 'from fiscal years 2001 through 2008, the Defense Department's reported obligations on all contracts for services, measured in real dollar terms, more than doubled—from roughly $92 billion to slightly over $200 billion.' This figure does not include Department of State or USAID contracts. See Commission on Wartime Contracting, above n 14, 8. The Congressional Budget Office (CBO) estimates that from '2003 through 2007, U.S. government agencies obligated a total of $85 billion for contracts principally performed in the Iraq theater … However, the $85 billion estimate does not capture the total share of US spending on Iraq that goes to contractors. CBO's estimate excludes the costs of contracts supporting operations in Iraq that are performed in countries outside the Iraq theater, including the United States'. In addition, CBO estimates that there was a further $10 billion in obligations for contracts performed in Afghanistan over the same period. See CBO, *Contractors' Support of US Operations in Iraq* (Washington DC, CBO, August 2008) 2.

The first of these forces arises out of the combination of the post-war demobilisations of the 1980s and the military downsizing after the cold war in the 1990s, which created an excess supply of men skilled and schooled in violence and ripe for commercial exploitation.[35] The second comprises the suite of reasons why states might prefer to supplement their 'official' military activities with support or ancillary initiatives. Core military spending can appear to be curbed; arguments as to greater efficiency can be proffered; statistics regarding military casualties can be reduced; expertise (especially for weak governments) can be contracted in and certain 'dirty' operations can be contracted out (to which, attractively, plausible deniability can be readily attributed);[36] the public's gaze can be averted;[37] and difficult political decisions can be avoided.[38] And the third constitutes the reasons why individuals would want to work for private military companies (PMCs), the most compelling of these being the simple fact that PMCs offer pay rates several times greater than those available in the regular forces. By offering rich rewards, such companies are able to attract some of the best and brightest soldiers from some of the premier fighting units in the world. Journalist Tony Geraghty, in his exposé of freelance soldiering, notes that in respect of the British Army's SAS, the haemorrhaging of skilled manpower to the private sector has been 'so severe ... that the regiment [has] had to make discreet appeals to its old comrades to stop poaching'.[39]

The corporatisation of the military—as with the corporatisation of any business activity—has leveraged the power, scope and application of the product, as well as exposing the business itself to greater scrutiny and (in theory, at least) to greater regulation. That said, few 'pure' PMCs—that is,

---

[35] See KA O'Brien, 'What Should and What Should Not be Regulated?' in S Chesterman and C Lehnardt (eds), above n 22, 31–32, noting the demobilisation of hundreds of thousands of soldiers in the former Soviet Union and the subsequent proliferation of private security companies in Russia since the 1990s; and see D Avant, 'The Emerging Market for Private Military Services and the Problems of Regulation' in S Chesterman and C Lehnardt (eds), ibid 181–82, noting the downsizing of militaries in the late 1980s and early 1990s with the end of apartheid and the cold war, which led to a flood of experienced personnel available for contracting.

[36] See O Jones, 'Implausible Deniability: State Responsibility for the Actions of Private Military Firms' (2009) 24 Connecticut Journal of International Law 239, 256 on the 'plausible deniability' point specifically, and generally, on the attractions of contracting PMCs in modern times, see D Isenberg, 'A Government in Search of Cover: Private Military Companies in Iraq' in S Chesterman and C Lehnardt (eds), above n 22; and T Geraghty, Guns for Hire: The Inside Story of Freelance Soldiering (London, Piatkus Books, 2008) ch 11.

[37] V Newell and B Sheehy, 'Corporate Militaries and States: Actors, Interactions, and Reactions' (2006) 41 Texas International Law Journal 67, 88–89.

[38] Indeed, for PW Singer this is the more likely driving force behind the privatisation of conflict than the costs savings arguments, which he characterises as a 'common myth'; as quoted in SL Schooner, 'Contractor Atrocities at Abu Ghraib: Compromised Accountability in a Streamlined, Outsourced Government' (2005) 16 Stanford Law and Policy Review 549, 553.

[39] Geraghty, above n 36, 13. He notes further, more forthright efforts made by the Ministry of Defence in the UK to warn soldiers of the drawbacks and dangers of joining PMCs, including poor equipment, unsatisfactory professional standards, and lack of life and disability insurance (14).

those that deal primarily in providing security in conflict settings, rather than those whose military activities are merely an arm of a much wider business (as, for example, is the case with Halliburton)—are publicly listed (and none are listed on the FTSE4Good). As their category label implies, most PMCs are indeed built upon private rather than public capital.

There are in fact many ways in which PMCs slip between the cracks of legal regulation. To a significant degree they exist in a politico-legal twilight zone,[40] which is both caused and perpetuated by what Human Rights First calls 'a culture of impunity'.[41] That organisation goes on to argue that 'the main obstacle to ending [such a] culture ... among private security contractors is not shortcomings in the law but rather the lack of will to enforce the law'.[42] Former Secretary Rice's Panel of Experts drew a somewhat different conclusion in its October 2007 report in respect of the specific circumstance of PMCs in Iraq. That report stated that 'the legal framework for providing proper oversight of Personal Protective Services (PPS) contractors is inadequate, in that the Panel is unaware of *any* basis for holding non-Department of Defense contractors accountable under US law' (emphasis added).[43] The truth would appear to lie somewhere in between these two views, in that there are inadequate incentive structures for enforcing the law, whatever its extent, in extraterritorial locations.

As such, we might ask: what are the problems, possibilities and peculiarities of holding PMCs/PPSs to account under home state or host state laws, or international law? How and why should it be done, and what are the implications?

V. THE LEGAL IMPLICATIONS

Max Weber's famous dictum,[44] which holds that states are best defined as entities that are able authoritatively to exercise a monopoly over the legitimate use of violence within their respective jurisdictions, is especially apt to the present discussion. Weber's preference for a functional definition (that

---

[40] Where states use PMCs to circumvent their obligations under domestic and/or international law, or engage them to undertake tasks that would otherwise be politically infeasible; see D Avant, above n 35, 185–89.

[41] Human Rights First, *Private Security Contractors at War: Ending the Culture of Impunity* (New York, Human Rights First, 2008) iv.

[42] Ibid iv. cf J Cockayne et al, *Beyond Market Forces: Regulating the Global Security Industry* (New York, International Peace Institute, 2009) 39, emphasising that inadequate investigative capacity in war zones and a lack of cooperation agreements with foreign governments are key factors in the paucity of prosecutions.

[43] Report of the Secretary of State's Panel on Personal Protective Services in Iraq, October 2007, 5 available at 2001–2009.state.gov/documents/organization/94122.pdf.

[44] M Weber, *Politics as a Vocation* (1919) in H Gerth and C Wright Mills (eds) *From Max Weber: Essays in Sociology* (London, Kegan Paul, 1947) 78.

is, de jure) over an institutional or teleological one (that is, de facto) does not, however, mean that he saw no value in these alternative perspectives of the state; rather, he simply did not see them as definitive. Thus, he and we are well able to appreciate that states have the authority, and indeed the need, to delegate aspects of their monopoly over violence. They do so, typically, to permit individuals to use 'force' in self-defence; they allow 'citizens' arrests'; they grant powers for the conditional use of force to quasi-public prosecutorial bodies (for example, those that combat white-collar crime; bailiffs; parole officers; and national park rangers); and they authorise security businesses to use forceful means within varying legal limits to provide services that stretch from protecting pubs, clubs and dignitaries, to fighting wars. There is no doubt that orthodox as well as heterodox theories of the state recognise the need both to delegate and to regulate that delegation. The task is how and to what extent that regulation can be made effective.

The war in Iraq is representative of three classic indicia of modern conflict: 1) internecine enmity and distrust fuel continuing violence and unrest long after the initial 'theatre' phase of a war has ended; 2) warfare is now guerrilla rather than classical; terrorist rather than trench; and 3) occupying forces are expressly committed to reforming the shattered political, social and economic system by rebuilding institutions of state and bolstering their respective capacities and competencies. And in respect of initiatives to combat terrorism and build peace in particular, private contractors, including military firms, are conspicuously and critically active. Thus, for example, as Elke Krahmann points out in respect of the war in Iraq, 'contracts over $50 million and $48 million were [initially] awarded for the training of the military and police forces respectively to DynCorp International and Vinnell (with MPRI as its subcontractor), and an additional $18.4 billion worth were approved by US Congress for further security sector reforms in 2004'.[45]

To be sure, the relatively recent increase in the prevalence of asymmetric conflict, and the increasing corporatisation of its form, have been important contributory factors to a sort of legal invisibility cloak thrown over so much of what PMCs do. But whatever the temporal, commercial or political reasons, the circumstance is abhorrent and, as such poignant events as Nisour Square illustrate, intolerable.

A. Domestic Laws

The municipal corporations laws of many states have little to say, specifically, about PMCs. The standard, generic regulatory framework that

---

[45] E Krahmann, 'Transitional States in Search of Support: Private Military Companies and Security Sector Reform' in S Chesterman and C Lehnardt (eds), above n 22, 94.

accompanies incorporation does little more than dress mercenaries in corporate garb and thereby remove a socially unacceptable and legally problematic tag. This is, all in all, a good return for—in the case of the UK—a trip down to Companies House and the £20 filing fee for a corporate licence. The normally attendant privileges of corporations—such as client confidentiality and privacy—also stand in the way of the use of corporate or commercial laws to secure effective oversight of PMCs.[46]

Criminal laws do, of course, draw boundaries beyond which corporations and their employees are prohibited from going. But typically, in cases of PMC 'home' states, these apply mainly intra-territorially. Generally, such extra-territorial exceptions as there are cover international crimes or treaty-based crimes committed by individuals such as torture, genocide, war crimes, hostage taking, hijacking, and child sex offences.[47] The criminal actions of PMCs, as corporations, are generally not well covered.[48] In any event, even where jurisdiction is extended extra-territorially, the greatest obstacle to prosecuting PMCs or their employees arises out of the serious problems of evidence-gathering in conflict zones, which are expensive to overcome.[49] As a result, few investigators or prosecutors have

---

[46] C Lehnardt, 'Private Military Companies and State Responsibility' in S Chesterman and C Lehnardt (eds), above n 22, 156.

[47] See C Ryngaert, 'Litigating Abuses Committed by Private Military Companies' (2008) 19 *European Journal of International Law* 1035, 1042 and fnn 37–38; and see further, C Doyle, 'Extraterritorial Application of American Criminal Law' (Washington DC, Library of Congress, Congressional Research Service, September 2007).

[48] One conspicuous but ineffective example of exceptional extra-territorial application is South Africa's Prohibition of Mercenary Activities and Regulation of Certain Activities in Country of Armed Conflict Act 2006. Other states with prohibitions on mercenary activity with extra-territorial reach include France, which prohibits mercenary activity by French nationals or residents abroad (Law No 2003-340 of 14 April 2003 relating to the repression of mercenary activity) and New Zealand, which, by the Mercenary Activities (Prohibition) Act 2004, prohibits the recruiting, use, financing and training of mercenaries by New Zealand citizens, residents or corporations abroad. By contrast, the UK's Private Security Industry Act 2001 and Australia's Private Security Act 2004 are limited to the regulation of domestic private security operators and do not cover security services for export. However, at least in respect of individual crimes, the Australian Crimes (Overseas) Amendment Act 2003 (Cth) extends Australian criminal law (specifically, Jervis Bay Territory jurisdiction) to Australians 'undertaking a task or project, or performing a function' in a foreign country on behalf of the Commonwealth, or pursuant to an agreement between Australia and the UN or another state where such agreement immunises the person from criminal proceedings in the foreign country. See the Crimes (Overseas) Act 1964 (Cth) s 3A.

[49] An example of the difficulties faced by prosecutors relying on evidence obtained on foreign soil is the dismissal of the indictment in *USA v Slough*. The Court held that statements obtained from the accused Blackwater employees by State Department officials soon after the shooting in Iraq were compelled under threat of loss of employment and could not be used against the accused in any subsequent criminal prosecution in accordance with their Fifth Amendment privilege against self-incrimination. The Court held that the prosecution had made improper use of those compelled statements (or evidence obtained from them) in its investigation and the preparation of its case. In particular, the Court held that the prosecution had failed to ensure that other members of the Raven 23 Convoy whose evidence was used to secure the indictment were not exposed to the compelled statements—which were widely

strong incentives to pursue such cases. On top of this, the criminal laws of 'host' states themselves are often inadequate or even by-passed by immunity provisions (as in Iraq), and are, in any case, by definition, stretched by the extant conflict.[50]

In respect of relevant military law, the picture is also murky. The US Uniform Code of Military Justice (UCMJ),[51] while principally governing the conduct of US soldiers, also covers crimes committed by 'persons serving with or accompanying an armed force in the field'. By a 2006 amendment,[52] the UCMJ was extended to cover such persons not only in times of war, but also during 'contingency operations', thereby covering the situations in Iraq and Afghanistan. Thus, contractors may be subject to military jurisdiction and court-martial for crimes under the UCMJ. However, questions still remain about whether the requirement that persons must 'accompany an armed force in the field' would cover non-Department of Defense (DOD) contractors such as Blackwater (which was contracted by the Department of State), and furthermore, whether subjecting civilians to court-martial would withstand constitutional challenge.[53] Only one case to date has been brought against an individual civilian contractor under the UCMJ, and since the defendant pleaded guilty the constitutional questions were not tested.[54]

An alternate basis for jurisdiction over contractors may be the special maritime and territorial jurisdiction of the US,[55] which extends federal criminal jurisdiction over crimes committed on certain territory such as US military bases, federal buildings, the high seas and, pertinently, 'diplomatic,

---

reported in the media—and that the evidence the witnesses gave was from their own recollection and not tainted by any compelled statements they had read. See Memorandum Opinion dated 31 December 2009 in *USA v Paul Slough et al*, Criminal Action No 1:08-cr-0360-RMU in the US District Court for the District of Columbia. The US government has lodged an appeal against the decision (Notice of Appeal filed 29 January 2010).

[50] There are also evident concerns in legislators' minds that restrictive legislation might operate against legitimate PMC activities (such as protection services) and freedom fighters. See Geraghty, above n 36, 291, 294 and 302.

[51] 10 USC §§ 801–946 (2010).

[52] National Defense Authorization Act for Fiscal Year 2007, HR 5122, 109th Cong. § 552 (2006) (enacted).

[53] See, eg, J Elsea, M Schwartz and K Nakamura, *Private Security Contractors in Iraq: Background, Legal Status, and Other Issues* (Washington DC, Congressional Research Service, 25 August 2008) 25–29, noting that 'any trial of a civilian contractor by court-martial is likely to be challenged on constitutional grounds' at 25. See also Commission on Wartime Contracting in Iraq and Afghanistan, *At What Risk? Correcting Over-reliance on Contractors in Contingency Operations* (Arlington, CWC, February 2011) 52, available at www.wartime-contracting.gov.

[54] Multi-National Corps–Iraq, 'Civilian Contractor Convicted at a Court-Martial' (Press Release, 23 June 2008) available at www.usf-iraq.com/?option=com_content&task=view&id=20671&Itemid=128. See further J Elsea, *Private Security Contractors in Iraq and Afghanistan: Legal Issues* (Washington DC, Congressional Research Service, 7 January 2010) 25 and fn 144.

[55] 18 USC § 7.

consular, military or other US Government missions or entities in foreign States', including the adjacent land. Such jurisdiction was successfully used to prosecute and convict a civilian CIA contractor who brutally assaulted an Iraqi man detained in a facility in Iraq controlled by US forces.[56] However, the strict geographic limitations of this jurisdiction render it inadequate as a general basis for contractor accountability, given that contractors are often operating outside US military or diplomatic facilities—such as Nisour Square, which is outside the diplomatic 'Green Zone'.

Therefore, the most promising basis for jurisdiction is the Military Extraterritorial Jurisdiction Act of 2000 (MEJA),[57] which extends criminal jurisdiction over members of the armed forces and persons 'employed by or accompanying the armed forces' outside the US, in respect of offences punishable by imprisonment of greater than one year. Prior to 2004, only DOD contractors were persons 'employed by the armed forces outside the United States'. However, by a 2004 amendment,[58] the MEJA was extended to include contractors of 'any other Federal agency ... to the extent such employment relates to supporting the mission of the Department of Defense overseas'.[59] The MEJA was invoked in the case of *USA v Paul Slough*, filed in December 2008, which was the prosecution of five Blackwater guards for manslaughter in respect of the deaths of 14 civilians in Nisour Square and the attempted manslaughter of 20 others.[60]

Private law can also operate as a restraint on the behaviour of PMCs, although not without some difficulty. Contract, occupational health and safety and labour laws are all generally of only schematic relevance on account of both the nature of the industry (that is, the inherent physical dangers of being a security contractor) and, again, the off-shore locations of

---

[56] *USA v David Passaro*, Criminal Action No 5:04-cr-211-BO, in the US District Court for the Eastern District of North Carolina, Jury Verdict of 17 August 2006. Conviction upheld by the Fourth Circuit Court of Appeals on 10 August 2009. See 'Court Upholds CIA Contractor's Detainee Abuse Conviction', *Agence France-Presse*, 11 August 2009.

[57] Military Extraterritorial Jurisdiction Act, 18 USC § 3261 (2000).

[58] National Defense Authorization Act for Fiscal Year 2005, HR 4200, 108th Cong. § 1088 (2004) (enacted).

[59] Whether this formulation of 'supporting the mission of the DOD' would include Department of State contractors like Blackwater, or CIA contractors, was not clarified by Congress. In 2007, the House of Representatives passed a bill (the MEJA Expansion and Enforcement Act of 2007) that sought to amend the MEJA to cover contractors of all US government agencies operating in connection with 'contingency operations' (ie, Iraq and Afghanistan) and removing the requirement that the contract 'support the mission of the DOD'. However, the legislation was never passed in the Senate. See further n 24 above and accompanying text. See also Elsea, above n 54, 22–23, who notes that 'depending on how broadly DOD's mission is construed, MEJA does not appear to cover civilian and contract employees of agencies engaged in their own operations overseas.'

[60] *USA v Paul Slough et al*, Criminal Action No 1:08-cr-360-RMU, commenced on 4 December 2008 in the US District Court for the District of Columbia. However, on 31 December 2009 the criminal proceeding was dismissed on account of tainted evidence being used to secure the indictment. See further n 49 above.

the bulk of their activities. But tort law can, and in some cases does, have the capacity to cover the activities of PMCs and their personnel. A number of cases were initiated in the US against Blackwater by the families of victims of the Nisour Square atrocity[61] under the 1789 Alien Tort Statute (ATS),[62] an enactment which gives US federal courts jurisdiction to hear tort suits brought by foreigners for conduct 'committed in violation of the law of nations or a treaty of the United States'.[63] The cases against Blackwater became ensnared in pre-trial discovery and motions for summary dismissal[64]— a familiar problem in ATS litigation brought against corporations—before recently being settled.[65] The difficulties of seeking tortious remedies are not confined to the injured and bereaved Iraqis. For there also seems to be an issue regarding the ability of security personnel themselves (that is, the US citizens employed by Blackwater) to sue the company in tort for injuries

---

[61] The Nisour Square cases were *Estate of Himoud Saed Abtan et al v Blackwater USA et al* (Civil Action No 1:07-cv-1831 filed 11 October 2007, US District Court for the District of Columbia) and *Estate of Mushtaq Karim Abd Al-Razzaq et al v XE (Blackwater) et al* (Civil Action No 3:09-cv-626 filed 26 March 2009, US District Court for the Southern District of California), which were consolidated and transferred to the US District Court for the Eastern District of Virginia on 2 June 2009 (*Abtan et al v Erik Prince et al*, Civil Action No 1:09-cv-617), and later consolidated with a number of other ATS cases against Blackwater for the purposes of pre-trial discovery and motions (*In re: Xe Services Alien Tort Litigation*, Consolidated Civil Actions Nos 1:09-cv-615, 1:09-cv-616, 1:09-cv-617, 1:09-cv-618, 1:09-cv-645, 1:09-cv-1017, 1:09-cv-1048, US District Court for the Eastern District of Virginia). Also see Matthew Dahl, 'Soldiers of Fortune—Holding Private Security Contractors Accountable: The Alien Tort Claims Act and its Potential Application to *Abtan, et al v. Blackwater Lodge and Training Center, Inc, et al*' (2008) 37 *Denver Journal of International Law and Policy* 119.

[62] 28 USC § 1350. Section 1350 was originally enacted in the Judiciary Act of 1789 as ch 20, § 9, 1 Stat 73, 77.

[63] The ATS in its entirety provides: 'The district courts shall have original jurisdiction of any civil action by an alien for a tort only, committed in violation of the law of nations or a treaty of the United States.'

[64] The length of some ATS claims against (well-resourced) corporate defendants is staggering. For example, the claim against Royal Dutch Petroleum/Shell for its alleged complicity in human rights abuses against the Ogoni people in Nigeria was originally filed in November 1996, and finally settled on the eve of trial on 8 June 2009. For a timeline of the various motions, appeals and interlocutory disputes between the parties over 13 years of litigation see the Center for Constitutional Rights' page at www.ccrjustice.org/ourcases/current-cases/wiwa-v.-royal-dutch-petroleum.

[65] The consolidated cases, *In re: Xe Services Alien Tort Litigation*, settled on 6 January 2010. While the parties did not disclose the settlement amount, media reports suggested that the family of each deceased received $100,000 and injured persons received $30,000. See M Baker, 'Company Once Known as Blackwater Settles Lawsuits Alleging Reckless Culture, Civilian Deaths', *Associated Press*, 7 January 2010. As at November 2011, another civil suit remains pending. The suit is being brought on behalf of three persons killed and three persons injured in the Nisour Square shooting and is based on North Carolina tort law or, in the alternative, Iraqi law. The suit was initially filed on 15 September 2009 in a North Carolina state court, and later removed to the federal district court on 15 October 2009. On 25 January 2011 the case was remanded back to state court; see *R. Daniel Brady et al v Xe Services LLC et al*, Civil Action No 5:09-cv-449, US District Court for the Eastern District Court of North Carolina, Order of Remand (25 January 2011). Blackwater/Xe has appealed the remand decision; see *In re: Xe Services LLC*, Docket No 11-1354, US Court of Appeals for the Fourth Circuit, Petition for Writ of Mandamus (18 April 2011).

they sustain while in Iraq. They have come up against two hurdles: the 'political question doctrine', a non-justiciability doctrine which precludes the courts from passing judgment on inherently political questions, such as military decision-making; and a federal common law rule known as the 'government contractor defence', which effectively extends the US's sovereign immunity from tort claims to military contractors.[66] Both doctrines have the potential to significantly limit the ability of injured contractors or their families to bring tort claims against their (or their relatives') employers.[67] While the purposes of the doctrines are to preserve the separation of powers and ensure the government's immunity from suit when exercising its discretion in complex military matters (whether directly, or through its contractors), their application has the unfortunate consequence of barring compensation claims by individuals in the employ of the government or its contracted agents.[68] The contradictory upshot, therefore, is a situation in which the government uses Blackwater's corporate status to shield itself from liability, while at the same time extending to Blackwater the immunity from suit to which, normally, only the state is entitled.

B. International Law

Despite the manifestly transnational dimensions of the business of PMCs, the reach of international law over contractors is flimsy or, more often, absent. As individuals, mercenaries are recognised only in a negative sense in international humanitarian law: that is, the protections typically afforded to official military personnel—in particular, prisoner of war status—are not extended to mercenaries. However, most PMC personnel do not meet the strict and technical definition of mercenaries under Additional Protocol I.[69] Accordingly, the status of PMC personnel under international humanitarian

---

[66] While historically the government contractor defence, as formulated by the US Supreme Court in *Boyle v United Technologies Corp* 487 US 500 (1988), applied to military *procurement* contractors, who manufactured equipment according to government specifications, the defence has more recently been held to apply to *service* contractors. See the discussion of the case law in B Davidson, 'Liability on the Battlefield: Adjudicating Tort Suits Brought by Soldiers Against Military Contractors' (2008) 37 *Public Contract Law Journal* 803; and J Jacobs, 'The *Boyle* Test is an Insufficient Standard for Determining Whether to Allow Private Military Contractors to Assert the Government Contractor Defense' (2008) 36 *Hofstra Law Review* 1377. Blackwater has also argued for the application of the government contractor defence and the political question doctrine in the various ATS suits brought against it arising out of the Nisour Square shooting, in an attempt to have the plaintiffs' claims dismissed.

[67] See further Davidson, above n 66 and Jacobs, above n 66.

[68] Ibid.

[69] Protocol Additional to the Geneva Conventions of 12 August 1949 and Relating to the Protection of Victims of International Armed Conflicts, opened for signature 8 June 1977, 1125 UNTS 3 (entered into force 7 December 1979) (Additional Protocol I) Art 47.

law remains contentious.[70] On one view, it is unlikely that private military contractors, who generally operate outside the military chain of command, would be considered 'combatants' or satisfy other criteria for the conferral of prisoner of war status under Article 4 of the Third Geneva Convention[71] or Article 43 of Additional Protocol I. Hence, PMC personnel are likely to be considered 'civilians', entitled to the protections of the Fourth Geneva Convention.[72] However, as 'civilians', if they take a direct part in hostilities and are captured by the enemy, they cannot claim the privileges of a combatant: chiefly, immunity from criminal prosecution for taking part in hostilities.[73] The UN Convention Against Mercenaries underscores this fact by requiring states parties to criminalise direct participation in hostilities by a 'mercenary' (as that term is defined in the Convention).[74]

As corporations, PMCs themselves—like all transnational business entities—operate within and between home and host state laws, rather than under any specific international legal regime.[75] There are recent international initiatives (including the UN Framework and Guiding Principles on Business and Human Rights)[76] that might address the potential lacunae this creates in terms of corporate responsibility for human rights infringements. However, these have taken little notice of the peculiarities of PMCs, beyond the role they play as security providers hired by extractive industry corporations[77] or in reference to the process that resulted in the Montreux Document on Private Military and Security Companies ('the Montreux document').[78]

---

[70] For an example of how reasonable (expert) minds may differ on the status of PMCs in international humanitarian law, see the report of the 'Expert Meeting on Private Military Contractors: Status and State Responsibility for Their Actions', organised by the University Centre for International Humanitarian Law, Geneva, 29–30 August 2005, at www.adh-geneva.ch/docs/expert-meetings/2005/2rapport_compagnies_privees. pdf.

[71] Geneva Convention (III) Relative to the Treatment of Prisoners of War, opened for signature 12 August 1949, 75 UNTS 135 (entered into force 21 October 1950).

[72] Geneva Convention (IV) relative to the Protection of Civilian Persons in Time of War, opened for signature 12 August 1949, 75 UNTS 287 (entered into force 21 October 1950).

[73] For a discussion of the potential classifications of PMCs under international humanitarian law, see L Doswald-Beck, 'Private Military Companies Under International Humanitarian Law' in S Chesterman and C Lehnardt (eds), above n 22.

[74] International Convention Against the Recruitment, Use, Financing and Training of Mercenaries, opened for signature 4 December 1989, 2163 UNTS 75 (entered into force 20 October 2001). There are 32 states parties to the Convention as at November 2011.

[75] See D Kinley and J Tadaki, 'From Talk to Walk: The Emergence of Human Rights Responsibilities for Corporations at International Law' (2004) 44 *Virginia Journal of International Law* 931, 937–49.

[76] See n 97 below.

[77] See the Voluntary Principles on Security and Human Rights at www.voluntaryprinciples.org.

[78] See Report of the Special Representative of the Secretary-General on the Issue of Human Rights and Transnational Corporations and Other Business Enterprises (hereafter SRSG), J Ruggie, *Business and Human Rights: Mapping International Standards of Responsibility and Accountability for Corporate Acts*, UN GAOR 4th sess, Provisional Agenda Item 2, UN Doc A/HRC/4/35 (19 February 2007) fn 54.

Of course, the potential for PMCs to violate human rights is well-recognised. Reports by the UN Special Rapporteur on Mercenaries and by the Working Group on Mercenaries that replaced it in 2005[79] have charted the particular and long-standing problems that the use of mercenaries pose for the right to self-determination in circumstances where peoples are under 'colonial or alien domination or foreign occupation'.[80] More recently, they have recorded the human rights impacts of the use of private military and security contractors in conflict zones.[81] And the infamous Taguba and Fay Reports detailed the human rights abuses of detainees in Abu Ghraib Prison at the hands of a number of employees of two security firms that were engaged by the US government to run the facility after the 'coalition of the willing' occupied the country.[82]

The fundamental regulatory challenge posed by the existence and operations of PMCs centres on the question of state responsibility. That is, to what extent is state responsibility under international law affected by the delegation to private operators of the public function and authority to exercise force? The broad answer is that, insofar as the conduct of private operators can be attributed to the state, that state's international obligations will persist in respect of such conduct. However, from this general proposition two further, more specific questions flow: 1) what are the determinants of such attribution; and 2) what is the practicability of states fulfilling their consequent obligations?

As regards what constitutes sufficient delegation to avoid responsibility, state practice is informative. For reasons of convenience, capacity and commerce, states—as indicated earlier—are keen to delegate their security competence, and have no real desire to maintain effective control, still less

---

[79] Working Group on the use of mercenaries as a means of violating human rights and impeding the exercise of the right of peoples to self-determination, established by the UN Commission on Human Rights in Resolution 2005/2, UN Doc E/CN.4/RES/2005/2 (7 April 2005).

[80] See, eg, the 1993 Report on the question of the use of mercenaries as a means of violating human rights and impeding the exercise of the right of peoples to self-determination, submitted by E Bernales Ballesteros, Special Rapporteur, *The Right of Peoples to Self-Determination and its Application to Peoples under Colonial or Alien Domination or Foreign Occupation*, UN ESCOR, 49th sess, Provisional Agenda Item 9, UN Doc E/CN.4/1993/18 (8 January 1993).

[81] See, eg, the Working Group's recent reports of country visits to the US and Iraq. S Shameem, Chairperson-Rapporteur, *Report of the Working Group on the use of mercenaries as a means of violating human rights and impeding the exercise of the right of peoples to self-determination* (Mission to the United States of America) UN GAOR 15th sess, Agenda Item 3, UN Doc A/HRC/15/25/Add.3 (2 July 2010); and JL Gómez del Prado, Chair-Rapporteur, *Report of the Working Group on the use of mercenaries as a means of violating human rights and impeding the exercise of the right of peoples to self-determination* (Mission to Iraq) UN GAOR, 18th sess, Agenda Item 3, UN Doc A/HRC/18/32/Add.4 (12 August 2011).

[82] AM Taguba, 'AR 15-6 Investigation of the 800th Military Police Brigade' (2004) at news.findlaw.com/hdocs/docs/iraq/tagubarpt.html; and GR Fay, 'AR 15-6 Investigation of the Abu Ghraib Detention Facility and 205th Military Intelligence Brigade' (August 2004) at news.findlaw.com/hdocs/docs/dod/fay82504rpt.pdf.

to retain responsibility. Further, as Chia Lehnardt notes, 'on those occasions where it has been alleged that international obligations have been violated, governments have explicitly or implicitly denied any responsibility for such wrongdoing, not on the basis that no breach of international law has occurred, but because any connection to the perpetrators is denied'.[83] Yet, there can be little doubt about the responsibility of states for the actions of their agents or delegates, when they are acting in a public capacity. The International Law Commission notes with approval in the commentary to its *Articles on State Responsibility* (ASR), the continuing pertinence of a 1929 statement made by the German government to a League of Nations conference that 'from the point of view of international law, it does not matter whether a state polices a given area with its own police or entrusts this duty, to a greater or less extent, to autonomous bodies ... the principles governing responsibility of the state for its organs apply with equal force'.[84] That said, the nature of 'contracting out' to PMCs today is such that state responsibility for their actions is not a foregone conclusion. On the one hand, the nature of typical state–PMC contracts means that PMCs are not 'organs' of the state (under Article 4 of the ASR). On the other hand, however, they might be considered to be 'exercising elements of governmental authority' (Article 5 of the ASR), or perhaps acting under the 'direction or control' of the state (Article 8 of the ASR). Articles 5 or 8 are the most likely bases for attributing PMC conduct to states, but everything turns on the facts of a specific case. For the conduct of private groups or entities to be attributed to the state on the basis of 'direction or control', the state must be exercising 'effective control' over the specific operations of the individual, group or entity. This was stated by the International Court of Justice (ICJ) in the 2007 *Bosnian Genocide* case, affirming its earlier judgment

---

[83] Lehnardt, 'Private Military Companies and State Responsibility', above n 46, 141. For example, the UK's attempts to distance itself from the actions of Sandline International in selling arms to Sierra Leone in contravention of a UN arms embargo, ibid fn 14. Consider also the US government's decision to permit a US company, MPRI, to enter into a military training contract with Croatia during its war with Serbia. MPRI's training was credited with transforming Croatian forces and leading to a series of important offensives in which they recaptured Croat territory. In effect, the US assisted an ally, but could claim neutrality by virtue of the fact it was MPRI, and not the US Military, which provided the training. See JC Zarate, 'The Emergence of a New Dog of War: Private International Security Companies, International Law, and the New World Disorder' (1998) 34 *Stanford Journal of International Law* 75, 106–08.

[84] J Crawford (ed), *The International Law Commission's Articles on State Responsibility: Introduction, Text and Commentaries* (Cambridge, Cambridge University Press, 2002) 101 (Article 5, para 4). This line of responsibility has also been reaffirmed in Part I of the Montreux Document: see Montreux Document on Pertinent International Legal Obligations and Good Practices for States related to Operations of Private Military and Security Companies during Armed Conflict of 17 September 2008, as annexed to a Letter dated 2 October 2008 from the Permanent Representative of Switzerland to the United Nations, UN Docs A/63/467 & S/2008/636, Part I, para 7. See further J Cockayne, 'Regulating Private Military and Security Companies: The Content, Negotiation, Weaknesses and Promise of the Montreux Document' (2008) 13 *Journal of Conflict and Security Law* 401.

in the 1986 *Nicaragua* case.[85] Certain arrangements may not qualify as 'effective control'. For example, a mere contractual relationship is likely to be insufficient for the state to be said to have 'effective control' over the conduct of the PMC (especially given that most PMCs operate outside the military chain of command). Further, while interrogating detainees might be 'exercising governmental authority', it is not so clear whether providing food or security services would fall within that concept.[86]

It should be added that, in the particular respect of international human rights law, there exists a growing body of jurisprudence (especially in the Inter-American Court of Human Rights and the European Court of Human Rights) which imposes 'due diligence' obligations on states to take such reasonable measures as to prevent, punish, investigate or provide redress for human rights violations committed not only by agents of the state but also by private persons within the state's jurisdiction.[87] All that said, the practicability of states fulfilling their obligations is another matter altogether, especially in light of the circumstances in which many PMCs operate—that is, in conflict zones, in weak or failed states, and where political stakes are high. Domestic scrutiny that would satisfy the standards of international law is unlikely to come from most host states, and is not very attractive to home states on account of the costs incurred (both financial and political) and the loss of flexibility (read 'deniability') that transparency would occasion. Looking to Iraq for indications of state practice in this regard is instructive. It is perhaps unsurprising to see, for example, the US government's blithe response to communication problems between the military and PMCs. That response was to employ another PMC to sort it out![88]

---

[85] *Application of the Convention on the Prevention and Punishment of the Crime of Genocide (Bosnia and Herzegovina v Serbia and Montenegro)* (Merits) [2007] ICJ Reports 43, paras 398–407, and referring to *Military and Paramilitary Activities in and against Nicaragua (Nicaragua v United States of America)* (Merits) [1986] ICJ Reports 14.

[86] See further Lehnardt, above n 46.

[87] The classic statement of these 'positive' or 'due diligence' obligations is by the Inter-American Court in the *Velásquez Rodriguez Case*, Judgment of 29 July 1988, Inter-American Court of Human Rights, (Ser C) No 4 (1988) at paras 172–74. In the European Court of Human Rights, in respect of the responsibilities that must be borne by states for their regulatory failures to prevent corporations from acting in ways that infringe on human rights, see *López Ostra v Spain*, App No 16798/90, Judgment of 9 December 1994, (1995) 20 EHRR 277; *Taskin v Turkey*, App No 46117/99, Judgment of 10 November 2004, (2006) 42 EHRR 50; and *Fadeyeva v Russia*, App No 55273/00, Judgment of 9 June 2005, (2007) 45 EHRR 10. For the broader implications of this line of reasoning see C Chinkin, 'A Critique of the Public/Private Dimension' (1999) 10 *European Journal of International Law* 387, 393–95, specifically on how human rights jurisprudence may be diverging from the general international law of state responsibility in this respect.

[88] Lehnardt, above n 46, 155–56.

VI. CONCLUSION

Failures in the legal regulation of PMCs are evident. Events like the Nisour Square killings highlight these failures and inject some political and ethical urgency into the concern to address the gaps. Barely two months before September 2007, a widely publicised Congressional Research Service paper noted, perceptively, the prevalence and utility, but also the serious regulatory problems, of the roles played by PMCs in Iraq.[89]

In the face of greater public scrutiny and criticism of PMCs, and the possibility that states might respond to redress the absence and inadequacy of domestic or international legal oversight, the industry has reacted, albeit in piecemeal fashion. An initiative of the Swiss government and the ICRC led to the adoption by 17 countries of the Montreux Document, which restates the relevant obligations under international law, as well as 'best practice' for states, private military corporations and private security companies to adopt.[90]

Within the field of corporations and human rights the soft law approach has, in practice and (presently) in rhetoric, been preferred over hard law.[91] It is therefore in some respects true to form that we look to the softer options; that is, trying to encourage PMCs themselves to accept voluntarily some degree of (self-)regulation, rather than attempting to force them to do so, which may result more in the sound of many well-meaning heads bashing against walls than anything else.[92]

Yet here too, PMCs' actions are less than encouraging. For example, Blackwater withdrew from the industry's peak body (the International Peace Operations Association (IPOA)) shortly after the Nisour Square incident not only to avoid scrutiny under the body's code of conduct standards, but also, it is claimed, because other member companies privately pressured Blackwater to withdraw from IPOA to avoid a review that would damage the reputation of all IPOA member companies.[93]

---

[89] J Elsea and N Serafino, *Private Security Contractors in Iraq: Background, Legal Status, and Other Issues* (Washington DC, Congressional Research Service, 11 July 2007) available at media.washingtonpost.com/wp-srv/world/documents/contractor_crsreport_091807.pdf.

[90] See Montreux Document, above n 84. For related information, including meeting records, see the Swiss Federal Department of Foreign Affairs website at www.eda.admin.ch/psc.

[91] On the politics of that preference see D Kinley, J Nolan and N Zerial, 'The Politics of Corporate Social Responsibility: Reflections on the United Nations Human Rights Norms for Corporations' (2007) 25 *Company and Securities Law Journal* 30.

[92] For a review of the degrees of timidity with which the UN, the OECD and the EU seek to encourage such self-regulation by PMCs, see N White and S MacLeod, 'EU Operations and Private Military Contractors: Issues of Corporate and Institutional Responsibility' (2008) 19 *European Journal of International Law* 965, 977–84.

[93] Cockayne et al, above n 42, 141–42. Cockayne further notes that as Blackwater's contract with the US Department of State was renewed in April 2008 it would appear that 'the company's withdrawal from IPOA had no real impact on its ability to contract with the US government', ibid.

The circumstances reduce, in our view, to the focal point of how states must lead and act—internationally and domestically[94]—in this field. And this includes how they react to the cries of the many private security companies (and some PMCs as well) for stronger regulation to demarcate more clearly the jurisdictional and responsibility boundaries, as well as to rein in the more roguish of the PMCs.[95] To be sure, there are a number of actors (state and non-state) upon whom various degrees of responsibility might and can be foisted. But for reasons of contractual relations, the nature of the activities and, above all, jurisdictional authority, it is states, individually and collectively, that must shoulder the primary burden. In this 'business sector' above all others, states have a responsibility to regulate to require compliance.[96] It is not enough to regulate by urging compliance in a typical soft law form. Nor is it tenable to rely on the possibility that desirable hard law approaches by states might be aided by an international legal initiative that establishes the human rights responsibilities of corporations[97] upon

---

[94] In a report of the UK Parliament's Joint Standing Committee on Human Rights, the Committee stressed the need for the UK government to exercise leadership in ensuring that businesses understand their responsibilities to respect human rights no matter where they operate (Part 11 'Conclusion', paras 309–10), including in respect of establishing an international regulatory scheme covering PMCs (Part 8, 'Specific Areas for Improvement', paras 269–75): *Any of Our Business? Human Rights and the UK Private Sector* (December 2009) at www.publications.parliament.uk/pa/jt200910/jtselect/jtrights/5/502.htm.

[95] See the statement (known as the 'Nyon Declaration') issued by three private military and security industry associations, calling for an international code of conduct: 'Industry Statement', issued by International Peace Operations Association (IPOA), British Association of Private Security Companies (BAPSC) and the Pan African Security Association (PASA) at Nyon, Switzerland (6 June 2009) available at www.icoc-psp.org/uploads/2009.06_-_Nyon_Declaration.pdf. Following the Nyon Declaration, the Swiss government convened a multi-stakeholder initiative which negotiated an International Code of Conduct for Private Security Service Providers, the text of which was finalised in September 2010. On 9 November 2010, the Code was signed by 58 private security companies from 15 countries at a ceremony in Geneva. As at 1 October 2011, there are 211 Signatory Companies from 45 countries. See further www.icoc-psp.org.

[96] As especially argued in respect of 'home' states by F Francioni, 'The Role of Home States in Ensuring Compliance with Human Rights by Private Military Contractors' in F Francioni and N Ronzitti (eds), *War By Contract: Human Rights, Humanitarian Law and Private Contractors* (Oxford, Oxford University Press, 2011) 93–110.

[97] As does the former SRSG, who dismissed the prospect of any such international initiative emanating out of the UN system, at least in the near future; see J Ruggie, 'Business and Human Rights: Treaty Road Not Travelled', *Ethical Corporation* (6 May 2008) available at www.ethicalcorp.com/content/john-ruggie-business-and-human-rights---treaty-road-not travelled. Though it must be said that Ruggie's tripartite 'protect, respect, remedy' framework that he has advanced instead does not preclude international cooperation; see Report of the Special Representative of the Secretary-General on the issue of human rights and transnational corporations and other business enterprises, J Ruggie, *Business and human rights: further steps toward the operationalization of the 'protect, respect and remedy' framework*, UN Doc A/HRC/14/27 (9 April 2010) paras 52–53. For the final report of the SRSG, containing the Guiding Principles on Business and Human Rights, see Report of the Special Representative of the Secretary-General on the issue of human rights and transnational corporations and other business enterprises, J Ruggie, *Guiding Principles on Business and Human Rights: Implementing the United Nations "Protect, Respect and Remedy" Framework*, Human Rights Council, 17th sess, Agenda Item 3, UN Doc A/HRC/17/31 (21 March 2011).

which all states (the weak and the strong) can draw or be measured against in their own separate efforts.[98] It is states that must promote and institute regimes that secure PMC accountability, drawing on international and domestic apparatus, on mandatory and voluntary initiatives, and on private and public law principles. This means recognising, as a first step, that many of the orthodoxies of legal categories are in need of change (though not so as to throw the 'centrality of state' baby out with the 'restrictive orthodoxies' bathwater), to keep pace with the political and practical changes in the field of private military enterprise.[99] After that, we might go about the process of implementation.

[98] This is argued by the first named author in D Kinley, *Civilising Globalisation: Human Rights and the Global Economy* (Cambridge, Cambridge University Press, 2009) 195–201. Interestingly, neither the EU nor the Council of Europe appears to agree with this uncompromising approach. Both entities are currently engaged in efforts to institute international regulatory frameworks covering the human rights responsibilities of corporations. Regarding the EU, see the European Commission, *Annexes to the Communication from the Commission to the European Parliament, the Council, the European Economic and Social Committee and the Committee of the Regions: Commission Work Programme 2010 'Time to Act'*, EU Doc COM (2010) 135 final, Vol II (31 March 2010) 20, which heralds a new Communication of the Commission on CSR with business and human rights as a central plank; and regarding the Council of Europe, there is the prospect of a Committee of Ministers Recommendation on business and human rights, which is presently winding its way through the processes of the Council of Europe's Parliamentary Assembly (see Committee on Legal Affairs and Human Rights, 'Human Rights and Business', H Haibach, Rapporteur, Doc 12361 (27 September 2010) and Parliamentary Assembly Resolution 1757 (2010) 'Business and Human Rights' (6 October 2010)).

[99] On the centrality of the state in international legal regulation and resisting the temptation to focus on non-state actors in the global economy as significant or even the principal sites of *direct* international legal responsibility for human rights abuses, see Kinley, above n 98, 222–28.

Index